# From Baghdad TO CHICAGO

Cover images:
Scene from Baghdad in the 1950's, left, and the
Tribune Tower on Chicago's Magnificent Mile, right.

# From Baghdad to CHICAGO

## Memoir and Reflections of an Iraqi-American Physician

## Asad A. Bakir

ARCHWAY
PUBLISHING

Archway Publishing books may be ordered through booksellers or by contacting:

Archway Publishing
1663 Liberty Drive
Bloomington, IN 47403
www.archwaypublishing.com
1 (888) 242-5904

ISBN: 978-1-4808-5771-1 (sc)
ISBN: 978-1-4808-5770-4 (hc)
ISBN: 978-1-4808-5769-8 (e)

Library of Congress Control Number: 2018902251

Print information available on the last page.

Archway Publishing rev. date: 07/26/2018

To my wife, Nadia Killidar
Without her gentility, grace,
forbearance, intelligence, and love,
this book would not have been possible.

# CONTENTS

# PROLOGUE

What is past is prologue.
—Shakespeare

I was born in Baghdad, Iraq, and lived there for twenty-eight years, where I finished medical school, served in the Iraqi Army Medical Reserve Corps, and did my medical internship. I then worked in England for eight months before coming in 1972 to Chicago to do my medical residency and renal fellowship. I have lived and worked in this interesting and dear city ever since.

I have lived through four generations of Iraqis, stretching from my grandparents to my children, experienced the dramatic upheavals that convulsed Iraq over the last sixty-five years, and seen the untold ruin they left behind. This book is a memoir of my life and times in Iraq and Chicago and my brief spell in England.

There is no bibliography at the end of this book, because it was not intended to be a scholarly work, only a memoir. Besides, a bibliography would have consumed at least fifty pages. The events described, however, are factual. A great many of them I have lived through, observed at close range, read about, or heard firsthand from family and friends. Readers whose interest is piqued by what I have related could always refer to a plethora of paper and online publications, radio, TV, and YouTube interviews to further pursue the subjects arousing their curiosity.

I have been careful to describe events as objectively as possible, in the scientific manner I have been accustomed to in my medical studies and career. When I discuss Shia-Sunni positions and interactions in modern Iraq and the Middle East, I have shunned sectarian and religious partiality because I have neither. My paternal grandmother, a brother-in-law, several cousins-in-law, and my best friends are Sunnis. Moreover, the wives of an uncle and a cousin of mine are Christian. Apologies in advance if my account is discomfiting for some readers, Arabs or Americans, for I have not intended to perturb anyone, but only to give a frank account of my experience and share my reflections.

I have used the customary American spelling of Arabic personal and place names; however, the first time a name appears, I often show in parentheses its Arabic pronunciation as best as I can; some Arabic sounds do not exist in the English tongue. All my translations of Arabic poetry are adaptations since a transliteration is almost impossible without losing the original connotation and nuance; and the all-important rhyme in Arabic poetry cannot be maintained in English. Furthermore, I am not a poet. When discussing medical subjects, I've had the general reader in mind but tried to present such material in a manner not boring to medical professionals.

I have an abiding love of history, and memoirs are pieces of history, so I hope the reader will be interested in my account of events from my earliest recollections at the age of four years to the present, a period spanning sixty-nine years. Alexis de Tocqueville said, "When the past no longer illuminates the future, the spirit walks in darkness," and Edmund Burke stated, "Those who don't know history are destined to repeat it."

# 1

# Beginnings

I was born in Baghdad, Iraq, in the fall of 1944. At the time, but especially in the 1950s, Iraq was on the threshold of becoming a modern country. Its beginnings as a state had been laid down by the British shortly after their triumph over the much weakened Ottoman Empire at the end of World War I (the "war to end all wars"), and the victors, in this case the British and the French, drew the borders of today's Iraq, Syria, Lebanon, and Palestine. The latter two had been parts of historic Greater Syria, known to the Arabs as Bilad al-Sham. The notion of a state with borders was an eighteenth-century European concept almost nonexistent in the East, and under the Ottoman Empire, today's Iraq constituted the provinces of Mosul, Baghdad, and Basra, the latter encompassing Kuwait.

Interestingly, many Arabs under the leadership of Sharif (Shereef) Husayn of the Hejaz, today part of Saudi Arabia, fought alongside the British against the Ottomans, perhaps one of the greatest historic mistakes the Arabs ever made. The sharif had been promised a free and united Arab kingdom under his rule once the Ottoman Empire was defeated. Indeed, there were many powerful voices in London advocating the creation of an Arab kingdom loyal to the British to serve as an obstacle to other powers, especially Russia, from gaining warm-water harbors or making designs on British India (the Great Game). Alas, Faisal Faysal), the Sharif's son (later King Faisal I of Iraq), understood upon traveling to Paris after the end of the war that the Sykes-Picot Agreement represented the abandonment of the British promises to his father. This, however, was not the first time the British betrayed the sharif.

On the other hand, the Shia (Shiites) of Iraq, who had no love lost for the Ottomans, fought with them against the British, who had landed an expeditionary force in Fao (at the northern tip of the Persian Gulf) in 1914 and were advancing north toward Baghdad. There are many heroic stories from those times, especially about the Battle of Kut, where the British were badly defeated, sustained heavy casualties, and had to withdraw from the city and wait for reinforcements. But there were also many casualties among the Shia fighters, and numerous prominent warriors met their death, among them the famous poet Mohammad Sa'eed al-Habbubi, who led a detachment of volunteers to fight the invaders. It was the history of the Shia repeating itself, always fighting for God and religion, regardless of the political consequences to themselves.

In 1920, there was a Shia uprising against the British, who had already entered Baghdad in 1917 and controlled most of today's Iraq. The Ottomans had withdrawn from the northern province of Mosul without a fight. This rebellion, known as the 1920 Iraqi Revolt (Thawrat al-Ishreen), was also joined by Sheikh (Shaykh) Dhari ibn Mahmud of the Sunni Dulaym tribe and many urban Shia and Sunni figures from Baghdad. There was again much heroism and sacrifice. Many of the Shia tribal chiefs—the most prominent among them Abdul Wahid Sukker, chief of al-Fatla tribe—spent their own money to equip the fighters and support their families. Initially they were successful, evicting the British army from large areas in the south and costing it large casualties.

The rebellion, however, was eventually crushed by British heavy guns, air power, and (according to some sources) poison gas and with help from other tribes that were either friendly toward the British or had been neutral but joined them when the British seemed to be winning the day. When Sheikh Sukker finally surrendered, he uttered a verse in his melodic southern dialect, "Ye Hsayn il-ta'yir madheeni," meaning "Oh Husayn, it's the flyer that did me in," apologizing to Imam Husayn, the AD 680 martyr of Karbala, for the defeat of the revolt. The British then destroyed al-Fatla tribe's dwellings and killed and imprisoned a great number of their men. Sheikh Sukker was tried in a British military court, treated badly, and spent time in several prisons before he was released.

Some time later, the British general Sir James Haldane met Sheikh Sukker, shook his hand, served him coffee, and lit up a cigarette for him. He applauded Sukker's courage and heroic history, told him the Arabs should be proud he was one of them, and gifted him a golden watch with a laudatory inscription. Sheikh Sukker died in October 1956, when I was twelve years old. Thousands attended his funeral, including notable personalities from across the Arab and Muslim world.

The end of the 1920 revolt reminded the Arabs yet again of the defeat of similar religiously motivated rebellions against the encroaching European powers in the late nineteenth and early twentieth centuries: Mohammad al-Mehdi against the British in the Sudan; Ahmed Arabi against them in Egypt; Omar al-Mukhtar (the Lion of the Desert) against the Italians in Libya; and Abdul Qadir Al-Jaza'iri against the French in the Maghreb.

There was another rebellion in Iraq, this time by the Kurds, who had inhabited north-northeastern Iraq for many centuries. They, too, had been promised by the British a state of their own and took up arms when the promise was not honored. The British managed again to crush the revolt by employing, among other things, poison gas dumped from airplanes.

After much work and political maneuvering, the British were finally able, in August 1921, to install Sharif Husayn's son, Faisal, who had been driven out of Syria by the French, as King Faisal I of Iraq. This marked the birth of the State of Iraq, which under British mandate joined the League of Nations, the forerunner of the United Nations. The British government undertook to secure Mosul (Musul) for the new Iraqi state and to protect southern Iraq, including the holy Shia cities of Karbala and Najaf, against the notorious Wahabi Bedouin raiders from Najd in today's Saudi Arabia.

The Wahabis were the followers of Mohammad Abdul Wahab, who preached in the late eighteenth century. They were rigid fundamentalists who did not recognize mediators between Allah and humankind, frowned on the building of shrines, considered the Shia and Sufis heretical, and viewed Christians and Jews as *kafirs* (infidels), notwithstanding the fact that the Koran (al-Qur'an) calls them "the people of the book" and assures them religious freedom, respect, and security. The Wahabis were later joined by Mohammad bin Saud (Sa'ood), the ancestor of today's Saudi monarchy, and raided other tribes of the Arabian Peninsula, destroyed villages, did much killing of fighting-age males, took the women as slaves, and instituted a reign of terror and coercive conversions to Wahabism.

Outside the Arabian Peninsula, the Wahabis frequently raided Karbala and Najaf in Iraq; desecrated the holy shrines; carried away gilded tiles, artifacts, and carpets; plundered homes; killed large numbers of civilians; and abducted the women into slavery. Najaf has the shrine of Ali ibn abi Talib (Imam Ali), the fourth caliph of Islam and the Prophet's cousin and son-in-law. Karbala is the burial place of Imam Ali's two sons, al-Husayn and al-Abbas, who were martyred in Karbla in AD 680.

The Wahabi raids had been so destructive and rapacious that the Ottoman Sultans dispatched several campaigns to subdue them, the last of which was led by Ibrahim Pasha, the son of the famous ruler of Egypt, Mohammad Ali al-Kabeer. These campaigns were largely ineffective because the Bedouins, when pressed, simply retreated and disappeared into the desert. The British were well aware of the dark Wahabi record—hence their stated commitment to defend the nascent Iraqi state against those marauding nomads.

After the installation of King Feisal I, there began a period of relative calm and progress. The Hashemite rulers of Iraq, so called because they descended from Beni Hashem, the family of the Prophet, were loyal to what became their country, and worked to forge a nation out of the disparate groups inhabiting the area within the British-drawn borders of modern Iraq. Faisal I himself was one of the kindest and most astute rulers of Iraq—thoughtful and balanced while being buffeted by British prerogatives on the one hand and nationalistic demands on the other, always steering a calculated and wise middle course. Yet he was disappointed by the passivity and at times the open hostility of many Iraqi factions. He later described the people inhabiting his kingdom as disparate, contending and feuding groups bound by nothing except their hostility to the ruler.

One of the consequences of the 1920 rebellion was the exclusion of the Shia from the officer corps of the nascent Iraqi Army and high civil bureaucracy. The Sunnis had generally occupied such positions during the long centuries of Ottoman rule and continued to do so. The Shiites, therefore, did not have much experience in statecraft, bureaucracy, or the formal military and security services. Furthermore, many refused to work in a British-mandated state for religious reasons, seeing the British as infidels—an attitude reinforced by the Shia clerical establishment.

Increasingly the Shia politicians, southern tribal Sheikhs, and religious leadership saw their people marginalized in the upper strata of the state, and the impression was further amplified during the reign of King Faisal's son and successor, King Ghazi (1933–39), who, unlike his father, was not astute or balanced, and had, moreover, harbored anti-Shia sentiments. Consequently, two Shia ministers resigned in late 1933 from Ali Jawdat al-Ayubi's cabinet because they considered the government inattentive to the interests of the majority Shia population in the expansive plain of the Gharraf River, a large branch of the Tigris in southern Iraq.

To make matters worse, parliamentary elections in August 1934 were engineered to reduce the opposition Ikhwan Party representation and exclude key mid-Euphrates Shia sheiks from the assembly. This led to a political alliance between the sheiks, the Ikhwan party, and the shrewd Sunni politician Taha Yaseen al-Hashimi. My father told me once that al-Hashimi was so canny that the Baghdadi Jews, renowned for their astuteness, referred to him as "Abu-dmaghain," meaning the man with two brains.

In January 1935, Ayatollah Mohammad Kashif al-Ghita' and prominent Shia tribal sheikhs convened to promulgate the People's Charter wherein they accepted the Iraqi State but emphasized the neglect of the Shia grievances by the Ayubi government. Meanwhile unrest flared across the mid-Euphrates region, and in March 1935, an uprising erupted in the city of Diwaniyya. The People's Charter was presented to the government and a petition submitted to King Ghazi to dismiss Ayubi, who, amid the continued unrest, was prevailed upon to step down to be succeeded by Jameel al-Medfa'i, who in turn resigned only two weeks later for failing to manage the mid-Euphrates turmoil.

The king then asked al-Hashimi, a rival to both al-Ayubi and al-Medfa'i, to form a new cabinet. This quieted the Diwaniyya uprising in one week, after which two prominent Shia rebel sheiks and a large contingent of their armed followers entered Baghdad to petition the king and parade their strength.

The Hasimi government, betraying its onetime political allies, began arresting prominent clerical followers of Ayatollah al-Gita' on May 6. This triggered a rebellion by the Rumaytha Shia tribes in Diwaniyya. General Bekr Sidqi, notorious for the Assyrian massacre of 1933, was assigned the task of quelling the uprising. He declared martial law in Diwaniyya, employed the Iraqi Army and Air Force to crush the rebellion, and on May 11 initiated the indiscriminate bombing of villages in Diwaniyya.

Soon afterward, the Muntafij tribes of Sug al-Shiyukh and Nasiriyya took up arms and cut the railway running from the city of Nassiriyya to Basra at the southern tip of Iraq. Their sheiks then traveled to the holy city of Najaf to sign a manifesto of the Shia tribes against Prime Minister Hashimi.

The government was alarmed by these rapid developments and offered to negotiate with Ayatollah al-Ghita'. This, in fact, was a strategy to divide the rebellious tribes, because while Defense Minister Ja'far al-Askeri was trying to negotiate a truce with the sheiks of the Muntafij tribes, General Sidqi's military operations against the Rumaytha tribes continued unabated until they were defeated on May 21.

As for the Muntafij tribes' uprising, the Shia governor of Karbala, Salih Jabr, who later became prime minister, convinced the Ayatollah to restrain the warriors and advise them to stop fighting, probably by hinting that they would otherwise be subdued by General Sidqi's forces, and promising the Ayatollah better times for the Shia once hostilities ended. Not every tribe, however, could be restrained, as their grievances were not addressed in good time.

A string of Shia uprisings therefore continued well into 1936, in one of which the rebels killed ninety army troops and shot down two military airplanes. Sidqi's forces crushed the rebellion without mercy, blowing up homes, carrying out public hangings, and rounding up civilians for jail. It was this same General Sidqi who led a coup d'état against the government in October 1936, and his collaborators offered to negotiate with Ja'far al-Askeri but murdered him when he arrived at the assigned meeting place.

In the final analysis, the Shia rebellions of 1935–36 did not represent an existential danger to the central government. They failed, as did the 1920 revolt against the British, because the balance of military power was overwhelmingly against them and even at the height of warfare they were divided.

Many years later, some Shia became army officers, but upon attaining the rank of captain or higher, were transferred to noncombat positions like provisions or other noncrucial administrative posts. The overwhelming majority of the officer corps were still Sunnis, but the rank and file was mostly Shia, including the ranks of sergeant and sergeant major.

In the civil administration, too, more Shia came to be ministers, but usually not of the sensitive ministries of interior or defense, although the director of public security in the late years of the monarchy, Behjet al-Atiya, was a Shiite. A brilliant engineer, Dhia' Ja'far, also a Shiite, was appointed minister of development, an important post in the nascent state. There were also three Shiite prime ministers during the monarchy: Sayyid Mohammad al-Sadr, who presided at the coronation of King Faisal II; Saleh Jabr; and Fadhil al-Jamali. On the whole, however, the Sunni Arabs constituted the overwhelming majority of prime ministers. They also occupied two-thirds of upper level government positions, and the Shia only one-fifth—the reverse of the Arab Shia-to-Sunni population ratio in Iraq. The Sunni Kurds had about one-seventh of such positions, so that 80 percent of the upper echelons of government were controlled by the Sunnis.

It seemed that the monarchy in the early 1950s made a political decision to get closer to the Shia, who constituted a majority of the Iraqi Arabs, so that although King Faisal II proposed to a Sunni Turkish lady, his uncle, the onetime Regent Abdul Ilhah, asked for the hand of the daughter of Amir Rabi'a, a powerful Shiite tribal sheik. Furthermore, Abdul Hadi al-Chalabi, the father of the late Ahmad al-Chalabi, was quite close to the ruling elite and a speaker of the senate, perhaps largely a symbolic post but a prestigious one nonetheless.

Nuri Al-Sa'eed was the most astute and experienced statesman in the history of modern Iraq and the main power behind the throne. He was Iraq's prime minister eight times between 1930 and 1958, and the architect of Iraq's foreign and most of its internal policies. He also had the allegiance of parliament, which he shrewdly managed to pack with loyal landlords and politicians. He had represented Ottoman Iraq in Majlis Al-Mab'oothan (the Assembly of Delegates) in Constantinople, and after the collapse of the Ottoman Empire in World War I, escorted Faisal from

Syria to Iraq. He loved the country, served it faithfully, was averse to corruption and tolerant of criticism, but became more authoritarian in his later years.

By and large the government ministers during the monarchical regime were Iraqi patriots with ability and integrity, and the Iraqi bureaucracy was clean, the least corrupt of any in the Middle East, including Turkey and Iran. Oil revenue was increasing in the 1950s, and the government established Mejlis al-I'maar (the Board of Development), which oversaw the building of important dams and bridges, and laid plans for other infrastructure projects and a modern university for Baghdad. The latter was to be built on an island in the Tigris River. Frank Lloyd Wright was among the architects who submitted designs.

The monarchy, however, faced many political and socioeconomic problems that it did not address effectively. The principal disadvantage for the regime was the public's deep anti-British sentiment and its perception that the regime was merely doing the bidding of the hated British. This was not unique to Iraq, for in most other Arab countries the masses perceived the governments coming to power after the collapse of the anticolonialist revolts as puppets of the foreign powers.

In Iraq there were popular urban demonstrations whenever it was time for treaty renegotiations with the British, often culminating in violence, casualties, and resignation of the cabinet. In one of those upheavals, Ja'far al-Jawahiri was killed by a police bullet. He was the brother of the most famous Iraqi poet of the twentieth century, Mohammad Mehdi al-Jawahiri, who eulogized him with profound grief and towering passion in a poem titled "My brother Ja'far." He recited it to a throbbing crowd of thousands that packed the historic Hayderkhana Mosque in the center of Baghdad. The poet likened the martyr's wounds to a mouth that can never be silenced. He decried the arrogance of the regime and prophesied a horizon stained with blood.

No reading Iraqi of that time did not know that poem, and many knew it by heart. Even I, hardly born at the time of the incident, had memorized it when I was fourteen. Its pulsating rhythm was magical and captivating, and I wanted to recite it at the annual high school elocution contest. It was turned down, however, and I was assigned a humorous poem to deliver instead.

Feelings of Arab nationalism and anticolonialism were mounting among the Iraqi Army officer corps, and discontent was spreading. There were coups d'état that the regime overcame. In one of them, the so-called Rashid Aali al-Gaylani's coup of 1941, the British bombed Iraqi Air Force bases, reoccupied Baghdad, and brought back the regent and Nuri Al-Sa'eed, who had fled during the turmoil. Four Iraqi rebel officers were executed while al-Gaylani fled to Saudi Arabia.

There was also unabated anger among the Iraqi military and public at the signing by the Iraqi and other Arab governments of the first truce in the 1948 war with the Zionist army. The Zionists, taking advantage of the truce, strengthened their ranks, improved their weaponry, and eventually defeated the Arab armies, thereby paving the way for the partition of Palestine and the establishment of the State of Israel. The Iraqi and Arab public and militaries saw their governments as having slavishly succumbed to the colonial powers and sold out Palestine.

Masses of Palestinian refugees streamed into Iraq and other Arab countries in the 1940s, and they kept the Palestine issue alive and burning among the Arab peoples and the media. I cannot remember any time in school when there was not one or more Palestinian students in my class, and they were usually among the top students. Like their fathers, they became competent and respected professionals, physicians, writers, poets, journalists, and teachers who influenced future politicians and militaries. The Palestinian mufti of al-Quds (Jerusalem), Ali Amin al-Husayni, had gone to Baghdad and become an influential figure, forming around him a nucleus of Arab nationalists, both civilian and military. He was one of the main motivating forces behind the 1941 coup of Rashid Aali and the four officers, all close friends of his.

There was, moreover, increasing resentment of the Regent Abdul Ilah among the public and the political class. As his nephew, Faisal II, approached maturity, and especially after the latter's coronation as king of Iraq in 1953, the Regent became much more interested in the affairs of neighboring Syria. If a union could be consummated between it and Iraq, he could then become the de facto ruler of Syria. Schemes were hatched, and money was promised and given to various Syrian opportunists, but nothing actually materialized except mounting anger by the Syrian public which was mostly Arab nationalist in orientation and becoming more so by the day. To make matters worse, the Regent developed the habit of interfering in the workings of the executive branch in Iraq. He was furthermore seen as ignorant of the realities of the Iraqi street.

Further alienating the public from the regime were the socioeconomic changes of the 1950s. Oil revenues increased considerably, leading to a widening gap between the rich, well-connected, and entrepreneurial upper middle class on the one hand and the fixed-income middle class of teachers and government employees on the other. "Connectedness" and nepotism became more prevalent—a theme brilliantly portrayed by a gifted and popular Iraqi playwright and actor, Yusuf al-Aani, in the play *The Yarn* and the movie *Sa'eed Afendi*, which I and most people of my and my father's generation had seen, enjoying its political wit and hilarity. Another even more popular Iraqi artist was the lyricist and singer Aziz Ali, who gave voice to the anti-British sentiment and socio-economic inequities in his widely popular satirical monologues broadcast from Radio Baghdad.

Last but certainly not least, the state of the Iraqi farmers left much to be desired. Intelligent land reform was badly needed, but hardly anything was accomplished along that line. The landowners were powerful allies of the political class, especially of Nuri al-Sa'eed himself, who habitually stacked the parliament with their numbers through clever manipulation of the electoral process. They repaid him by voting in favor of his agenda and thwarting the proposals of his political opponents.

The regime, moreover, failed to spell out its political and socioeconomic objectives and did not form a political party to market its policies to the public. It was too slow to adopt the emerging tools of mass media and political propaganda to sway public opinion to its viewpoint. Its benign neglect of economic inequities helped the communists make significant inroads into the lower middle class, the poor, the workers, and even the peasantry. Furthermore, the regime's inattention to the rising tide of Arab nationalism and anticolonialism, especially after the debacle in Palestine, facilitated the spread of these fervent ideologies among the military and the urban public.

Fatefully, into this boiling ferment of Arab nationalism stepped the gigantic figure of Gamal Abdul Nasser. In 1952, he toppled King Farouk (Faruq) of Egypt in a military coup, set up a republic, and shortly thereafter had the British evacuate Egypt (*al-Jala'*, meaning the "pullout"). It is difficult now to describe the immense popularity of this event, not only in Egypt, but also in Iraq and the Arab World, indeed the entire Third World. Nasser was a charismatic leader and an accomplished speaker who plucked at the neuralgic cords of anti-imperialism, Arab nationalism, unity, and nonalignment with either the Western or the communist powers, a position he named "active neutrality" (*al-Hiad al-Ijabi*). He became a hero of the nonaligned block comprising Nehru of India, Sukarno of Indonesia, Tito of Yugoslavia, and Nkroma of Ghana. Nasser's speeches were hugely popular, and Iraqis and other Arabs waited impatiently to hear him on the airwaves.

He was a master rhetorician, adept at connecting with the audience. His speeches often went on for more than an hour, and his favorite targets were the Hashemite dynasties of Iraq and Jordan, King Saud bin Abdul Aziz al-Saud of Saudi Arabia, and al-Habib Bourguiba of Tunis. I was once listening to a speech of his when some in the audience shouted, "How about Hussein, Oh Rayyis (leader)?" They meant King Hussein of Jordan. The quick-witted Nasser immediately retorted, "It is a sin to stab at a corpse," to general laughter.

Nasser also had at his disposal a powerful propaganda apparatus in the form of Radio Sawtul Arab (the Arab Voice) with its star announcer, Ahmad Sa'eed; Radio Cairo; and a number of large circulation newspapers and magazines, especially *Al-Musaw'wir* (the *Photographer*) and *Aakher Sa'a* (the *Last Hour*) that were widely read in the Arab countries. Arab regimes, including Iraq's, began to feel threatened by this new wave and mounted their own largely ineffective media campaigns for the people's hearts and minds.

I have been convinced for a long time, but admittedly not in my teens and twenties, that Nuri al-Sa'eed understood that Iraq was still a weak nation in need of an alliance with Great Britain and the West to safeguard it, not just against the Soviet Union, but also against Turkey and Iran, both of which had fought over

Iraq for over two millennia. He also recognized that Iraq, with fifteen per cent Kurdish population, and with Turkey to the north and Iran to the east, could not choose history over geography and join the chorus of Arab nationalism and unity that Nasser was trumpeting. After all, there had been no history of long-lasting Arab unity, even when the Arabs were the dominant global power. There were instead contending and competing powers in Iraq, Syria, Egypt, and Andalusia.

Nuri al-Sa'eed, an Arab himself, maintained friendly relations with the Arab "brethren," but he worked on securing Iraq as a nation that would enjoy safety and prosperity by minding its own special geography and demography. In 1954, he and his cabinet decided to join the Baghdad Pact, which, besides Iraq, included Britain, Turkey, Iran, and Pakistan. It appears Nuri's intention was to neutralize Turkey and Iran, to fend off Soviet ambitions, and to confront the Nasserist wave.

Ironically, Nasser's Egypt was interested in joining the pact, provided, among other things, that it be named the Cairo Pact. Nasser dispatched a "Free Officer" colleague of his, Salah Salem, to discuss the issue with Nuri al-Sa'eed in a meeting in Sersenk in northern Iraq. Salah could not understand why Nuri was preoccupied with Soviet influence. He told Nuri the Soviet Union was too far from Iraq to be a cause of concern, upon which Nuri ordered his adjutant to fetch a map and dutifully showed Salah that it was only a fifteen-minute flight from the southwest Soviet Union to northeast Iraq. Furthermore, Salah did not seem to know that in the days of Czarist Russia there was actually a Cossack regiment in northern Iraq, fighting the Ottomans during World War I.

The discussions did not bear fruit, and Salah returned to Egypt. Shortly thereafter, the mighty Egyptian propaganda machine unleashed a continuous torrent of attacks on the Baghdad Pact. Meanwhile, Nuri Al-Sa'eed broadcast a long speech on Radio Baghdad, which I still remember. It extolled the benefits to Iraq of the Baghdad Pact and articulated his famous sentence "Dar al-Sayyid ma'moona." (The esquire's home is safe.)

The idea of the Baghdad Pact did not fly well with many in the Iraqi political class because of suspicion of British designs, Arab nationalist sentiment, and because competing politicians were jealous of Nuri and intent on limiting his power. Mohammad Ridha al-Shibibi, a prominent member of the Senate and a famous poet and nationalist, stood up in the Assembly and accused Nuri of "tying up Iraq to the wheel of imperialism." Nuri, upon hearing this, went to see al-Shibeebi at his chambers in the Senate to pacify him.

In 1956, Nasser announced the nationalization of the Suez Canal Company, thus triggering the tripartite military attack on Egypt by Britain, France, and Israel, the latter occupying most of the Sinai Peninsula in a short time, but vacating it later at the behest of President Eisenhower. There were massive student demonstrations in Iraq and most other Arab countries in support of Egypt. I was eleven years old then, and I remember standing outside my home and watching a student procession out of a high school located just behind our house. There were roaring shouts of "Long live Egypt," "Long live Gamal Abdul Nasser," and "Down with imperialism," and I suddenly found myself joining the chorus. We all loved Nasser in those days; so did our fathers.

Nevertheless, when my father heard the uproar outside, he called me in. His words still ring in my ears: "You are still a kid. You should mind your studies, pursue useful hobbies, and spend time with your siblings. Don't be swayed by ambitious politicians

who exploit the passions of the young and the mob to
office." I was upset by the admonition but did not repl
days, boys my age simply did not talk back to their par

The turmoil in Iraq resulted in some violence and th
eight people across the country, mostly policemen. Sch(
shuttered, and later Nuri al-Sa'eed himself went to the A'(
High School, a hotbed of Arab nationalism, to address
dents. He told them that Iraq was doing far better than Eg
that Nasser had nothing to offer them except rhetoric.

The tripartite attack on Egypt came to naught and i
caused the collapse of Anthony Eden's British cabinet. Hov
it greatly enhanced the popularity of Nasser, not only acros
Arab and Muslim world, but also among the peoples of the n
independent nations of India and several African countries
1958, Nasser visited Syria, where he received a hero's welco
Shortly thereafter, Egypt and Syria forged a union, the Uni
Arab Republic, later joined by Yemen, with Nasser as Preside
In response to that, Iraq and Jordan entered into a merger, tl
Hashemite Union. King Faisal II of Iraq and his cousin Kin,
Hussein of Jordan were both great-grandsons of the late Shari
Hussein of Hejaz.

MAP OF IRAQ 1925-1958

# 2

# Early Childhood

My very first memories go back earlier than 1948 when I was a little under four years old, living with my mother and younger brother in my maternal grandparents' house in Kadhimiya, a northwestern district of Baghdad. My father, Abbas Bakir, a young physician, had gone away to Switzerland to get a degree in tropical diseases. Two of the Shia (Shiite) Twelve Imams, Musa al-Kadhum and Mohammad al-Jawad, are buried in the famous Kadhimiya shrine, popularly called al-Kadhum. They were descendants of the Prophet Mohammad's daughter Fatima al-Zahra and his cousin Ali ibn abi Talib, the fourth caliph (khaleefa) of Islam. The town was therefore always congested with Shia pilgrims, some coming in caravans, others on foot from all over the Muslim world. In those days, many Sunni Muslims from Baghdad also visited al-Imam al-Kadhum, whom they respected and hoped would answer their pleas.

Many of the pilgrims settled in Kadhimiya because they venerated the place, and it was very hard, costly, and often risky to make the trek back to their homeland. To make a living, many found work as household hands, often a woman and her husband or a young offspring if she was a widow. So until 1963 we almost always had at least two Iranian helpers, usually a woman and her son, who in time became part of the family. The woman took care of us, the children, and the housework; her son worked around the house, took care of the garden, ran errands, took us out on walks, and often played janitor in my father's clinic.

These people, originally simple villagers, were clean, polite, and delicate, always addressing the male members of our family, children included, as *Agha*, meaning "Sir," and the female members as *Khanum*, meaning "Madam." We became quite attached to them and learned their rustic Persian dialect. When their sons or daughters came to marrying age, my parents or grandparents helped them with money, furniture, and gifts. Even after they left our household, went on their own, and often prospered, they would still call on us regularly, offer their assistance, and run errands—so loyal and grateful they were.

Vividly do I remember my grandparents' house in Kadhimiya, where I spent my very early childhood. It was a beautiful three-story brick house, built (God only knows when) in the Islamic style of the time. It had an open central courtyard in the middle of which stood a well and a tall date palm towering up to the level of the third story. The rooms in the upper two floors were skirted by a narrow balcony looking down on the open courtyard. Above the third floor was the *sat'h*, a flat roof fenced off by a not-too-high brick wall, punctuated by elegant promontories equidistant from each other. The sat'h also had a room where the mattresses were stored during the hot summer days, to be taken out immediately after sunset and placed on metal spring beds spread out on the roof. Air conditioning had not then been invented, and we, like most other Iraqis, slept on the *sath* in the summer.

The house also had a basement (*sirdab*) twenty-four steps underground, the perfect place for the indispensable early afternoon siesta, when outdoor temperatures in July and August would rise to 50 to 55 degrees Celsius (122 to 131 degrees Fahrenheit). The *sirdab* was nevertheless so cool that we often covered ourselves with bedsheets. The equally indispensable watermelons were also stored in the sirdab, after the outer green skin layer was scraped off with a sharp knife; this rendered the watermelons cool enough to savor but not too cold to lose their distinct aroma, as they do nowadays when kept in the refrigerator.

Among my most precious memories is sleeping on the sat'h in those lovely summer nights. By the time I got to bed, the mattress would be pleasantly cool. I would lie down and look at the wonderful summer sky, occasionally peppered by flitting clouds through which the moon seemed to sail, now being eclipsed, now emerging in its full glory. In the clouds I discerned various figures: an old man with an imposing nose, fluffy white hair and a long beard; a horse-drawn carriage; a dancing woman; a roaring lion. And I waited wide-eyed for the figures to transform into different ones.

The moon, too, seemed to me like a human face with its two eyes, a nose, and a mouth drawn out to one side. I gazed at it, wondered if it was anything like the earth, and doubted it was as far as I was told; it just seemed so close. I had learned by then that the full moon was the middle of the lunar month, the half moon was either the seventh or the twenty-first day and the thinnest crescent the very first day. I would also look for the Big Dipper, which my uncle had shown me how to find. We called it *Benat Ne'sh*, meaning the "girls behind the coffin," referring to the stars forming the tail of the trapezoid-shaped "coffin," the appellation no doubt reflecting the generally pessimistic Middle

Eastern cultures. Late at night it would get cold, so I would cover myself with the *lahaf*, a cotton wool-stuffed quilt, and enjoy the luxurious feeling the lahaf provided, allowing me to savor the late cool and caressing summer night while keeping my body comfortably warm.

Another favorite memory is the cockcrow at dawn, a sound, in a strange and soothing way romantic, indelibly heralding the eternal cycle of day and night, oblivious of seasons, happy or miserable times, the rise and fall of empires and natural or man-made disasters; a sound I miss nowadays and relish whenever I hear it again on my travels to the Middle East or Mexico.

As for the *sirdab* (basement) siestas, I enjoyed those, too, but I always woke up as soon as the other family members did and never lingered in the basement after they'd gone upstairs. The household helpers had stuffed my mind with stories about snakes, especially the males (*irbeeds*) taking refuge from the heat in the nice, cool crevices, slithering in the dark. I had also heard the story of the huge black *irbeed* that had once appeared at the edge of my father's cot, then only a tender babe, ready to snuff out his life, had it not been for the house's black tomcat, which promptly pounced on the *irbeed* and killed it. Cats were therefore welcome to prowl around the house because they would not only dispose of mice but also the occasional fearsome *irbeed*.

My loveliest memory from those days was of my maternal great-grandmother, Big Bibi, who lived, mostly in near-sleeping mode, in a spacious room on the third floor. She was of great age and bedridden, but her mind was quite sharp during her wakeful hours, when she invariably asked to see me, so I would excitedly skip up the stairs to her room because I loved her and relished the stories she told me. Often I asked her to repeat the ones I liked most. On the fruit tray at her bedside, she often had a pomegranate cut into triangles, displaying the glistening crowns of the ruby-red seeds. We called each of those triangles a rooster's comb. Big Bibi would give me one or more of them to eat, and would tell me the rooster would soon begin to crow in my belly, laughing weakly as she said so. I knew she was only trying to entertain me, so I giggled but never waited for the cockcrow.

She would also hold my hands and tell me about the three lines of the palm: the life line—I would live long; the happiness line—I would be happy; and the creases at the base of the thumb, which told her I would have only two children—quite amazing, as I do have only two children now. She would also play with me in her own sedentary way by grabbing my fingers one after the other, reciting, "Sa'oodi (my pet name), this is the little finger; it is playful and carefree. This is the ring finger; it will fetch you a beautiful wife. This is the third finger; it will stand you tall among your friends. This is the index finger; it will make you a doctor like your dad. And this is the thumb; it will bring you two children." She would then tickle me under the armpit, sending me into convulsive laughter. Even today I remember clearly the wonderful babyhood time I spent with Big Bibi.

Then one day she did not ask for me. I was about to dash upstairs to see her, but was held back by my grandmother (Little Bibi). "Big Bibi has a bad cold; you cannot see her because you'll catch it." It was the same thing the next day and the day after. In my child's heart, I began to have dark forebodings and suspected the family was hiding something from me. The fourth day one of the household helpers took me to some family friends to play with the children. Back home the next day, I again wanted to go upstairs to see Big Bibi, but the family told me she'd gone on a journey.

I felt my chest tighten and my heart about to burst, and I

broke into convulsive sobs, screaming, "You are lying to me; she is too old to go on a journey. She is dead; I know, I know." It took them all a long time to persuade me that she'd gone to a better world and that we will all join her there, Allah willing, when our time comes.

Kadhimiya was an old and conservative town. The houses, separated by narrow medieval alleys, had bay windows that almost touched each other across the alley. Everyone knew everyone else, and gossip was rampant. The people, mostly Shia, persecuted for thirteen centuries, had the "minority complex," judging each other severely, spreading rumors, and resenting members of their own community who achieved success and national recognition. My father was a successful young physician, acknowledged as an outstanding diagnostician and respected for his merits and his father's reputation among the Kadhmawis, but the restrictive social environment caused him to move us across the Tigris River to A'dhamiya, while keeping his practice in Kadhimiya because "These are my townsfolk, and I will continue to serve them."

He was also probably reluctant to shut down his busy practice in Kadhimiya. Early in his career, a woman was brought to his office, pale, unconscious, and seemingly dead. He immediately injected a sugar solution into a vein, whereupon she woke up and asked, "Where am I?" Her incredulous family burst out in unison, "Praise be to the Prophet and his family. The Hajji's son has resurrected our daughter!" *Hajji* (pilgrim), referred to my paternal grandfather, Hajji Bakir, who'd been to Mecca on pilgrimage. The news swept the old town like fire in dry hay, and my father's practice took off to the stars.

A'dhamiya was the nicest district of Baghdad when we moved there in 1950. It had wide streets, traffic circles, a movie house (there was none in Kadhimiya), and a more modern and relaxed atmosphere. My mother discarded the abaya (chador) she had worn in Kadhimiya, and we, the children, became more relaxed and at ease, not being diligently watched and judged by all the Kadhmawis who knew us, our parents, and several generations of our ancestors.

The grammar school, Najeeb Pasha al-Namoothajiya, which I went to in A'dhamiya was a public school, but *namoothajiya,* meaning "model." All classroom teachers were women. Grammar school in Iraq was six years, spanning the ages of six or seven to twelve or thirteen, and ending with a nationwide test the pupils had to pass to be accepted in high school. We had English in the second year, music classes in piano and violin given by famous Iraqi musicians, and a drama team, where some of my classmates and I would go with Ammu (Uncle) Zaki to the Radio Baghdad studio to air children's plays for the serial program *Ammu Zaki.* After lunch break at the school, we were given milk and biscuits and put to half an hour's nap.

Najeeb Pasha was a mixed school, and I still remember some of the pretty girls whom I was quite fond of. They must be grandmothers or even great-grandmothers now. The pupils generally came from the upper and middle echelons of society, but schools were generally more democratic. There were no zoning regulations, and many students from poor families could be found attending the best public schools. A case in point: The son of the school's head janitor was a classmate of mine. This was socially healthy in that it allowed us to interact with children less fortunate than us and lessened the chance that we'd grow up to be arrogant elitists.

Memories from Najeeb Pasha stand out crisp and clear after more than half a century. I remember my first school trip to Samarra, north of Baghdad, with its famous spiral brick minaret, which I climbed with great gusto, to the horror of many students and a few teachers. At the time there were no guardrails around the spiral staircase, which seemed to me to be ascending toward the "seventh stratum of heaven." Samarra is the city where two of the twelve Shia imams are buried in a famous shrine that al-Qaida operatives blew up in 2006, intending to trigger a sectarian war. They succeeded, for the incident resulted in immense slaughter of both Sunnis and Shia.

I also recall the religion class in fourth grade. I was then ten years old. One afternoon we were reading from the Koran (Qur'an) when a sentence aroused my curiosity: "And if He wished, He would have guided you all to the true path," *He*, of course, being Allah. I asked the teacher, a good-looking but serious woman in her early forties, why Allah would not guide us all. Wasn't that a better fate for his children than Jahannam (hell) for those He chooses not to guide? She did not answer me but gave a hiccup of a laugh, then smiled benevolently. My child's instinct told me that she agreed with me. But then she said, "We mortals are not to question the wisdom of Allah, which is entirely beyond our limited comprehension. Think of it like this: Without darkness we would not appreciate light, and without evil we would not rejoice in the good." Such daring questions of mine were largely tolerated because of my good scholastic performance, my neat handwriting (which I inherited from my mother), and my melodic *tajweed* (intonation) of the Koran in religion class.

I made many friends in Najeeb Pasha. One of them, Ahmad Shibib, was the son of Palestinian parents. He, too, was very good in *tajweed* and Arabic. He invited me to his home one day and showed me his parents' beautiful orchard, where they had lovingly planted all the citrus fruits of their Palestinian homeland and tended them with the love and nostalgia of reluctant emigrants.

Very large numbers of Palestinians had come to Iraq in the late 1940s and thereafter. Another dear friend was Nabil Omar Ali, the son of a famous army officer, noted for his courage, integrity and patriotism. Nabil is my only childhood friend whom time and distance have not separated from me.

We continued, of course, to go to Kadhimiya to visit relatives and friends. To me it seemed too far from A'dhamyia although the two districts faced each other across the Tigris River, and the distance from our A'dhamiya home to the center of Kadhimiya could not have been more than one and a half miles. The ancient bridge connecting the two towns rested on floating barges, and it wasn't until several years later that a modern bridge was built. A cousin of my parents, Miss K, used to take me with her when she visited the Kadhimiya shrine. She was a spinster who had lost her hearing after contracting meningitis in childhood. Her speech was garbled, but people could understand it if they paid close attention; her mother and I always understood her perfectly well. She was, however, quite intelligent and ready of wit, and she loved me. My first experience of the Kadhimiya shrine was quite memorable.

The shrines of Iraq, like the ancient temples of Mesopotamia since Sumerian times, stand in the middle of the town, surrounded by the bazaar (*sug*), and bristle with ceaseless human activity inside the shrine and outside in the bazaar. The gilded-dome Kadhimiya mosque had four huge gates that led into an open courtyard surrounding the shrine. Before leaving the courtyard to enter the shrine, I had to take off my shoes and deposit them with the *keshwanchi*, the man who watches over the shoe racks. Then I entered an open, wide outer corridor having several massive double doors leading into an inner roofed corridor. The doors were covered with silver plate carved with intricate floral and arabesque designs and excerpts from the Koran or the Hadith (Hadeeth), the sayings of the Prophet. On both sides of each set of double doors hung a plaque displaying the "Permission to Enter" script I had to recite out loud before entering.

"May I enter, O' Allah? May I enter O' Messenger of Allah?" a plea I had to repeat to each of the Twelve Imams. The inner corridor, too, had massive double doors leading into the inner sanctum. These doors were much more ornate, with at least one set covered with carved gold plate. The shrine itself stood at the center of the inner sanctum. It was gilded and heavily decorated. Masses of humanity ambulated around the shrine, touching, kissing and clinging to it. I felt sorry for Miss K as she struggled to navigate me around very carefully lest my little body be crushed by the teeming crowd. The space around the inner sanctum was not wide, being rimmed by long rows of people at prayers.

I can never forget my first impression of those pilgrims, the look on their faces of passionate awe, quiet veneration, or vocal pleas often mixed with their tears. I remember to this day the face of a tall, imposing man, possibly in his forties, bearded and mustachioed, wearing the Arab headdress and long robe, clinging to the shrine, his whole body shaking with silent sobs. There were people from Kadhimiya itself, from towns all over Iraq, and from other Arab and Muslim countries, especially Iran, speaking different dialects and languages, yet they were all transformed into a single mass of spiritual humanity.

On the way in and out of the mosque, Miss K reminded me that many people there knew our family, so I had to stick to etiquette and be sure to say *"al-salamu alaykum"* (Peace be upon you) to all adults who came our way. Salam was to be rendered by the younger to the older and the pedestrian to the sitting. In case someone rendered us a *salam*, Miss K explained, I was to reply with a longer and kinder one, "Wa alaykum al-salam wa rehmetu Allah wa' barakatuhu." (And peace be upon you and Allah's mercy and blessings.)

Another lasting impression from this period was my first encounter with the Ashura ceremonies covering the first ten days of Muharram, the first month in the Muslim lunar calendar, when Imam Husayn was martyred in Karbala on the tenth day that month in AH 61 (AD 680). Hence the name Ashura derived from *ashra*, the number ten in Arabic. My mother had taken me with her to Kadhimiya to visit her parents for a few days, and while there the home help couple, husband and wife, begged her to let them take me to see the Muharram ceremonies. Imam Husayn was the son of Ali ibn Abi Talib, the fourth caliph of Islam, the Prophet's cousin and the husband of his daughter Fatima al-Zahra. All the Twelve Imams issued from Ali and Fatima, and are therefore descendants of the Prophet himself through his favorite daughter. They are therefore called Ahlul Bayt, the "People of the House" (of the Prophet).

As a child of seven or eight, I was awed and deeply affected by the Ashura ceremonies. I saw young men beating hard at their chests and flagellating themselves. On the tenth day, to the beating of drums and the sound of bugles, they wounded their foreheads with sharp, curved steel lances (Qamat), causing blood to trickle down their faces and bodies. Before the tenth, there were also passion plays and processions depicting the family members of Imam Husayn and his mercenary killers, chief among them, al-Shimr ibn al-Jawshan, who was always dressed in glaring red, in contrast to the spectators in black. In fact, almost all Shia women of my grandmother's generation wore black at least for the first ten days of Muharram, but usually for forty days (al-Arba'een) after the martyrdom of Imam Husayn.

For readers not acquainted with the Karbala paradigm: Imam Husayn lived in Hejaz when the people of Kufa, then the capital of Iraq, pleaded with him to come and save them from the depredations of the Umayyad caliphs, and they intended to proclaim al-Husayn as caliph. Al-Husayn's father, Ali ibn abi Taleb, had moved the capital from Mecca to Kufa in Iraq to be closer to what had become the center of gravity of the young Muslim Empire, including at the time Greater Syria and Egypt, both conquered from the Byzantines, and Iraq, and a large part of Persia, taken from the Sasanids. Mu'awiya ibn abi Sufian, the founder of the Umayyad dynasty, had been the governor (Wali) of Syria for a long time, and he did not recognize Ali as caliph. Ali was assassinated while praying at the Great Kufa Mosque, whereupon Mu'awiya proclaimed himself caliph.

Mu'awiya then proceeded to pursue Ali's followers in Iraq. There were many killings, amputations, and disappearances, and the ones who were not eliminated were bought over by Mu'awiya, who was at his best in that game. Likewise in Egypt, which was pro-Ali at the time, the Umayyads extirpated his prominent followers, including the governor he had appointed, Mohammad ibn abi Bekr al-Siddiq, son of the first caliph after the Prophet. They grabbed the governor, stuffed him in a donkey's hide soaked in oil, and set it on fire. Mu'awiya also had his preachers curse Imam Ali on the pulpits after Friday's prayers, a practice that continued for many years until it was stopped by the caliph, Umar ibn Abdul Aziz, who was a grandson of Umar ibn al-Khattab, the second successor caliph to the Prophet.

After Mu'awiya's death, his son Yazid became caliph. He was dissolute and spent much time drinking and hunting. It was during Yazid's rule when al-Husayn proceeded to Kufa with his family and a few of his loyalists. He had sent ahead of him his cousin Muslim ibn Aqeel to Kufa, where thousands of people received him with great enthusiasm and prayed behind him. The Umayyads got to work, rounding up most of Husayn's loyalists and buying up the perfidious ones. In the end, they killed Muslim and threw down his body with showers of coins from the Minaret of the Kufa Mosque. There were no phones, wireless, or cell phone messaging in those days to quickly alert al-Husayn of his cousin's fate.

On his way from Mecca to Karbala, al-Husayn was advised by several of his advocates to turn back because they were certain he had no chance against the formidable Umayyad forces. One of those friends, a distant relative, was the chief of the Beni Asad tribe, which had emigrated from the Arabian Peninsula to southern Iraq in the year AH 19 and were related to the late Prophet. He informed al-Husayn that all his advocates in Kufa had been killed, imprisoned, or bought. Husayn gave him the famous refrain he'd given to others: "If Muhammad's religion would only be reborn by my demise, let the swords take me." Hence the similarity to the plight of Jesus Christ, both events evoking the concept of the triumph of blood over the sword, or as Edward Gibbon put it, "And on the final day Jesus met Caesar in the arena, and Jesus won."

The Umayyad army, reported to be 5,000 to 30,000 strong, surrounded Al-Husayn's camp of 70 to 150 family members and warriors and cut it off from the Euphrates River so that his people withered from thirst. His infant son, crying from dehydration, was shot by an arrow that killed him instantly. The men fought on horseback or on foot until they were all killed, including the thunderous Al-Abbas ibn Ali,, Husayn's half brother. Only one of Husayn's sons, Ali, was spared because he seemed to be in the throes of death, but he miraculously survived and was later acclaimed as Zayn al Abideen (the Model of Worshippers) for his intense religiosity.

Husayn himself was stabbed many times until he fell. He was then decapitated and the horses driven over his body until nothing remained of him except the severed head and the skeleton. This was the man who was a model of human sanctity. His grandfather, the Prophet, was very fond of him and had said, "He who loves al-Husayn loves me, and he who hates him hates me," and "al-Hassan and al-Husayn are the knot of my household." (Hassan was Husayn's older brother.) Thus ended the saga of Karbala on Muharrum 10 of the year AH 61, corresponding to October 10, AD 680. It decidedly separated the advocates of Imam Ali and his descendants (Shi'at Ali) from the Sunnis. The Shia have been commemorating the first ten days of Muharrum (Aashura) ever since.

Al-Husayn's head was taken back to Yazid in Syria, along with the weeping Hashemite ladies, including al-Husayn's elder sister, Sayyida Zayneb. The head was then sent to Egypt to convince its pro-Ali populace that al-Husayn had indeed met his death. The tragedy surrounding the deep mourning of Sayyida Zayneb alarmed many people in Syria, especially the elderly who remembered her as a child in Hejaz, so she was sent to Egypt where she stayed with some friends of her departed father Ali ibn Abi Talib. She became ill from long, unremitting grief and died not long afterward. She and her brother al-Husayn are much beloved by the Egyptians, and both have large mosques in Old Cairo that are always teeming with pilgrims and visitors. In fact, there is a popular saying that an Egyptian may make a false oath, but never when he swears by "the head of our master al-Husayn."

So it was that the Arabs slaughtered and mutilated the direct descendants of their prophet barely fifty years after his death, a prophet who had infused them with the force of heaven itself and took them out of the darkness into the dominions of Byzantium and Persia, the dominant and most civilized empires of the age. The murder of al-Husayn and his living memory were the prime cause of the later demise of the Umayyad dynasty of Syria. His son Zayn al-Abideen carried the imamate line down to the twelfth imam, Mohammad al-Mahdi.

The talk about Karbala brings to me another memory. My paternal grandfather, Hajji Bakir, used to travel to Karbala to visit the shrines of Imam Husayn and his half brother Al-Abbas, and he would stay at the home of one of his friends, as was the custom in those days. He insisted on taking me with him. It seems that I was the favorite among his many grandchildren; he would tell his wife he loved me more than his own son Abbas, my father. When the two *eids* (feasts) came, Eid al-fitr at the end of the fasting month of Ramadhan, and Eid al-Adha at the end of the pilgrimage to Mecca, he would give me double the cash gift he gave to my siblings and his other grandchildren and always chose me as his little companion on his trips to Karbala.

What I particularly remember about those trips are the awe-inspiring visits to the shrines, far exceeding my experience in those of Kadhimiya. My grandfather and I would walk through narrow centuries-old alleys lined by shops that sold every item imaginable: foods, spices, amazing Persian sweets, textiles, beautiful Persian prayer rugs, amber rosaries, and a host of other artifacts. A donkey-drawn cart would pass us by, sometimes splashing lingering rainwater at my grandfather's long tunic, and I would dutifully stoop and rub it off with my handkerchief.

Grandpa's Karbala hosts, clad in their long robes and turbans, looked just as imposing as he did. He would introduce me to them as "my grandson Sa'di," another nickname of mine. "Welcome

Sa'ad," they would reply, easily guessing my real name, addressing me as an adult. After we'd gone to sleep, I would wake up about four in the morning to the sound from the bazaar of the huge wooden mortars that strong muscular men wielded to pound the hot *hareesah* in steal cauldrons. *Hareesah* was a delicious dish of oatmeal and macerated meat that many households in Karbala would order, especially in the winter, during religious holidays or when they had guests. My grandpa's hosts would serve us in the morning the delicious *hareesah* in large dishes topped with molten lamb's fat, cinnamon, and sugar, and I loved it so much that I kept at it until my grandpa gave me a certain side glance to indicate it was time to stop before I would grudgingly stop eating. Of course I still love *hareesah*, and it's so much easier to prepare in these times of electric blenders.

I and my two younger brothers were very close to my two maternal uncles and had much fun whenever we were with them. When I was between ages seven and twelve, my older maternal uncle, Abdul Husayn, would take me with him to the movies. One time when I was seven we were watching a Hollywood movie at Cinema Roxy on al-Rasheed Street. The film's title escapes me now, but I clearly remember a romantic scene where the hero was waxing eloquent about his love for the beautiful heroine. I was waiting expectantly for him to kiss her, but he seemed too timid to do so.

I then got frustrated and blurted out to my uncle, "Why doesn't he kiss her, Uncle, what's he waiting for?" The audience around us broke out in loud laughter, some turning their heads to see the audacious child who made the comment. My uncle was embarrassed, but I felt the audience was glad that in my child-hood candor I had expressed their own thoughts. Finally, after many not-so-subtle clues by the heroine, our brave hero actually lowered his face to hers and gave her a passionate kiss. The audience laughed again, many turning toward me to make sure I was happy with the outcome.

When I was seven or eight, Uncle Abdul Husayn taught me to play backgammon. At first I counted the slots as I moved the checker, but every time I did so, he would give me a gentle slap on the hand, saying, "Don't count the slots. Just scan them quickly and place the checker where it belongs. This will boost your arithmetic." He was also a great humorist. We and also the adults laughed hard when he told us his seemingly inexhaustible stories and jokes. So we always waited anxiously for Friday to arrive, when he would come to visit us. He and my other uncle, Abdul Amir, were very close to my mother, their only full sister, and treated her with great tenderness.

We also had a wonderful time with the younger maternal uncle, Abdul Amir. We jumped into his bed, rode on his back, and the three of us—our two sisters were not born then—performed impromptu plays that he recorded on his Grundig tape player, one of the first to arrive in Baghdad. We kept the tapes and would play them every once in a while until a burglar stole them along with my father's gold Movado watch. We could not understand why he'd taken the tapes, but when he was caught many days later and brought before our cousin, the district attorney, he surrendered the tapes but swore by Allah he had not stolen the watch. My cousin let him go, but kept the tapes. He would not give them back to us, and whenever I asked him about them he would smile and say, "I will give them to you when you've grown up and become a man, and they will remind you how naughty you were as a kid." I never saw them again.

My mother, Amira Abdul Razzak, saw to it that we kept abreast of our homework and excelled at school. She often tutored

me and my brothers in English and math. She would go surreptitiously to Najeeb Pasha School to ask the teachers how we were
doing and tell them not to be lenient with us simply because they
were friends of hers. Like almost everyone else in those days, and
nowadays too, she was superstitious, always wary of the "envious
eye," so she would often burn Syrian rue (*perganum*) seeds over
burning charcoal in a brazier and recite a special sura from the
Koran to ward off the evil eye, which surely directed its gaze
toward her three boys born in succession and now doing well at
school. We liked the crackling of the rue seeds over the coals, but
tried to escape our mother's ritual to no avail.

What we really loved was to cuddle in winter with my mother
in a circle, with blankets covering our legs. In the middle of the
circle stood the same brazier with the burning charcoal, this time
topped by cooking chestnuts which we picked up, removed their
shells, and ate with gusto. The occasion was also a wonderful
story-telling time.

We also had a good time with my mother's three aunts,
Munira, Thamina, and Amani. They loved us and told us stories
from the old times. They often slept over at our home for many
days, and we enjoyed the busier environment. Aunt Thamina was
very religious. To her, extreme cleanliness meant holiness, so she
insisted on kissing us before she took her ablutions because we
were not allowed afterward to come near her for the remainder of
the evening. Her ablutions and prayers took an eternity, and we
joked among ourselves that her prayers were longer than Imam
al-Hassan's (the elder brother of Imam Husayn, famous for his
long, meditative prayers). The part we really enjoyed about all of
this was the wickedness we displayed when we went in a close
circle around Aunt Thamina while she was praying, pretending
we were about to touch her, prompting her to articulate *"Allahu*

*Akbar"* (God is greater) each time we came close to her because she could not interrupt her prayers to ward us off.

When Aunt Thamina stayed at our home, she saw to it to wake me up before sunrise to perform my predawn prayers, a habit of hers that I did not enjoy in the least. One time I got up reluctantly and murmured, "But, Aunti, it's too early; I can do it later," to which she retorted, "But, son, missing the predawn prayers is like burning a thousand villages." I responded, "How about the Prophet's saying that one good deed is worth the prayers of a thousand years?" She replied, "And what good deed have you done so far?"

When I was still a student at Najeeb Pasha School, Queen Alya, the widow of King Ghazi and mother of the king-to-be Faisal II, died. Our feared principal, her mouth quivering and face clouded by sorrow, announced the news at a gathering of all the students. The young Faisal was therefore doubly orphaned before his maturity. There were public mourning ceremonies, and the famous Egyptian Qur'an reciter, Abdul Basit Abdul Samad was invited to Baghdad where he intonated glorious Koranic suras in both the A'dhamiya mosque of Imam Abu Hanifa (Haneefa) al-Nu'man and the Kadhimiya mosque—recitals I've always considered masterpieces of the their genre. I later got a tape recording of the reading at the A'dhamiya mosque, which I greatly cherished and kept for many years until it was lost during a house move.

In 1953, not long after the death of Queen Alya, the young Faisal attained his maturity and was crowned King Faisal II of Iraq. His maternal uncle Abdul Ilah had ruled the country during his nephew's minority.

THE SPIRAL MINARET (AL-MALWIYA) IN SAMMARRA, IRAQ,
COURTESY OF NATIONAL GEOGRAPHIC MAGAZINE.

THE KADHIMI'YA SHRINE IN THE 1950's.
COURTESY OF STEVE McCURRY.

My paternal grandfather, Hajji Bakir

# 3

# Baghdad College

When I graduated from Najeeb Pasha in 1956, my parents had to choose the "right" high school for me. The best one was Baghdad College, a private school established by the American Boston Jesuits in Baghdad in 1932. My father was opposed to my going there because he felt the school had a missionary agenda, but my uncle, Dr. Farhan Bakir, having recently returned from graduate training at Georgetown, was impressed with the American educational system and persuaded my father to send me to Baghdad College. There was an admission English test in my days, but the interviewing Jesuit father felt I did not need one, so I was quickly accepted in the school with many assurances to my father that I would be happy there.

High school in my time was five years. The first three (middle school) was followed by a national exam, whereupon the high-scoring students would proceed to study math and the sciences in the next two years (secondary school, science branch). The lower scorers would study arts and the humanities (secondary school, literary branch). At the end of secondary school there was yet another, much more intimidating national test. The high scorers in the science branch could apply to medical (six years) or engineering (five years) colleges, but the lower scorers would only be accepted in colleges of law, commerce, business administration, or agriculture.

I don't think that was a good or a fair system, for one because the future career of a pupil was more or less decided at the childish age of fifteen, when many pupils may very well be late bloomers. Much more importantly, however, the system perforce relegated to secondary status the essential studies of agriculture, economics, finance, and business administration, all crucial disciplines for national economies.

Baghdad College was indeed a superb high school, equal to any in the US. It had elegant buildings, spacious, well-groomed fields, a good library, up-to-date laboratories, and knowledgeable, intelligent, and dedicated teaching staff. And although it had many student societies and sporting activities, scholastic excellence was emphasized over and above all else. There were monthly "reading of marks," which all the students, their parents, and the faculty attended. Blue and yellow ribbons were given to the first and second ranking students in each class, and testimonials for the best achieving students in individual subjects.

The fathers (priests) at Baghdad College were dedicated, and most were excellent teachers. They had come to Iraq and adjusted to its continental weather with very hot summers and dry, cold winters, sandstorms in the spring and summer, and temperatures in July and August soaring to 113 to 131 degrees Fahrenheit (45 to 55 Celsius). They lived simply and traveled second class on public buses. And they knew their students well and remembered them long afterward.

Our principal was Robert Sullivan, SJ, serious and

intimidating. When he called us to his office to discuss some issue, we knocked at the door, which opened electrically. This in itself was somewhat sobering since no other door in all of Iraq did so at the time. He asked me once if I had any comments about the curriculum, and I offered some suggestions. He said, "But we've been doing this for five hundred years," to which I responded, "All the more reason for making some changes." He was not amused. A problem for me was that ever since my childhood I somehow always spoke my mind, especially to power. My father once told me: "You will succeed in whatever field you choose as long as you like it. Just don't venture into the diplomatic service."

In English class, Sidney MacNeil, SJ, read to us Poe's "The Telltale Heart" so theatrically that we got goose bumps. He almost never gave any student more than nine out of ten, so it was quite remarkable that he gave me nine and a half for a simple sentence I wrote: "Shakespeare was a shrewd businessman"—which he thought was excellent owing to the element of surprise in the last word.

Robert Farrell, SJ, was a newcomer to Baghdad when he was assigned as our homeroom teacher, Class 3A. A spoiled and always splashingly dressed student, the son of a wealthy landlord, made a lot of trouble during class, and I saw that Father Farrell was quite frustrated by that. I was in a way a class leader and was embarrassed that one of our classmates had behaved so badly on the first day for a new teacher. When the class ended, I shot at the student: "A monkey in silk is still a monkey." I had heard Marlon Brando say that line in the movie *Viva Zapata*, and it had appealed to me. I saw Father Farrell forty-five years later at a Baghdad College reunion in Framingham, Massachusetts. I did not recognize him at first, but he called me by my first name. He then told me he'd always repeated to his US students my proverb about the monkey in silk. That is what I meant earlier when I said the fathers never forgot their students. As for the proverb, I have to give credit where credit is due, to Viva Zapata's screenwriter.

In 2D, Joseph Fennell, SJ, taught us chemistry. He had his own method of getting certain facts to stick in our memory. He had a habit of placing his right index finger on the right side of his nasal ridge while asking a student in a twangy voice, "Why would a horse refuse to stop by a glue factory?" The student would scratch his head and look around for some stealthy assistance, when Father Fennell would say, "Because they would grab it and make glue out of its bones." How can one forget that?

Outside of class, Father Fennell would instruct us on archery—great fun. He once saw me walking by myself and figured I was immersed in thought, so he asked me what I was thinking about. I said I found science incompatible with religious teaching. I asked him, "If we seek the truth, shouldn't we look to science and science alone?" He gave me a forgiving smile and said, "The ultimate truth is out of our reach because our science is often limited by our preformed notions and prejudices, and what we take now for facts may later prove to be wrong."

I saw him forty-six years later, also at the Framingham reunion. He lived in a retirement home for the Jesuit fathers and was blind from macular degeneration. I told him who I was. He smiled, his eyes no longer projecting his active mind, and asked me, "Have you found the truth yet?" I laughed and said, "Not a bit closer to it now than when I was fourteen." He let out a weak laugh; he was too frail.

Mathematics with a passion was given to us by William Sheehan, SJ, who used to say "A mathematician is lazy," meaning that we should attempt to take the shortest possible path toward solving problems and not get lost in long and tortuous maneuvers.

When he got tired of writing on the blackboard, he would grab his right wrist with his left hand, flexing and extending his right hand. He was baffled as to why the class erupted in suppressed laughter whenever he did so. Little did he know that in Iraqi custom that particular gesture was an obscenity directed only at a hated foe.

My biology teacher was S. T. Gerry, SJ, who was attached to his pipe. At times he manned the school's bookshop, when he often skipped lunch. Later in the afternoon, he would say he was hungry and immediately produce an apple, which he devoured with great gusto, not forgetting to say, "An apple a day keeps the doctor away." He also oversaw the Scientific Society and would take us beyond the Sedde (dam) in Baghdad to fish for paramesia and other unicellular organisms in the muddy puddles of the area. The Sedde was an earthen dam built by the Ottoman governor, Nadhum Pasha, to protect Baghdad when the Tigris crested in April. When the river later receded, it left behind large pools of stagnant water.

We would then take our catch back to the biology lab at the school to examine the various creatures under the microscope and make notes. Father Gerry would then go round, look down each student's microscope and at his notes, and write down his own remarks in a book he carried with him. One afternoon we stole into his office to look at the notes he jotted down about us, and discovered that yak was a favorite word of his because he used it often. He would write, "X.Y. is a nice young man but quite a yak." We then had a good laugh at the expense of the yaks.

Frederic Kelly, SJ, who taught us physics in the senior grades, was a graduate of the Massachusetts Institute of Technology. He was tall and walked fast, with the palms of his hands facing forward. And he was passionate about his subject. One day while giving a class on electromagnetism, he held a light bulb in the middle of a magnetic field, whereupon the bulb instantly lit up, prompting a back-seat student from southern Iraq to shout in Arabic a common expression of pleasant surprise: "Praise be to the Prophet Muhammad and his kin!" sending the whole class into a spasm of laughter, to Father Kelly's utter loss as to the cause of the merriment. He did not understand Arabic and could not possibly know that Iraqis and other Arabs would utter that very sentence when sighting what seems to be a miracle.

Our Arabic teacher in senior high school was Mr. Mohammad Husayn al-Shibibi, himself a poet. He was an eccentric but intelligent and warm man. He was popular with the students, whom he stratified into two groups: the *taratra* (clowns) and the *abaqira* (geniuses), not naming the segment in the middle. Both groups, however, were fond of him, owing to his good humor, kindness, and passionate love of Arabic poetry. He had a ruddy face, a large central bald spot surrounded by thick red hair, and wore wide-rimmed reading glasses and an impressive mustache. When he asked a question, he would first scratch his head while simultaneously flexing his knees, thus shortening his height, a habit that always gave us cause for suppressed amusement.

He would hold *taqfiya* (rhyming) competitions in class and also out on the lawn during lunch breaks. In classical Arabic poetry, the last word of each verse must rhyme with the last word in all other verses. Recognition went to the first student to come up with the correct rhyme. The students found these exercises to be great fun.

Once, toward the end of the school year, he invited the class to a rhyming luncheon at his home. The poem was by his favorite poet, Abu al-Tayyib al-Mutanabbi, a tenth-century

Iraqi poet from Kufa, and possibly the greatest of all Arab poets. At the end of the contest, he presented the winners with books, which he dedicated with a few lines of verse lauding the qualities of the winning student. My prize was a book about (whom else?) al-Mutanabbi by an accomplished Lebanese author, Joseph al-Hashem. The book has been with me for fifty-six years now, the pages fragile and yellowing. I still cherish it and reread it every few years, and it reminds me of the dear late Ustadh (teacher) and his unforgettable gift to us, his former students.

The name al-Mutanabbi literally means "he who claims to be a prophet," and the man was indeed a prophet among the poets. Many of his verses and half verses have long been famous Arabic proverbs. He once suffered from a nocturnal fever which he described thus:

> My visitor must be shy, for she only comes in the
>     dark.
> I offered her my limbs and innards as well.
> She spurned them, dwelling in my bones
>     instead.
> The doctor says it must be something I ate,
> That my ailment is surely from the food I
>     partake,
> But his books tell him not of a thoroughbred
> Wilting from long indolence.
> Having galloped amid the legions of the foe,
> Raising one dust storm after another,
> He is now leashed, unable to roam, gallop,
>     or eat.

Each verse (Bayt) in a traditional Arabic poem is composed of two halves written on the same line but separated by a space: *al-Sadr* (front) is the right half of the line, and *al-A'jz* (back) is the left half (since Arabic script goes from right to left). It is the last word of the *A'jz* that must rhyme with all its counterparts in the other verses. In my adaptation into English of Arabic verses, I will keep the *Sadr* and *A'jz* on the same line unless they are too long to be fitted in one line, in which case I would have the two halves succeed each other from above downward, as I've done above. The prerequisite rhyming of all the last words of the *A'jz* is impossible for me to render in English, but I've done my best.

He addressed another famous verse from a poem to the ruler of Syria, Sayful Dawla al-Hamdani:

> Credit me if one recites you a poem for I am the
> songbird, he the echo.

It was Baghdad College that kindled my interest in America. The way the fathers taught, interacted, and joked with us was so different from the set rules of Iraqi and Arab societies that I saw America as a genuinely New World. I pictured myself visiting there or doing graduate work.

The material we covered was new and fascinating to me. We read Shakespeare, Poe, O'Henry, Ogden Nash, Jack London, and Washington Irving, and were taken by "Rip Van Winkle," and "The Legend of the Sleepy Hollow." We had *Aesop's Fables*, *Grimm's Fairy Tales*, *Prose and Poetry for Boys and Girls*, Nesfield's *English Composition* and Francis Donnelly's *Model English*, books one and two. The latter showcased some of the most beautiful pieces of English literature, including a passage by Washington

Irving I memorized at the time; it impressed upon my young imagination the natural beauty of America:

> On no country have the charms of nature
> been more prodigally lavished. Her mighty
> lakes, like oceans of liquid silver; her
> mountains with their bright aerial tints;
> her valleys teeming with wild fertility; her
> tremendous cataracts, thundering in their
> solitude; her boundless plains, waving with
> spontaneous verdure; her broad, deep rivers,
> rolling in solemn silence to the ocean; her
> trackless forests, where vegetation puts forth
> all its magnificence; her skies, kindling with
> the magic of summer clouds and glorious
> sunshine; no never need an American look
> beyond his own country for the sublime and
> beautiful of natural scenery.

I still have in my study Father Donnelly's two-volume book from 1958, peppered with the scribbles, notes, and comments of a fourteen-year-old. In fact, I pick up the two volumes every now and then and reread the passages I most cherished as a boy, a kind of reminiscence, I suppose.

Of the friends I made at Baghdad College, Namik Hazim Namik especially stands out. He introduced me to Western classical music. I had had some exposure to it from a few movies and Radio Baghdad, which occasionally played Korsakov's *Scheherazade*, Tchaikovsky's *Marche Slave*, the popular segments of Bizet's *Carmen*, some of Donizetti's famous pieces, or one of Liszt's Hungarian rhapsodies. Namik, however, was a different story altogether. He had plunged with great zest into the Western classics, listened to them with rapture, and read about the lives and times of composers and conductors. He designed an elegant bar graph depicting the career span of the famous composers, with his initials boldly displayed overhead.

He had a studio-like room with huge loud speakers and gave regular concerts he invited his friends to. I still remember Namik's concerts, and they've always had a special place in my heart, as has Namik himself. We used to get together and listen to the music over drinks, beer, or A'raq in late high school and college. We would exclaim "Allah," the forerunner of the Spanish "Olé," to give vent to our rapture. Namik would often stand up and play conductor. I heard Tchaikovsky's *Pathetique* for the first time in one of the early concerts as the wondrous melodies merged with the tepid breeze of a beautiful summer evening, transporting us all to an enchanted planet. Another concert of his was my first introduction to Beethoven's Ninth Symphony, and I can never forget the impact on my senses of that masterpiece. It was then that I understood what some author meant when he said a man who has heard the Ninth is not like one who has not.

Another dear friend from Baghdad College was Ali al-Haydari, who (like me) was later accepted in medical school. His father was a learned man with a keen interest in a wide range of Arabic poetry from classical to modern and had an extensive library. He used to lend me some poetry books, which I quite enjoyed reading, often memorizing large segments of different poems. One of those books that I loved and remember some of its poems to this day was by the Lebanese Bshara al-Khoury, so called al-Akhtal al-Sagheer, the Little Akhtal, after a famous Arabic poet from Umayad times in the seventh century AD.

When I reflect on the past, as I often do nowadays, I see that Baghdad College changed my life in many more ways than I'd ever admitted to myself before. By early 1958, Baghdad College's reputation for excellence had spread far and wide. This was acknowledged in a visit to the campus by King Faisal II, his uncle and onetime regent Abdul Ilah, the prime minister Nuri al-Sa'eed, and several other cabinet members. I think there was also a political message behind the visit. The astute Nuri saw the setting sun of the British Empire and the blinding sunrise of American power, and it made sense to pay a royal visit to Baghdad College, an institution clearly identified as American.

Nuri had met earlier with President Eisenhower, and the two men had a long, friendly chat. Iraqis, my father included, were talking about Nuri's fraying relations with the British. He had extracted from them higher payments for Iraqi oil, and in a meeting with the British Prime Minister Harold McMillian, he is rumored to have brought up the subject of Kuwait, became heated, and banged the table. He, like other Iraqi political leaders who came after him, considered Kuwait part of Iraq. About four decades before, the British had drawn a line in the sand, separating Kuwait from Iraq, thus denying Iraq effective access to the Persian Gulf waters and, as it turned out later, a large fraction of its oil wealth.

Furthermore, Fadhil al-Jamali was getting more attention in Iraqi political circles as he was seen to be closer to the Americans than to the British. When he was young, he secured a scholarship to do graduate studies in the United States and while there married a fine American woman. After he returned to Iraq, he served as minister of foreign affairs and later as prime minister. He was a highly educated man and one of the signatories to the

United Nations Charter. However, there was not enough time for the Iraq–US relation to blossom, for dark clouds had gathered beyond the horizon, and very few people had predicted the coming storm.

*All the images in this chapter, except the images on pages 57, 58 and 59 are the courtesy of the Jesuit Archives of the Northeast, and Central US, with special thanks to Dr. David Miros, Ann Rosentreter and Michael Benigno.*

THE AUTHOR UPON ENTERING
BAGHDAD COLLEGE, AGE 12

ROBERT FARRELL, SJ,
HOMEROOM CLASS TEACHER,
BAGHDAD COLLEGE, 1959

JOSEF FENNELL, SJ, MY
CHEMISTRY TEACHER,
BAGHDAD COLLEGE, 1958

MUHAMMED HUSAYN AL-
SHIBIBI, MY ARABIC TEACHER,
BAGHDAD COLLEGE, 1960

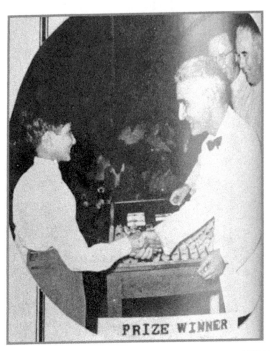

BAGHDAD COLLEGE: THE AUTHOR RECEIVING A SCHOLASTIC PRIZE FROM
MR. ABDUL HAMEED KADHUM, IRAQ'S MINISTER OF EDUCATION.

KING FAISAL II OF IRAQ INAUGURATING A DEVELOPMENT PROJECT;
TO HIS RIGHT IS MINISTER OF DEVELOPMENT MR. DHIA' JA'FAR.
IMMEDIATELY BEHIND HIM IS HIS UNCLE ABDUL ILAH, THE EX-REGENT.

KING FAISAL II, RIGHT, AND NURI AL-SA'EED,
LEFT, VISITING BAGHDAD COLLEGE, 1958.

BAGHDAD COLLEGE: KING FAISAL II STANDING
BETWEEN THE PRINCIPAL ROBERT SULLIVAN, SJ, LEFT,
AND THE RECTOR MICHAEL MCCARTHY, SJ.

BAGHDAD COLLEGE: FROM LEFT TO RIGHT: MINISTERS FADHIL AL-JAMALI, ABDUL WAHAB MERJAN AND ABDUL AMIR ALLAWI.

BAGHDAD COLLEGE: CLOCKWISE FROM LEFT TO RIGHT: REGENT ABDUL ILAH, KING FAISAL II, MICHAEL MCCARTHY, SJ, ROBERT SULLIVAN, SJ AND MINISTER OF EDUCATION, KHALIL KENNA.

From left to right; the author, Namik Hazim Namik and
Mani' al-Sa'doon at one of Namik's home concerts, late 1950's.

Iraqi scene from the 1950's.

BAGHDAD IN THE 1950'S: AL-RASHEED STREET, THEN
THE CITY'S MAIN COMMERCIAL ARTERY. COURTESY
OF NATIONAL GEOGRAPHIC MAGAZINE.

IRAQI WOMEN IN THE 1950'S BALANCING ROUNDED WOODEN YOGURT CONTAINERS ON THEIR HEADS ON THE WAY TO CUSTOMERS' HOMES. COURTESY OF NATIONAL GEOGRAPHIC MAGAZINE.

The Sassanid Arch of Ctesiphon, the highest unsupported brick arch in the world, Salman Pak (al-Mada'in) southeast of Baghdad.

The author, 17, in the final year at Baghdad College, 1961. Courtesy of the Jesuit Archives of the Northeast and Central US.

# 4

# The Demise of the Monarchy: July 14, 1958

The Arab world in the 1950s was undergoing a great ferment that resulted in a crescendo of nationalist and anticolonial fervor, punctuated by the 1952 coup d'état in Egypt. Nasser's charged speeches were enthusiastically received by millions of Arabs, through the pervasive influence of his personality and his media. The public mood was given a powerful boost by the tripartite assault on Egypt in 1956, the smoldering Palestinian problem, and the ongoing war of liberation in Algeria.

Millions of Arabs knew of Jameela Bouhaird, the legendary woman of the Algerian resistance. Her pictures populated schools, public bus stations, newspapers, and magazines. Other millions flocked to see the famous French movie *The Battle of Algiers*. Not surprisingly, therefore, within a decade after the coming of Gamal Abdul Nasser, three military coups toppled the regimes in Iraq, Sudan, and Libya.

I was a fairly happy fourteen-year-old in the summer of 1958, enjoying the holiday after my second year at Baghdad College. If I forget everything else, I can never forget that fateful day, July 14, 1958. I was at home when we heard Radio Baghdad broadcast "Declaration Number One" by the Revolutionary Command Council announcing the overthrow of the monarchy and the establishment of the Republic of Iraq.

The rhetoric was intense and threatening, and I sensed the country was in a state of war. It became clear quickly that the two main figures leading the coup were Staff General Abdul Kareem Qasim and Staff Colonel Abdul Salam Arif, the latter calling for the elimination of the "traitors." King Faisal II, on the threshold of marriage, and his uncle Abdul Ihah forbade the royal guard from overpowering the mutinous troops besieging the palace, which they otherwise could have easily accomplished. The rebels promised the king, the reagent, and their household safe passage, but officer Abdul Sattar al-Ubusi shot them as they were about to leave the palace, on orders, it is said, of Colonel Abdul Salam Arif. The royal corpses were dragged in the streets and mutilated by the mob. The royal ladies, like their male kin, Hashemite descendants of the Prophet, came out in their nightgowns, raising up Koran-clasping hands. They were shot too.

Nuri al-Sa'eed was missing, and the coup leaders were not sure if he was in hiding or had fled the country. A curfew was declared, and the Army set up checkpoints and was looking for Nuri everywhere. I remember an evening when my father and I tuned in to BBC Arabic. The newscaster said that Nuri al-Sa'eed was still missing, that his whereabouts were unknown, but it was thought he was somewhere in Kadhimiya. My father's eyes almost popped out, and he blurted, "They (the British) are tipping the Army about Nuri's whereabouts."

Nuri al-Sa'eed was indeed in Kadhimiya but had left it shortly thereafter. Neither luck nor the British, however, saved him as they had in previous coups. As he fled Kadhimiya, he was caught about five miles to the south, in al-Battaween district, and shot on the spot. He was secretly buried, but his corpse, too, was exhumed by the mob, mutilated, and dragged in the streets. One cannot help but recall the time of the French Revolution—Charlotte Corday at the foot of the Guillotine in 1793, exclaiming before her decapitation: "Oh liberty! How many crimes are committed in thy holy name."

It was revealed much later that the Iranian Secret Service (Savak); King Hussein of Jordan; the Turkish prime minister, Adnan Menderes; as well as the Iraqi Army chief of staff, Rafiq Arif; and the director of Iraq's Department of Security, Behjet al-Atiyya, had all known of plans afoot for a military coup by certain officers of the Iraqi Army. Even Aziz Ali, a popular Iraqi composer and singer of political monologues, delivered on Radio Baghdad in early 1958 a song beginning with the line "Hadhi al-sena sena; mu mithil kul sena," meaning "This year is a year unlike any other."

Timor Bakhtiar, chief of Savak, and Adnan Menderes, prime minister of Turkey, conveyed the information through civilian messengers to the regent, Abdul Ilah. They could not use direct official channels because the two countries, like Iraq, were members of the Baghdad Pact, which included Britain. Abdul al-Hadi al-Chalabi, speaker of the Iraqi senate, was visiting Iran shortly before the July 1958 coup. He delayed his departure out of courtesy to his hosts, who insisted that he postpone his return to Baghdad.

King Hussein of Jordan, a cousin of King Faisal II, felt so strongly about the issue that he informed officer Rafiq Arif himself. Arif reassured the king that the matter was mere rumor and that he did not doubt the loyalty of the Iraqi Army to King Faisal II. King Hussein, however, insisted that his message be delivered, and Arif promised to do so, but it is improbable that he did because he himself knew the other Arif, Abdul Salam, was involved in such coup plans. More about this shortly.

In fact, Behjet al-Attiya, the security chief under the monarchy, had submitted reports to Nuri al-Sa'eed about General Qasim's involvement in suspicious activities, reports that Nuri dismissed, exclaiming, "Oh, not Karrumi!" a loving rendering of "Kareem," Qasim's first name. The reports from Iran and Turkey reached the reagent, Abdul Ilah. He sent them to the British ambassador in Baghdad and was told they were not factual but rumors intended to damage senior Iraqi officers to make it easier for a communist takeover of the government.

It turned out that the British ambassador had espoused a plan for the military to take over the government, the candidates being either Chief of Staff Rafiq Arif himself or Ghazi al-Daghestani, another senior officer. King Faisal II was to remain on the throne merely as a symbolic monarch. Rafiq Arif admitted in the revolutionary people's court, set up shortly after the July coup, that he had been quite aware of the coup plans and that he protected the officers involved because he shared their ideology and aspirations. It seems that Qassim and Arif had cleverly beat him to the prize.

The British must have recognized the shakiness of the Iraqi monarchical regime in the face of the Arab nationalist fervor and the popularity of Egypt's Nasser. They knew the fascination of the Arab masses with strong military rulers, were very worried about the grass root strength of the Iraqi Communist Party, were annoyed by Nuri al-Sa'eed's recent oil negotiations and his bringing up the subject of Kuwait, and resented the burgeoning establishment's tilt toward the US. They decided, therefore, that it was time to change the scenery in Iraq. Those who disagree with my argument must ask themselves how it happened that the British and the other Baghdad Pact member states stood idly by during the violent toppling of a regime they themselves had pledged to defend as the central member of the Baghdad Pact.

Back to the revolution. The general public and the political class, which did not participate in the atrocities, were nevertheless quite jubilant about the end of the monarchical regime, mainly because the mainstream resented its foreign policy. Demonstrators flooded the streets in support of the revolution; messages of congratulation and gratitude for the leaders swamped Radio Baghdad; and poets, men of letters, and artists sang their praises. It was felt that Iraq had thrown off the British yoke and would soon join the United Arab Republic of Egypt and Syria, thus providing a powerful boost to the cause of Arab unity, socialism, and nonalignment.

Gamal Abdul Nasser congratulated the "brotherly nation" of Iraq, its leaders, and its people. The Egyptian media trumpeted the Iraqi Revolution and prophesied the fall of the other puppet Arab regimes. And Radio Sawtul Arab broadcast charged nationalistic poems sung by famous singers, including, no less, the inimitable Dame Um Kulthum as she rendered Mohammad Hassan Ismail's poem:

> I saw in your newborn dawn the glow of steel
> > chains melting,
> Oh Baghdad, the fortress of lions, the Mecca of
> > eternal glory.

Qasim and Arif, perhaps with the advice of civilian contacts, showed political sagacity by quickly setting up a largely ceremonial triumvirate Presidency Council comprised of a Sunni Arab, Mohammad Najib al-Rubay'i, a respected retired general; a Shiite Arab, Mohammad Mehdi Kubba, a former head of the Istiqlal (Independence) party; and a Kurd, Khalid al-Naqshabandi, a retired officer, governor of Arbil, and a member of the prominent Sufi Naqshabandi clan. The cabinet of ministers was also assorted to include prominent figures of the political opposition to the monarchical regime, now labeled the *al-ahd al-ba'id*, the "extinct era."

Two cabinet members came from the National Democratic Party, which espoused democratic politics and had a membership of educated middle- and upper-middle-class professionals. It had been founded by the well-known and respected Kamel al-Chaderchi, who was for a while a political prisoner during the monarchical regime. The party, however, was never as well organized or regimented as the Communist or even the Ba'th Party. One cabinet member each came from the Istiqlal and the Ba'th parties, and one was a Marxist economist. Only one Free Officer was given the politically unimportant Ministry of Social Affairs.

The cabinet choice, however, alienated the fourteen senior Free Officers who had been active in the conspiracy to topple the monarchy, as most of them were senior in rank to Colonel Arif. The real power was vested in General Qasim, who became prime minister, commander in chief of the armed forces, and minister of defense. Colonel Arif was second in command as Qasim's deputy in all those posts, and he handled the sensitive portfolio of minister of interior.

Just a fortnight after the military coup, an interim constitution was promulgated, and a permanent document was promised in good time after a popular referendum.

Iraq was declared a republic and a member of the Arab League, with Islam as the official state religion. The Presidency

Council was to execute the powers of the presidency, which were practically symbolic, and both the executive and legislative powers were vested in the ministerial cabinet. There was no parliament. There had been early pronouncements about the army returning to the barracks and the establishment of democratic civilian rule, but no statement to this effect was made in the interim constitution, and no commitment to detach the army from politics.

As with many other revolutions, a people's court was quickly established to try members of the extinct era. This was a kangaroo court presided over by Fadhil Abbas al-Mehdawi, a relative of General Qasim. The public prosecutor was another military officer, Majed Mohammad Ameen, who was said to be a communist. The court was open to the public, and was packed with spectators of different political stripes. There were orators among the audience and poets, too. Every now and then someone in the audience would stand up in the middle of the proceedings to deliver with great passion and eloquence a fiery speech or poem imbued with the love of freedom and the motherland and fervent denunciations of colonialism.

The chief judge, al-Mehdawi would himself waxed eloquent at the beginning or during the trial on various political and revolutionary topics having nothing to do with the case at hand. The content of his outpourings was crude and nearly ignorant. The public prosecutor too engaged in similar though more articulate and focused speeches. The proceedings were shown on Iraqi television (in black and white in those days), and millions of people glued themselves to the TV sets at home or at the famous *qahwas*, teahouses serving tea, gossip, backgammon, and dominoes.

The accused included famous Iraqi personalities of high integrity and accomplishment. Prominent among them was Professor Fadhil al-Jamali. During his trial, he had to withstand al-Mehdawi's moronic taunts but nevertheless displayed exemplary grace and forbearance. He ended up in prison, and when later released, he was welcomed in President Bourgaiba's Tunisia and given the chair of Islamic philosophy at the university. His American wife, who had mastered Arabic and become a Muslim, was also a teacher.

Staff General Omar Ali, an outstanding army officer, a regimental commander who had proven his ability, courage, and wisdom, had refused to join the July coup because he would not betray his oath of allegiance to the crown. Many of the revolutionary officers had once been under his command, including Colonel Arif, of whom it was said that Omar Ali had a low opinion. General Ali had at one time been on service in Northern Iraq, when he captured a notorious bandit, Khulepeeza, who had eluded several past officials. During his trial in the people's court, the bandit's wife, a woman seemingly of ill repute, was brought to testify against General Ali to the cheers of the spectators. Al-Mehdawi lauded her as a *munadhile*, a freedom fighter. He, too, was given a prison term and shared the cell with al-Jamali.

Sa'eed al-Qazzaz, a Kurdish minister of the interior, a man of integrity and honesty, was also a victim of the court. A man among the spectators rose up to direct at him an abusive and vulgar poem; al-Mahdawi obviously permitted it. When the judge asked al-Qazzaz if he'd known his accuser, it turned out that this sublime poet had been at one time in dire straits, had approached al-Qazzaz during al-Qazzaz's visit to his town and appealed for help, which the minister promptly rendered by ordering the hosting official to give the man a job. Al-Qazzaz was sentenced to death by hanging. He gave a brief statement upon hearing the court's sentence: "When I stand at the gallows, I will see at my feet those who don't deserve to live." He was hanged.

As with other revolutions, differences between its main figures soon bubbled up to the surface. General Qasim was not about to gift Iraq to Nasser because that's what a "United Arab Republic" would have entailed. Qasim identified with the larger Arab causes, but was first and foremost an Iraqi nationalist and saw himself as the new ruler of Iraq. He also recognized the diversity of the Iraqi population and showed no bias in his choice of candidates for important government and other posts. Hence there were suddenly many highly qualified Shiites, Kurds, and Christians in the various ministries and the University of Baghdad.

In fact, a Mandian, *Subbi* in the Iraqi dialect, the brilliant Professor Abdul Jabbar Abdullah, an MIT graduate and a student of Albert Einstein, was appointed by Qasim himself to be dean of Baghdad University despite the objection of President al-Rubay'i that the professor was a *Subbi*. Qasim had no bigotry. To him the professor was an Iraqi, and that was that. Mandians, *Sabi'a* in formal Arabic, are ancient people of southern Mesopotamia who sanctify John the Baptist and had baptized their children in Iraq's rivers for close to two millennia. They are peaceful, patriotic, intelligent, and artistic—and the best silversmiths in Baghdad. Interestingly, their facial features always reminded me of the ancient Sumerians of southern Mesopotamia, and I have no doubt that they, like many other southern Iraqis, must still have plenty of Sumerian DNA.

Qasim also embraced the Kurds. The new emblem of the Republic of Iraq included the Arab sword and the Kurdish dagger. Qasim, not knowing he would come to regret it, invited Mulla Mustafa al-Barazani, father of the current president of Iraqi Kurdistan, Mas'ud al-Barazani, back to Iraq from his exile in the Soviet Union. Mulla Mustafa and his Barazani followers had fled to the communist Mahabad Republic in northern Iran after the failure of their rebellion in Iraqi Kurdistan in the 1940s, and upon the collapse of Mahabad in 1947, they were granted asylum in the Soviet Union. Furthermore, Qasim also had a loyal Kurd, Taha al-Shaykh Ahmed, in his innermost circle. A popular song at the time was "Kurd we' Arab fedd'i hzam," meaning the Kurds and the Arabs were bound by one belt.

Qasim was very popular. People spontaneously put up his photos in their homes and offices, and throngs literally lifted up his Khaki station wagon when he visited the various neighborhoods of Baghdad. They also liked his nationalist policies, his love of country, his long working hours, and his austere lifestyle. And the poets sang his praises. Young people volunteered in their tens of thousands to join the Popular Resistance force (al-Muqawama al-Sha'biyya), which was established in August 1959.

Colonel Arif, on the other hand, played the Arab nationalist card. He made no secret of his desire to add Iraq to the United Arab Republic comprising Egypt, Syria, and Yemen, under the leadership of Gamal Abdul Nasser, whom he told during a visit to Cairo that Qasim was a transient figure, a statement quickly leaked to Qasim. He also toured Iraq and gave immature speeches about Arab unity, singing the praises of Nasser and almost never mentioning Qasim.

Arif had a following of Arab nationalists and Nasserists, mostly among the Sunni Arabs who espoused the same cause. In the first year of the revolution people in most Baghdad neighborhoods painted portraits of Qasim on the perimeter walls of their homes, but there were almost none in A'dhamayia, the citadel of the Baghdadi Sunnis.

Hanna Batatu, in his massive book *The Old Social Classes and the Revolutionary Movements of Iraq*, argues that the July 1958 coup was actually an expression of the alarm of the *Sunni triangle*, the homestead of the great majority of the Iraqi Army officer corps, at the rising power of the Shiites during the later years of the monarchical regime. The Sunnis, a minority among the Iraqi Arabs, felt they could retain a commanding position in an Iraq that was part of a larger Sunni-majority political union. In that sense, they were quickly alienated from General Qasim—his mother was rumored to be a Shiite—whose policies they saw as antithetical to their historical hold on power.

On the other hand, most of the Shiite poor, the Kurds, and the minority Christian and Subbi populations were pro-Qasim as they felt their citizenship rights would be better protected in an independent Iraqi state. Furthermore, the Iraqi Communist Party, perhaps the largest and best organized of any Arab party at the time, allied itself with General Qasim, who cleverly used the communists and their sympathizers to fend off the Nasserist elements.

A popular refrain of communist-organized demonstrations was "Your republic, oh Kareem, for shame that it becomes an *iqleem!*" Kareem, Qasim's first name, and *iqleem* (province) rhyme, almost always a requirement of slogans. The party's motto was the poetic *Watanun Hurrun we' Sha'bun Sa'eed*, meaning "A Free Homeland and a Happy People." Their flagship was *Ittihad al-Sha'b* (the *People United*) daily newspaper, which was well written and produced, and enjoyed a wide circulation.

The Shiites, however, were not a monolithic block. The landowners in southern Iraq, the affluent, and the religious resented Qasim, mainly because they saw him allied with the communists. A great many educated middle- or upper-middle-class Shiites were Arab nationalists and Nasserists, and some, like Fu'ad al-Rikabi, were in the top echelons of the Iraqi Ba'th Party. Moreover, the religious elements dreaded the communist tide and were alarmed when their children joined the Peace Partisans or the Popular Resistance force, which were rightly perceived as communist-influenced organizations.

Thousands of Shiite men sought the advice of Say'id Muhsin al-Hakeem, the Grand Ayatollah at the time, as to whether some of their "communist" offspring can inherit them. Of course most of those offspring had almost no idea what communism was all about, and they were merely motivated by patriotism, the restless idealism of the youth, or simply their attraction to General Qasim. Ayatollah al-Hakeem then issued a *fetwa* (obligatory religious directive), similar in authority to a papal bull, that such offspring could not inherit their fathers because "communism is blasphemy and atheism."

Hence there developed a politicosocial rift between a very large pro-Qasim faction, mostly poor Shiites, Kurds, and communists, and a much smaller pro-Arif pro-Nasser faction, mostly Sunni Arabs, middle- and upper-class secular as well as religious Shiites and Turkmen, the latter having had a historic antagonism to the Kurds. The Ba'th Party, very small at the time, but even more conspiratorial and violent than the Communist Party, also allied itself with the Arab nationalist pro-Nasser forces. The party's ideology was Pan-Arabist and fascist. Its motto was *Umma Arabi'ya Wahida thate Risala Khalida*, meaning "One Arab Nation with an Immortal Message." Notice again the rhyme, this time of *wahida* and *khalida*, the feminine adjectives for "one" and "immortal" respectively. A motto is never effective if it does not possess the unbeatable power of the rhyme.

The Ba'thists' other motto was *Wihdetun, Hurryyatun, Ishtiraki'yatun,* meaning "Unity, Freedom, Socialism." Note that unity preceded freedom and socialism. These were all foggy ideas lacking defined concepts, but effective rhetorical slogans for mass appeal. The socialism part of the motto was supposed to indicate Arab socialism, a term also mouthed by Nasser, but it's never been clear to me or anyone I know what exactly the difference was between the Marxist-Leninist and Arab brands of socialism.

The antagonism between Arif and Qasim worsened as Arif kept up his public speeches about Arab nationalism, Nasserism, and also, in September 1958, a call to revive the Revolutionary Command Counsel. Qasim, having ignored Arif's speeches at first, eventually removed him from the posts of deputy commander of the armed forces, deputy prime minister, and minister of the interior.

Qasim also attempted to get Arif out of the country by offering him a position as the Iraqi ambassador to West Germany, which Arif refused. In October 1958, Qasim called him to his office to persuade him to accept the post. The meeting lasted all day. At one point, Arif, typically impetuous, pulled out his revolver from his belt—a move Qasim interpreted as an assassination attempt. At the end of the stormy meeting, Arif complied and left for Bonn, but he returned three weeks later amid whirling rumors about a plot against the regime. In early November, not even four months after the July revolution, Arif was arrested on charges of conspiracy to assassinate General Qasim and overthrow the government. At his trial he denied the charges, but was given the death sentence, which was commuted to life in prison upon the recommendation of the court, no doubt suggested by Qasim himself.

In September 1958, the Qasim administration announced two of its most revolutionary and modernizing acts. First, it revoked the Tribal Disputes Code (*Qanoon De'awi al-Asha'ir*), which had dispensed for tribal people legal judgments sensitive to their ancient traditions, and replaced it with the formal civil law that applied to all citizens. This did not sit well with the tribal chiefs, who had hitherto enjoyed uncontested authority over their tribesmen; nor even with the tribes themselves, who had for centuries practiced the traditional internecine raids, and honor and revenge killings.

Second, and far more repugnant to the landowners, was the revocation of the Law of Rights and Duties of Cultivators, which was semifeudal, the lot of peasants indebted to their landowners having been long-term or indefinite servitude. The Agrarian Reform Law (*Qanoon al-Islah al-Zira'i*) to dismantle feudalism (*Iqta'*) and redistribute agricultural land was announced on September 30, 1958. It limited landlord holdings to 250 acres of irrigated land or 500 acres of rainfall land. Landowners were to be compensated over twenty-five years with 3 percent–yield government bonds. The peasants would be each given 7.5 to 15 acres of irrigated land or double that for rain-fed lots. They were to pay 120 percent of the land price to cover distribution costs over twenty years at 3 percent interest. The peasants would keep 50–75 percent of the crop. As I will explain later, the Agrarian Reform Law was well intentioned, but beside alienating the landowners, it produced negative agricultural and socioeconomic outcomes that have beset Iraq to this very day.

Even before the announcement of the Agrarian Reform Law, the peasants in Kut and Umarah in central and southern Iraq were excited by the revolutionary rhetoric and went on a rampage, pillaging and destroying landowners' property and homes and burning accounts and rent documents. The communists joined this movement to disable the landlords and gain the loyalty of the peasants, whom they organized into associations in which the communists assumed leadership roles. These associations were subsequently united to form the National Federation of Peasants

(*Ittihad al-Jam'iyyat al-Fallahiyya*), which the communists insisted should assume the function of land distribution.

To go back to the politics of the revolution, the ousting of Arif was followed by a coup attempt by Rasheed Aali al-Gaylani, who, after a failed coup in 1941, fled the country into exile in Saudi Arabia, then spent fifteen years in Egypt, where he met Nasser. He returned to Iraq shortly after July 1958. He now had a following of army officers loyal to Arif, but also including some Ba'athists, Arab nationalists, Nasserists, and landowners averse to communist influence and the Agrarian Reform Law. The coup plan was discovered in December 1958, and the ensuing trials revealed that Rasheed Aali was working for a union with Nasser and that the plotters had received money and weapons from the United Arab Republic. Rasheed Aali was sentenced to death but was not executed.

Following this episode, the Arab nationalist ministers resigned from the cabinet and were replaced by leftist supporters of General Qasim. Meanwhile, the communists worked on consolidating their power. They infiltrated the news media and trade unions; showed their unflagging support for General Qasim, whom they started calling al-Za'eem al-Awhad (the Sole Leader); established the Peace Partisans (*Ansar al-Salam*) and the World Youth Organization (*Munadhemet al-Shabeeba al-Aalami'ya*); and later infiltrated the Popular Resistance force set up in August 1959. Qasim, for his part, started to refer to Iraq as "*al-Jumhuriya al-Iraqiya al-khalida* (the Immortal Republic of Iraq), which meant they could forget about union with Nasser.

Nasser, in his powerful public speeches and his propaganda machine, started to blast Qasim and "the communist puppets" (of the Soviet Union). Qasim, true to his style, did not extend the courtesy of a rebuttal. This further frustrated Nasser. He grew petty, and in one of his long-winded public speeches he kept asking, "Why would Qasim not answer us?" These outbursts by Nasser, his attacks on Qasim, and the public knowledge of his support of the Iraqi anti-Qasim elements diminished him in the eyes of most Iraqis who had previously adored him, and his star began to fade in the Mesopotamian sky.

The Egyptian Embassy in Baghdad was distributing money to Arab nationalist and even Ba'athist factions to help them organize, publish, and recruit. Nasser also understood the demographics of Iraq and attempted to appeal to the Iraqi Shiites by inducing the Cairo Azher University, the most important religious center of Sunni Islam, to add to its curriculum the Ja'feri jurisprudence promulgated by Ja'fer al-Sadeq in the ninth century, and followed by practicing Iraqi Shiites.

Another military coup against Qasim was now in the making. The main figure was Abdul Wahab al-Shawwaf, commander of the Mosul garrison. The other important actors in the plot were Nadhum al-Tabaqchali, the commander of the army's Kirkuk Regiment; Rif'at al-Haj Sirri, the chief of military intelligence; and Ahmad Ajeel al-Yawer, the chief of the large Shammar tribe. He hated the communists and resented agrarian reform. Last but not least, Nasser's United Arab Republic was to provide arms and a radio transmitter to announce the revolution.

Qasim must have gotten wind of the conspiracy because he allowed Aziz Shareef's communist Peace Partisans to converge on Mosul on March 6, 1959, to celebrate the anniversary of their founding. A quarter million of them swarmed the city. There were confrontations and clashes between the communists and the Arab nationalists, who were aided by the Shammer tribesmen. Al-Shawwaf arrested the communist leaders, and when their followers marched to release the prisoners, they were fired upon by Al-Shawwaf's troops.

Al-Tabagchali and al-Haj Sirri did not deliver on their promise to aid al-Shawwaf. The radio transmitter from the United Arab Republic arrived too late and was too weak for satisfactory transmission. Also, a plan to bomb Radio Baghdad fizzled out. Qasim, on the other hand, authorized his devotee Jalal al-Awqati, commander of the air force, to bomb al-Shawwaf's Mosul headquarters. Al-Shawwaf was wounded in the air raid and was taken to hospital to treat his injury, but while there he was killed by a Kurdish orderly. Many of al-Shawwaf's officers were killed or escaped to Syria, and the Shammer tribesmen vanished into the great desert.

The communists and their Kurdish allies then committed great atrocities, killing hundreds of Arab nationalists. Many members of wealthy old Mosul families were killed and their homes ransacked. Almost twenty people, some uninvolved in the revolt, were executed on the orders of a makeshift court set up by the communists. Al-Tabagchali, al-Haj Sirri, and eleven other officers were arrested, tried, and sentenced to death. Qasim, who had previously blocked the execution of Arif and al-Gaylani, yielded this time to communist pressure and let the Mosul officers be shot. The tragic significance of the Mosul episode was that it unleashed with lethal violence the heretofore restrained grievances that different factions harbored toward each other.

Relations with the Soviet Union were strengthening. Significant economic, military, and cultural exchange agreements were signed. Iraqi students went to Russia for graduate studies, and Soviet military and technical advisers streamed into Iraq. Most of them were impressed by the Iraqi middle-class standard of living, which they said was far better than their own. A Russian physician assigned to the hospital where my father worked told him he could not understand why the Iraqis needed the Soviets.

He also turned out to be a Shiite from one of the Soviet Muslim republics, I don't remember which, and insisted that my father take him to visit Kadhimiya to pay his respects at the shrine. My father had to oblige him, although he himself had rarely visited the Kadhimiya mosque.

Soviet publications flooded the bookshops and the famous al-Mutanabbi Street book stands: an Arabic translation of Marx's *Das Kapital*, books on dialectic materialism and history, books by Lenin and Stalin, the weekly magazine the *Soviet Union*, and most interesting to me, Arabic translations of numerous works of the nineteenth-century giants of Russian literature.

To cap it all, Qasim announced in March 1959 Iraq's withdrawal from the Baghdad Pact. Nasser, too, had forged close relations with the Soviet Union, which financed the Aswan High Dam project and was supplying the Egyptian armed forces with military hardware, tanks, and MIG fighter jets. In Egypt, however, there was no communist party with the strength, organization, and grass roots that the Iraqi Communist Party possessed and used to propel and disseminate the communist lore and cause.

On World Workers Day (Labor Day), May 1, 1959, the Communist Party was instrumental in organizing a procession of over one hundred thousand souls along al-Rasheed Street, the main historic thoroughfare in the center of Baghdad. I remember we were watching the event on television. Every labor union, artisan guild, and peasant association streamed down the long street carrying its special poster, along with pictures of Abdul Kareem Qasim, who, after all, was not a communist himself. The participants and the thousands of cheering onlookers clogging the street and sidewalks were happy and truly jubilant in expressing their love of Qasim. And although the Communist Party had organized the procession, the majority of the participants and the cheering crowds were not communists, and it is doubtful that they even understood the precepts of communism. The people were simply displaying their devotion to Qasim, and it was clear that he was very popular among the majority of Iraqis.

However, a minority consisting of Arab nationalists, Nasserists, Ba'thists, the Iraqi Army officer corps, and the aggrieved landowners perceived the events in Iraq as a communist takeover. This was reinforced by the incessant blaring of the Nasser propaganda machine and the paranoia of Western mass media, with their usually superficial knowledge of other lands and their preconceived generalizations. At a time when the Cold War was at its peak, this obviously raised sirens in the United States and its NATO and Middle Eastern allies, resulting in a torrent of publications in those countries warning of a Bolshevik putsch in Iraq, with eye-catching drawings displaying the map of Iraq surrounded by jail bars colored red, or under the banner of the hammer and the sickle.

Following the collapse of the Mosul revolt, there was yet another plot, this time hatched by the Ba'thists, to kill General Qasim. The foremost actors were Fu'ad al-Rikabi, Colonel Saleh Mehdi Ammash, General Najeeb al-Rubay'i and Ayad Sa'eed Thabit. Siddeeq Shanshal, a previous Qasim minister and some officers were also apprised of the conspiracy, and several thugs, among them Saddam Hussein, Abdul Kareem al-Shaikhly, and Ali al-Zaybeq, were chosen to train for the killing.

In a classic gangster operation, the motorcade of General Qasim was trapped by two trucks that blocked a segment of al-Rasheed Street in Ras al-Qarya. Then the killers, among them Saddam Hussein, unleashed their bullets on his car. He was wounded, but was rushed to Dar al-Salam Hospital, where he was attended to and eventually recovered. Some conspirators, among them al-Rikabi, Saddam, and al-Shaikhly, fled to Syria, at the time part of the United Arab Republic under Nasser. Others, including Thabit, were captured and tried. Some were acquitted, while others were handed the death sentence and imprisoned, but none were actually executed.

There were widespread spontaneous celebrations of Qasim's survival, manifested by the traditional slaughter of sheep to distribute the meat to the poor, a thanksgiving act called *sedeqe*. I was fifteen at the time, and I remember I was going to my father's office in Kadhimyia when I felt quite uneasy in the stomach at the sight of all the slaughtered sheep on the sidewalks. The greatest of Iraqi poets, Mohammad Mehdi al-Jawahiri, recited a ringing poem to some one hundred thousand spectators in the Scouts Stadium (Sahet al-Kashafa) in Baghdad, rejoicing in Qasim's recovery and advising him against leniency toward the conspirators.

The communists, having gained in political power, wanted to neutralize or cow their enemies, and they chose Kirkuk as another stage to accomplish that. Most of the city's inhabitants were Turkmen, central Asian peoples, not Seljuq or Ottoman, who had settled in Iraq in late Abbasid times in the tenth century and afterward. Two dynasties of theirs, the Aq Qo'unlu (the White Sheep) and the Qara Qo'unlu (the Black Sheep) had for a time ruled much of Iraq after the collapse of the Abbasid state. The Turkmen were loyal Iraqis—studious, enterprising, and conservative. The prominent families in Kirkuk were mostly Turkmen: merchants, landowners, bureaucrats, businessmen, and good military officers. There was a long-standing hostility between them and the Kurds, exacerbated after July 1958 by the Kurds gaining much more power with the return of Mulla Mustafa al-Barazani and the Kurds' alliance with the communists.

To celebrate the first anniversary of the July 14 Revolution in

Kirkuk, the communists transported thousands of their followers to the city for a huge procession. They also counted on the support of the Kurds who lived in the countryside around Kirkuk, the Kurdish Democratic Party, and the Kurdish workers in the oil company. Clashes predictably broke out, leading to the death of at least thirty Turkmen. Over a hundred were injured. The Kurds were the main perpetrators.

The Kirkuk episode alienated General Qasim from the Communist Party. He described the events of Kirkuk as barbaric, without mentioning the party by name. Unlike the case in Mosul, there had been no military conspiracy in Kirkuk against Qasim, and he likely perceived that the communists had abused their power and were using the mob to intimidate their opponents. Perhaps he also felt he was about to lose control of the situation, so he decided to strike. Over the eight months following the Kirkuk episode, the prominent communist Abdul Qadir Isma'eel al-Bustany was tried and jailed, the communist newspaper *Iti'had al-Sha'b* was shut down, three pro-communist ministers were dismissed or resigned from the cabinet, and the Popular Resistance force was disbanded.

The latter force was largely composed of younger people, some of whom had communist sympathies, but few were true card-carrying members. Some were simply opportunists, a common phenomenon in Iraq and perhaps in most other countries, but the majority were simply young people riding the revolutionary tide and enamored of Qasim. There were, as always, thuggish elements among the force. I remember one day when I was at Baghdad College, a student plucked out a small picture of General Qasim someone else had nailed into a tree, threw it on the ground, and stamped on it—an ultimate insult in Iraqi custom.

The following day a wave of alarm traveled through the

campus as some thugs from the Popular Resistance forces on bicycles swarmed over the well-manicured fields of Baghdad College. They dismounted and, not finding the student who desecrated the photo of the Sole Leader, picked up a few Arab nationalist and Ba'thist students whom they somehow identified, and beat them up in front of the other students. They then warned the "reactionaries" to watch out, remounted their bikes, and left. Nothing of the sort had ever been seen before at Baghdad College.

The waning of the honeymoon between Qasim and the communists galvanized the Arab nationalists and Nasserists, who saw that Qasim was not a communist after all. He had actually never been. They promptly feigned love for the Leader, and Qasim's pictures suddenly appeared on the walls of A'dhamiya and other Sunni neighborhoods. The dark side to this was the beginning of surreptitious revenge beatings and killings in predominantly Sunni neighborhoods of "communists," onetime members of the Popular Resistance forces, the Peace Partisans, the World Youth Organization, and oftentimes their uninvolved relatives and friends.

Meanwhile, the promises made at the dawn of the July 14 Revolution of a constitution, parliament, and the military returning to their barracks were never fulfilled. A Law of Associations in January 1960 allowed the formation of political parties, but students, government officials, and military officers were prohibited from joining. Qasim managed to play off factions within each party against each other, creating subservient rump parties that were licensed by the Ministry of Interior to the exclusion of the parent parties themselves.

Rump Communist and National Democratic parties thus came into being. They did not represent the majority of the membership and were therefore practically impotent. The Kurdish

Democratic Party (KDP) was also given a license, as well as the Islamic Party, which was fiercely anticommunist, and had the support of the Grand Ayatollah Sayyid Muhsin al-Hakeem, the top Shiite Mujtahid in the Najaf Hawza. With dictatorship increasingly entrenched, Qasim became more withdrawn, remote, and isolated. His mass appeal was slowly ebbing, but the communists, though chastised and diminished, continued to support him, albeit not with the same previous fervor. As the year 1961 folded, most political parties ceased to be functional.

When I graduated from Baghdad College in the summer of 1961, the Qasim administration had promulgated far-reaching social and economic policies. I was only seventeen then, but I recognized that the changes were quite revolutionary, some of them the first of their kind in the Middle East, and with the potential to result in long-term transformations in Iraqi society. I also listened intently to my father, his relatives, and his friends when they discussed those policies, often heatedly, and I often jumped uninvited into the fray to offer my opinion.

I have already mentioned the revocation of the codes in effect under the monarchy regarding tribal disputes, rights and duties of cultivators, and the announcement in September 1958 of the Agrarian Reform Law. The latter was the most significant and well intentioned. However, not only did it not succeed, but it actually led to a progressive decline in agricultural output that has continued to haunt Iraq to this day.

The landlords were stunned by the promulgation of the law. They had not been consulted beforehand because they were perceived by the revolutionary regime (much of the middle class and the political parties) as having been exploitative of the peasants and a pillar of the extinct era. Moreover, it is not the habit of revolutionary regimes anywhere to consult with segments of society they have come to obliterate. The landlords, not surprisingly, did not cooperate. They put their equipment and water pumps under lock and took up residence in the cities.

The state did not have enough qualified personnel or the experience to undertake the redistribution of land and the arbitration of water rights. Neither did the peasant cooperatives set up by the government. The efficiency of the landlords in providing management, credit, and seed was grossly underestimated by the revolutionary regime, as was the historic role of those landlords, who were also tribal chiefs and had for centuries arbitrated intra- and intertribal conflicts and commanded respect and obedience.

Hence, even by 1963, only one-third of the expropriated land had been distributed. The peasants were at a loss and began a mass migration to the cities, mainly Baghdad, where they formed a large unskilled proletariat. Meanwhile, the land was neglected and left to salinate. By 1961, Iraq, where organized agriculture was invented in Sumerian times more than five millennia ago, could no longer export barley. More sadly, it imported almost half of its needs of wheat and rice.

A milestone law that the Qasim administration promulgated in December 1959 was the Personal Status Law (Qaanoon al-Ahwaal al-Medeni'ya) to improve the standing of Iraqi women. It set the minimum marrying age at eighteen, thereby delegalizing child marriage; prohibited polygamy, except when approved by a judge, and then only in very special circumstances; and banned arbitrary divorce. In many cases, a Sunni man had been able to divorce his wife by simply saying, "You are thrice divorced" (*taaliq bil thelaath*), and the wife would almost always lose custody of her underage children. Divorce was harder in the Ja'feri Law to which the Shia subscribed, in that the man had to bring at least two witnesses to testify under oath to the truthfulness of the husband's reasons for divorce.

The fourth and perhaps the most daring part of the Personal Status Law addressed a woman's inheritance right. In Muslim religious law (*Sheree'a*), a male offspring inherits twice as much as the female. Moreover, a Sunni, but not a Shia man, who has no male offspring will be inherited by his male brothers, which is why many wealthy Sunni men who had only daughters had converted to Shi'ism. Under Qasim, indirect legal means were employed to give women equal inheritance rights, and this applied to both Sunnis and Shia.

Needless to say, women were dizzyingly happy about the law, but most tried not to display their pleasure to their male relations. Even in Egypt, where Nasser was waging a furious media war against the Qasim regime, prominent women's rights advocates like the famous writers Ameena al-Sa'eed and Aa'isha Abdul Rehmaan came out in praise of the Iraqi law.

In fact, there was a noticeable empowerment of women under the Qasim regime. He appointed Nazeeha al-Dulaymi minister of municipalities in one of his cabinets, the first woman in the entire Mideast to assume a ministerial position. Women became much more active in politics and social affairs and established the Iraqi League of Women, constituted by educated teachers and other professionals and chaired by a highly educated woman lawyer, the sister of one of my classmates in Baghdad College. Moreover, there was a remarkable rise in the number of young women entering graduate education. One-third of my class in medical school were women.

The Qasim administration also issued laws aimed at easing the burdens of urbanites with limited income, the lower middle class and the poor. Taxes were lowered for those groups, price controls placed on basic foods, penalties defined for merchants making exorbitant profits, the work day reduced from nine to eight hours, pay raised for overtime work, residential and commercial rental prices lowered, and evictions were made much more difficult.

Another important achievement of the Qasim government was the clearing of the Baghdad slums. Well into my late teens there were vast slums of mud houses located mostly beyond Nadhum Pasha's dam (al-Sedde). But there were also numerous slums in the city itself, since there were no zoning regulations. These mud huts were miserable dwellings, lacking toilets and clean water, and inhabited by Arab immigrants from the southern countryside.

The government undertook a massive project of demolishing the slums and building simple and clean brick dwellings so that several mini-cities arose where the wretched slums had existed. The largest of those cities was named Revolution City (Medinat al-Thawra). The name was changed to Saddam City under the Ba'ath, and yet again to Sadr City after the 2003 US invasion, in memory of the late Muqtada al-Sadr's father, who was the religious leader and advocate of the Shia poor.

But more about the Qasim era later.

STAFF GENERAL ABDUL KAREEM QASIM, RULER OF IRAQ, 1958-
1963, DELIVERING A SPEECH AT AL-HIKMA UNIVERSITY.
COURTESY OF THE JESUIT ARCHIVES OF THE
NORTHEAST AND CENTRAL US.

# 5

# The Arab Renaissance: 1798–1960

Chance had perhaps favored my generation, at least during our formative years. I grew up at a time of an Arab renaissance, if I may call it that. The period between the Napoleonic invasion of Egypt in 1798 and the early 1960s, especially the interval between the two world wars, saw a resurgence of Arab intellectual output, notably the art of the novel, hitherto unknown in Arab letters; romantic and political poetry; daring and scholarly historic and social writings; painting; reformist religious thought; and public education.

In 1908, Bishop Louis Ma'loof produced the first modern Arabic dictionary, *Al-Munjid* (*The Rescuer*), an accomplishment that may be likened to that of Johnson's English dictionary. It went into forty-one editions. Later, Elias Anton Elias published his *Al-Qamus al-A'sri* (*The Modern Dictionary*), probably the first English-Arabic dictionary in the Arab world. Mr. Elias intended to familiarize Arab readers and students with the English language and appoint the Arabic words most closely corresponding to their English counterparts. He therefore helped to modernize the language itself by endowing old words with new meanings pertaining to science, industry, and technology.

Accomplished men of letters in Lebanon and Egypt were studiously translating the gems of Western literature and science into Arabic. Upper- and middle-class readers and the educated youth were devouring these works and becoming advocates of this or that school of literature, political science, philosophy, or painting. It was a thrilling and dizzying period for Iraqis and Arabs, and it promised to open expansive new vistas.

I was an avid reader from my early childhood. I read everything my parents got me, and later, in the last two years of Najeeb Pasha School, I would go during the summer break to the famous al-Muthanna Bookshop on al-Mutanbbi Street, the literary artery of Baghdad. The bookshop had a large main floor, a basement, and an upper floor. I would wander there, bewitched like a child in a candy shop, enjoying the smell of paper -I still do- moving between the rows of books: poetry, novels, history, and translations of world literature, unaware of the passage of time or of the browsers around me.

One day I must have been totally immersed in this enterprise because I did not notice that the bookshop had shuttered for the siesta break. I became apprehensive in the large, convoluted place, with the deafening silence surrounding me, so I hurried to the phone and called my father's cousin, a lawyer whose office was across the street from the bookshop. He called one of the bookshop's employees, who rushed to let me out. After 2003, al-Mutanabbi Street was burned down by the Wahabi al-Qa'ida terrorists who wanted to stab at Iraq's literary heart and obliterate a treasured landmark of Baghdad, but it was later rebuilt. I am almost sure, however, that it has lost its old charm in the process.

When I got older, in Baghdad College and afterward, I would go to the Baghdad Public library, housed in those days in a quaint domed building sitting astride Bab al-Mu'adham, a busy city square. It later moved to a much smaller house on a side street in A'dhamiya, a telltale sign of the insidious decline of intellectual life in Iraq. I also became a regular client of McKenzie's, the main bookshop offering English publications, located on al-Rasheed Street, at the time the main commercial avenue in Baghdad. A few years later, another important English bookshop, which I also frequented, opened in al-Bab al-Sharqi, later named Tahreer Square.

While in grammar school at Najeeb Pasha, I read the stories of the Egyptian writer Kamel Geylani. These were all in Arabic and came in groups: Arabic stories, stories from *One Thousand and One Nights* ("Aladin and the Magic Lamp," "Ali Baba and the Forty Thieves," etc.), English stories (*Robinson Crusoe, Gulliver's Travels*), Shakespeare's plays rendered in prose, Indian stories, and more.

The Arabic of Mr. Geylani was beautiful. His style and the pictures, though only in black and white, left me dreaming of those faraway places, the fabulous characters, and the magical adventures: Aladin (Ala'uldeen), the genie having granted his wish, flying off to China atop the magic carpet; the romantic Chinese palaces and the awe-inspiring pagodas; that strange and fascinating land beyond India. The Prophet Mohammad had said, "Seek thou knowledge even as far as China," a vast country, remote, romantic, and inviting to a child's imagination.

Then there was al-Sindabad (Sinbad) and his exploits on land and sea, and Indian stories of wise animals counseling kings.

*Robinson Crusoe* filled me with amazement at man's tenacity at survival, and I was fascinated by the intelligent noble savage, Friday, recognizing for the first time that man, "barbaric" or "civilized," is only a product of his environment. This latter theme I also found in another wonderful story, *Hay ibn Yaqdhan*, written more than three centuries earlier by the Andalusian Arab philosopher Ibn Tufayl, also rendered for children by the incomparable Kamel Geylani.

*Gulliver's Travels* gave me endless joy, but also made me question the wisdom and goodness of our species. A string of deep and sad cynicism runs through all the stories: the giants' King of Brobdingnang outraged by tiny Gulliver's proud account of the warfare methods of our race; the endless agony of the immortals in Luggnagg; then on another island the detestable and greedy humanoid Yahoos, ruled by the Houyhnhnms, the noble talking horses. I later learned that Jonathan Swift went mad in his last years and recoiled at the sight of man. Of Geylani's Shakespeare's stories, my favorite at the time was *The Merchant of Venice*, Taajir al-Bunduq'iya in Arabic, for the pure and noble friendship between Bassanio and Antonio and the loving intelligence of Portia.

When I was older, I was of course reading Shakespeare in English and was naturally taken by his great tragedies, *Hamlet*, *Julius Caesar*, *King Lear*, *Macbeth*, and *Othello* in that order. We studied *Julius Caesar* in Baghdad College, and I memorized a large part of it. Among my favorite verses were Cassius's "The fault, dear Brutus, is not in our stars, but in ourselves, that we are underlings"; Caesar's "A coward dies a thousand times before his death, but the valiant taste of death but once"; and Antony's "O judgment! Thou art fled to brutish beasts and men have lost their reason." Now, so many years since, I can recite from memory only parts of that speech by Antony. Among my other favorite verses are of course the ones starting with "To be or not to be" from *Hamlet*, and "Tomorrow, and tomorrow, and tomorrow" from *Macbeth*.

Returning to Baghdad in 1977 to visit my family and friends after an absence of six years, I rushed to the extensive library I had left behind to look for Kamel Geylani's books, but alas, they had vanished like many others, pillaged by well-meaning relatives who "borrowed" them for their young ones but seemingly never returned them. Much later, in 2003, I traveled to Egypt with my wife and two adult children. Even then I was still looking for Geylani's books, just for the memory. I even remembered the address of the publishing house, but it was not there. It had probably shut down and the books gone out of print.

In early high school, a series of books by the title *Awladuna* (*Our Children*) provided me with agreeable translations of *Robin Hood, Ivanhoe, The Prince and the Pauper, The Treasures of King Solomon*, and *Age of Exploration*. My favorite among these was *Robin Hood*, and among the title character's coterie, Brother John. I still remember the romantic picture I formed in my mind of the Sherwood Forest, its tree branches and leaves flapping in the autumn wind, hugging and hiding Robin Hood and his jovial band.

There were, moreover, well-illustrated books on scientific subjects: the principles behind the workings of the light bulb, telephone, telegraph, radio, and television and the age of the dinosaurs, all of which filled me with a fascination I remember to this day. It was these latter books that made me realize for the first time that science has its own romantic aspect, perhaps not as warm as literature, but more intriguing and intellectually engrossing.

The period of the Arab renaissance also saw religious reformists like Jamal al-Deen al-Afghani of Afghanistan, Mohammad Abdu of Egypt, and Mohammad Ali Sharia'ti of Iran. Then there was the "dean of Arabic letters," the blind Egyptian Sorbonne graduate Taha Hussein, who dared to suggest that the language of the Koran is essentially the same as late pre-Islamic Arabic poetry, thereby provoking a furious storm of indignation by the millions who believe the Koran was not created, but is indeed the Word of the Creator, Allah himself. There was also the Iraqi poet Jameel Sidqi al-Zahawi, who dared to call for the abandonment of the black chador (*aba'*) covering women from head to ankle, and the *pooshyia*, the black fenestrated face cover. He, too, received a deluge of rebuttals, most of them quite abusive.

The "prince of the poets" was the ingenious Egyptian Ahmad Shawqi, with the immense versatility of his themes, spanning religion, politics, history, romance and humor. Several of his poems were sung by the greatest of the Arab singers, the incomparable Dame Um Kulthum, the "nightingale of the East," to the music of the most accomplished Arab musicians, standing tall among them Riadh al-Sunbati. Um Kulthums's Thursday evening concerts, broadcast from Cairo, were eagerly awaited by all and sundry in Baghdad. Friends got together over *araq*, the strong local spirit made from fermented dates, and *mezza* (appetizers) to enjoy the concerts; my father and later I were also devotees of her concerts.

The famous Egyptian singer and musician Mohammad Abdul Wahab, often called al-Ustadh (the Maestro), also immortalized Shawqi by singing some of his poems, among them "Qays and Layla," accompanied by the marvelous lady singer Asmahan, originally from Lebanon. The poem tells a popular old Arab story of thwarted love. Qays, incidentally, was himself a poet, Qays ibn al-Mullawah, wandering in the desert night, reciting in verse his passion for distant Layla. Shawqi's inspired poems, rendered into sublime music and delivered by those virtuoso singers, are outstanding classical gems of the Arab renaissance. Another singer of that same caliber was the Lebanese lady Fayruz, who delivered in a celestial voice beautiful songs to the music of the Brothers Rahabani.

Now in my older age, I go back to those songs every three or four months, plug the CDs into the player in my study or car, travel back in time, and enjoy the beauty of the Arabic language. The poetry, the nuances of the language, the music and the singers' virtuosity invariably recharge my subconscious zone, nowadays called the "hard drive."

One of the greatest Arab poets was the Iraqi Mohammed Mehdi al-Jawahiri who captivated the populace by his political poetry. He was born in Najaf, a descendent of a literary line of poets and clerics. I particularly like these lines from an old poem of his because they demonstrate the sixth sense, denied to us mortals, that great poets seem to possess.

> The South took fright; the scheming of
>     Kharijites, they said
> The North protested; incitement by the
>     neighbors, they declared
> The proud Center rioted, not wanting to be
>     outdone
> Hence the puzzled spectators of a wretched
>     scene
> Inquired, "Who, prithee, are the owners of this
>     domain?"

South, North, and Center refer to the corresponding parts of Iraq. Kharijites are people who parted company with Iman Ali. One of their numbers later assassinated him while he knelt at prayers. "They" refers to the Iraqi authorities.

Now, almost a century later, al-Jawahiri's portrayal of the condition of Iraq and Iraqis has unfortunately not changed.

Another verse of al-Jawahiri:

> He who remarks my hair is prematurely grey
> To him I say, "Tis only the dust from the fray"

And contemplating death:

> The puzzle of life and enigma of the mind
> Is the turning into mere dust
> Of the thing that we call Thought

> And at age seventy, talking to himself,
>     lamenting the mockingly fast passage of
>     time:

> What is it that you fear
> What is it that you desire
> When seventy years have sped by
> Like dashing steeds at the races

Al-Jawahiri, like many other Arab poets before and after him, pendulated between praising and denouncing the rulers, but he was nevertheless tolerated and often honored by the monarchy for his poetic genius. King Faisal I appointed him to a cultural post at the royal court, and the reagent Abdul Ilah, after hearing Al-Jawahiri recite a poem, stood up, took off the *Wisam al-Ra-fidayn* (medal of the two rivers) he was wearing, and placed it on the poet.

The 1958 Revolution embraced al-Jawahiri and its leader,

Abdul Kareem Qasim, who visited him at his home, proclaimed, "I am proud to visit the home that bred the Revolution," later appointing him the head of the "Journalists' Guild." After Abdul Kareem Qasim survived the assassination attempt, al-Jawahiri gave a ringing recital of one of his most famous poems at the packed Kashafa (Scout) Stadium in Baghdad. He congratulated the Leader on his survival and pleaded with him to be firm with the conspirators:

> Conjure the scene in reverse and take notice
> Of what they would've wreaked had they
>     triumphed
> Would Mercy be found in their lexicon?
> Or remembrance of Kareem and his votaries?
> By God, they would've hunted Zayd while
>     seeking Za'ida
> And at the stake burned Amer while casting for
>     Umar

He was prophetic yet again, for at the start of the 1963 CIA-sponsored Ba'athist coup d'état Qasim was murdered, and arbitrary incarcerations and killings were perpetrated on a massive scale.

It is ironic that al-Jawahiri himself later ran afoul of General Qasim. A workers demonstration had been harshly handled by the police, so the poet approached Qasim to argue for the laborers' cause. In an emotional moment, he said to Qasim reproachfully, "The police of Nuri al-Sa'eed again?" He was then subjected to yet another kangaroo trial and released on a measly bail of one dirham (sixty-six US cents at the time), a premeditated insult. Fearing for his life, he eventually sought safety in Czechoslovakia, where he remained as if in exile. Feeling homesick, he composed a touching poem, remembering his beloved Tigris river:

> I salute you from afar; please return my greeting
> Oh Tigris of plenty, Oh mother of all gardens
> Thirstily I seek you, like the pigeons sheltering
> Betwixt your waters and the rich muddy bank

Many years later he tired of exile and went to Damascus, where the Ba'athist regime, which hated its counterpart in Iraq (and vice versa), welcomed him. Poets, after all, had been honored throughout Arab history, not just by their devotees but also by rulers intent on immortalizing their legacy and spiting their enemies. He lived there many more years and died in his late nineties. The Saddam regime, having earlier stripped him of his Iraqi citizenship, did not grant his wish to be buried in his birthplace of Najaf, so he was interred in Damascus. At his funeral a hundred thousand mourners marched behind his coffin to bid farewell to the Arabs' greatest poet.

There was also the innovative Iraqi poet Bedr Shaker al-Sayyab, whose tragic life was cut short by tuberculosis. He adopted a less rigid verse in many of his poems, was in the vanguard of the modern Arab poets, and was much admired by my generation. Lady Lamee'a Abbas Umara is another outstanding Iraqi poet whose themes range from romantic love to politics to longing for her beloved Iraq that she had to leave. She has a beautiful voice full of passionate energy, and it's a real treat to listen to her moving recitals, more like a song.

Another talented and popular Iraqi poet was Mudhaffar al-Nawwab. He composed in both formal Arabic and the Iraqi dialect. His poetry was intense and passionate. One of his sad romantic poems, "Al-Rail we' Hamad" ("The Train and Hamad"), composed in the dialect of southern Iraq, was rendered into a melodic song loved by all Iraqis. He fled the Iraqi Ba'ath rule, lived in Libya for a while, then moved to Damascus, where he was very popular among the Syrians. In one of his famous poems, he berated some of the Arab rulers, declaring that a pig's sty was cleaner than the cleanest of them.

The child prodigy Tunisian poet Abul Qasim al-Shabi, like Mozart, died young. A famous heroic poem of his was put to a dynamic song. Here are select verses of it:

> When the people strive to reclaim their life,
>     destiny will surely yield;
> Their chains shall snap, and the darkness will
>     recede.
> But those who recoil from the heights will
>     forever dwell in the caves.
> When I asked the Earth, "Oh Mother, do you
>     hate our kind?"
> Of my children, she said, I love the ambitious
>     and those daring the tides,
> For the air bears not the dead bird, nor the bees
>     kiss the dead flower.

The Syrian poet Nezar al-Qebbani said, "My poetry shall not kiss the hand of the Sultan." He composed daring love poems as well as political poetry. In the latter he confronted the Arabs and their rulers with their own demons. My and succeeding generations of Arabs love his poetry and his moral courage. More about him later.

There were also the storywriters and novelists, the best of

them Egyptians. The Nobel laureate Najib Mahfouz (Nejeeb Mahfoodh) wrote in the 1950's his magnificent trilogy, *Bayn al-Qesrayn*, *Qasr al-shawq*, and *Al-Sukkariya*, all names of Cairo districts (*Palace Walk* is the title of the English translation), describing the life and times of three generations of Egyptians. The novel had very close resonance for the peoples of the Arab East (the Levant and Iraq). I remember reading it in my teens and not putting it down until I finished the last volume of the trilogy while I should've been studying instead for the all-important baccalaureate, a difficult and intimidating national examination given to all senior high school students in Iraq, one that would decide a student's future career path.

Mr. Mahfouz wrote many other excellent and engaging novels, most of them, like *Palace Walk*, in the realist style. In *Miramar*, he portrays the newfound privileges of the revolutionary class that toppled King Faruq of Egypt in 1952. In *Awlad al Hara* (*The Neighborhood Kids*), the Great Jabalawi, the master of a lofty palace, is always talked about with awe but never seen, and three prominent characters in the story are metaphors for the Prophet Mohammad, Jesus Christ, and Science. This latter story is now being vehemently denounced by the Islamists of Egypt.

Today, the dentist-novelist Ala' al-Aswani is the only worthy Egyptian successor to Mahfouz and may have even surpassed Mahfouz in his novel *Imarat Ya'qubian* (*The Yacobian Building*), which was rendered into an excellent movie. He also wrote another excellent story, *Chicago*, in which he describes the life of some first and second generation Egyptian Americans and, indirectly, the long arm of the Mubarak regime. Al-Aswani had undertaken graduate training in dentistry at the University of Illinois at Chicago, and has a busy dentistry practice in Cairo, Egypt.

My wife and I met him when we were invited by my Egyptian

friend Dr. Wagih Izzat Nessim to a reception given to the author by the Egyptian American Association. Al-Aswani is a charming man indeed, highly educated, and has been a resounding voice against fake religiosity and an advocate of religious tolerance and respect for human rights and individual freedoms.

Another Egyptian writer was Ibraheem Abdul Qader al-Mazini, who wrote highly entertaining stories with a mixture of wit, sarcasm, and humor. In his book *Ibraheem, the Writer*, he said he had already chosen the words for his epitaph:

> Oh, visitor to my lonely grave
> Read thou the words on my tombstone
> Here my bones will forever rest
> How I wish they were yours not mine

Another book, *Ibraheem the Second*, he dedicated "To every Tahiyya, whose patience with her spouse is sometimes sorely tested." Tahiyya in the story was Ibraheem's wife.

There was also the playwright Tawfeeq al-Hakeem, who penned interesting, thought-provoking, and daring plays like *The Wise Man's Donkey* and *The Tree Climber*. In *The Tears of Iblees* (a synonym for Satan), Iblees becomes quite exasperated with everybody cursing him whenever there is a calamity. He goes to the chief Muslim imam, then the Christian patriarch, then the Jewish rabbi, weeping, begging to convert, bitterly complaining that humans blame all their vicissitudes on him while forgetting their own greed, jealousy, and belligerence. He is rejected in succession by all three figures, who are greatly alarmed by his sincere wish to convert. They firmly turn down his tearful pleas, reminding him that the whole edifice of their creeds will collapse if he turns to the true path, and (implicitly) their business will collapse as well.

In my early years at Baghdad College, I came to read the great Coptic Egyptian writer and thinker Salama Musa. In *Ha'ula' Allamooni* (Those Who Taught Me), he wrote about the lives and works of the major European writers, philosophers, and scientists of the nineteenth and early twentieth centuries: Charles Darwin, George Bernard Shaw, Ernest Renan, Friedrich Nietzsche, Havelock Ellis, and others. The chapter on Darwin, and Musa's later book *The Theory of Evolution and the Origin of Man* struck my young mind like a thunderbolt. I read it again and kept thinking about it.

A few years later, in 1960, I purchased the Modern Library Giants' one-thousand-page edition of Darwin's *The Origin of Species and the Descent of Man.* I remember sitting long hours reading it while my neighborhood friends would be playing marbles, backgammon, or chess, and my mother reminding me to concentrate on the school curriculum.

The book changed my mind's life forever. I placed it in a prominent place in my library, like a sacred text, and I took it with me when I left Iraq in 1971. Its pages have only now begun to yellow, a testimony to the superb quality of the Modern Library books and my tender care of them. But then I've always treated my books with the care one gives to children.

No wonder then that I got excited when Cinema Granada in Baghdad showed the movie *Inherit the Wind* about the "Monkey Trial" in 1925 of John Scopes, the substitute teacher in Dayton, Tennessee, who talked to his class about evolution. It was marvelously played by two of my favorite actors, Spencer Tracy as the defense attorney Clarence Darrow, and Fredrick March as William Jennings Bryan, the three-time US presidential candidate, who argued for the prosecution. I saw it twice in Baghdad and two more times twenty-five years later in Chicago. A wonderful classic.

In Egypt today, only a few people know more about evolution than did the court audience in Dayton in 1925—this more than half a century after Salama Musa published his book on evolution and the great interest it aroused then among the educated classes in Egypt and the Arab world. In 2009, Alexandria was one of the cities participating in the worldwide celebrations of the 150th anniversary of the publication of *Origin of Species*, and the meetings were attended by practitioners and PhD students in the fields of biology, physiology, and medicine.

A BBC reporter randomly interviewed attendees as they left the meetings, asking them what they thought about the theory of evolution. Only a few had any meaningful knowledge of it, some had not heard of it, and one person supposed there was some truth to it, but was uneasy about its incompatibility with the Koran and the Sharia.

This is a telltale sign of the intellectual decline that has occurred over the last half a century, not only in Egypt, but in most other Arab countries, the result of dictatorship, the curbs on the freedom of speech, the decline of educational standards, and the rise of religious fundamentalism—the latter often abetted by Sadat and Mubarak in Egypt and Saddam during the last twelve years of his reign in Iraq. Far more airtime was given, especially in Egypt, to religious programs on government-controlled TV, satellite, and radio stations, where religious clerics harangue the audience with their tenth-century outpourings.

From the last decade of the nineteenth century to the 1960s of the twentieth, Cairo teemed with literary activity. A common saying was: "Cairo writes, Beirut publishes, and Baghdad reads." There were serial publications like *Al-Mukhtar* (*Selections*), *Al-Hilal* (*The Crescent*), and *Iqra'* (*Read*), the latter featuring beautifully written stories, often romantic or nostalgic, about interesting personalities and epochs in Arab history.

One such *Iqra'* book was *Faris Beni Hamdan* (*The Knight of the Hamdanids*) by Ali al-Jarem about the life, times, and poetry of Abu Firas al-Hamdani, a proud Arab prince, poet, and warrior, and a cousin of Saiful Dawla al-Hamdani, the most prominent ruler of the Hamdanid dynasty (AD 890–1004), which ruled Syria and northern Iraq, and spent much time, energy, and resources checking frequent attempts by Byzantium to recapture territory it had lost to the early Muslim conquerors. The great poet al-Mutanabbi himself lauded Saiful Dawla in some of his most memorable poems. Dame Um Kulthum sang one of Abu Firas's famous poems, addressing himself:

> I see you scarce of tears; patience being your
>     merit.
> Does love not command you one way or
>     another?
> Yes, I am pining and turmoil besets my soul,
> But the likes of me declare not their woes.

Yet another book in the *Iqra'* series, *Abu Nu'as*, by Abdul Haleem Abbas, was about one of the most talented, colorful, and irreverent Abbassid era poets, who often wrote about wine and women. The poet is popular to this day. In fact, there is a famous street in Baghdad by the Tigris River named after him. It had many restaurants serving *araq*, wonderful *mezza*, and the ever popular *masgoof*, freshwater fish out of the Tigris, placed on skewers planted in the earth in a circle, and cooked slowly by a fire raised at the center. From our late teens onward, my close friends and I had memorable times in Abu Nu'as Street. If we had our drinks and *mezza*, but did not order the fish, we would stroll to a nearby place for *pacha*, various parts of lamb boiled in water, another very popular dish in Iraq. In one of Abu Nu'as' famous poems, he pleads with a friend not to admonish him for his drinking habit:

> Admonish me not, for that per se is temptation,
> But cure me with her who caused my affliction.
> Yellow is her color, and sorrows near her not.
> Touching her, a rock will sense the pleasure.

The word for wine in Arabic can be either masculine (*khemr*) or feminine (*khumra*), and Abu Nu'as naturally preferred the feminine form. The wine in this case was obviously not red.

Another book of Ali al-Jarim that I liked in my teenage years, not one of the *Iqra'* series, was *Hatifun min al-Andalus*, (A Caller from Andalusia) about the romantic poet of Muslim Spain, Ibn Zaydoon (AD 1003–1071) and his legendary platonic love for the poetess Wallada bint al-Mustakfi, the beautiful daughter of the Ummayad caliph, Muhammad III of Cordoba. On a trip to Spain in 1994 with my wife and two teenage children, we were surprised to find in the middle of a square in Cordoba a memorial stone for Ibn Zaydoon etched with one of his romantic poems in the original Arabic.

Indeed, Al-Jarim's stories were lovely reading for a young person, evoking the Arab past: its heroism, poetry, romance, and sad eventual decline. Several decades later, in Chicago, I would pick up from my bookshelves those tattered and yellowing books and read them again with nostalgia for that period of my life and those epochs of the Arab past. I must copy them before they completely fall apart.

There were also prominent Egyptian women of letters. At about age eleven I read Ameena al-Sa'eed's Arabic translation of Louisa May Alcott's *Little Women* and enjoyed it immensely. I still remember my favorite characters in the book, Jo and Lawrence. Twenty-seven years later I recommended the book to my two children, but I don't think they read it.

Another Egyptian woman writer was Ai'sha Abdul Rahman, also known as Bint al Shati' (Daughter of the Coast), who wrote an interesting book about Sukayna, the daughter of Imam Husayn, expounding on various aspects of her life, nearly unknown to my generation or even my father's. She wrote about Sukayna's intellect, learning, and literary salon, and her marriage to Mus'ab ibn al-Zubayr, who shared her father's fate when he rebelled against the Umayad caliphate. As I related earlier, both Ameena and Ai'sha were advocates of legal and inheritance rights and higher education for women, and they had the courage to applaud Abdul Kareem Qasim's Personal Status Law.

In Baghdad, Ali al-Wardi was one of the most interesting writers in the age of the Arab renaissance. Incidentally, he happened to be a classmate and friend of my father. Likewise, his son Hassan was a friend and classmate of mine in medical school. Even as a boy in Kadhimi'ya, Ali was an avid reader. An uncle of his employed him to help keep shop but let him go after a while because Ali spent most of the time reading books in a small backroom instead of attending to customers.

He pursued his studies and got a scholarship at the American University in Beirut, where he received his bachelor's degree in 1943. He later got masters and PhD degrees in social sciences from the University of Texas. In his time, this was a rare event, as most Iraqi students went to England for postgraduate studies.

Perhaps he felt social studies were emphasized and possibly more advanced in the United States.

Ali al-Wardi was the first author in Iraq and possibly the Islamic world to examine, in the light of Western scholarship, the history of early Islam, the Iraqi personality, and the more recent centuries of Iraq's history. His writings were an eye-opener for me in my late teens and early twenties and for countless others, not just of my generation, but my father's as well, because he presented history not in the propagandist "Arab nationalist" fashion taught at school, but with a clear-eyed analysis of the times, the socioeconomic, religious, sectarian, and psychological forces shaping mass movements and their leaders. And he wrote much of that in the form of interesting stories; he was an outstanding raconteur.

In the booklet "Shakhsiyet al-ferd al-Iraqi" ("The Personality of the Iraqi Individual") and in his later book *Wu'adh al-Salateen* (*The Sultans' Preachers*), both published in the early 1950s, al-Wardi argued that many Iraqis, even in the large urban centers, had tribal roots, albeit of various vintage, and that the tribal character and ethos were an integral part of their ostensibly urban makeup.

Hence the average Iraqi would go to the mosque, practice the religious rituals and engage in good deeds, but would meanwhile retain many tribal characteristics: bearing long grudges; pining for revenge; favoring family and kin above all else ("my brother and I against my cousin, and my cousin and I against the outsider") regardless of the merits of each; hospitality at all cost, even beyond one's means; and extreme sensitivity to any real or perceived offense to his honor.

The Iraqi would thus manifest the double urban-tribal personality. The tribal component would gain ascendency in times of political, social, or economic upheaval. Whenever the central authority teeters, the "desert" will rise and the "city" recede. Of course, geography is ignored only at one's peril, and it so happens that almost all urban centers in Iraq, astride the Tigris and the Euphrates rivers, are near the edge of the desert. In fact, civilizations in Iraq have always been threatened by the desert Bedouins, and a plethora of Assyrian texts and slabs keep referring to battles with the *Arabu*, meaning the desert Arabs.

The persistent Bedouin characteristics, al-Wardi argues, are especially prominent among the more recently settled tribes along the lower Tigris and Euphrates rivers in southern Iraq. The tribes had habitually raided each other. The victorious takes off with the possessions of the vanquished and these raids (*ghazawat*) were seen as heroic undertakings necessary for the survival and standing of the tribe. The Bedouin male, therefore, gloried in such endeavors and viewed manual work with contempt, including farm labor.

In peacetime the tribe is usually busy moving its livestock from one grazing land to another, and on special market days in nearby villages the tribal women trade animal products and hand-woven rugs for other necessities. Water is of course always scarce in the desert, so it would be foolhardy for the Bedouin to wash himself or his few articles before he and his livestock have had enough to drink. Even then, the surplus, if any, would more wisely be stored rather than used for washing.

We can therefore see why the farmers and villagers of southern Iraq, especially those of recent settlement, were not hardworking and often looked at farm labor as a humiliating chore. Common sayings among them were "vegetable planter" or "onion planter," derogatory epithets directed at the farmers. The men would be seen sitting in *qahwas* (tea houses), chatting, drinking tea, and playing backgammon or dominoes while the women worked hard on the fields or carried milk, milk products, rugs, or straw articles to sell at homes or at the marketplace. Occasionally some woman might be seduced and would pay for the slip with her life in an expeditious honor killing. And despite Qur'anic and Hadith emphasis on honesty and cleanliness, stealing was not necessarily viewed as a sin since it was akin to the Bedouins' pillaging raid, and cleanliness was often seen as a luxury.

Owing to those lingering bedouin traits, the Iraqi farmer during the monarchy worked mostly out of fear of the landholders, but even then he seldom worked the land all four seasons, unlike his Egyptian counterpart. Nevertheless, Iraq was an exporter of food and food products. When the well-intentioned Agrarian Reform Act of the revolutionary Qasim government dismantled the feudal system, many farmers neglected the land, which quickly salinated. Oil income was increasing, so thousands upon thousands of farmers seeking other employment migrated to the cities, especially Baghdad, swelling it with unskilled urban proletariat. Consequently, as early as the late 1960s, Iraq, which had invented agriculture in the fifth millennium BC, was importing not only grain but also animal feed.

When I read al-Wardi's books, I was impressed by his analysis. I could see its veracity while watching the behavior of the people around me, friends and classmates, students of different political affiliations, and social or political leaders of various stripes. My father and many others of his generation were also admirers of al-Wardi's works, but that is not to say the author was universally popular, for he caused consternation among the more traditional and religious elements and received loads of hate mail, especially from his fellow Kadhmawis. The authorities, too, viewed him warily, not the lenient monarchy, but the forces that toppled it, especially the later Ba'thist regime, which stripped him of the chairmanship of his department at the university in favor of one of his onetime pupils.

In my mid to late twenties, I began to read al-Wardi's *Lamahat Ichtima'iya min Ta'reekh al-Iraq al-Hadeeth* (Social Vignettes from the Modern History of Iraq) in six volumes. This was a fascinating work. In it he reviews the recent centuries of Iraq's history, shedding light on the brutality of rulers, not just to their own people, but also to each other. An endless list of rulers grabbed power through conspiratorial or military means, then routinely blinded the ones they displaced before killing them or dumping them in lightless dungeons for what was left of their wretched lives. This was probably the practice of the times, but we never read about that in school.

He also presents interesting aspects of the birth of the Bahai (Baha'i) faith in Iraq. He surveys the devastating outbreaks of plague and cholera that decimated the populace, so much so that at one time the population of Baghdad was reduced to only thirteen thousand souls, mostly Christians and Jews, because, unlike the Muslims, they quarantined themselves in their neighborhoods during the epidemics. The survivors could hardly find any carpenters, blacksmiths, or other craftsmen to attend to their needs. Many of those horrendous outbreaks were caused by pilgrims flocking to Iraq to visit the numerous holy shrines. Governments often tried to quarantine the pilgrims to make sure some did not have the early stages of a fatal disease, but the clergy protested vehemently, calling the preventive attempts un-Islamic and causing the authorities to back down.

In that same work, al-Wardi reviews the history of the 1920 revolt against the British, mainly by the Shia tribes of the Euphrates, and discusses the religious and tribal mores that influenced the beginning and the course of that famous rebellion. One large tribe, for example, joined the rebels because its chief perceived an insult to his honor by a British major who clearly did not understand the Muslims' view that dogs are unclean. The officer had let his beloved dog loose to wander among the tribal notables he had invited to his place. When the dog brushed against the chief of a respected large tribe, the Sheik kicked it away.

"Why did you kick my dog?" the major inquired.

"Because it is dirty," retorted the Sheik tensely.

"I am afraid it is cleaner than you," answered the arrogant major.

The Sheik sprang up to his feet, his face radiating red-hot anger, and roared, "And you call yourself a major? My ass," and he left in a huff to summon his tribe.

In fact, some tribes were neutral or friendly toward the British, but later joined the rebellion because of British ignorance of tribal mores and sensitivities or the shaming of a neutral tribe by the belligerent ones. Again, al-Wardi was nearly the first author to discuss these important events in Iraq's history in his charming and often daring storytelling style.

Aziz (Azeez) Ali was another famous and talented Iraqi. He was an employee in the Department of Customs during the monarchy, but also composed and sang lyrics, which he called monologues, in the local Baghdadi dialect. His songs were stinging, satirical, mostly humorous, sometimes sad, and highly popular then and now with Iraqis of all stripes. He aimed his satire at the authorities, old folk superstitions, and what he considered to be the ailments of Arab and Iraqi societies. Every Wednesday we would tune in to Radio Baghdad, government-owned and operated, to listen to his highly insightful and entertaining monologues. He sang only one monologue that I know of immediately after the toppling of the monarchy by the 1958 military coup, which he enthusiastically welcomed, but was largely never heard of again—a testimony to the tolerance of governments of the extinct era.

Here is an excerpt from his poem "We are lost," one of the sad monologues:

> Lost in the desert and befuddled we are;
>> befogged are those who have no guide.
> We headed West, got tired and frail, yet never
>> made it home.
> But to turn East, agony awaits and a red demise,
> And to top it all, our chiefs are either deaf, or
>> their ears are stopped.
> We dance for whomever beats the drum, and
>> skip after him in joy,
> Then he drops us in the midst of the road,
>> neither dead nor alive.
> We kept bragging; we sang our ballads and
>> recited the poems,
> But when danger alighted, it found us stunned;
>> and we dropped the flag.

Another monologue, "Doctor," was also very popular and remains so to this day; here are excerpts of it:

> Never, Doctor, had I or my kin been ill, seen a
>> healer, or taken pills.
> The last few years, however, we have ailed and
>> suffered.

Chronic our malady has become; it has blotted
   our joy.
By God, Doctor, won't you heal us?
From ourselves has our ailment arisen. Give us
   hemlock, if it be good medicine.
Diseases of the body your potions may ease, but
   ours is the ailing of the soul.
Treat our soul, prithee, if you could; fulfill,
   Doctor, our hope.
From you we seek not poems nor soothing
   words, but deeds that give us a cure.

Aziz Ali himself composed the music for his monologues. His voice had a memorable bass quality, and he always had an excellent chorus of female and male repeaters that added force and emphasis to the lyrics. Almost every new song of his created a political stir, and he was at it for over a quarter of a century.

He humorously relates in his autobiography that after he finished singing at Radio Baghdad studio one Wednesday, the station director came up to him to say that the Pasha, as Prime Minister Nuri al-Sa'eed was called, happened to be visiting the studio and wanted to see him.

Aziz was wary but nevertheless dragged himself to see the prime minister, who asked him, "Why do you incite the people against us? At any rate, what kind of work do you do?" "I'm a customs employee, Pasha," Aziz replied. "Wonderful, so we pay you to defame us," retorted the Pasha curtly.

Aziz was fairly distraught by the experience and stopped going to the studio for a few Wednesdays until the station director called to reassure him and asked him to resume his program. The director later told Aziz that he was visiting Nuri one Wednesday evening, when Nuri tuned in to Radio Baghdad to listen to Aziz. Then Nuri turned to the director and said, "Listen to the man; he is making fun of me again." Aziz, however, kept up his schedule at Radio Baghdad.

He also relates that when politicians were out of office, they used to call him to express support for his broadcasts but invariably tried to muzzle him when they returned to office. But that's a staple of Iraqi politics, and seemingly of politicians the world over.

The flame of the Arab renaissance began to flicker with the advent of the revolutionary military regimes that came to power after 1952. Military officers turned heads of state were much less tolerant than the civilian kingly rulers and expected blind obedience from their ministers and subjects as they have long been accustomed to from their inferiors in the army. They were also much less educated, inexperienced in local and global politics, did not appreciate the worth of the more illustrious members of society, and were even wary of them. They therefore introduced the police state model, first begun in the Arab world by Egypt's Gamal Abdul Nasser, who acquired it from his colleague in the nonaligned block, Joseph Tito. Nasser was also a friend of Nehru, but he was not inclined to follow Nehru's example.

Corruption, that ancient malady, eventually spread through those totalitarian bureaucracies like cancer, and the ruled became restless, disaffected, and angry. They could not voice their opposition in an open forum because there were hardly any licensed political parties to give them voice. All opposition was deemed traitorous by the rulers. Hence the people flocked to the mosque, where Islamism was conceived and born. The renaissance thus gave up its last breath, not knowing if and when it will rise again from the dead.

AL-MUTANNNA BOOKSHOP ON AL-MUTANABBI
STREET, BAGHDAD IN THE 1950'S.

# 6

# Medical School

**M**y years in medical school were the least happy of my life. In my late teens and early twenties, my soul was beset by a torturous tumult, exacerbated by four major events that led to bleak political outcomes and massive violence, all of which depressed me, dashed my optimism about the future of Iraq, and imbued me with cynicism, a trait unnatural to me.

Furthermore, it was not my wish to go to medical school, but my father pressed me to do so because he thought medicine suited my temperament, that I would make a notable physician and continue a line of accomplished doctors. I eventually abided by his wish because I loved and respected him and knew he had my best interest at heart. Moreover, it was rare in those days for an Iraqi boy of seventeen to defy his father's wishes. Incidentally, when I finished Baghdad College, I changed my name from Sa'ad (happy) to As'ad (happier), wishful thinking perhaps, because I got tired of the fathers at Baghdad College calling me Sa'ad, which sounds like *sad*, and did not want that to stick when I went abroad for postgraduate study.

In my days, the Medical College of Baghdad was the only medical school in the country, so I came in contact with students from different parts of Iraq, many having different dialects, nuances of speech, and to a lesser extent even social habits. The college was and is still free, but it accepted only the top-scoring students in the national baccalaureate exam given at the end of high school. Many outstanding students in my class came from relatively poor or limited income families.

I always marveled at these less fortunate students' tenacity and perseverance as they took notes in the lecture room or sat for hours on end in the library, studying English textbooks of the basic sciences they had taken in Arabic at public high schools. They had the dictionary close at hand, looked up the meaning of at least one word in each line, and jotted it down in the margin.

Many lived in crammed circumstances. I would see them studying in a public square or garden under the light poles or in popular tea houses, oblivious to the surrounding noise of people, the radio and television, and the constant clicking of dice against the backgammon boards. This reminds me even today of the Iraqi culture's emphasis on education and scholarly accomplishment and their importance to rich and poor alike.

A third of my class were girls—a phenomenon uncommon at the time, not just in other Arab countries, but also in Europe and North America. The girls were generally more studious than the boys and did very well in class. They had less distractions as they did not go out as often as the boys, and then only to visit relatives or friends. They often accompanied their mothers to the *qabools*, once-monthly women-only receptions given by lady friends or relations. Girls never went out with boys or other girls to the movies, theater, or other public places of entertainment. They did so only with their families. A few went with their families to private clubs, but in my days, the Ilwiyya Club was just about the only respectable and elegant club in Baghdad.

But we mixed with the girls in medical school, worked with them in laboratory or clinical groups, and often had lunch with them in the school's cafeteria. As in this county, college provided a good opportunity for boys to meet girls and fall in love. The boy would then ask his parents, if they consented, to visit her parents to ask for her hand, to be followed by engagement and marriage if all went well. Mixed marriages between different sects and ethnicities happened fairly often.

The majority of girls in my class were quite modern and wore the latest fashions. A few who lived in conservative neighborhoods would deposit the *abayas* (chadors) in their closets on arriving to school and put them back on when heading home. There were only three Muslim Sisters who covered their heads and outside the classroom interacted only with three Muslim Brothers. This circle of six students almost never socialized with the other students, who likewise pretended not to notice their little group.

The medical college faculty in my days was entirely Iraqi except for three members, who taught some of the basic sciences: Mr. Terrent, a Welshman, for physics; Mr. Roesebik, a Dutchman, for organic chemistry; and Mr. Slipka, a Czech, for embryology (the study of the development of the human embryo). I apologize to them and the readers if my spelling of their names is not accurate; it has been a long time. A fourth professor, Mr. Tala't, an Egyptian, visited for a brief period and taught us the physiology of the respiratory system.

Mr. Terrent, the physics teacher, was a brilliant but eccentric Welshman, who had in earlier days worked at the Ernest Rutherford lab in England. Many students, however, thought he was not a good teacher. He would come into the auditorium, scan the students, then strike the desk with his index finger and say, "Ah, didn't work this time; next time perhaps," meaning that the molecules of his finger did not fuse with those of the desk, in which case he wouldn't have been able to pull his finger away from the desk. He was a devotee of quantum theory.

One day, while he was talking about the center of gravity, he leapt onto the top of the desk, lay flat on his back, and started to push his body over the edge of the desk until his head and chest hung in the air and started to sway up and down like a seesaw—all to demonstrate to us the concept of the center of gravity, which we'd learned three years earlier in high school and was even then quite easy to grasp.

Another time he was discussing the simple harmonic motion, which we were also quite familiar with, when he said to a student, "You are swimming toward the river bank with your head submerged, and suddenly you find yourself trapped under a docked boat. You can't break loose and you are running out of breath. What do you do?"

The student replied mischievously: "I am getting really scared now, sir. What do I do?" (There was laughter.)

Mr. Terrent: "You lift your back gently against the bottom of the boat, then you bring it down. You repeat the maneuver a few times. The boat begins to move up and down, and as it moves up, you slide out from underneath it, raise your head above the water, take a deep breath, and swim to shore. So if you did not know about the simple harmonic motion, you would be quite dead now, wouldn't you?" More laughter.

As Mr. Terrent talked, he would observe the students, and if he saw one talking to his neighbor, he would immediately throw the blackboard eraser at him like a dart, often missing and hitting the unsuspecting neighbor.

The chemistry teacher, Mr. Roesebik, was a kind man who knew his subject well but was not a dynamic teacher, and we had to strain our ears to hear him. It was as though he was talking to himself. It was rumored among the students that he'd initially come to Baghdad on a limited teaching assignment but decided to stay on when his wife, long infertile in Holland, conceived after their arrival to Iraq. Mr. Roesebik must have considered the happy event a signal from heaven for him to stay put and serve the country.

One time during some political unrest at the college, the security forces invaded the campus and started to herd the students out of the school and toward the nearby Ministry of Defense for the sole leader, General Qasim, to address them. Many students were still in their white lab coats, and one of them even had a tray holding a brain he'd been dissecting in the anatomy hall. Other students were fleeing in all directions. It was then that Mr. Roesebik packed six students into his car and drove them off campus, telling the security henchmen with perfect composure they were his lab technicians. An Iraqi assistant of his sheltered more students in the lab itself under the same pretense. The student body never forgot the two men's kindness.

Mr. Slipka, the embryology teacher, was a soft-spoken Czech. He was a handsome man, like most Slavs I'd seen, men and women, but I always detected in his face the sadness, perhaps even the depression, of intelligent men coming from totalitarian states. There were many communist block professionals in Iraq in General Qasim's days, and all the ones I'd seen bore the same facial expression: It seemed they wanted to say something but wouldn't or couldn't. They were friendly and warm, but one could see restraint in their faces, gestures, and body language. When they drank, they became merry and recounted funny stories, laughing uproariously, but never discussed the politics of their home countries or Iraq's. I also felt that Mr. Slipka, an accomplished embryologist, was happy to be in Baghdad and not in Czechoslovakia. After all, Iraqi politics didn't matter much to him, a foreigner. He liked the people, enjoyed teaching his Iraqi students, and didn't have the Czech secret police watching him.

The students liked Mr. Slipka. At the end of his embryology course, we presented him with a set of Parker pens, which he greatly appreciated. He thanked us profusely, poetically, and told us, his eyes tearing, that he would never forget us or his time in Iraq.

The Republican Hospital (al-Musteshfa al-Jumhuri) was the teaching hospital for the University of Baghdad Medical College. It was known to the public as *al-Majeediya,* after the Ottoman Sultan Abdul Majeed, during whose reign it was built. It had large wards, like other public hospitals of the period, and like most other hospitals in Iraq, provided free medical care. The patients were of mixed socioeconomic background, but the majority were poor or of limited means: peasants, the urban poor, and lower-middle-class professionals and craftsmen. Quite often, however, there were affluent patients who had serious or rare diseases, but there were no private wings or rooms for them, as was the case in many hospitals in England. The attending physicians were bright and experienced, usually the best in the country, and almost all on the faculty of the medical college.

We were let loose on the wards in the third of our six school years, where we came to see a wide spectrum of diseases, many quite common in Iraq, the Middle East, Asia, and Africa: parasitic diseases, especially bilharziasis, malaria, amebiasis, giardiasis, hookworm and cysticercosis (hydatid cyst); bacterial diseases like streptococcal infections, often bequeathing rheumatic fever and heart valve disease; tuberculosis; typhoid fever; brucellosis (Malta fever); cholera; and anemias peculiar to Iraq and the Mediterranean region.

Bilharziasis in Iraq is caused by a parasite called Schistosoma haematobium, which flourishes in the marshy areas and rice paddies in the south of the country. Infected individuals shed its eggs in the urine, thereby contaminating the soil. The eggs then infest a species of snail inside which they grow into an immature form (larva) of the parent parasites, and then break out of the snail to penetrate the foot skin of the shoeless peasants and their sons wading in the rice paddies. The larvae grow into adult worms inside the human body, then copulate, the male hugging the larger female in a long groove in his slender body, and the eggs are deposited in the urinary passages and the bladder of the unsuspecting human host, causing inflammation and bloody urine.

The peasants, seeing their sons urinating blood for the first time, would proudly proclaim them to have become "men," just as the menarche of a girl would make her a "woman," which is why Iraqi physicians called this type of hematuria (bloody urine) the "male menarche." The chronic inflammation of the urinary passages often leads to scarring and obstruction, ultimately causing kidney failure. Schistosomas are as ancient as the people of the Middle East, their eggs having been detected in the bladders of Egyptian mummies.

Malaria is caused by a parasite, Plasmodium, which infects the female anopheles mosquito and resides in its salivary glands. When the mosquitos bite humans, they inject their saliva into the bloodstream. The parasites head to the liver, undergo further development, then infect human red blood cells, causing them to rupture.

The infected patients have fever and rigors, and in a type of malaria caused by Plasmodium falciparum, may develop "black water fever" where the hemoglobin released from destroyed red blood cells spills into the urine, giving it a very dark color. In this type of malaria, the patient may develop severe involvement of the brain, culminating in coma and death (cerebral malaria). In an exemplary collaboration between the Iraqi health authorities and the UN World Health Organization (WHO), malaria was eradicated in most of Iraq by 1966 through comprehensive mosquito control and treatment of infected patients. Alas, the disease came back with the intensification of the Kurdish war in the north, and the infected soldiers took it back to central and southern Iraq.

We also saw quite a few cases of sickle cell anemia, especially in patients from Basra in south Iraq. It is caused by a mutated gene that renders the red blood cells more resistant to the malarial parasite. This is a double-edged sword, however, because the product of the mutant gene, the sickle hemoglobin, will itself cause destruction of red cells as it precipitates inside them in tactoid shapes that disrupt the cell membranes. Under the microscope, the cells no longer display their normal doughnut appearance but look like sickles. The disease is a good example of the frequent blindness of protective genetic endeavors.

Hookworm, Ancylostoma duodenale, was a common cause of anemia in Iraq, especially among the poor and the peasantry. The parasite larvae penetrate the exposed skin of humans to be carried in the blood to the lungs. They are then coughed up and swallowed, ending up in the small intestine where they mature into the adult worms that attach themselves to the lining of the intestines with hook-like teeth. This causes minute daily blood loss which nevertheless results in severe anemia as well as protein loss after months and years of infestation. The female worm lays about twenty-five thousand eggs a day. They pass out in the stools into the soil and infect other people.

The anemic children exhibit a craving for clay, which would worsen their anemia by interfering with iron absorption from the intestines. From my early days on the wards I still remember a young boy of nineteen whose fingernails were concave upward (spooning), so that the nail could actually hold a drop of water; he had a potbelly from protein loss, and heart failure—all signs of severe anemia from hookworm infestation.

The flat hydatid worm, Echinococcus granulosus, was another parasitic scourge. The adult worm lives in the intestines of dogs and other canines (the definitive hosts) and discharges gravid (pregnant) segments full of eggs with the dog's feces, contaminating the soil, grass, and vegetables. When cattle (the intermediate host) or man eat contaminated food, the eggs pass into the intestines, mature into *oncocysts* that penetrate the intestinal wall to gain access into the bloodstream and settle in various organs, especially the liver and lungs, but also the brain, where they grow into large cysts that crowd out normal tissue. The worm's life cycle is repeated when canines or humans eat the cyst-infested organs of cattle. To make matters worse, cow and sheep organs, especially liver and brain, are popular food items in the Middle East.

The cysts may grow as large as a basketball and may rupture, releasing many daughter cysts, which often cause anaphylactic reactions and shock. Large cysts, especially in the brain, may cause serious compression consequences and have to be removed by careful, delicate surgery to avoid rupture and dissemination of daughter cysts. The disease could even be fatal. A close lady friend of my mother died from brain cysticercosis.

Tuberculosis (TB for short, *tederrun* in formal Arabic, and *sill* in the Iraqi dialect) is caused by Mycobacterium tuberculosis, an acid-resistant rodlike bacterium (bacillus) that is spread by droplet transmission. It was quite common in Iraq. Its dissemination is aided by congestion in the old towns: pilgrims streaming in from lands from India to Morocco, and the close living quarters. In times past and until the years of my childhood and adolescence, two or more generations of a family lived in the same house, so an infected member would transmit the disease to others. Grandparents or parents may have a chronic cough. "Oh well, it's a cold or cigarettes or street dust," it was said, when in fact it was often tuberculosis. The children in the family would be easy prey of the disease.

Until the early 1950s, there was no effective treatment for tuberculosis. Patients were advised to live for a while in high and dry places. The financially able would travel to Switzerland. Doctors prescribed very large doses of vitamin D. Patients who did not improve had air injected around a lung to collapse it or had a lung or a part thereof removed.

An uncle of mine contracted tuberculosis when he was a young man and went to Switzerland for treatment. He ended up having a lung and a half removed. When he woke up after surgery, he saw a beautiful young nurse sitting by his bedside, weeping.

"Why are you crying my dear?" he asked.

"I was looking at you, so young, so far from home, all alone after having this big surgery. I could not hold back my tears," she said apologetically.

He immediately fell in love with her. When he recovered, he asked her, "Would you marry me?"

Her answer: "You have to meet my parents first."

Her parents quizzed him about his religion and told him they were Christian. Did he believe in Christ? He said there was more than ample mention of Christ in the Muslim holy book, the Koran. To the Arabs he was Isa al-Maseeh (Jesus the Messiah), and that too many Muslim Arabs were named after him. Muslims revere Jesus as a great prophet, believe that he was immaculately conceived, that he spoke while still a babe in the cradle, and that he cured lepers.

Thus did my uncle win his Swiss wife. She was indeed a wonderful woman. She went back with him to Iraq; learned Iraqi in no time at all (by itself an exceptional achievement); and was solicitous to his parents and his youngest sister, who had Down syndrome, all of whom lived in his house. When the children grew up and left home, she almost adopted a young girl, a daughter of her husband's nephew. She took the child along wherever she went, so the little girl learned to speak fluent French.

She traveled with her husband and children to Switzerland almost every summer, and when they came back, she always brought me amazing Swiss chocolates, a great weakness of mine to this day. In my Baghdad College years, I would visit her and my uncle whenever I felt oppressed by one thing or another, and we would talk about all manner of interesting topics, especially French literature. She was intrigued by my partiality to Stendhal, especially his novel *The Charterhouse of Parma*. She was perceptive and always recognized my dark moods however hard I tried to hide them. She managed to soothe me by talking about subjects dear to my mind.

She was also very fond of my father and considered him the best diagnostician in the country. He spoke French to her, having learned it while studying in Switzerland in 1948. One day when I was sixteen, he told me she did not think it healthy for me to have read Plato's *Republic*. "Too young for that," she had said.

"What do you think?" I asked.

"It was healthy if you understood it," he answered.

So it was that my uncle's tuberculosis brought to our larger family this wonderful woman from faraway Switzerland, a woman

I've seen since my childhood as possessing the double gifts of an engaging mind and the kindest soul.

Another kind of tuberculosis existed in Iraq as well. This was caused by Mycobacterium bovis, which infected cows and other ruminators and was usually contracted by drinking the milk of infected cows. In medical school, we saw many patients with bovine tuberculosis, which often caused scarring and narrowing at the junction of the small bowel and the colon, producing a characteristic "string" sign on x-ray.

Because of widespread TB during my childhood days, all grammar school students were vaccinated against the disease by injecting into the skin of the upper arm, overlying the deltoid muscle, a much-weakened form of the bacterium, the BCG vaccine, Bacillus Calmette-Guerin, so named after two French bacteriologists. This was akin to introducing a mild localized tuberculous infection at the site of the injection, causing a small ulcer that kept discharging for several weeks before it healed, leaving a round scar.

The BCG vaccine thus stimulated the host's immune system to block tuberculous infection upon exposure. A measure of immunity is a positive skin reaction to the injection into the skin of the forearm of a purified protein derivative of the tubercle bacillus (PPD). This matter often created problems for Iraqis seeking work in the United States, especially in the field of health care, as I was. We had to have PPD skin testing for TB and therefore had to explain that the positive reaction was not the result of an infection but of the previous vaccination. Many, myself included, had to show the scar over the deltoid muscle.

By the time we finished medical school, the incidence of TB had decreased dramatically because of improved public health conditions, better public education, vaccination, and (importantly) the discovery of effective drugs. When I left Iraq in 1971, the disease was no longer common.

When I was twelve years old, I began to have fevers. Large nodes came up in my armpits and groin that ached so much that I, usually not given to tears, used to weep from pain at night. My father was told I needed to have a lymph node biopsy to make a diagnosis of my ailment, but he resolutely said it was Malta fever (brucellosis), a bacterial disease caused by Brucella melitensis and acquired by cows, which in turn transmit it to humans who drink their milk. In my childhood days, milk was delivered to homes by woman peasants. It was not pasteurized, and when infected milk was not heated well enough, the person consuming it would catch the disease.

My father treated me with two antibiotics known to be effective against brucellosis. The fever disappeared, and the lymph nodes melted away. It was an interesting demonstration to me at an early age of the great value of experience in clinical diagnosis, and I recollected it much later when a story was told to me of an eminent European professor who visited China and was making clinical rounds at a hospital there.

The professor was shown a patient who had widespread skin lesions, so he got into an elaborate description of the lesions, giving them fancy names and discussing a plethora of possible diagnoses. It was then that the Chinese physicians standing around him smiled graciously, whereupon their senior member told him politely, "Professor, around here we call this smallpox." Europe had at the time eradicated smallpox, so the famous professor had only read about it in textbooks but never seen a case.

Cholera, though not endemic in Iraq during my medical school years, nevertheless erupted in an epidemic form that reached Baghdad shortly thereafter. Dr. Mahmud Thamer, who had recently returned from the US, was a brilliant physician and lecturer who gave us the nephrology (kidney disease) course, and was the reason why I decided to specialize in nephrology after my internal medicine training. He had an office practice outside his appointment at the medical school, as did many other faculty members, and had become popular because of his knowledge, modesty, and superb bedside manners. When the cholera epidemic alighted, he closed his busy office and went to the Tuwaitha Hospital where he attended to the cholera patients referred there for treatment. Many had become so dehydrated from the severe diarrhea that their kidneys shut down.

In the mid-1960s, in Iraq as well as most other countries, including the USA, patients with kidney failure died of the affliction. Dialysis treatment was available only on a sporadic basis. In many countries, only wealthy patients could afford the expense of the treatment. Although medical care was free in public and teaching hospitals in Iraq, the necessary equipment or special fluids needed for dialysis were scarce.

Dr. Thamer introduced peritoneal dialysis to our teaching hospital and got us interested in the physiochemical principles underlying the treatment. Bottles containing special fluid were warmed up in a water bath heated to body temperature before the sterile fluid was poured through a catheter into the abdominal cavity where it would remove the noxious substances that accumulate in kidney failure. Dr. Thamer would dip his index finger in the warm water and guess its temperature. He was always very close to the thermometer reading. We were fascinated by this novel dialysis procedure.

While rotating at the pediatric hospital during the fifth year of medical college, I was struck by the dramatic scene of a whole ward full of "yellow children" with jaundice. The whites of their eyes and their skin had turned deep orange. The flood of such patients occurred around March, the fava bean season. These children had a deficiency of a certain enzyme, glucose-6-phosphate dehydrogenase, which caused their red blood cells to burst (hemolytic anemia) upon eating the beans. The hemoglobin released from the damaged cells turned into bilirubin, the pigment that stains the skin and conjunctiva yellowish green, hence the name *favasim* given to this type of hemolytic anemia.

The treatment was only supportive, and mothers were educated about favasim. The children thus affected would have to avoid the much-loved fava beans for the remainder of their lives. This was always sad news to the children and their parents because fava beans, *bagilla* in the Baghdadi dialect, are popular in Iraq. They are eaten boiled or cooked with rice and dill. Vendors used to roam the streets with their carts to sell the delicious boiled *bagilla*. Certain drugs, including some used to treat malaria and lupus, may also cause the hemolytic anemia in patients having the enzyme deficiency.

Another hemolytic anemia with deep jaundice affecting many Iraqi children was thalassemia, also called Mediterranean or Cooley's anemia. The red blood cells are small and contain too much fetal hemoglobin, causing the cells to burst. The bone marrow, expanding to make more red blood cells to compensate for the destroyed ones, changes the shape of the facial bones, resulting in a Mongolian appearance to the face of affected children, hence the fourth name for this malady, Mongolian anemia, having nothing to do with the Mongols.

There are three grades of severity of thalassemia, the most severe being incompatible with life beyond the second decade. Those children, many of them already teenagers, presented a painful sight that I remember to this day, and most of them knew they would not survive. The less severe grades of thalassemia will only manifest as mild or moderate anemia with small red blood cells and is frequently seen in the US in patients of Italian and other Mediterranean descent. It usually causes no harm.

There were memorable doctors among the medical school faculty. Most of them had postgraduate degrees from Britain (London or Edinburgh), but in my later years at the school and during internship, more came back from the United States after several years of training there. A few had both a British degree and work experience in the US.

In the Department of Medicine there was Dr. Mahmud al-Jaleeli, with his vast knowledge, keen memory, and diagnostic acumen. Dr. Farhan Bakir had obtained a postgraduate degree from Britain, but had also trained at Georgetown. He introduced to the teaching hospital important modern practices such as morbidity and mortality conferences and the diabetes clinic. He was an outstanding diagnostician, had a special interest in pulmonary diseases, and was an expert on hydatid lung disease. He later became chairman of the Department of Medicine and recruited brilliant new staff members. He was physician to several of the successive rulers of Iraq, their families, and many of their friends, and there was hardly anyone in Iraq who had not heard of him. His students went on to become prominent physicians and always remembered him with love, admiration, and awards.

I have already talked about Dr. Thamer, a keen intellect, a great teacher, and a modest gentleman. Another outstanding teacher was Dr. Mohammad Ali Khalil, who taught us endocrinology (ductless glands), a fine human being with impeccable manners and keen intelligence. He was probably the most gentlemanly Iraqi I have ever known. He and his family from Kadhimiya were old friends of my family, and he himself was at times personal physician to my parents.

Dr. Taleb al-Istarabadi also taught us endocrinology and endocrine physiology. He was brilliant, temperamental, and another fine teacher. Patience was not one of his virtues, however. One time, while he was giving a lecture in the auditorium, a female student came in a little late and was indecisive as where to sit, so she kept moving up and down the rows, distracting the other students. "Would you kindly stop skipping up and down like a mountain goat?" Dr. Istarabadi blurted to general laughter.

Another dynamic teacher was Dr. Artin Qantarchian, who taught us neurology. Later during my internship, I encountered Drs. Mehdi Murtadha in internal medicine, Lu'ay al-Nuri, and Salman Tajuldeen in pediatrics, Hikmet Habib and Hamed al-Mundhiry in hematology, and Tahseen al-Salim in clinical pathology, all outstanding personalities and exemplary teachers.

In the Department of Surgery there was the famous Dr. Khalid Naji, much liked and remembered by many generations of his students. Eccentric he was, but a challenging and dramatic lecturer, fine diagnostician, and always on the dot in recognizing able students. He was often harsh and sarcastic, but we could all see he was a kind man who greatly cared about his students, his teaching mission, and his patients. One day we were with Dr. Naji at the outpatient clinic where he was instructing us on performing some minor surgical procedures, so we were busy with our needles and sutures. A much anticipated soccer game was to take place later in the afternoon between Iraq and Hungary, which had a formidable team at the time. Dr. Naji let us leave a little early to catch the game, saying while laughing uproariously, "Take the sutures with you; you'll need them to stitch our team's net. Those Huns will tear it to pieces." He was right, of course; Iraq's team was beaten by the Huns.

I made many lifelong friends at medical school, among them

Mazin al-Khateeb, who was with me at all subsequent stages of our life and whose late parents were very dear to me; also Emil Totonchi; Ridha al-Ansari; and Amer al-Juburi. They are all in the US now, and have been for many years. Our children were born in the US, and we share many memories, both happy and sad. Time and place have, however, separated me from other dear friends and group mates like Namuk al-Khateeb, Aram Chopanian, and Ara Awanais.

Looking back, I can confidently say that the University of Baghdad Medical College was in my days (and for three decades, from the 1940s through the 1970s), the best medical school in the Middle East and many other countries in Asia, Eastern Europe, and Africa, excepting the universities of South Africa. It received students from different Arab countries: Jordanians, Palestinians, Kuwaitis, Yemenis, Sudanese, and Saudis. It gave them an excellent medical education and put up most of them in boarding houses for almost no fees. Those students graduated and returned home to man budding medical schools or establish successful practices. In fact, many among the Iraqi medical graduates and some faculty members who had left Iraq were crucial in building the medical education and health care institutions in Kuwait, Jordan, Saudi Arabia, the United Arab Emirates, and Oman.

My time in medical school, and the years closely bracketing it, witnessed five stormy events: (1) the collapse of the union between Egypt and Syria in September 1961; (2) the anti-Qasim Ba'thist coup in February 1963; (3) the Arif-Nasserist takeover of November 1963; (4) the Arab-Israeli war of June 1967; and (5) the second Ba'ath coming in July 1968. The following chapters discuss some of these events.

My father.

Mazin, left, and I at
the Baghdad Medical
College yard.

With friends at the Baghdad Medical College cafeteria: clockwise from left to right: Mazin al-Khateeb, myself, Aram Chopanian, Arkan al-Zahawi, Amer al-Juburi and Ridha al-Ansari.

With friends in an open-air restaurant on Abu Nu'as Street on the bank of the Tigris River. Clockwise from the left: Amer al-Juburi, Mazin al-Khateeb, Ridha al-Ansari and the author.

# 7

# The Collapse of the United Arab Republic

By 1958 the Syrian Communist Party under the leadership of Khaled Baktash had gained a strong following. Interestingly, this development, occurring during the peak years of the Cold War, alarmed not only the Western powers and their Middle Eastern allies, but also Egypt's president, Gamal Abdul Nasser. He met with the Syrian rulers and prompted them to get rid of the communists, but he was told that only a union with Egypt would save Syria from a communist takeover.

There was popular support in Syria for union with Egypt, especially among the Arab nationalists and even the Ba'thists, who practically ruled the country at the time and shared Nasser's themes of Arab unity and socialism. Furthermore, Nasser was especially popular in Syria, also in the rest of the Arab world, after surviving the tripartite assault of Britain, France, and Israel in the 1956 Suez war.

The union of the two countries, the United Arab Republic (UAR), was proclaimed in February 1958, with Nasser as president. He dissolved all political parties, including the Ba'th, since he had no intention of sharing power with the Ba'thists, and his Syrian henchman Abdul Hameed al-Sarraj became the head of the National Union, the only official party, a replica of its counterpart in Egypt. Al-Sarraj launched a brutal liquidation of the communists with reports of many of their ranking members "disappearing in tubs of nitric acid." However, Egyptians, not Syrians, controlled most of the power positions in the administration, the armed forces, industry, and oil.

The formation of the UAR almost caused a state of panic for the US, Britain, and their Arab allies. It prompted a union between the Hashemite states of Iraq and Jordan in that same February, ironically only five months before the July 1958 coup that toppled the Iraqi monarchy.

Saudi Arabia was giving money to the Bedouin tribes in Syria to prevent them from declaring allegiance to Nasser. And civil war erupted in Lebanon in May 1958 between Nasser's advocates—the Muslims and Druze—and his opponents—the Maronites headed by the Lebanese president, Camile Sham'oon. Last but not least, American forces landed in Lebanon and British troops in Jordan.

Nasser had not coveted Lebanon but felt nevertheless obligated to help his followers, so he authorized Syria's al-Sarraj to provide them with money, arms, and military training. Eventually the Americans persuaded President Sham'oon not to run for another term, and General Fu'ad Shehab assumed the office. He met with Nasser, who explained to him that he was not interested in unity with Lebanon, but did not want the country to be an operational base against the UAR. A deal was therefore struck whereby

Nasser ceased military support for his Lebanese advocates, and the US gave a dateline for withdrawal from Lebanon.

In July 1961, Nasser initiated in Syria a far-reaching nationalization program without consulting the Syrians, who before the union with Egypt had enjoyed a flourishing private sector economy. Banks, insurance companies, the cotton trade, heavy industries, and import/export companies were all nationalized. A limit of 103 to 203 acres was placed on private land ownership. A 90 percent income tax was levied on annual incomes exceeding ten thousand pounds. Workers were given a 25 percent share of company profit, and the workday was reduced to seven hours without pay reduction. These measures led to stagnation and erosion of Syrian industry and agriculture.

Syria before the union had a self-sufficient economy and for five years a democratic government. Three and a half years into the union, the private sector economy had almost disappeared; industry and agriculture had withered; the Syrians had no real say in directing their affairs; and they suffered under a dictatorial rule. The merchant class feared extinction. There was an old saying in Iraq that no ruler of Syria could survive without the blessing of the merchant class.

So it was that unrest sprouted, especially among the military class, which resented the hegemony of Egyptian high brass, and in September 1961, a group of officers staged a coup and declared Syria's independence from the UAR. The new government offered to rejoin the union on better terms for the Syrians, but was rebuffed by Nasser, who even considered sending troops to Syria to subdue the new government but changed his mind when he discovered that all his Syrian allies had been defeated.

It is curious that Nasser did not exert more energy to prevent the Egypt-Syria divorce at a time when he was battling Qasim of

Iraq and other Arab rulers for political power, beating them with the stick of Arab unity. Except for diehard Arab nationalists and spellbound Nasserists, the irrevocable failure of the Egypt-Syria union indicated to the Arab and Iraqi middle class and politicos that Arab unity to Nasser was simply a slogan he employed to achieve his and Egypt's hegemony and to use the pliant Arab states fallen under his sway as a nonaligned block to play off the superpowers against each other.

# 8

# Toward the End of the Qasim Regime

It was the third year of the Qasim era when I entered medical school. As I've already mentioned, Qasim was now more isolated and less popular. The communists, while no longer adoring him, continued to give him guarded support. The Arab nationalists and Ba'athists feigned friendliness but were actually organizing and planning to overthrow him. The majority Shia followers of Grand Ayatollah Sayyid Muhsin al-Hakeem were not favorable toward him, and he had no reliable support in the army.

Furthermore, like the Monarchical regime he had toppled, and unlike Egypt's Nasser, Qasim failed to establish a political party or organization that propagated his socioeconomic and political agenda and recruited loyalists among the middle class and the poor. In the final analysis, as popular as he'd initially been with the majority of Iraqis, he had neither the vision nor the political experience to lead a country as complex internally as

Iraq and as critical to neighboring countries, particularly Turkey and Iran, and to the global powers. The one superpower friendly toward him, the Soviet Union, was nevertheless more focused on its relationship with Nasser's Egypt.

Qasim and his cabinet of technocrats were at that time engaged in negotiations, begun earlier in his tenure, that had far-reaching consequences for Iraq. First and foremost were the protracted discussions with the Iraq Petroleum Company (IPC), a conglomerate of British Petroleum (BP), and the major US, Dutch, and French oil companies. The monarchical regime had concluded an agreement with IPC, ironically not published until July 14, 1958, for the company to relinquish to the Iraqi government 40 percent of its concession lands not hitherto prospected.

The Qasim administration, however, requested the surrender of 75 percent of the concession territory, to increase gradually to 90 percent; also 50 percent of the profits and 20 percent ownership. The IPC and its parent companies were not ready to agree to those terms, for Iraq at the time was one of their least important oil producers, and they did not want to set a precedent for other Middle Eastern oil states.

The negotiations did not come to fruition, so in October 1961, Qasim issued an ultimatum to the IPC, stating that Iraq will forgo the demand for 20 percent ownership in return for the relinquishment of 90 percent of the concession territory and partnership with the IPC in the development of the remaining 10 percent. The IPC did not oblige, hence the declaration by Qasim in December of Public Law 80, which stripped the IPC of 99.5 percent of its concession lands, allowing it to operate only in the areas already in production. He also set up the Iraqi National Oil Company (INOC), which could make its own deals with other foreign companies to develop the acquired lands, including the very rich Rumayla fields in Basra.

Although Public Law 80 would have far-reaching positive consequences for Iraq in later years, its immediate effects were negative in that the battle with the IPC was costly and led to a slump in oil production that placed Iraq behind the Gulf producers. More importantly, as most Iraqis speculated, the IPC and its foreign shareholders were now determined to get rid of Qasim, a desire only strengthened by the emergence of the Kuwait crisis.

Kuwait had been part of the Ottoman Vilayet (province) of Basra. In 1899, the British signed an agreement with the ruler, Mubarak al-Sabah, making Kuwait a British Protectorate, and in 1922, after taking over Iraq from the defeated Ottoman Empire, drew a border between Iraq and Kuwait in a manner that restricted Iraq's access to the Persian Gulf to only thirty-six miles (fifty-eight kilometers) of swampy land, thereby blocking the prospect for Iraq to have deepwater harbors and become a naval power. In 1923, the British reaffirmed the border arrangement. King Faisal I of Iraq did not agree to this but had no power to change it since Iraq was under British mandate.

In June 1961, Britain and Kuwait agreed to terminate the 1899 treaty, and Kuwait was declared an independent state. General Qasim, like Nuri al-Sa'eed before him, made noises about Kuwait being part of Iraq, and on July 25, 1962, he laid claim to the emirate and declared its Amir a Qa'im Maqaam (administrator), accountable to the *mutaserrif* (mayor) of Basra. He had planned a military takeover of the emirate, which somehow never materialized. It was widely circulated among Iraqis that the commander of the First Army Regiment in southern Iraq was a friend of the Emir of Kuwait, who had showered him with plenty of gifts, cars included. The commander, it was believed, had marched his troops to the Kuwaiti border and just sat there.

British troops landed in Kuwait to protect its "sovereignty," and the Arab "brethren" rose to the rescue of the "State of Kuwait," assembling a force to replace the British troops, who were an uncomfortable reminder of the colonials. Even Nasser, who had made a career of Arab unity—one land stretching from the Atlantic Ocean to the Persian Gulf—recognized Kuwait, so intent was he on frustrating Qasim and retaining the status of the all-Arab star. More Arab countries recognized Kuwait, which was then admitted to the Arab League, upon which the Qasim administration ceased all cooperation with the League and recalled its ambassadors from several countries that recognized Kuwait, including Lebanon, Jordan, Tunisia, and the USA.

Iraq's relations with Turkey and Iran had likewise deteriorated after Qasim took Iraq out of the Baghdad Pact in March 1959. The relations with Iran worsened even further because of the Shatt al-Arab issue. Shatt al-Arab is a wide river formed by the confluence of Iraq's two great rivers, the Tigris and the Euphrates, at the town of Qurna, a little north of Basra. It runs southeastward toward the Persian Gulf and forms a geographic divide between the southeastern extremity of Iraq and the Iranian province of Khuzistan, populated by ethnic Arabs.

In December 1959, Iran expressed its dissatisfaction with a 1937 agreement that had drawn the border at the low water mark on the Iranian side but in return had given Iran the right to navigate the midchannel line for eight kilometers (five miles) around the important Iranian port of Abadan and allowed military vessels to sail up the river to anchor at Iranian ports.

Qasim's reaction to the Iranian complaint was to nullify the 1937 agreement and claim sovereignty over the eight-kilometer midriver line around Abadan. Iran protested that the midline of the channel should be the boundary between the two countries. The bitter contention led in early 1961 to the cessation of shipping along Shatt al-Arab. Further complicating the acrimonious affair, Qasim laid claim to the Iranian Province of Khuzistan, calling it Arabistan, and his cabinet renamed the Persian Gulf the Arabian Gulf. Eventually the two countries agreed to settle their differences by negotiation and possibly arbitration. Qasim's relationship with the Shah of Iran had nevertheless soured considerably.

On the internal front there was a cooling followed by deterioration of the relationship between General Qasim and Mulla Mustafa al-Barazani and his Kurdish Democratic Party (KDP). Mulla Mustafa was beginning to suspect that Baghdad was not serious about Kurdish autonomy and travelled to the Soviet Union to air his complaint. While he was gone, Qasim incited the Zeebaari Kurds, longtime adversaries of the Barazanis, to move against the latter. Upon returning from Moscow, Mulla Mustafa left Baghdad to his native Barazan in Iraqi Kurdistan and defeated the rebellious Zeebaris.

The situation vis-à-vis the Barazanis became intense, and by the time I entered medical school, Qasim had bombed the village of Barazan, initiating the Kurdish war, which dragged on without any demonstrable gains by the Iraqi Army, but in fact caused increasing demoralization among its rank and file, and a general disappointment among the public who perceived Qasim's strategy to be dead-ended.

# 9

# The First Ba'th Coming and the Fall of Qasim

Despite the difficulties and political disappointments Qasim experienced in 1961 and 1962, a large section of the Iraqi population still liked him and felt he was a hardworking, incorruptible nationalist leader bent on serving the country and guarding its interests. They clearly favored his position on the oil negotiations and the Kuwait affair. What his advocates did not perceive was his lack of political insight and understanding of big power and oil politics. Furthermore, he had not forged a political organization or party that marketed his policies, nor had he cemented support among the upper echelons of the armed forces. Last but not least, he was not making headway against the Barazani Kurdish rebellion.

On the other hand, the Ba'thists and Arab nationalists were getting better organized and, as always, supported politically and financially by the Nasser regime. They also approached the leadership of the Kurdish rebellion and promised them autonomy for Kurdistan once they toppled Qasim. Last but perhaps most importantly, the CIA provided them with several hundred million dollars and the names of five thousand "communists" listed for liquidation. A great many Iraqis were certain of the CIA involvement but were criticized by the few as being conspiracy theorists who, however, were vindicated some fifty years later when documents were declassified and the big CIA "donation" became public knowledge. I for one read a full account of it in the New York Times.

As I mentioned before, Qasim, in July 1959, had denounced the violence perpetrated in Kirkuk by the communists and their fellow travelers. The Ba'thists and Arab nationalists took that to mean the end of the Qasim-Communist honeymoon and unleashed violent acts, including murder against real or perceived communist individuals. The violence spread to high schools and colleges, where there were frequent bloody fights between students of different political persuasions—often classmates. An incident in medical school, which has ever since seared my memory, was a clash between medical students where Coca-Cola bottles in the college cafeteria were broken and the sharp glass edges used as weapons.

Collaboration between the Ba'thists, Arab nationalists, their allies in the military, and Abdul Salam Arif, cemented by CIA funds and intelligence, eventuated in the military coup of February 8, 1963, which coincided in the Muslim lunar calendar with the fourteenth day of the holy month of Ramadan, one of the three *al ash'hur al hurum* (forbidden months) during which the Muslim religion prohibits the spilling of human blood. The occasion is still referred to as Black Ramadan by the majority of Iraqis. The main supporters of the coup hailed from the provinces of Mosul and Anbar. The Ba'thists were the real power behind the coup because they were the best organized and the most ruthless. The putsch started with the assassination of Jalal al-Awquati, Qasim's air force commander.

Shortly after the launching of the coup, thousands of Qasim's supporters, including communists, gathered at different places in Baghdad, but mainly in Tahreer Square. My late close friend Qusay Adwa, who was at the site, told me that Qasim actually drove out there. The throngs pleaded with him to give them weapons to fight off the coup forces, but he retorted: "No, no. You will only steal the revolution." He sent for Ali Ghalib Aziz, whom he had appointed to the command of the Fifth Brigade, charged with protecting Baghdad, but he was informed officer Aziz was not at home. The coup commanders ordered tanks to roll over the people coming out to support Qasim and used heavy guns to shell for three days the district of Kadhimiya, which was home to many of Qasim's advocates. The rebel forces killed thousands of people in military operations against lightly armed or unarmed opponents of the coup.

Incredibly, Qasim simply hunkered down in the fortified Ministry of Defense, where he had been residing, and did not lead the strong military contingent housed there to fight the rebel forces. Had he done so, he would have had a good chance of defeating the coup. Eventually the Ministry of Defense was overwhelmed, and Qasim and two of his most loyal companions, Taha al-Shaykh Ahmad, a Kurd, and Abdul Kareem al-Jidda, an officer from A'dhamiya, were killed. The latter fought to the "last bullet" before he fell.

I was nineteen years old then, and I can never forget the terrible scene on television when a soldier grabbed dead Qasim's limp head by the hair and spat at his face—a dead commander in chief to whom the soldier had sworn allegiance. Thus had history come full circle from the killing in July 1958 of the royal family and Nuri al-Sa'eed by the rebel forces of Arif and Qasim to the killing less than five years later of Qasim himself.

It is telling of Qasim's leniency, however, that in November 1958 he had commuted Arif's death sentence and never subjected him to long or harsh imprisonment. He had let go many conspirators and kept in sensitive military positions officers who were ill disposed toward him, eventually collaborating to overthrow him. In the context of the violent Iraqi history, Qasim was far less bloody than the rulers who succeeded him. Nevertheless, his behavior in the last two years of his presidency, and especially during the March coup that toppled him, showed him to lack focused thinking and decisive leadership.

Colonel Fadhil al-Mehdawi, the chief judge of the People's Court set up in the summer of 1958, was also killed and his mutilated face shown on television, a gruesome sight. It was said that he was beaten to death by shoe strikes to his head and face. The public prosecutor at that court, Majid Mohammad Ameen, was also murdered.

The young Ba'thists sought a well-known Nasserist figurehead for the presidency, so they appointed Abdul Salam Arif, whom they immediately promoted to field marshal. Taher Yahya, previously a Tikriti police officer with no military field experience, was made chief of staff, and another Tikriti army officer, Ahmad Hassan al-Bakr was appointed prime minister. Such has been the comical tragedy of Iraqi politics ever since.

Behind this window dressing, however, the real power resided with the Ba'th party under the leadership of Ali Saleh al-Sa'di, who assumed the post of deputy prime minister and minister of interior. He had been a wayward youth and a thug and later developed into a clever and ruthless Ba'athist organizer and conspirator. A widely circulated story about him was that he was fond of imbibing *arag Hibhib*, not from a glass, but from a gallon-size container. Arag, as explained earlier, is one-hundred-proof booze made from fermented dates, and Hibhib, the town in Diyala Province where al-Sa'di hailed from, was famous for producing the powerful potion.

The Ba'thists also dominated the Revolutionary Command Council, which had the power of removing cabinet ministers and, when deemed necessary, assuming the role of the commander in chief of the armed forces. In effect, the council had unlimited and unchecked powers. Thus began a terribly bloody chapter in the modern history of Iraq.

The payoff by the coup actors to the US and Western interests was delivered swiftly. It included the extermination of the communists, the recognition of the State of Kuwait, and the near reversal of Qasim's Public Law 80 pertaining to oil policy.

The Ba'th party set up the national guard, a militia politically more powerful than the regular army. Beside the five thousand names of "communists" obligingly provided by the CIA, thousands of others, mostly Shia and often victims of personal vendettas or false reports by opportunists, were murdered, subjected to harsh imprisonment and brutal torture, or shot at night in their own neighborhoods.

Hundreds of "communists" were packed in a sealed train headed for Nugret al-Salman (the Hole of Salman), a notorious prison in the southern Iraqi desert, where would-be escapees would almost certainly die from heat stroke and dehydration. The train had no air conditioning and not enough water to drink. The ill-fated passengers simply perished. Prisons could no longer hold all the detainees, so many were incarcerated in school buildings. Corpses were regularly seen floating on the Tigris, among them the strangled teenage son of al-Shibibi, our beloved Arabic teacher in Baghdad College, who was never a communist. He may have sympathized with the Qasim administration but had never announced it, at least not to his students.

National guard thugs also raided after midnight the house of al-Shibeebi's brother, Shaykh Mohammad Ridha al-Shibibi, a famous poet and a prominent senator under the monarchy, and rounded up his daughters. Al-Shibeebi is reported to have looked at the assailants in agonized disbelief, then said, "May Allah be merciful to Nuri al-Sa'eed's soul." When the guardsmen asked him why he said that, he replied, "I have just remembered an occasion when Nuri said to me, 'Our shaykh, you have often criticized me in the senate. Please remember that this country is a garbage can, and I am its airtight lid. Whoever comes after me will make rags out of your turban.'" Al-Shibeebi added sorrowfully, "He was right." Unabated, the atrocities disturbed the people and reminded them of the prophetic warning the great al-Jawahiri gave Qasim in the poem he recited at the Scouts Stadium following the attempt on Qasim's life in 1959.

Meanwhile, there was a widespread purge of Shiites from government ministries and the universities. Arif himself was a sectarian Sunni and did not seem careful to hide the fact—this in a country where the majority of the Arab population were Shia. Hassan al-Alawi, a Shiite journalist, author, and at the time a Ba'thist, relates that he and Taleb Shibib, another Shiite Ba'thist, went to a meeting that was also attended by Abdul Salam Arif. When the two entered, he turned to them and said, "Al-Rafidha have arrived." *Al-Rafidha* means "rejectionists," a term used by bigoted Sunnis to describe the Shia, who presumably reject the successor caliphs after the Prophet except for the fourth, Ali ibn Abi Talib, the Prophet's cousin and his son-in-law.

Another population segment victimized by the coup authorities and the Ba'thists was the large Iraqicized Persian community in the country, mostly concentrated in the shrine cities of
Kadhimiya, Karbala, and Najaf. This community had two or more
generations of descendants born in Iraq. They looked, talked, and
lived like other Iraqis; many did not speak Persian; and many had
intermarried with Iraqi Shia Arabs living in those same cities.
They were shopkeepers and merchants. The less fortunate among
them worked as home helpers, like the woman and her son who
lived in our home, and gardeners who were prized for their skill,
honesty, and cleanliness.

The new government expelled these people en masse. Many
of them went back to Iran, a country only their ancestors or elders
had known. Entire families were thus rendered refugees in a new
country, threatened with the prospect of poverty and destitution
and having to struggle to eke out a living and secure schooling for
their children, who did not even speak Persian. Many among the
young, desperate for jobs, were recruited into Savak, the Shah's
secret service. The inhumanity of this act by the coup authorities
boded ill for the future and was undoubtedly motivated by sectarian bigotry.

The new government was intent on forging a closer relationship with the West, especially the United States, and on
fostering a friendly attitude toward Kuwait. The latter donated
thirty million Iraqi dinars ($100 million US at the time) to the
Iraqi government, a measly gift from an emirate floating on oil.
The Ba'th slogan "One Arab nation with an eternal message" was
forgotten when the party reciprocated by officially recognizing
the State of Kuwait.

Neither the monarchy nor the Qasim administration would
have even contemplated this colossal betrayal of the national

interest. In fact, their refusal to do so was one of the main reasons for their demise. Every Iraqi recognized that, and there was a common saying that "Kuwait is the tomb of any Iraqi ruler who dares lay claim to it." The other advocates of Arab unity—the Arab nationalists in the government, President Arif chief among them—did not raise any objections to the Kuwait transaction. Ironically, the recognition of Kuwait occurred at the same time the Iraqi government was getting ready to negotiate an Arab union with Egypt and Syria.

Then there was oil again, the black source of modern Iraq's travails. Qasim's Public Law 80 had expropriated the concession lands of the Iraq Petroleum Company (IPC). The coup government got the Iraq National Oil Company (INOC) to restore to the IPC all the expropriated lands with proven oil reserves, including the Rumayla field, and concluded a joint venture agreement with IPC, where the latter had a controlling interest. In other words, the new government fulfilled for the IPC all the demands Qasim had rejected.

On the social front, the government proceeded to dismantle the progressive legislation enacted by the Qasim administration. Indeed, one of its earliest acts was the revocation of the Personal Status Law that had granted women inheritance rights equal to men's and made the practice of arbitrary divorce and polygamy much more difficult.

The Kurdish problem again: As I mentioned earlier, the Kurdish Democratic Party (KDP) had been in contact with the Ba'th before the 1963 coup and had agreed to lend its support to a new regime in return for Kurdish autonomy. The Ba'th emphasis on Arabism, however, sensitized the Kurds, so Barazani demanded in March 1963 what amounted to a federated Kurdish state comprising the provinces of Sulaymaniya; Arbil; oil-rich

Kirkuk; and parts of Mosul and Diyala provinces, where the Kurds were a majority; a regional Kurdish government; parliament; an army regiment; a frontier force essentially composed of his Peshmerga fighters; and a Kurdish vice president in Baghdad. The Kurds saw that the Ba'th was not ready to accede to those demands, but the negotiations continued.

Driven by a vacuous ideological romanticism, oblivious to Iraq's geography and demographics, misguided by imagined rather than factual history, and dismissive of the lessons of the failed union between Egypt and Syria, the Iraqi Ba'th, in collaboration with its Syrian counterpart, nevertheless concluded in April 1963 an agreement with Egypt's Nasser, committing to some kind of future Arab union between the three countries. This was triggered in March 1963 by the coming to power in Damascus of the Syrian Ba'athists, who sought for their own reasons a new union with Nasser and summoned the help of their Iraqi comrades to facilitate the agreement.

It was unlikely that Nasser would actually pursue such a union. He distrusted the Ba'th, disliked their fanatical ideology, and was wary of wading into the quagmire of Iraq's internal problems. Nevertheless, the Kurds were even more alarmed by the announcement of the April agreement and pressed harder their demands. The negotiations between them and the Iraqi Ba'th stumbled before halting. The atmosphere became tense. When the Kurdish delegation in Baghdad was arrested, war broke out again.

Unlike Qasim's limited and largely defensive military policy in Kurdistan, the Ba'th went full blast with heavy guns, tanks, and air power. They inflicted massive civilian casualties, bombed grain fields, destroyed conquered villages, and began an Arabization strategy, settling Arab tribes in Kurdish areas and relocating Kurds to non-Kurdish regions of Iraq, including the south, where they fell prey to bilharziasis and other parasitic diseases to which they lacked natural immunity. None of these stratagems produced tangible military gains for the government, and by late winter 1963, the Kurds had actually regained their positions. This created disaffection among moderate army officers and several ministers, who turned against what they saw as the futile Ba'ath policy in Kurdistan.

Making matters worse for the Iraqi Ba'th party was its own split in mid to late 1963 into three factions. A militant wing, led by Ali Saleh al-Sa'di, advocated totalitarian party control, Marxist-like socialism (the slaughter of the communists notwithstanding), centralized economy, collective farms, and workers' control of the means of production. This faction controlled the notorious national guard.

A second faction was more moderate, receptive to gradualism, and willing to work with non Ba'thists who shared a similar orientation. It was led by Hazem Jawad and Talib Shibeeb and included men to whom Ba'thism was only skin deep—more political opportunism than ideological creed—like Taher Yahya al-Tikriti and militaries such as Hardan al-Tikriti. Yet a third smaller wing was headed by army officers Ahmed Hassan al-Bakr, another Tikriti, and Saleh Mehdi A'mmash. It was sort of center-right, but tried nevertheless to mediate between the two other wings to safeguard party unity.

At the sixth Ba'th Party conference, held in Damascus in October 1963 to elect the members of the Pan-Arab Command (Syria and Iraq), al-Sa'di's militant wing won most of the seats assigned to Iraq, to the chagrin of the party founder Michel Aflaq. The Pan-Arab Command, however, was not the same as the Regional Command for Iraq, where the moderates called for a conference to elect eight new members. During the conference, several army Ba'thists took the meeting by storm, forcing the election of a moderate command and shipping off into exile al-Sa'di and four of his associates.

An Iraqi American friend of mine, an outstanding physician who now practices in the US, was in those days a prominent Ba'thist, but decent, intelligent, and patriotic. He once related to me that in those times of Ba'th Party disunity in late 1963, he was chosen by his colleagues to travel to Damascus to meet with Michel A'flaq. His own position was that democratic procedure be maintained in the internal workings of the party, but A'flaq told him that "the party should go with the A'sker (the Ba'thist army officers) because they have the guns."

The expulsion of al-Sa'di led to serious chaos and instability as his loyal national guard went on a rampage for a whole week, and his friends in the air force bombed the presidential palace, prompting the moderate Iraqi Ba'thists to appeal to the Pan-Arab Command in Syria, whereupon Michel Aflaq and Amin al-Hafidh arrived in Baghdad, declared the November elections of the Regional Command null, and exiled two prominent moderates to Lebanon. This affair further weakened the political standing of the Ba'th Party, as most Iraqis resented the Syrians' interference in Iraq's affairs.

President Arif, himself not a Ba'thist but a declared Arab nationalist, became increasingly alienated from the Ba'th. The Ba'thist military officers were closer to the Arab nationalists and the moderate Ba'thists. They did not share the militant aspects of Ba'thist ideology, resented the national guard, and were mainly interested in regaining political power for the Army. Taher Yahya and Rasheed Muslih left the party, while al-Bakr, Hardan and A'mmash stayed on but sided with Arif. Except for A'mmash, all four military Ba'thists hailed from Tikrit.

The bloodletting that followed the February 1963 coup, the atrocities perpetrated by the national guard, the deadlocked war in Kurdistan, the turning of Nasser against the Ba'athists, the Iraq Ba'th Party split, the Syrian Ba'th intrusion, and the subsequent exile of the prominent members of the Iraqi Ba'th regional command were the factors that doomed the Ba'th Party rule and made it easy for President Arif to step in and take over. All it took was a day of military operations and some aerial bombardment by Hardan al-Tikriti, nominally a Ba'thist himself, and his friends in the air force. Thus ended in less than ten months the first Ba'th government of Iraq.

# 10

# The Arab Nationalists and Nasserists in Power

Abdul Salam Arif announced the formation of the Revolutionary Command Council, bringing the country back under the control of the army. He appointed himself president and commander in chief of the armed forces and was promoted to field marshal, a recurring comical practice following coups by military adventurers. He gave himself almost unlimited powers, dissolved the hated Ba'th militia (the national guard), interned the Syrian Aflaq, the Ba'th Party founder, and his associate al-Hafidh, and appointed Taher Yahya of Tikrit prime minister.

The moderate Ba'thist military officers who had aided Arif were rewarded with important posts. They came mostly from Tikrit, a small town north of Baghdad on the Tigris River, and were often blood relatives and very cohesive. Chief among them was Hardan, who was made minister of defense, and al-Bakr, appointed vice president. Less cohesive but more numerous were

Arab nationalist and Nasserist officers, among them Arif Abdul Razzaq, made commander of the air force.

These officers and others had probably calculated that once Arif came to power, they would manipulate him like a puppet, or else replace him with one of their numbers, counting on Arif's reputation for simple-mindedness. But Arif had matured since the days of the first coup of 1958. He became less impetuous, more calculating, and a better operator and conspirator. He appointed his brother Abdul Rahman Arif acting chief of staff and commander of the army's fifth brigade, and a fellow officer from his original hometown of Ramadi, Sa'eed Slaibi, as commander of the republican guard.

To discredit the Ba'thists, all that Arif had to do was to allow the publication of a booklet detailing the atrocities they'd committed in 1963, with photos showing the methods they used to torture political prisoners to force false confessions: strapping down inmates on nail mattresses; suspending them for hours on end by the hands or feet; beatings with hard rubber cords; electric shocks to the teeth, nipples, and genitals; sleep deprivation; burning the skin with live cigarettes; avulsion of finger and toenails; and mock and real executions in full view of other detainees.

Less than six months after assuming power, Arif dismissed Hardan and abolished the post of vice president, transferring al-Bakr, who had no experience in foreign affairs, to that very ministry. Al-Bakr resigned shortly thereafter, hoping to topple the regime once the opportunity arose. That and the purge of Ba'thists from government and the dissolution of the national guard left the authority in the hands of Arif and the Nasserists. The positions of power drew mainly from the Sunni Arabs, including those who'd supported the Mosul rebellion against the late Qasim. The important civil posts were in the hands of younger people much more committed to Nasser's model of political and socialist engineering.

Arif surrounded himself with Nasserists to cement his anti-Ba'thist regime and secure the support of Nasser. His spokesmen reiterated that Iraq would be looking forward to unity with Egypt as the April 17 agreement had intended. In January 1964, he had a long and cordial meeting with Nasser in Egypt, but neither ruler seemed in a rush to implement a political union. Nevertheless, the Nasserists were further galvanized by the event and kept pressing for union.

In December 1963, it was announced that there would be a future political union between Egypt and Iraq to include the presidents and prime ministers of both nations, and in May 1964 there was an agreement on a joint military command, followed in September by the influx into Iraq of several thousand Egyptian troops, ostensibly to conduct joint maneuvers, but in fact to fortify the Arif regime in the aftermath of a failed Ba'thist coup attempt.

In May 1964, the government announced a new provisional constitution resembling that of Egypt, but with more emphasis on Islam than socialism. Plans were also afoot to elect an Arab socialist union like the one in Egypt to bolster Arif's political base. This did not materialize because neither the leftists nor the Ba'thists were allowed to join. The National Democratic Party supporters were interested only in real (not staged) elections, and the merchants, landowners, and clergy were wary of any socialist edifice.

The Nasserists, however, kept pushing the socialist agenda, and in July 1964 the government declared the nationalization laws, which were engineered mainly by two Nasser acolytes, Khayr al-Deen Haseeb, the governor of the Iraq Central Bank, and his cousin, Adeeb al-Jader, the minister of industry. These laws were quite sweeping in that they meant to shift Iraq's economy from the private sector to state control, not just the means of production but also commerce.

Two stages of these laws nationalized the banks, insurance companies, and the cement, textile, flour, vegetable oil, and tobacco industries. They gave the government import/export monopoly over such items as cars, machinery, durable goods, spare parts, pharmaceuticals, and even staples like sugar and tea. Workers and other officials at all companies were to get 25 percent of the net profit, participate in the running of the company, and have representation on the board of directors. No individual investor could own more than ten thousand dinars ($28,000 US) worth of stock in any company. Income and inheritance taxes were raised.

These laws proved to have a long-lived impact on the economy of Iraq and were unfortunately the most durable legacy of the Arif-Nasserist period. They struck a blow to the merchant class, among which the Shia were prominent. Beside the loss of nearly all political power after the ascent of Arif in November 1963, the loss of economic power rendered the Shia community paralyzed and voiceless. The power of its landowners had disappeared with the Land Reform Law of 1958, and it lacked any meaningful presence among the army high brass. This left it vulnerable to the whims of a Sunni military establishment that continued to neglect and weaken it for the next forty years.

The nationalization laws essentially transferred wealth from the merchants, businessmen, and entrepreneurs to top government and military officers, their relations, and friends, eventually culminating in crony capitalism for the ruling group and socialism for everyone else. The consumers suffered because there was no adequate governmental cadre to replace the private sector. Furthermore, the government agents were salaried officials, not private merchants interested in improving sales and profits, and would not respond appropriately to the laws of supply and demand.

Thus began an era of interrupted supply and recurrent scarcity of food items, durable goods, building materials, and services; arrogant officials lording it over the customers; the spread of bribery and corruption; long consumer lines; and black markets, with the trend worsening over the next four decades. This was in fact one of the main factors that eventually alienated the middle class and the masses from the postcolonial "revolutionary" regimes.

To address the festering Kurdish problem, Arif met with Mustafa al-Barazani in early 1964, and they agreed on a ceasefire, general amnesty, reinstating Kurds in the armed forces and the government, and recognition of Kurdish national rights in the constitution. But this created a rift between Barazani and the intellectuals of the Kurdish Democratic Party (KDP), like Jalal al-Talabani and Ibrahim Ahmad, who, perceiving the Arif government to be weak, pushed for Kurdish autonomy. The rift evolved into a complete split by mid-1964, when Talabani, Ahmad, and another twelve like-minded party members were thrown out of the central committee.

The KDP therefore lost most of its educated urban leaders, but Barazani and his followers consolidated their control of the party. The Talabani faction took refuge in Iran, whereupon Barazani protested to the Shah, who, recognizing Barazani's strength and wary of the active cooperation between the KDP and its Iranian counterpart, decided to side with Barazani, so that he, the Shah, would call the shots. Iran began to provide significant armaments to the Iraqi KDP, and Barazani improved the arming and training of his Peshmerga fighters, turning them into a formidable force that controlled almost the entire Kurdish countryside and the mountainous Iraqi borders with both Iran and Turkey. The large Kurdish cities, however, remained under government control.

By October 1964, Barazani now felt strong enough to make further demands. The Kurds had also been alarmed by the Iraqi government's union negotiations with Egypt and its plan to form an Arab socialist union in Iraq. Barazani demanded Kurdish autonomy and the conversion of his Peshmerga fighters into an official border force. The Arif government refused both demands, and by April 1965 hostilities resumed. Relations with Iran became very tense, as Iraq accused it of providing arms and refuge to Kurdish fighters, while Iran protested that Iraqi armed forces were violating Iranian border villages in their pursuit of the Peshmerga.

The honeymoon between Arif and the Nasserists grew stale early in 1965. The Nasserists' nationalization laws and the attempted establishment of the Arab socialist union were unpopular in Iraq. Arif had used the Nasserists to neutralize the Ba'athists, just as Qasim before him depended on the communists to subdue the Nasserists and Arab nationalists. When Arif took the helm in Iraq, he probably recognized that union with Egypt was more a dream than reality and was, like the late Qasim, loath to yield real power to Nasser. The latter, moreover, had grown much less interested in union in view of his experience with Syria, his impression that the Arif regime was still vulnerable vis-à-vis the Ba'thists in the wake of their attempted 1964 coup, and the persistence of the Kurdish problem.

In foreign policy, the regime was much friendlier to the West but also managed to maintain good relations with the Soviet Union. The Iraqi armed forces had for several years purchased Soviet light and heavy weaponry and MIG fighter jets, so Arif needed to maintain the supply of weapons and spare parts. The Iraqi armed forces had also adopted the Soviet military strategy of static defense. The Soviet Union cooperated, not withstanding the mass killing of Iraqi communists throughout 1963, and supplied Iraq with more MIG-21 jets, a surface-to-air missile system, Iraq's first medium jet bomber, and a nuclear reactor.

In July 1965, Arif made his move against the Nasserists. To forestall a backlash by their numbers in the military, he promised the Nasserist Arif Abdul Razzaq, commander of the air force, the position of prime minister. He then let go the pro-Nasser cabinet ministers as well as Prime Minister Taher Yahya, who was shielding some socialist economists, especially Khayr al-Deen Haseeb, the maestro of the nationalization laws. Arif then installed three of his loyalists in key positions. One, Abdul Razzaq al-Na'if, also from Ramadi, was in military intelligence. The other two became commanders of the Baghdad garrison and the Republican Guard.

In September 1965, while Arif was attending an Arab summit in Morocco, Arif Abdul Razzaq attempted a coup, but this was swiftly aborted by Abdul Salam Arif's brother, Abdul Rahman and Sa'eed Slaibi, the chief of military intelligence. Abdul Razzaq was quietly shipped off to Egypt. When Arif returned, he appointed Abdul Rahman al-Bazzaz prime minister, the first civilian to occupy the post since July 1958.

Al-Bazzaz hailed from a respected family and was well known to the Iraqis of his generation. He was married to the daughter of Mulla Najm al-Deen al-Wa'idh, a prominent and highly respected Sunni cleric. Al-Bazzaz was an Arab nationalist of old credentials, having been in the 1930s a member of two Arab nationalist clubs, and he was imprisoned during World War II for his support of Rasheed Aali. He became a lawyer with a degree from the University of London, dean of the Baghdad Law College, a diplomat in London and, under Qasim, ambassador to Egypt, another sign of Qasim's open-mindedness, since he was well aware of al-Bazzaz's history and his affinity for Nasser.

During al-Bazzas's tenure, there was a marked dilution of the Nasserists' socialist programs. Khayr al-Deen Hasseeb resigned as governor of the Central Bank, and Shukri Saleh Zeki, an antinationalization economist, became prominent in the cabinet. He stimulated the private sector by allowing various private factories, encouraging joint projects with foreign capital, and revising interest rates to encourage savings and investment. Private sector production rose, the budget deficit decreased, and the value of the dinar rose. In other words, Zeki was cognizant of economic realities that took other socialist regimes in Egypt, India, and China up to three decades to recognize.

This was also a time of increasing civilian role in the government. Ministers and prominent officials, as under the monarchy and the Qasim regime, were often accomplished professionals, usually recommended to the prime minister by the dean of the University of Baghdad. The military National Revolutionary Council was dissolved. Above all, the government and the prime minister were by and large men of integrity, not soiled by corruption, in contrast to the preceding cabinet of Taher Yahya, known to Iraqis as the "Thief of Baghdad." But even Taher was mild compared to what came afterward. This "civilian" period, if I may call it that, did not last very long, as Arif died in a helicopter crash in April 1966.

Arif was never popular with most Iraqis. They did not think he was intelligent or charismatic, and they resented his earlier boyish rashness. Older Iraqis abhorred his role in the murder of the royal household, and the younger ones could not forget that he killed Qasim. The Shia resented his sectarianism, and the Kurds were wary of his Arab union rhetoric. After he died, an uncharitable joke circulated that "He was born a Muslim, died a Hindu, and was buried a Christian" because he was incinerated (cremated) in the helicopter blowup, and his remains were placed in a wooden coffin for burial (Christian), unlike the Muslim practice of depositing the shrouded body directly into the grave.

After the death of Abdul Salam Arif, there were three candidates for the presidency, including Arif's brother, Abdul Rahaman, also a military officer, and Prime Minister al-Bazzaz. The army obviously wanted to hold on to power, so Arif was "elected" president. He was a mild man, not endowed with a strong personality or a talent for scheming, so the ambitious brass thought him easy to manipulate.

There was a running joke about the second Arif, too. Returning from a trip, he disembarked at Baghdad airport, surrounded by his security detail. A curious crowd gathered outside the airport, and an older woman dashed toward him, kissed his hand, and kept repeating, "May Almighty Allah preserve you."

The security men were alarmed and kept pushing her back, saying, "Go away, woman; you aren't allowed here. What do you want?" She promptly replied, "Oh, dear brothers, I am just praying for his safety, lest something happen to him and we get Abdul Samee' for President." Abdul Samee' was the third Arif brother. He operated a laundromat in Adhamiya not far from our house.

Abdul Rehman al-Bazzaz submitted his resignation and was asked by President Arif to form a new cabinet. This essentially continued the policies of the first al-Bazzaz cabinet, but the political currents were this time more turbulent, and Arif II was weak and inadequate at balancing the various factions competing for power. Hostilities had resumed in Kurdistan a year before the first Arif's death. In April and May 1966, the Barazani Peshmerga fighters defeated the Iraqi Army at the important battle of Handrin, forcing it to withdraw from a strategic mountain pass, thereby consolidating control of their autonomous area. This victory resulted in the June 1966 accord with the government of al-Bazzaz, who was trusted by the Kurds.

The 1966 agreement stipulated the constitutional recognition of Kurdish nationality, the rights of the Kurds to self-government, the use of Kurdish as the official language in Kurdistan, the inclusion of Kurds in the national armed forces and civil service, and the allotment of funds for reconstruction in Kurdistan. The accord, not destined to materialize, angered the anti-Kurd and Arab nationalists in the military, who moreover resented the loss of executive power to the civilian al-Bazzaz government. Furthermore, the civilian Nasserist elements were livid at the dilution of their socialist programs and the dismissal of their ministers.

There was yet another coup attempt by the Nasserist officer Arif Abdul Razzaq, who had somehow slipped back to Iraq from exile in Egypt. He was supported by like-minded army officers, especially some from Mosul who were involved in al-Shawwaf's aborted coup against the late Qasim. Razzak's forces bombed several military camps around Baghdad, the presidential palace, and briefly occupied Radio Baghdad's broadcasting station, denouncing on the air al-Bazzaz's government with the hackneyed phrase "agents of imperialism."

The coup failed within two days because Arif II had gotten wind of it. The Baghdad Brigade did not betray him, and he himself led the Republican Guard and crushed the coup forces advancing on Baghdad. The ringleader Razzaq was arrested in Mosul by Arif loyalist officers, but was spared the bloody retribution common to the Ba'ath practices of 1963. He and his military and civilian accomplices were imprisoned for no more than two years.

Relations between President Arif II and Prime Minister al-Bazzaz began to cool steadily. The army brass loathed the relative longevity of the civilian cabinet, and the Nasserists and Arab Socialists were pressing President Arif for a change of government. Furthermore, Arif probably resented the fact that al-Bazzaz's popularity among the general population far exceeded his own, so he eventually asked for al-Bazzaz's resignation in August 1966.

Naji Taleb followed al-Bazzaz as prime minister. He was one of the original Free Officers who had conspired to topple the monarchy, and a moderate Arab nationalist. He was not a threat to the contending political forces. As a Shi'ite, he was not a competitor in the eyes of the high brass. He was not effective because he could not satisfy the full agenda of the Arab nationalists and socialists.

Taleb abrogated al-Bazzaz's accord with the Kurds, which resulted in sporadic warfare. Furthermore, there arose during his term economic difficulties because Syria shut off for three months the pipeline that carried Iraqi oil to the Banias terminal on the Mediterranean. The IPC had precipitated the incident by refusing to pay Syria retroactive dues. Taleb finally gave up and submitted his resignation in May 1967.

Arif II himself formed the next cabinet, becoming both president and prime minister. He appointed four deputy prime ministers: a Sunni, a Shiite, a Kurd, and the recurring Taher Yahya, who was actually the strongest of the four. But the positions were largely ceremonial and devoid of real power. The cabinet was a loose group of mostly military officers representing different interests and clans. The long-promised parliament never came into being, and like the monarchy, the Qasim and the first Arif regimes, there was no political structure or party to build support for the government, which in this case was not popular with the majority of Iraqis. The Shia had been almost completely marginalized, and the Kurds had picked up arms again.

What about the Ba'thists? The Iraqi Ba'th party, having committed political suicide in November 1963, thereby losing power to the first Arif, was still embroiled in an internal power struggle well into 1965. Although Ali Salih al-Sa'di had been exiled, he kept trying to dominate not only the regional but also the Pan-Arab Command. In Iraq he was opposed by officer Ahmed Hassan al-Bakr, who sided with party founders Michel Aflaq and Salah al-Deen al-Baytar to gain more legitimacy and also (as I said before) because Aflaq preferred military coups to achieve a Ba'th takeover of the state.

In February 1964, the seventh Pan-Arab Ba'th congress in Damascus expelled al-Sa'di and his faction and appointed al-Bakr a member of the Pan-Arab Command and Abdul Kareem al-Shaikhly head of the Iraq Regional Command. There was another hiccup in September 1964 when, after the failure of an attempted Ba'thist plot against the first Arif, the remaining Iraqi Ba'th leaders, including al-Bakr, were rounded up, imprisoned, or sent into exile.

In Syria, on the other hand, the Ba'th was still in power, but now beset by internal struggles of its own. After the collapse of the Egypt-Syria union in 1961, there was a crop of young military Ba'thists led by Salah Jadeed, an Alawite, who was more focused on a Syrian rather than a Pan-Arab agenda. The group enjoyed strong support from a former officer, Ameen al-Hafidh, who dominated the Regional Syrian Command and the government but was opposed by the old guard headed by Aflaq and al-Baytar.

The eighth Pan-Arab Ba'th Party congress in April 1965

failed to resolve the differences between the Jadeed group and the old guard, and in February 1966 Jadeed took over the Syrian state through a military coup in which al-Hafidh was wounded. The new rulers kicked out Aflaq and al-Baytar from the party and the country and imprisoned the old guard of the Pan-Arab Command, electing new members to suit their agenda for Syria.

The Iraqi Regional Command was mostly on the side of the old guard, but many members were ambivalent about the events in Syria. After the Jadeed coup in Syria, there was an unsuccessful attempt by the Iraqi Command to convene another Pan-Arab congress to resolve outstanding differences and maintain party unity.

This was the moment when Saddam Hussein stepped into the limelight, as he organized a special meeting of the Regional Iraqi Command that resulted in a victory for the anti-Syrian faction, electing al-Bakr secretary general and Saddam himself assistant secretary general. The split between the Iraqi and the Syrian parties was now complete. Al-Bakr and Saddam came to play a deciding role in the affairs of the Regional Command. They were both from Tikrit, and other Tikritis, both military and civilian, came on stage as well. Other prominent members came from the city of Samarra.

The resolution of the internal struggle for power allowed the Iraqi Ba'th to concentrate on its clandestine activities, developing a militia and intelligence network and infiltrating mass organizations of students and teachers. Saddam had begun to organize the notorious Hunayn Brigade (Qatta' Hunayn), trained for assassinations and other acts of political violence and sabotage. The Ba'th was again readying itself for another, more durable power grab.

By this time, I was twenty-two and shared a great many Iraqis' political malaise and cynicism about the series of coups and changes of government. I saw nothing behind those events other than ambitious military adventurers and their civilian cohorts hustling for power, privilege, and the country's oil wealth. The slogans they adopted—Arab nationalist, Nasserist, and Arab socialist—were all devoid of intellectual and moral content, especially among the military, and were only meant to justify the quest for power and riches. No faction seemed to be above crass opportunism or bribery by foreign powers, which had only their own interests at heart. It all reminded me of some verses by an Iraqi poet from A'dhamiya, Hafidh Jameel. In one of his moving poetry volumes, *The Pulse of Conscience* (Nabadh al-Wijdan) he had said:

> Do you hope for restraint from predators
> Tugging at the corps of a country?
> This is the land of wonders,
> Where to seek a just measure
> Is the quest of a simpleton.

But there was more yet to come.

# 11

# Al-Nekseh: June 1967

The swift victory of Israel over Egypt, Jordan, and Syria in the Six-Day War of June 5, 1967, was a tsunami that struck the Arab psyche. It was called the *Nekbeh* (disaster) but the name was later diluted to *Nekseh* (setback). Most Arabs had not expected it, but in hindsight it was inevitable, for it was a clash between two military forces, one modern and First World, the other ossified and Third World. More significantly, however, the outcome of the June war exposed the ailments of the Arab world, its rulers, and its militaries.

Most people are unaware that the original cause of the June war had to do with water resources, but the trigger in 1967 was the closure by Nasser of the Strait of Tiran, thus denying Israel the use of the Eilat seaport, which gave it access to the Gulf of Aqaba and the Red Sea. But it is not my purpose to delve into the details of that affair here.

The outcome of the war put up to the Arabs a mirror reflecting the problems besetting their preenlightenment and preindustrial societies, the absence of democratic practice and freedom of expression, and the demonization of political opposition. The ruling class of military or ex-military officers (the case in 1967 Egypt, Syria, and Iraq) was far behind the times in military knowledge and experience. They were not among the better-educated members of society and had a poor grasp of the strength of the Israeli military machine, its intelligence capabilities, and the dimensions of superpower politics in the Cold War years. If Egypt had an independent legislature, opposition political parties, free press, or institutions of third thought, Nasser might have been dissuaded from going to war in 1967.

Unlike Turkey or Iran at the time, the high brass in post-monarchical Arab countries was not a military "aristocracy" that well understood its obligations to the nation. It lacked respect for civilian governments and was always ready to take over by a coup d'état. A great many Arab army officers had gone to military school because other colleges rejected them for poor performance in high school. And only a small fraction of graduating officers went on to the Staff College, which had a more demanding curriculum.

Political power was a zero-sum game where the winner takes all. The ruler labeled any opposing party as unpatriotic or, more ominously, an agent of imperialism or Zionism, so political opposition was persecuted, went underground, and became radicalized. Hence there was only the ruling clan versus the underground opposition.

The ruling clique, as in Iraq and Syria in 1967 and afterward, arose from insecure minorities. So it populated the important positions in the army, security apparatus, and ministries with members of its own sect, clan, or tribe, often relatives and close friends, regardless of merit, experience, or integrity. Promotions of military and civilian figures were based on those same considerations as well as blind loyalty to the ruler. And no one would ever tell the emperor he had no clothes. Very often, therefore, the reality was not one of national states but rather tribes with flags.

Rhetoric always outpaced deeds and military readiness. Poetry replaced reality, and the glorious Arab past crowded out the less glorious present. For many years before 1967, the Egyptian, Syrian, and Iraqi armed forces had been infiltrated by Israeli agents and moles who contributed invaluably to the Israeli victory of 1967. The Arab military leadership seemed not to be well informed of Israel's military capability, strategy, and tactics. The military rulers, being the product of coups d'état, were probably more interested in securing their rule and guarding against counter-coups than in taking on Israel, a convenient foe that they were always "preparing to defeat," a useful ploy to divert public attention from the lack of representative institutions, the suffocation of individual rights and initiatives, and the endemic corruption.

The Egyptian, Syrian, and Iraqi armies were largely supplied by the Soviet Union. The military academies taught Soviet-style military strategy and tactics of fixed positions and defensive war, unlike the Israeli strategy of nimble and preemptive warfare that also uses the element of surprise to maximum and devastating advantage, as when, on the first day of the war, the Israeli air force destroyed the bulk of Egypt's war planes parked without cover on the runways.

That operation alone decided the fate of the conflict. Crucial strategic and tactical decisions by top Arab officers, including Nasser himself, were often so amateurish as to be tragic, causing untold Arab casualties. And Nasser deceived both the Jordanians and the Syrians by telling them his forces were prevailing and drawing them into a war for which they were not prepared, one that resulted in the loss of the West Bank, including East Jerusalem, and the Golan Heights.

It is likely that Israel would not have attacked Jordan or Syria (especially not Jordan) had they not joined Nasser in what was already a lost war. Incidentally, Arif II sent a token force to fight alongside the Jordanians to no great effect, while the Israeli Air Force bombed the almost unprotected military base at H3 inside Iraq.

Only five days after the war's beginning, all of Sinai, the Gazza strip, the West Bank of the Jordan River, East Jerusalem, and the Golan Heights were lost, and the three Arab combatants readily signed a ceasefire, not even entertaining a protracted guerilla war of the Algerian, Chinese, or Vietnamese type.

Nasser gave another speech in which he declared he would resign and hand the mantle over to "my brother and friend" Zakariyia Muh'ey al-Deen, who was known to be pro-American. This was followed by tumultuous demonstrations in Egypt, the throngs shouting, "No, oh Nasser, no." Nasser of course would not disappoint his loving populace, so he changed his mind and stayed on. Although millions of Arabs continued to love him, his aura would be greatly diminished for the remainder of his life. The Nekseh, I think, killed him, for he died a little over three years afterward, in September 1970, reportedly from a heart attack. There was, however, a widespread rumor among Egyptians and other Arabs that he was poisoned at the behest of Anwar al-Sadat, during the hospitalization.

Five million Egyptians jammed the streets for his funeral. Countless Arabs wept bitterly, and many young people, men and women, took their own lives upon hearing the news of his death. He was to the Arab masses and intelligentsia a towering symbol of anticolonialism, Arab nationalism, and independence. He had expelled the British from Egypt and returned to it the vital Suez Canal. The urban poor and the peasantry were better off during his rule than they'd been for many centuries. Above all, he was the first Egyptian to rule his country in a thousand years. The BBC interrupted its programing to announce his death and delve into a discussion of how great a leader Nasser was.

Nasser, like Qasim but unlike the astute Nuri al-Sa'eed, did not quite comprehend the power of the West and the resources of its allies and puppets, foremost among them Saudi Arabia, which had bled him white by supporting his antagonists in the Yemen war. He overestimated the willingness of the Soviet Union to seriously confront the US and NATO to prevent Egypt's defeat in June 1967. He also grossly underestimated Israel's military readiness and short-war strategy while overestimating the competence of his generals and their tactics. In the final analysis, however, the Arab world etched the defeat of Nasser in its thick scorebook as yet another massive injury for which the culpable West will have to answer.

Going back to the Nekseh, the famous and popular Syrian poet Nazar Qabbani crystallized the whole debacle of June 1967 and its agony in his poem "Footnotes on the Book of the Nekse" and followed up with several other poems. He was an innovative poet who, unlike a great many others, did not play up to the rulers. This is how he described himself in a poem:

> Pigmies and mercenaries have cursed me
> Because I don't wipe the shoes of the Czar;
> Because I battle the plague in my besieged town;
> Because my poetry in its entirety is a war
> Against the barbarous horde.

From his "Footnotes:"

> I announce to you the death, my friends,
> Of the old language and the ancient books
> And the words of whoring, satire, and slur
> And the thought that led us to the rout.
> Oh, children from the Ocean to the Gulf,
> Accept not our thoughts.
> Ours was the time of fraud and dancing on the
>     ropes.
> You are the generation to conquer the loss.

On the fifth anniversary of the Nekseh, Qabbani composed a short poem, "Personal Address to the Month of June." Here are excerpts of it:

> Be, June, a blowup in our old skulls;
> Sweep off a thousand words.
> The proverbs and the ancient rhymes
> Tear up our threadbare robes.
> Shoot your bullets at the past.
> Since God was hanged at the city gate,
> There is no merit anymore
> In blasphemy or faith.

# 12

# The Second Coming of the Iraqi Ba'th

The June 1967 debacle reflected poorly, not only on the states bordering Israel, but also on all other Arab governments, including that of Arif II of Iraq, with its anemic response to the war effort and the negligible and inconsequential support it provided to its Arab "brethren" at war while the Iraqi high brass were relaxing in the seats of power and privilege. It exposed the regime's slogans about Arab unity for the balderdash that it was. This further added to the perception that the government was weak and incompetent, prompting Arif to appoint a new cabinet, headed yet again by Taher Yahya, during whose tenure there was a resurgence of the Nasserist socialists and the return of Khayr al-Deen Haseeb and Adeeb al-Jader.

Now that there was a strong anti-American and British sentiment in the country following the Neskseh, and perhaps to burnish its Arab nationalist image, Yahya's cabinet, largely influenced by Haseeb, al-Jadir and their civilian cohorts passed, in August 1967, Public Law 97, which granted the Iraq National Oil Company (INOC) exclusive rights to develop the unexplored lands and barred the IPC from the oil-rich Rumayla field.

This was followed shortly thereafter by the passage of Public Law 123, which placed INOC under the jurisdiction of the president of the republic. Al-Jadir was made the company's president and Haseeb a member of the board of directors. Pro-American/IPC officials were let go, and INOC announced it would develop the Rumayla field itself. IPC rejected these proclamations and threatened to sue any party purchasing the Rumayla field oil.

In November 1967, INOC signed a service contract with the French state-owned oil company ERAP to explore for oil outside of Rumayla, in return for which the French company would buy a fraction of the oil at a favorable price, and would also sell INOC's share of the oil on the world market for a commission. The French after the Nekseh were not viewed with the same jaundiced eye as the Americans and the British. They had no history of mandate over Iraq, were not seen as pro-Israel in the June '67 war, and were not as obdurate negotiators as the IPC. Further antagonizing American and British interests, INOC announced in December 1967 that the Soviet Union would help it develop the all-important Rumayla field. Work actually began in April 1968.

Adding to the chagrin of the Americans and their votaries in Iraq, INOC signed another ERAP-like oil agreement with a Yugoslav company but, perhaps more significantly, awarded to an ERAP subsidiary a concession to explore Iraq's ample sulfur deposits in the Western desert. Such a concession had been keenly sought by a US group, Pan American, headed by a onetime US assistant secretary of treasury, Robert Anderson. Predictably, this was the time for yet another coup d'état. The military and the

Ba'th party—both ever opportunistic, power hungry, and not averse to foreign financing—got to work.

As I have already explained, the Iraqi Ba'th party had resolved its internal squabbles and elected a new regional command with al-Bakr as secretary general and Saddam as assistant secretary general. Furthermore, and in response to the Syrian Ba'thists electing their own Pan-Arab Command and expelling the founders Aflaq and al-Baytar, the Iraqi Ba'thists in February 1968 formed their own Pan-Arab Command, reinstating Aflaq as Secretary General. This was largely a symbolic move because Aflaq at this stage had no real influence on the course of Iraqi power politics. The Iraqi Ba'thists simply wanted to portray themselves as the original Ba'thists.

Thus the party of Unity, Freedom, Socialism, and One Arab Nation with an Eternal Message split into two highly antagonistic Pan-Arab Commands. In fact, the vitriolic polemics employed by the one against the other far outstripped their rhetoric against the "Zionist enemy." Henceforth the two commands were always engaged in plots and subversion against each other. For some obscure reason, the politicos labeled the Iraqi Ba'th "rightist" and the Syrian one "leftist."

Many among the Iraqi high brass had become jealous of the political influence of the civilian socialists headed by al-Jadir and Haseeb. Among these officers were the crucial Ramadi clansmen of President Arif, namely, Abdul Razzaq al-Na'if, deputy director of military intelligence, and Ibrahim al-Dawood, commander of the Republican Guard. They were also opposed to Prime Minister Taher Yahya, ostensibly because of his corruption and cronyism, but mainly because he was protecting Haseeb and al-Jadir.

The Ba'thists used Sa'dun Ghaydan to approach al-Na'if, al-Dawood, and Rajab Abdul Majeed, a Nasserist officer who, like the other two, also hailed from Ramadi. Ghaydan commanded a tank group in the Republican Guard, so al-Dawood was his boss. Seemingly neither he nor al-Na'if recognized in early 1968 that Gaydan was an undeclared Ba'th sympathizer—a mole if you like. Alongside the approach to the military, the Ba'ath was busy preparing the ground for regime change, so there was a student strike and a demonstration, arranged by al-Bakr, calling for the resignation of the government.

Al-Bakr also brought together thirteen retired officers, including former prime ministers and other officials, five of whom were Ba'thists. Together they submitted a petition to President Arif demanding the dismissal of Prime Minister Yahya, the formation of a revolutionary coalition government, and a legislative assembly. Arif II did not heed their demands. Al-Na'if and al-Dawood therefore agreed to launch the coup, provided that al-Naif got the premiership and al-Dawood the Ministry of Defense. After all, what was another coup for a military that had made a career of it? The Ba'thists al-Bakr and Ammash were to become president and minister of interior respectively.

On July 17, 1968, about a month after I graduated from medical school, the coup started with al-Na'if's force taking over the Ministry of Defense and al-Dawood's the Baghdad radio station. Ghaydan, the nimble conspirator, opened the gates of the republican palace to the Ba'thist officers; al-Bakr and Hardan, both Tikritis; and Ammash. Meanwhile, the Ba'thists ordered their loyalist Tenth Brigade and the militia to march on Baghdad, not heeding al-Naif's efforts to block the move. No adventure movie could have surpassed that show, which ended late at night with Arif's abdication and exile to England wherefrom he later went to Istanbul, eventually settling in Cairo where he could speak the language.

Thus twice, first in February 1963 and then in July 1968, the US and its ally Britain paved the way for the Iraqi Ba'th to wrest power in Iraq. The immense suffering of Iraqis under the first Ba'th regime in 1963 would pale in comparison to what followed in the second coming.

Seared by the memory of its reversal of fortune in 1963, the Ba'th in 1968 proceeded quickly to consolidate power. It had little national support and no more than five thousand registered members. The Tenth Brigade was moved to Baghdad. It was commanded by Hammad Shihab, a Tikriti relative of al-Bakr. Al-Dawood was sent to inspect the Jordanian front, and Hardan, another Tikriti, filled in for him, thus taking charge of the army in addition to his command of the air force. Of Ba'thist officers who had been previously laid off, 117 were brought back to active duty. Then, only a fortnight after the July 17 coup, in a classic case of treachery, al-Na'if was invited to lunch with al-Bakr at the presidential palace where he was confronted by Saddam Hussein, leading an armed gang of Ba'thists. Al-Na'if was shipped off as ambassador to Morocco and later into exile.

Thus this second post–July 17 government was almost entirely military, and the Tikritis occupied crucial positions. The five members of the all-powerful Revolutionary Command Council were all military officers, three of them from Tikrit. Military men occupied the posts of president, prime minister, minister of defense, and minister of interior. All except the last were from Tikrit. Last but by no means least, Saddam, the future Stalin, was the operator behind the curtain, commanding the Hunayn Legion, which perpetrated acts of intimidation and assassination of potential, presumed, and imagined political foes.

# 13

# The Military Reserve College

About two months after the second Ba'th coming, our medical school graduating class had to join the Military Reserve College, a compulsory requirement predating the revolutionary regimes. We had to attend the college for six months of military training and classes, graduating at the rank of second lieutenant in the Iraqi Army Medical Reserve Corps, then serve as physicians for a year in the various military units. I always wondered why graduating doctors were not inducted into the reserve corps after finishing medical residency and gaining more experience, but the army seemed to follow its own wisdom.

We were enthusiastic about the event, occurring just over a year after the Nekseh of June 1967. For some reason the graduating engineers that year were not called except for a few returning from scholarships in the United Kingdom. There were, however, a large number of Ba'thist recruits with little educational background who were to graduate in six months as deputy officers. As it happened, they were soon thereafter promoted to full officers to replace the non-Ba'thists, mostly Arab nationalists and Nasserists, who had been retired by the new Ba'th government.

Our welcome on the first day was noteworthy. We were called to assemble in a bungalow to be addressed by an army captain who was also to give us an orientation and introduction to military life. The officer swaggered in. He was blond and heavy, had small, sunken, bland blue eyes, a thick brush-like mustache, and a somewhat protruding belly. He flexed his elbows, so his arms were not straight at his side (as an officer's arms should be), and he looked like the neighborhood thug much more than an army captain. He did not say hello, good morning, or welcome. He simply growled at us. He rambled for half an hour. At the end he said, "Do not ever think I'll be easy on you because you are doctors. I will wipe the floor with you if you step out of army discipline."

We had witnessed a live act that greatly enhanced my understanding of one of the reasons for the Nekseh. This officer could not forgo his grievance at not having been a doctor or a "professional," so he had it in for us. He did not understand that we were happy to serve his and the nation's army. He could not have been proud of his position because he clearly had an inferiority complex. We, on the other hand, did not expect any thanks for having joined the Military Reserve College—doing so was compulsory. But we certainly did not expect to be insulted by this thug posing as an Iraqi Army captain. And what about his senior officer who assigned him this "orientation" task?

For our living quarters we were assigned to several bungalows, each holding sixty men. There was the bugle call early in the morning; shaving and showering under cold water; and a quick breakfast of two boiled eggs, bad tea, and bread so hard it would cause head injury if tossed at someone. This was quickly followed by a thunderous injunction of *Inhadh* (Get up)! Then it was the forty-minute parade march: *Yes-yum, yes-yum,* the Arabic short for left-right, left-right, while the corporal shouted, "Where is the lion's hand? Show me the lion's hand," referring to the arms' swing during the parade march.

Then there were the teaching circles with our corporal, a pleasant and kind man. He would talk about the various hand arms, stating for example that the length of a certain rifle was X centimeters without the bayonet and Y with the bayonet mounted. The problem was that Y was less than X. Then I would remark, "Corporal: It must surely be the other way around." He would see the comment as irreverent and would shout, "Asad, don't argue. Run to the sand barrier and back." So I would, lest I end up in the school jail for insubordination.

The classes were generally boring, and the teachers lacked passion for their subject. Even we could see that the strategy and tactics lectures were woefully outdated. Moreover, there was no discussion of the military operations in Iraq in the twentieth century, the 1914 British landing in Fao, the Shu'ayba and Kut battles, the 1920 revolt, or any of their historic and tactical lessons.

Likewise there were no lectures about guerilla warfare, notwithstanding its ample twentieth-century examples in China, Cuba, Algeria, and Vietnam. The only interesting lecturer was a young and arrogant staff captain who was presumably an expert on nuclear war, but we could not see the relevance of the subject for a nonnuclear underdeveloped country, especially when the traditional warfare classes were so pathetic.

The officer corps was almost entirely from the Sunni triangle of the provinces of Baghdad, Mosul (now Naynawa or Nineveh), and al-Dulaym (now al-Anbar). The rank and file were mostly from the Shiite parts of Iraq. The officers often abused the soldiers with derogatory language and occasional kicks. We were all pained to witness that, perhaps because we had never been in the army.

During the six months of training, we had only one target training session with the Kalashnikov rifles, then the darling automatic weapon of the Iraqi Army. Surprisingly, I did well at hitting the target, seeing that I had never before held even a simple revolver. The remainder of our time was spent in daily parade marches, useless sessions with the corporals, and boring classes. There was no training in physical feats like jumping over obstacles, climbing walls, crawling under horizontal bars, or swimming in turbulent currents. We and the few engineering graduates complained to the officers that the Israeli army trains its reserves— among whom are countless engineers, physicians, and men with science degrees—to drive tanks, fly planes, parachute, and operate radar systems. So why were we doing all this marching? They smiled or laughed patronizingly but did not answer the question.

Before the first Ba'th coming in 1963, the Iraqi reserves used to spend several weeks in *faradhiyat* (hardship training) at inhospitable locales, often in harsh weather conditions, where they had to learn the art of survival in wartime: sleeping in simple tents with almost no amenities; killing hares, snakes, mice, and even rats to cook for food; and learning to function under conditions of sleep deprivation. Not so, ironically, after the Nekseh.

As our graduation date approached, the parade march training intensified. Finally on graduation day, Colonel Dawood al-Janabi, the commander of the Military Reserve College, surveyed our final march with immense satisfaction and thanked us and the training corporals for a job so well done. Was the march the purpose for our recruitment into the reserves? My other memory is of our sergeant major briskly saluting each of us on graduation day. We were now his superiors. I was somewhat saddened by that and forgave him all the running orders he'd given me during training. We were soon to be assigned as physicians to various military units across the country.

With Mazin, right, after graduation from
the Military Reserves College, 1970.

# 14

# The Army Medical Reserve Corps

Upon graduating from the Military Reserve College, I was assigned as an internist to the physician corps at the headquarters of the Iraqi Air Force, almost across the street from the Military Reserve College. That was a stupendously boring time of my life. There was hardly anything for us to do, and I don't remember having seen a single patient there. I became quite restless, not having been accustomed to a life of torpor.

Our senior officer was fat, relaxed, and lacked any spark of ambition. There were many *khafar* (alert) days when we had to sleep on the premises for no obvious reason. We were not at war, but it suited the authorities to maintain an atmosphere of crisis to keep everybody on his toes. Israel was certainly not about to bomb Iraq, but I suppose there was always the likelihood of another coup. The Ba'th had not quite finished purging the army of "undesirable" elements. This time the party had come to stay.

Its leaders said so themselves: "Gi'na li nebqa," meaning "We've come to stay."

On those numerous *khafar* days, our senior officer sat on the side of his bed in his pajamas and elegant robe de chambre, watched a movie on a hand-held TV set he was very proud of, and chatted with us about all sorts of trivia. I didn't think he was a Ba'thist himself. He was too polite and civil for that, so I couldn't quite understand why he was there in the first place, but I guessed he was probably related by blood, marriage, or friendship to someone in the higher echelons of the Ba'th.

The Ba'th meanwhile was consolidating its hold on power, using the recipe of ruthlessness and fear common to other fascist parties old and new. There were executions and public hangings, the most horrid of which was the display of several people who'd been hanged on trumped-up charges of being CIA or Israeli agents. Their limp corpses were suspended from the light poles at Tahreer Square in Baghdad, swaying in the wind. Among the hanged were several outstanding personages noted for philanthropy, thought, and good deeds.

Prominent among those victims were the Shiite merchant Haj Abdul Husayn Jita of Basra, famous for his charitable works, and the Jew Izra Naji Zelkha, philanthropist and the scion of an old Basra family, of which another member later established the famous Mothercraft stores in England. Many other Shiites and two Christians were likewise murdered. When I saw the hanging corpses on Iraqi television, I felt an intense nausea and quickly turned off the TV.

The cynical and typically fascist element about that episode was that the Ba'th, which had twice grabbed power with CIA funding, was now hanging prominent citizens without even the semblance of a fair trial, based on ludicrous charges of collaboration with the CIA or Israel. To me this was the ominous "writing on the wall." Furthermore, between 1969 and 1973, hundreds of Shiites were killed, among them, in 1970, Rahi Abdul Wahid Sukker, son of the hero of the 1920 Revolt against the British occupation.

Back to the Air Force Command Headquarters. One day we were all informed that President Ahmed Hassan al-Bakr was to visit the site and give a speech. Needless to say, all had to attend unless they valued their life very lightly. We attended the event, expecting to see the president, but guess who showed up? Saddam Hussein. Saddam had just returned from yet another Arab summit in Morocco about the Palestinian problem after the *Nekseh*. The audience room was large and had at the front was an elevated stage upon which he strutted with the characteristic swagger of the neighborhood thug. The front rows were packed with senior army brass, the stars on their shoulders shimmering, but since the stage was high, they seemed to be sitting at Saddam's feet while he was looking down upon them. The layout must have been intended to produce that very effect.

He talked down to the high brass. He mentioned that nothing much was achieved at the summit and declared, "Hitler said if a hundred cowards convened for a hundred hours, they would not make a single heroic decision." I didn't know if Hitler had actually said that, but I was not surprised that Saddam was quoting a psychopathic mass murderer, for he was one himself. His other favorite figure, by the way, was Stalin. The high brass took the patronizing and almost insulting remarks gracefully. Not one of them uttered a comment or a question.

After a brief stay at Air Force HQ, I was transferred to the main military hospital in Kirkuk (Kerkuk). The city itself was about 80 percent Turkmen at the time. The Kurds inhabited large swaths of the countryside, and several towns were inhabited by Shiite Turkmen.

There was ongoing military action against the Barazani Kurdish rebels (Peshmerga), but other Kurds were fighting for the Iraqi government. The hospital was large and well equipped. Two competent doctors with postgraduate degrees from England ran the departments of internal medicine and surgery. Medical corporals knew well the endemic diseases and their standard treatment and were of great help to me in my work at a large and busy outpatient clinic. I also attended to hospitalized patients in a regular ward and to others in what was called *Redhet al-Humayyat*, the "Fevers Ward." Jaundiced patients with hepatitis and others with meningitis and various infectious diseases were admitted to that isolation ward.

I still remember a young soldier with severe jaundice (he had yellow eyes and skin) in the Fevers Ward. I assumed he had hepatitis A, which is common in Iraq and is transmitted by food or water contaminated by the causative virus. His disease was so severe that he lapsed in and out of coma, unusual for hepatitis A. I attended him frequently and almost gave up on him, but he began to improve after three or four weeks, was almost fully recovered by six weeks, and back on duty a month later.

He might have had hepatitis B, a blood-borne virus discovered in 1967, but the blood test to detect it was not available to us in 1970, at least not at the Kirkuk Military Hospital, and there was no treatment for the disease at the time. Hepatitis C, caused by another blood-borne virus, and currently the most common type of hepatitis in the US, was not discovered until 1989. I've always marveled at the fact that these discoveries and many more have occurred just within the span of my medical career.

Another patient I remember clearly was a middle-aged

corporal who was admitted to the general medical ward because of severe shortness of breath from congestive heart failure. He was known to the ward staff as Kaka (Brother) Rasul, being a Kurd. He was in great distress, so I called the hospital pharmacist to see if he had the new diuretic drug furosemide (Lasix), which had just arrived in Iraq. The pharmacist had a few samples and sent me two ampoules that I administered intravenously to Kaka Rasul over a period of six hours. He put out a torrent of urine, and his breathing was no longer labored, becoming quite normal after four hours. He was so relieved he kept showering me with thanks and calling on Allah to bestow upon me a long life, a plea the Muslims' God hears billions of times every day.

I was amazed how powerful this new diuretic was; it was indeed revolutionary. Before 1968 (when I was in medical school) we were still using Mersalyl, a mercury-based diuretic, which is actually toxic to the kidneys. This was replaced by chlorothiazide, a better and safer diuretic, but none was nearly as potent as Lasix, in my opinion one of the seminal achievements of German chemistry in the twentieth century.

It was getting late in the evening, so I left Kaka Rasul and went to bed. I went to see him early the next morning. He was lying peacefully in bed, his eyes closed, his white face serene, a shadow of a smile on his lips. He was dead. I was beside myself, but managed nevertheless to contain my deep sorrow. I said to myself that he probably died from a heart attack or blood clots in the legs shooting up to the lungs or abnormal heartbeats. Could the Lasix have caused the potassium in his blood to dip so low as to cause his heart to stop? We could not in those days get a *stat* (immediate) blood potassium value. For a long time afterwards I was tormented by the thought that in my enthusiasm to relieve Kaka Rasul's heart failure with Lasix, I might have caused his death from a fast-dropping potassium level. Even now, for-ty-seven years later, the thought still nags at me every once in a while. I'll never know the answer.

The patients I saw at the clinic mostly had diarrheal diseases. A great many others were malingerers whose sole object was to get a few days' sick leave to get away from the war. I accommodated them as best as I could and earned their sincere gratitude. This was a self-punishing behavior on my part because they always came back to me seeking more sick leave time. It took me a few weeks before I learned to harden enough not to oblige them.

I owe to the patients, however, my experience in quickly discriminating the symptoms of malingering from those of real ailments. Quite new to me, and very educating about human sex-uality, was the number of patients who had superficial injuries to the groin and genital area after having attempted intercourse with mules, thereby incurring the animals' powerful kicks. Countless mules were employed in the Kurdish war for their amazing agility on the high cliffs and their legendary endurance.

There was nevertheless plenty of spare time that I filled, ini-tially by joining in the activities of fellow officers: billiards, poker, small talk, and the Officers Club for dinner, drinks and movies. An episode at the Officers Club demonstrated early in my career the importance of acquired natural immunity. One of the med-ical officers at the hospital was a delicate creature, the only son of overprotective parents. He had never eaten out at a restaurant. His adoring mother always prepared his meals and shipped him delicious and wholesome sandwiches.

One evening he went out with us to the Officers Club. We had the usual *arag* or whiskey, then ordered kebab and other items. He was cautiously hesitant about ordering his food there and said he'd rather eat back in his room. With the cruelty of youth, we started to tease him and insisted that he "be a man and an officer" and eat with us. He was a gentle and obliging soul, so he did.

Next morning we all felt fine, but he had excruciating abdominal pain and bloody diarrhea from acute amebic dysentery, necessitating admission to the hospital, the administration of intravenous fluids, and specific treatment for the amebic infestation. We felt guilty and foolish about the whole episode and were at his bedside much of the time, yet he was pretty gracious about the whole affair and happy to be our friend.

Amebic disease, caused by the parasite Entameba histolytica, was and still is very common in Iraq, and I think a great many Iraqis had developed natural immunity to it. Many have the one-cell parasite in an inactive cyst form in the colon. If the immune system weakens for any reason, the parasite breaks out of the cyst and invades the lining of the colon, causing flask-shaped ulcers, much pain, and bloody diarrhea. When amebic cysts in contaminated food are ingested by a person not previously exposed to the parasite, they are much more likely to transform into the active mobile form, thus causing the acute illness our unfortunate friend suffered, to our shame.

I also used to go to the *qahwas* for tea and a game of dominoes with the locals. Most of them were Kurds who almost always beat me at the game, so the tea was on me. One of them would always leave at six in the evening. One day it seemed to me he had lingered past his regular time. I looked at my watch and saw it was ten past six, so I said, "Kaka: It's already past six." He smiled furtively, thanked me, got up, and left. I never saw him again. Was he a Peshmerga? But I was surprised at the friendliness and warmth of the local Kurds. Many of them addressed me as Dr. Beg, a respectful appellation, despite my being the "enemy."

I was beginning to be concerned that I would forget the more complex aspects of medical science and physiology I'd learned in medical school and on the wards of the Baghdad teaching hospital, so I immersed myself several hours a day in studying specialty medical textbooks. But this was not enough to ease my restlessness, so I accepted the offer of a local physician who had asked me to take over for him two evenings a week. I was a little wary even as I agreed to do so because I had to stay in my military uniform when I went to his office and would not finish work until fairly late in the evening when the Army presence was usually much thinner and the rebels most active.

As it turned out, I loved the time I spent in that office practice in Kirkuk. No one but a physician would have as good an opportunity to learn the traditions, folklore, habits, and superstitions of a community. The Kurdish patients and their families were nice, trusting, and grateful, and for the first time after medical school I felt I was doing something useful. One incident, however, sears my memory to this day.

A tall, hardy Kurd walked into the office one evening carrying a whimpering two-year-old girl. He said she'd had some diarrhea for a few days and became so weak she stopped walking. While I examined her, she kept meowing feebly like a newborn kitten, was prostrate, and could not move her legs. I was fairly incensed and raised my voice at her father. "This baby has been ill for a long time, but you waited until she could no longer walk before you brought her here. She has polio, infantile paralysis." The impetuousness of youth.

He gave me a pained but forgiving smile and said, "Dr. Beg, for two weeks now I haven't been able to leave my house. If a single bird flew by us, the planes would zoom down and rain on us their bombs." I was mum and ashamed.

After Kirkuk I was transferred to the military clinic in the center of Baghdad. The atmosphere there, far removed from the war theater in the north, was much more relaxed, and my colleagues and I could actually go home after work, but we had to sleep there when we were on call. The clinic director, Colonel Ghazi Hilmi, an ophthalmologist, was a pleasant and personable man. Corporal Nu'man, was the Ba'thist commissar at the clinic, and everyone took note of that and tried to be on Nu'man's good side, but the man was actually quite pleasant and respectful of the medical staff. We did not think he'd submitted any negative political reports about us.

I had many free evenings while at the Baghdad military clinic, so I welcomed the opportunity to do some office practice. One of our parasitology teachers in medical school, himself a physician, had an office in the west side of Baghdad, on the west bank of the Tigris River, in an area inhabited mostly by people originally from Tikrit (Tikreet), the hometown of the ruling clan. He must have been ill or otherwise occupied and wanted me to run his clinic, so I agreed to do so. It was understood that I would bill for my services.

My experience at the clinic was valuable, not medically and certainly not financially, but in expanding my social education. My patients were not only the locals who already lived in the area, but also their relations and clan members who would come from Tikrit or Beiji to visit and stay with them for a while. Much more than the locals, these visitors were strictly provincial and tribal. They knew hardly anything about the rest of Iraq and its peoples. Some had not even heard of Basra, Iraq's third-largest city and only harbor. They were quite poor and as conservative socially as they had been centuries earlier.

A female patient would come accompanied not only by her husband but also by one or more female relatives, and there was absolutely no possibility of her baring any part of her body for physical examination, which was therefore not too informative, conducted as it was from behind at least two layers of clothing. The husband would sit menacingly erect in his robe and headgear, scanning his wife and her female relations for any "impropriety."

Many of those patients were poor or had very limited means, so I did not charge them. I therefore ended up spending out-of-pocket money to keep the office going, and despite my wish to help that community, I decided against bankruptcy and left the office three months later for another physician to take over. At any rate, the date was nearing for the start of my medical internship at *Medinat al-Tib* (Medical City) Hospital in central Baghdad.

# 15

# The Medical City Hospital

We were held up in the Army Reserve Medial Corps longer than the recruits in previous years but were finally released in late 1970, whereupon I started my internship at the Medical City Hospital, the teaching facility of the University of Baghdad Medical College. This new hospital had in fact replaced the old Mustashfa al-Jumhuri (the Republican Hospital) where we had our clinical training during medical school.

My first three-month rotation was in internal medicine under the supervision of Drs. Farhan Bakir and Mehdi Murtadha, and Senior Resident Feryad al-Haweezi. My cointern was Mizhir. Dr. Murtadha was an outstanding physician, a superb teacher, and a kind man. His bedside manners were exemplary. One time before he started his rounds, a patient of mine complained to me of a toothache, so I told her I'd fetch her an aspirin, but I didn't return to her immediately because I was held up by the rounds. After about five minutes, Dr. Murtadha left us, headed to the medicine cabinet, took out an aspirin tablet, and gave it to my patient, to my utter embarrassment. He'd obviously heard her complaint, and I deserved the reminder that the patient comes first.

We worked hard and liked what we did. My cointern Mizhir was a convivial man with a heart of gold, fair with curly hair and an ever-present smile despite the hard work. We became close friends. When we were on call, we admitted several patients and had to present their cases the next morning along with the basic laboratory tests, many of which we performed ourselves: urinalysis, hemoglobin level, microscopic examination of a drop of blood or specimens of sputum, stool, or fluid obtained by lumbar puncture (spinal tap). We did electrocardiograms, inserted intravenous lines, catheters in the urinary bladder, and tubes via the nose into the stomach. The attending physicians were excellent, firm, and demanding. During the daily patient care and teaching rounds, there was no pampering of house staff, and admonishment or worse came promptly for tardiness, incomplete workups, inadequate knowledge, or lapses of common sense.

We learned much from Drs. Bakir and Murtadha, and later from two US-trained physicians who joined in our ward rounds: Drs. Hikmet Habib and Hamid al-Mundhiry, who demonstrated to us the dynamism of clinical rounds in the US and herded us to laboratories to look at blood or pathology slides or the x-ray department to examine films. I believe that those two excellent physicians were recruited by Dr. Farhan Bakir, who had himself done postgraduate training in the US.

My first fatality during the internal medicine rotation was the aged mother of Dr. Mohammad Ali Khalil, who expired shortly after admission from a stroke that was probably hemorrhagic. It was a painful sight to behold Dr. Khalil, an outstanding physician and teacher and beloved of all the house staff, coming in to visit his mother and struggling to contain his sorrow behind a quiet dignity and habitual gentility.

There were other unpreventable deaths that saddened me immensely and kept me wondering if I could have done anything else to prevent them. I would lose my appetite and not sleep soundly for many nights after losing a patient, especially one who had stayed long in the hospital. The wisdom at the time was that physicians must keep a kind professional distance from patients and their families to guard against the inevitable denial that would cloud their objective assessment of a patient's prospects. To me that seemed impossible to achieve. It took me many months to adapt to the sight of patients suffering and dying after long and intractable maladies.

During my neurology rotation (the discipline was part of internal medicine), Abdul Rahman al-Bezzaz, the onetime prime minister under the two Arifs and the first civilian to occupy the post after the 1958 coup, was admitted in a state of coma. He had been imprisoned and tortured by the ruling Ba'thist government, an event that most probably precipitated the stroke and coma, as he was known to be afflicted by familial hypercholesterolemia, a condition of very high blood cholesterol that per se causes premature stroke and heart attack.

Another event I witnessed during my neurology rotation was the admission to a private room of Medhat Ibrahim Jum'a, a prominent Ba'thist who was Iraq's ambassador to Kuwait. The diagnosis was nervous breakdown. Jum'a was a childhood friend of Hardan al-Tikriti, the ex-air force commander and a relative of al-Bakr and Saddam. He lived in Algeria at the time, a safe distance from the reach of the two men whose favor he'd lost when he joined Arif's camp.

Just before, Jum'a had invited his childhood friend Hardan to visit Kuwait. Hardan obliged; he was happy to see an old friend. Jum'a took him around, and after one of their excursions around the eight-year-old desert state, Hardan stepped out of the car to receive a well-aimed bullet to his forehead.

Jum'a was shaking violently and sobbing as he related the episode to a senior neurologist. "Doctor, as soon as he stepped out of the car, the bullet hit him right between the eyes," Jum'a said, almost wailing. The neurologist thus made the diagnosis of nervous breakdown.

On that same day, I was making evening rounds with my cointern. I knocked at the door to visit Mr. Jum'a. "*Tafaddhal* (Please come in)," he said. Upon entering, I found Jum'a in an elegant robe de chambre, surrounded by a retinue of friends. They were sitting around a table, drinking whiskey, playing cards, and laughing uproariously over some jokes. "Come join us for a drink, Doctor," Jum'a said to me with the laughter about to fade out of his face. I apologized, explaining that I did not drink while on duty and withdrew.

"That was the briefest nervous breakdown I've ever seen," I commented laughingly to my cointern. It was rumored that al-Bakr or Saddam had given Jum'a one million dinars (then worth $3.3 million US) to invite Jum'a to Kuwait where "destiny" had been waiting for him.

My cointern was a fine young woman who also happened to be the daughter of a friend of my father. I used to joke with her by calling her Dejerine, which sounded elegantly feminine, although it was the surname of a man, Louis Dejerine, a French physician who, along with Joseph Landouzy, had described the Landouzy-Dejerine type of familial muscular dystrophy. She was amused by the name and in turn called me Landouzy.

She and I used to study in the evenings after finishing rounds. One evening the heat was intolerable despite the air conditioner churning on. So I got up and opened a window. After a while a janitor showed up and started to shout at us about the open window and about the place being hot because the interns always opened the windows. He got up on a stool and slammed the window shut. My patience was thinned out by a long day's work, the heat, and the man's incredible insolence in the presence of a young lady, so I gave him a berating I thought he fully deserved. He left cursing and threatening.

The next morning I was summoned to the office of the hospital's medical director, Dr. Merdan Ali, who admonished me for the previous evening's episode even though I fully explained what had happened. He said that despite my excellence as a physician, I was a hot-headed young man who did not know what was good and safe for himself. He said the janitor was a party member. Many Ba'th Party members were employed around the hospital to spy on physicians and report antiparty comments. Most would not shrink from fabricating such reports. Many physicians, even senior ones, were intimidated by them, and some would even flatter them. The fact that the medical director himself, a pleasant and benign man whose intention was to protect me, called me to his office about the incident showed me yet again the handwriting on the wall and fortified my intention to leave Iraq as soon as the opportunity presented itself.

Among my favorite rotations at the Medical City Hospital was that of pediatrics. Beside the fact that I loved children, I was also intrigued by the special aspects of their diseases, their primordial survival reflexes, their not totally welded skulls at birth, and the congenital diseases that might afflict them, especially those of the heart. Even their normal electrocardiograms were different than those of adults. Furthermore, the attending pediatrician at the time, Dr. Lu'ay al-Nuri, a member of a prominent

Mosul family, was one of my favorite physicians and teachers. He had extraordinary intelligence, sharp clinical acumen, superb teaching ability, and outstanding bedside manners. It was a pleasure to round with him and observe how he approached the children, examined them, and talked to their mothers.

Four children in particular I still remember now, forty-six years later, as though I'd only seen them yesterday. One was five-year-old Mustafa, the youngest patient with Hodgkin's lymphoma in Iraq. He was a handsome and lovable Kurdish boy, with puffy cheeks from treatment with steroids, always smiling, and incurably curious. He would jump on the chart cart as we made rounds and would not listen to our pleas to get off. The other children looked forward to his "rounds," and his cheerful bubbly spirit lifted theirs. Slowly and inexorably, however, Mustafa became less responsive to treatment and began to waste away. His cheeks sank and his eyes bulged, his vivacity was replaced by apathy and listlessness, and his vibrant spirit evaporated into nothing. His death was one of the saddest episodes in my entire medical career.

Another child, Sufian, was only three years old, the only son of a Yazidi family from Sinjar in northern Iraq, the ancient home of a large Yezidi community. He had a lung infection that would simply not resolve with antibiotics. The chest x-ray did not show a foreign body obstructing an airway, in which case secretions would accumulate in the lung segment behind the obstruction and get infected repeatedly. We did not have chest tomography at the time, where we would be able to look at many thin sections of the lung, and computed axial tomography (CT) scan and magnetic resonance imaging (MRI) were not even invented. The poor child suffered for a long time, having fevers, shunning food, wasting away, constantly coughing and expectorating, turning quite blue during the coughing bouts.

We did not at the time have flexible bronchoscopes that we could introduce into the airways to search for inhaled foreign bodies, tumors, or inflammatory tissue, but the chest surgery service had one rigid bronchoscope, which one of their nimble residents introduced into little Sufian's bronchial tree and, lo and behold, discovered a watermelon seed blocking a tiny airway behind which festered the debilitating infection. The seed was removed and little Sufian subsequently made a quick recovery and resumed his baby talk and endless giggles like all other babies. Obstructions by inhaled watermelon seeds were frequent in children.

Two days later, four people appeared on the ward: two women, a man, and another big man with a commanding presence and a thick black mustache—Sufian's father. He sought me out, showered me with thanks for saving his only son's life, and presented me with a large sack of freshly picked pistachios, still having the green fleshy outer skin and looking quite enticing. Pistachios were highly prized in Iraq and very expensive. I thanked him but apologized that I could not accept the gift because my attendance on his son was my duty.

Like all other Iraqis and Middle Easterners, Sufian's father was quite offended by my declining his gift, seemingly oblivious or dismissive of the residents-in-training ethical code. He was mollified only when I said I would accept his gift and have a taste of the pistachios because they were irresistible but would give the sack to the nurses who'd worked long and hard to take care of Sufian. Beaming with a wide smile, he saved face by saying the gift was mine and what I did with it was entirely my own business.

He then grabbed my hand, wanting to kiss it, whereupon I reflexively withdrew it, saying "*Astaghfir Allah* (I beg Allah's pardon)." It seemed absurd that this big and intimidating man would want to kiss the hand of a twenty-seven-year old medical resident.

He left holding Sufian to his breast, surrounded by his whole retinue amidst hearty jubilation. I wonder what's happened to Sufian since. He must be forty-six years old now if he has survived the suicide and truck bombings by Al-Qa'ida or the subsequent massive slaughter of Yazidis by ISIS.

Another child I remember from those days was brought by his mother because he had some skin and scalp lesions, and we found that he had enlarged lymph nodes as well. We examined him thoroughly and discussed various possible diagnoses but could not quite settle on one. Dr. al-Nuri recommended a lymph node biopsy. I called Dr. Tehseen al-Salim, a pathologist who had just returned from postgraduate training in the US, described the patient to him, and said we needed a biopsy. He agreed. Two days later, Dr. al-Salim appeared on the pediatric ward, asked to see the patient, and subsequently requested that we join him for a discussion of the child's case.

The child, he told us, had Hand-Schuller-Christian disease, in those days also called histeocytosis-X and nowadays known as Langerhans cell histeocytosis, which could affect not only the skin, but the bones and other organs as well. The fact that the condition was described by European physicians and yet we saw it in an Iraqi boy confirmed my belief even then of humans' common origin, the admixture of their genetic pool during millennia of migration, and the "mistakes of nature" manifesting themselves in rare diseases affecting people in regions vastly distant from each other. At any rate, we were all quite taken by Dr. al-Salim's discussion of the pathology of the disease, and it was the first time we'd seen a pathologist come up to the medical floor to discuss a biopsy case with the clinicians. We understood that to be a product of US training.

Another boy in his mid to late teens was brought in because

his legs had grown so weak they could barely support him. We examined him, then did a lumbar puncture (spinal tap) and decided he had Gullain-Barre syndrome, an autoimmune disease that causes paralysis of the legs, often ascending to the arms and chest muscles. We were fairly terrified when the paralysis spread up to the boy's arms. He then started to have difficulty breathing and was almost suffocating. We had no respirators at the hospital in 1971, and out of desperation retrieved from storage an old, almost-forgotten *iron-lung* machine that had been used in the past to treat respiratory paralysis in patients with tetanus.

We could not believe our eyes when the ancient machine saved the boy's life. At long last he began to recover slowly, eventually moving his legs in bed. Then one day he got up from bed with some help, staggered a little as he stood up, and hesitated before he actually took a few steps, keeping his feet wide apart. He could not believe he was walking again and burst into a staccato of laughter mixed with joyful tears. The nurses and many of us joined in the lachrymal display, with hugs going all around.

I was interested in pediatrics even more than in adult internal medicine, and I spent the last stretch of my internship year at *al-Tifl al-Arabi* (the Arab Child) hospital in Baghdad. I loved children, their innocence, and their innate instinct about adults, manifested by giggling and spreading out their little arms to hug some or shrinking, crying, and kicking to fend off others. They possessed that elemental natural instinct shared by other mammals but lost by most adult humans. I marveled at their endless curiosity, the way they observed, almost studied, objects and people, and how they attempted to execute various tasks. I could almost sense how the nerve tracts in their brains, their intelligence, were being formed.

Mothers stayed with their hospitalized children. Many were

worn out by poverty, illiteracy, and frequent pregnancies—this in a country that had invented agriculture and writing and was now floating on oil. Many mothers, still in their reproductive years, had shriveled breasts from undernutrition and long periods of lactation following their numerous pregnancies. Breastfeeding their infants was therefore inadequate, so they resorted to concentrated, sweet Nestlé milk mixed with water, the reason many such infants were almost wasted. The attending physicians spent much time educating the mothers about issues of infant nutrition and dissuading them from using the Nestlé product. Legitimate infant formulas were dispensed to them, but there was no mechanism for follow-up or continued provision of these formulas after the babies were discharged from hospital.

The experience at al-Tifl al-Arabi was valuable to me. The senior resident was a dynamic and charismatic young Kurdish woman of aristocratic lineage. She strutted around and issued orders to both mothers and nursing staff, and everyone did what she said. They saw she was kind and caring. More memorable yet was the attending physician on our service, Dr. Hisham al-Salman, a true gentleman—intelligent, knowledgeable, caring, and a great teacher, with impeccable bedside manners. I still remember his interesting clinical rounds.

After rounds he and I would discuss social and sometimes political issues. He liked my manner of speech and asked me one day what I intended to do after my internship. "I want to get away from the *ru'b* (terror)," I said.

He nodded; it was clear that he, too, was suffocating under the Ba'th, but he laughed and said, "Your tongue is a sword. Please make sure it won't cut your own throat!" We both burst out laughing. Not too many years afterward, he was tortured to death in one of Saddam's prisons.

# 16

# Escape from Fascism: England

I had always intended to undertake postgraduate study and training in the US, and my desire to do so was only strengthened by
the increasing Ba'thist control of thought and speech throughout
the Iraqi educational system, from grammar school to the institutions of higher learning. The general atmosphere was suffocating
and resembled that of the Soviet Union, Germany, and Italy
during the rise of Stalin, Hitler, and Mussolini.

The generation of young Iraqi physicians before mine would go
for postgraduate studies to Europe, mainly the United Kingdom,
most often paid for by Iraqi government scholarship grants to
outstanding applicants. But my generation was more interested
in the USA, a younger giant having no detested colonial history
in the Middle East, offering vast horizons of opportunity and
mobility across a whole continent, and engaging in cutting-edge
research and training in all fields of science and medicine. In the
case of a Baghdad College alumnus like myself, another significant factor was my happy experience of education and life at the
college during my teenage years.

It was difficult for young physicians to leave Iraq, ostensibly because the government wanted to prevent a brain drain, but this was actually a habit of postmonarchical governments resenting physicians and other potentially independent earners and taking a perverse pleasure in harassing them; also a demonstration of control over people's careers and means of livelihood. Such control had already been secured over the public workers, who comprised the great majority of employees in the civil, military, and police bureaucracies, education, and the large work force in the oil and other state industries.

To go to the US for graduate medical training, we first had to pass the Educational Council for Foreign Medical Graduates (ECFMG) test, a two-part medical and English exam, not given in Iraq since 1967, when the center where it had been administered was burnt down in the aftermath of the Arab-Israeli war. I therefore had to take the test somewhere outside Iraq, and applied for a two-week leave to travel to Lebanon. A friend and classmate of mine pledged a bond with the Ministry of Health to guarantee my return. Ironically, he left the country not long after I did, a source of great amusement to both of us. I did not want to ask my father for money, so I applied for and received a three-month salary advance, which totaled only ID 200, at the time equivalent to $660 US.

I did not intend to linger in Lebanon, despite the loveliness of the country and its wonderful and witty people. A close friend and classmate of mine, Mazin al-Khateeb, had managed to leave Iraq for England, where he was doing locum tenens in casualty (emergency room medicine) at Harold Wood Hospital in Essex, twenty minutes by train from London, and he secured a similar position for me at the hospital.

I landed in London in October 1971 and was surprised to

see an old childhood friend, Harith al-Jamali, waiting for me at the airport. He was also a relation on my mother's side and a classmate in Baghdad College. I was delighted to see him. It was the first time I saw London, and as we drove on I could not but marvel at its impressive architectural landmarks: solid, imperial, and dignified. There was history at every corner. It reminded me of the saying, "England is London."

I got to Harold Wood Hospital, Gubbins Lane, Essex, exhilarated to see Mazin again, and went to work two days later. Mazin and I lived in a cozy three-bedroom house on the large hospital lawn called the Crescent. A pleasant post-middle-age but hardy lady kept house and at times cooked for us. She was a kindly woman and a good storyteller, relating to us much about Gubbins Lane, the hospital, past and present medical staff, and other entertaining trivia. She liked and mothered us.

Another Iraqi physician of our class joined us at Harold Wood shortly after I arrived. He had been a bright and accomplished medical student, warmhearted and gentle, but he became terribly homesick shortly after he got to England, so much so that he was clearly depressed, ignoring his appearance, and becoming almost disheveled. Although Mazin and I tried to cheer him up, his condition did not improve, and he decided to go back to Baghdad, where he regained his former happy disposition and had a successful medical career. It was the first time I saw a severe case of homesickness, which incidentally was common among Iraqis who went to study in England. Perhaps it was the lack of sunshine, the constant rain or fog, and the much different and seemingly passionless British.

Besides me and Mazin there were seven other Iraqi physicians at the hospital, three couples and a lady physician. She was a few years ahead of me in medical school and possessed what I'd call a "Sumerian" intelligence and the warmth of Mesopotamia. She was labeled a "communist" while in medical school and subjected to much harassment during the Ba'thist era. Except for our homesick friend, these other Iraqi doctors seemed happy and contented at Harold Wood. One of them called London "the mother of cities." However, they mixed mostly with their own kind.

The work in casualty was not hard. The emergency room was not really a trauma center, but the work was interesting, and it gave me a chance to know the British. The patients were well dressed and carried themselves with dignity. I remember a child of nine who was brought in by his mother after he'd accidentally cut his finger with a kitchen knife. He was dressed in a two-piece suit, answered "Yes, sir" or "No, sir" to my questions and did not utter a sound while I was stitching what was a deep wound, but I saw him pursing his lips with each stitch. The patients, adults, and children alike, showed much restraint and stoicism, but that was 1971 and the "tight upper lip" of the Englishman had not at the time gone out of vogue. The nurses were very kind and comforting to patients and never handled any of them perfunctorily.

I did not intend to stay long in Harold Wood, so as soon as I found my way around, I took the twenty-minute train ride to Liverpool Street Station in London and then to the Sick Children's Hospital on Great Ormond Street. I had a letter of recommendation from Dr. Lu'ay al-Nuri to Dr. Dennis Cotton. A young, intelligent, and polite physician met me at his crammed office and informed me with sadness that Dr. Cotton was no longer at the hospital. He had been struck by an errant car as he was strolling with his young daughter on a sidewalk; they were both killed.

At any rate, he told me apologetically that there were no positions available for me, and many of their house staff had already achieved their MRCP (Member of the Royal College of

Physicians) degree in medicine before starting at the hospital. A common problem for foreign physicians was the dearth of positions in medicine and surgery, so they often did a succession of locum tenens jobs in different hospitals. Even for British physicians, promotion from a registrar position to consultant was often unattainable unless a sitting consultant retired, died, or relocated. This was a common factor in driving foreign and even British physicians to head to the US if they could manage it.

At Harold Wood, the house staff did not work as hard as we had at the Medical City Hospital in Baghdad, but then Harold Wood was a much smaller place. Many of them had breakfast, midmorning tea break, lunch, and a second tea break in midafternoon at the Doctors' Mess (lounge), which had a long dining table, a TV set, and a draft beer barrel with a faucet. They partook of the beer quite liberally, so that the barrel had to be regularly replenished. The cook at the mess was an agreeable Irish woman, pretty but fairly large, with heavy makeup and dirty fingernails. The latter and the bad food made it almost impossible for me to eat hardly anything at the mess.

Neither did I eat much anywhere else the first three months. The food our housekeeper prepared was healthy but bland. Having been accustomed to good Iraqi cuisine for twenty-seven years, I found it pretty hard to stomach the English food, and I lost fifteen pounds (6.8 kilograms) before I found my way to the Indian, Greek, and Middle Eastern restaurants. My cousin Ali Mohammad Bakir, who was also in London, directed me to a particular Greek food stand in Oxford Circus that served delicious kebab akin to *sha'wir'ma* in Iraq and gyros in the US.

On my initial encounter with Englishmen (as contrasted with the women), I almost thought they belonged to another genus of Homo sapiens. It seemed to me that they had none of the transparency, warmth, or friendliness of the Iraqis, other Middle Eastern and Mediterranean people, nor of the foreigners who lived in Iraq: the Boston Jesuits at Baghdad College, Russians, East Europeans, or Indians. The medical house officers at Harold Wood would sit at the mess in the morning with their heads hiding behind newspapers and would hardly talk to each other. When I or other Iraqi physicians entered the mess and said good morning, only some of them would return the greeting in barely audible decibels from behind their newspapers.

I was curious about the phenomenon and kept asking myself: "How is it that these men are so bland and remote? After all, theirs is the country that produced Shakespeare, Milton, and Dickens. Is it racism? Is it the lingering arrogance bequeathed by the bygone British Empire? Or are they simply inhibited? I asked one of their more accessible numbers about this. He was promptly apologetic and said, "Believe me, it has nothing to do with your being a foreigner. We are like that. When I meet someone I like and we become friends, it takes me at least six months to even consider placing my hand on his shoulder." So I postulated they were just inhibited and internalized their feelings. Not so were the English women, especially the nurses, who were genial, warm and often garrulous.

My impression about the men was confirmed when Mazin and I threw a Saturday-night party at our house and invited the physicians and nurses. The men drank much, laughed constantly, told boldly nonconservative jokes, and then late at night went out on the lawn, linking together to form a choo-choo train, all the while laughing uproariously. One of them drove his minicar and parked it right across the entrance to one of the hospital wards. The following Monday morning, however, they were quite sober at the mess, again hiding their heads behind their newspapers.

The Irish and the Welsh, however, were different in that they were more like Iraqis: transparent, passionate, talkative, and friendly. Among them were some of my first friends in England. Perhaps it was the Gaelic DNA that they shared with the Scots, who were also warm and amicable but somewhat direct. My friend Mazin, talking to an orthopedic consultant at the hospital, asked him, "As an Englishman, what do you think of …" whereupon the consultant, taking umbrage, blurted, "Beg your pardon, sir. I am a Highlander." Mazin apologized but felt better when the consultant gave him a beaming smile and a wink.

In the winter of 1971/72, I did a six-week locum tenens as registrar in pediatrics and neonatology in Liverpool at the Millroad Maternity and Oxford Street Hospitals. The latter was where the Rh factor immune globulin RhoGAM had been developed. A pregnant woman lacking this red blood cell factor would develop antibodies to it if her fetus possessed it. Those antibodies would destroy the fetus's red blood cells, causing what is known as *hemolytic disease of the newborn*, with yellowing (jaundice) of the baby's skin and eyes. If the disease does not reverse with conservative treatment, the infant's blood must be exchanged lest permanent brain injury occur from deepening jaundice. RhoGAM suppresses the maternal immune response to the fetus Rh factor thereby mitigating the chance for the development of this potentially serious disease.

While in Liverpool I saw for the first time a case of anencephaly, where a newborn had a large part of its brain, skull, and scalp missing. It was let to expire at birth because it could not have survived. The condition results from defects of the neural tube during embryonic development. It seemed to be more frequent than usual in Liverpool.

The pediatric care at both these hospitals was exemplary, but my time in Liverpool was not a happy one. For six weeks it was cloudy and gray with frequent drizzles. I never saw my beloved sun and became homesick for the first time since my arrival in England. A car ferried me between the two hospitals, passing by entire blocks of grim and blackened buildings. The driver, a pleasant man in his fifties, must have noticed the sullen look on my face, for he commented, "From the years of the war, governor, they've never cleaned things up. I was in the British Army in Germany, and as soon as the war ended, I saw those Germans come out in droves to clean up the rubble, carting away smashed bricks and broken glass. But look at us here," he finished, pointing at the black blight. I was happy to return to Harold Wood when my six weeks in Liverpool came to an end.

I was impressed by the British high standard of medical schooling, clinical training, and bedside manners. As in Baghdad, the physicians always attempted to make a clinical diagnosis with as few auxiliary tests as possible. They did not allow dogma to cloud their common sense, of which they had plenty. They were very kind to the elderly and to very young patients and displayed much patience and forbearance in handling them. They did not resort to futile and often toxic therapies for the terminally ill.

Returning to Harold Wood, I spent the spring of 1972 doing another locum tenens in the same pediatric specialty. One time I attended to a little girl who was admitted because of seizures from high fever. After she recovered and was discharged, her mother invited me to their home for dinner. She picked me up at the hospital and drove up to her house, where I met her husband, who was general manager of Ford Motors operations (or was it GM?) in that area. It was a cozy home, and I enjoyed the best English meal since my arrival to England the previous October, a wonderful pot roast followed by a baked tart.

When I told the husband I intended to go to the US, he laughed and said they'd make me work very hard over there. "Imagine," he said, "I had taken off a two-week vacation for a trip to the country with my family, and in the middle of the vacation—and on a Friday, too—I got a call from the company telling me I had to get back to London for a meeting the next morning, on Saturday, mind you, with this important American company executive who'd just flown in from Detroit! I told them to forget it; I would not return before the end of my vacation."

"I am glad you were not fired," I said good-humoredly. "Of course not; this is England," he retorted. Remembering something, he added: "I was watching an interview with some American CEO on the tele (television) the other day. He'd been to Germany, and the interviewer asked him what he thought of the Germans. He replied that he liked the way they relaxed." My host then burst out laughing and said, "And we think the Germans are work maniacs."

I spent an interesting evening with the friendly couple. I was reminded again that one cannot quite understand other people without having been to their homes. The evening got late, but his wife insisted on driving me back to the hospital, not heeding my protestation that I could easily take the train.

Another memorable event was when I had to transfer an infant with respiratory distress to Great Ormond Street. I accompanied the seriously ill baby in the ambulance. The car was going at a reasonable speed, but I was too anxious about the infant and told the ambulance driver we needed to make haste. "You have it, governor," he said, turned on the siren, and sped like a rocket. I am fairly brave, but I had not been as frightened in my entire life before that afternoon. I was on tenterhooks while clutching the infant's cot. The driver was going in the wrong direction through one-way streets, crossing over islands, and doing all sorts of turns and twists. And sure enough, he got to Great Ormond at roughly the speed of light. I emitted a deep sigh of relief that the baby and I made it in one piece. I shook the driver's hand, and congratulated him on his superlative skill during the most dangerous cruise I'd ever had. "You haven't seen anything, governor. I was an ambulance driver during the London blitz and was much younger and more daring then," he said, laughing heartily.

There was at Harold Wood an Indian pediatric consultant, Dr. Nauth Missir, who would make rounds with us and discuss the more challenging cases. He was a fine physician and a gentleman, and I learned much from him. Sometimes we met him at Old Church Hospital in Romford, a much larger place, which had many more patients. It was there that I first saw a baby with hydrocephalus, staggering under the weight of his large head and breathing laboriously. I could never forget the appearance of that unfortunate child. The condition occurs when the normal circulation of the fluid inside the brain is blocked; the fluid therefore accumulates and, unless drained, causes pressure injury to the brain. Romford was only two train stops from Harold Wood, and as the train approached I still remember the baritone voice of the announcer: "The train will stop at Romford, Stratford, and all stations to Southend."

At Harold Wood Hospital, there was a ward for patients with terminal cancer. They were kept free of pain with potions containing opium and various alcoholic cocktails, and when a patient expired they would call a house officer to pronounce the patient dead. The hospital was staffed by consultants, registrars, and senior and junior house officers. No general practitioners (GPs) were on staff, as is the case in the US. They saw patients only at the office. When a GP's patient was discharged from the hospital, I would call the GP to apprise him of the patient's diagnosis, hospital course, medications, and prognosis before he got a copy of the patient's record from the hospital.

I enjoyed my time at Harold Wood. One of its most attractive features was its proximity to London, where I would often go to see the historical landmarks, watch plays featuring famous British actors, and visit the British Museum. The first time I visited it, in late autumn 1971, I was awed by its vastness, the articles it contained, and how well they were arranged and exhibited, and naturally I was beside myself with excitement in the Mesopotamian sections. The artifacts, sculptures, wall slabs, jewelry, and cylinder seals brought to me an almost-living history of ancient Iraq, a vibrant record handed down to Iraqi high school students—sadly, in dry, unimaginative textbooks.

At the museum I saw a wonderful necklace of cylinder seals from different periods of ancient Iraq that the archeologist Austen Henry Layard had given to his wife, Enid. She was wearing it when she and her husband were dining with Queen Victoria, who could not help but admire the necklace. Naturally, Enid took it off and beseeched the queen to accept it as a gift. I thought it interesting that Queen Victoria had overlooked the fact that the artifact had been stolen from Iraq, yet did not hesitate to accept it. But wasn't that the same thing the British privateers (pirates), Sir Francis Drake for one, had done when they looted Spanish and French galleys and were rewarded for that with knighthood?

In retrospect, this filching of Mesopotamian antiquities destined for museums in London, Paris, and Berlin was probably a blessing in disguise, for could we imagine what would've become of them had they remained in Iraq during and after the US invasion of 2003 or when ISIS took over the Iraqi province of Nineveh? Moreover, the *valis* (administrators) of the Iraqi provinces in Ottoman times displayed no alarm at the pilfering of ancient artifacts by European archaeologists in the nineteenth century. It is said that when Layard wanted to ship the famous Assyrian winged bulls to London, he asked the *vali* of Mosul for his permission to do so. The *vali* laughed hard upon receiving the request and granted it, relating to his retinue how this "crazed" Englishman was all about transporting a heap of stones out of Mosul all the way to England.

Besides London's various wonderful museums, there was of course the theater, a long-term passion of mine. To my utter delight, I saw some of my favorite British actors in the flesh on stage, like Kenneth More in *Getting On* in Queen's Theater in 1971. I kept returning to London in later years, and watched Alec Guinness in 1976 play Jonathan Swift in *Yahoo* (I was sitting in the first row) and Lawrence Olivier in 1984 doing *King Lear* at the Barbican. It is only on stage that the talent, skill, and dynamism of these great actors came into full expression, largely because they responded to the reaction of the audience.

Mazin rented a yellow Volkswagen that we drove around to explore Essex and other places around London. We drove once to the historic districts of Ongar and Fyfield and stopped for a few drinks and sandwiches at a quaint pub where Charles Dickens had written a large part of *David Copperfield*. We later drove the little car to Cambridge to see its famed university. To me London was and remains the most interesting city of the modern world, but then I speak English, not French, Spanish, or Italian.

The time finally arrived for the ECFMG test, so I, Mazin, and my cousin Ali headed to Seymour Hall to take it. We passed the test and started applying for residency programs in the US. It so happened that my cousin Dr. Ja'far Hussein and his wife, Lilly, lived in a Chicago suburb. They had trained at Cook County

Hospital in Chicago, and Lily was an attending physician at the hospital. They stressed that all three of us should apply to Cook County because it had an immensity of clinical and pathological material and that we'd learn during our residency there far more than at any other place. So we applied to "County" and were accepted, but we were informed we had to take an English test when we arrived there. Moreover, I was interested in Cook County Hospital for other reasons I will mention a little later.

When I got the letter of acceptance from Cook County, I headed to the American Consulate in London to get my J-1 Exchange Visitor Visa. A memo in my Iraqi passport indicated that I could travel anywhere in the world except the USA, Israel, and Syria, the latter a result of the nasty divorce between the Iraqi and Syrian Ba'th parties. I felt I had to bring the memo to the consul's attention. He looked at it, waved his hand dismissively, said: "Oh, don't worry about that," and promptly stamped the passport.

As I was about to leave England, I reflected on my life and experience during those eight months. The English in general are intelligent and resourceful people. When I was there, they were polite, tolerant, restrained, and paid much attention to proper behavior in public places. For example, they would gather around the Speakers' Corner in Hyde Park and oftentimes would be harangued by a demagogue, a fool, or even a deranged speaker. They would listen, smile, or laugh, but I never heard any booing or saw a fight break out, at least not during the time I lived there.

When I would stop a man to ask for directions, he would go to great lengths to make sure I wouldn't get lost. He might point with his index finger to show me where a building stood, but would apologize beforehand for having to point. I also discovered that once an Englishman or woman got to know me and decided to befriend me, that person made a loyal and lasting friend.

After all, a small nation had invented the industrial revolution that changed the course of human civilization; built an empire so vast the sun never set on it; produced a great many of the most formidable minds of the Enlightenment and the scientific age: Newton, Shakespeare, Darwin, Dickens, George Elliot, Paine, Crick, and many others; spearheaded the institution of Parliament; and matured into a tolerant state where thinking men and women did not die for their writings, and where Voltaire and Marx would go without fear of persecution. Last but not least, it inspired the American Founding Fathers, and made its tongue the global language of the modern world.

# 17

# Cook County Hospital, Chicago, USA: Part I

Toward the end of May 1972, I was getting ready to travel to Chicago to start residency in internal medicine at Cook County Hospital. I was quite excited about that because I was greatly interested in the hospital, having read about its long and rich history. The hospital is named after the county of Cook, the largest in Illinois, and one of the largest in the US. Its forerunner was a small almshouse in a Chicago public square that the Cook County government, henceforth referred to as "County," opened in 1835 to house the sick and the poor.

In 1836, Dr. Daniel Brainard, who trained in New York, came to Chicago and built a reputation for being an excellent physician and surgeon who performed painless operations. He was the first US physician to use ether anesthesia. He founded Rush Medical College, believed that both science and religion should be taught for free, was an advocate of health care for the poor, and championed for Tippecanoe Hall. This was a warehouse at Kinzie and State Street that County purchased in 1847 for $846 and converted into a hospital, Tippecanoe Hall. There were at the time epidemics of scarlet fever and smallpox, and a hundred patients with various contagious diseases were crammed in the building, so County in 1851 paid a local farmer to move some of the hospital patients to a farm on Irving Park Road.

Drs. George Amerman and Joseph Ross, both outstanding physicians, were the godfathers of Cook County Hospital. They led a vigorous drive for a public hospital. In 1858, they leased a building on Arnold and Eighteenth Street and contracted with County to attend to the poor. But in 1861, the federal government converted the facility to a military hospital renamed Desmarres Eye and Ear Hospital. After the Civil War, the two doctors returned to run the hospital and kept pushing for a larger permanent facility to provide "care for the indigent poor" and "clinical instruction of students."

So the Old Cook County Hospital (CCH) opened in 1866 on Arnold and Eighteenth Street to serve a larger number of patients, Chicago's population having grown in the 1850s from twenty-nine thousand to one hundred thousand. The county budget for the hospital was ten thousand dollars a year. It quadrupled in four years.

The first admission to the hospital was a Danish immigrant with cholera. He transmitted the infection to many hospital workers before he died from the disease. The first operation there was a leg amputation undertaken by Dr. Amerman on a sailor with chronic infection of the tibia.

The first intern at the hospital (1866) was Dr. Nils Quales, who was born in Norway. He practiced veterinary medicine before emigrating to America in 1859. He attended Rush Medical College, and in the Civil War served as a soldier in the Union Army. After he finished his internship at CCH, he was appointed city physician of Chicago, and later went into practice in Wicker Park. In the Great Chicago Fire of 1871, he and his wife dashed around in an express wagon and managed to rescue sixty-seven men from the Marine Hospital. The king of Norway made him a knight of Olaf in 1910, four years before his death at age eighty-three.

The first woman intern at CCH (1881) was Dr. Mary Elizabeth Bates, a graduate of the Women's Medical College of Chicago (later Northwestern University Medical School), where she also taught after finishing her training. She later went into general medical practice in Denver. She was a strong advocate of women and children's rights.

In the 1890s, Dr. Christian Fenger taught the latest antiseptic techniques at CCH, and Dr. Nicholas Senn, the author of twenty-three books on surgery, lectured there. In 1891, Dr. Joseph B. Lee interned at CCH and was pained by the high death rate of women during childbirth. He made it the object of his career to improve hospital obstetrical practice and home deliveries and was one of the founders of the University of Chicago's Lying-In Hospital. He succeeded in making childbirth much safer for Chicago's women before his death in 1942.

The first operation on a human heart was undertaken at CCH by Dr. Daniel Hale, who also participated in the establishment of forty hospitals for African Americans. The first African American physician to join CCH medical staff was Dr. Austin Curtis, who later became professor of surgery at Howard University Medical School.

In 1910, Dr. James Herrick of Rush Hospital was the first in the US to describe sickle cell anemia in a dentistry student from the island of Grenada, whom he saw while rounding at CCH.

He described the sickle-shaped red blood cells first seen by his resident under the microscope and hypothesized, correctly as it turned out thirty-nine years later, that the sickling was caused by an abnormal hemoglobin in the red cells. He published his excellent clinical paper in the Archives of Internal Medicine.

The era of Dr. Karl Meyer at CCH started in 1914. He was one of the founders of the Hektoen Institute for Medical Research, Cook County Graduate School of Medicine, and the International College of Surgeons, a member of the University of Illinois Board of Trustees and medical superintendent of CCH. He was a leading surgeon who performed an incredible one hundred thousand operations during his long career, one of the first successful gastric resections in 1933, and developed surgical techniques for dealing with the complications of peptic ulcer.

During Dr. Meyer's tenure, CCH became a leading teaching hospital where much breakthrough research and training were accomplished. It had the first blood bank and trauma unit in the US and one of the first burn units. These two units sustained the tradition of excellence and remained among the best in the country. Dr. Meyer retired in 1967, five years before my internship at the hospital, but I frequently heard people talk about him, remembering his time. In the first year, the other interns and I lived in Karl Meyer Hall, the interns' residence on Wolcott Street named after him.

In 1916, the middle of World War I, the main hospital building on 1835 West Harrison Street was completed. It was eight stories high, had 2,700 beds, and occupied an entire block. During the last year of the war it was filled to capacity with the victims of the influenza pandemic that killed 520 people in Chicago, 550,000 in the US, and 51,000,000 worldwide, far more than the number of the troops killed in combat.

In 1928, Dr. Richard Jaffe ran at CCH the best pathology department in the country. He was a brilliant lecturer and author of 119 publications. His Thursday morning lectures were attended by a large audience of medical students, house staff, and physicians from all over the Midwest.

Dr. Bernard Fantus interned at CCH in 1900, later becoming the first among the outstanding physicians of the twentieth century. In 1937, he established the first blood bank in the country at CCH. When County purchased the old West Side Hospital on Harrison and Ogden in 1940 and converted it into outpatient clinics, it named it the Fantus Clinic in honor of Bernard Fantus. Three years later, County also purchased the McCormick Institute for Infectious Diseases and converted it to laboratories for the newly formed Hektoen Institute for Medical Research, hoping thereby to attract government and private grants to support research and teaching.

In 1948, as in the 1920s, tuberculosis was widespread in the inner city, with 350 new cases reported in 1948 alone. Many patients were treated at CCH, and County undertook a major effort to stem the spread of the disease, part of which was the screening with chest x-rays of twenty-four thousand people in suburban Cook County.

In 1949, babies weighing under 5.5 pounds were considered premature and were transferred in incubators to CCH. County authorities battled a wide array of diseases—polio, typhoid, and rheumatic fever—using immunizations, educational, and school health programs.

In 1960, Dr. Leonidas Berry was among the most prominent gastroenterologists in the country. He was a Rush Medical School graduate, then in 1946 the first African American internist at CCH. He cocreated the Eder-Berry gastroscope to obtain tissue from the stomach and was the first American gastroenterologist to use fiber-optic gastroscopy. He was at one time the president of the New York Academy of Medicine and a recipient of an award from the National Association for the Advancement of Colored People (NAACP).

In the 1960s, the cardiology team at CCH, treating patients with myocardial infarction (heart attack), publicized its important finding that shock (very low blood pressure) in some such patients was not always the result of damage to the heart muscle but often simply due to hypovolemia (dehydration). The team also treated many patients with alcoholic heart disease (cardiomyopathy) and demonstrated that the condition improved after prolonged bed rest, which was in fact due to the interruption of alcohol intake during the long hospitalization.

To me the history of CCH was a glorious catalog of outstanding physicians directing their minds, experience, knowledge, and research findings toward serving the poor indigents and underprivileged—a characteristic of great physicians throughout history.

DR. BERNARD FANTUS. COURTESY OF CARYN STANCIK,
EXECUTIVE DIRECTOR OF COMMUNICATIONS, COOK
COUNTY HEALTH AND HOSPITAL SYSTEMS.

DR. KARL MEYER. COURTESY OF CARYN STANCIK.

# 18

# Cook County Hospital: Part II

I arrived at Chicago in late May 1972 and showed up at Cook County Hospital's Main Building at 1835 West Harrison Street. The temperature was above ninety degrees Fahrenheit, and the humidity was suffocating. The weather that day was like that of Basra in southern Iraq. I never minded the summer heat of Baghdad because it was always dry, but I had never adapted to humid heat and loathed the sensation of sweat never evaporating and clothing sticking to the skin like some adhesive patch. I had always considered human life in the hot, humid subtropics and tropics as a marvelous triumph of our species and was quite unpleasantly surprised that Chicago, at 41.88 degrees latitude, could feel like a sauna even before the start of June. I almost regretted leaving London.

There was a fairly long line of prospective interns waiting to be processed and take an English test. A tall, blond, very attractive young woman was directing some of us hither and thither. Most fortunately for me she said, "You don't need the English test; your English is better than mine," for which I thanked her, as the exemption would obviously shorten my stay in the sauna. We were to spend a few days in orientation and would reside at Karl Meyer Hall. The hospital had four buildings at the time: the main building and three others, A, B, and E, with a total bed capacity of twelve hundred. In 1972, one in five US physicians had been through County at some stage of their clinical training or afterward, and hundreds or even thousands of international physicians had also trained there. It was therefore well known not just in the US but also the world over.

It was a time of political turmoil at the hospital (CCH). The powerful Cook County Board under the leadership of the politically consummate Mr. George Dunn had lost the custody of the hospital to the newly formed Health and Hospital Governing Commission, which appointed Dr. James Haughton, a Jamaican American, as director. He fired the chairman of medicine, Dr. Ralph Gunner, an eminent cardiologist, who went to Loyola University Hospital, followed by two of his staff physicians, Drs. William Towne and Henry Loeb, and later, a pulmonary specialist, Dr. Harold Levine. The latter three joined the staff of Hines Veterans Administration Hospital, affiliated with Loyola.

Dr. George Dunea, a kidney specialist, acted as chairman of medicine at CCH for a brief period before Dr. Quentin Young was appointed to the post and held it for the next twelve years or so. The Cook County Board, however, could never forgive the loss of a political prize as huge as CCH, and kept the pot boiling with budgetary crises year after year until the hospital returned to its lap a few years later.

I enrolled in the three-year straight medicine program, which entailed a year of internship and two years of residency in internal medicine and its subspecialties. As I related earlier, I had graduated from medical school four years earlier, had served as a physician in the Iraqi Army Reserve Corps for almost two years, done a year's rotating internship at the main teaching hospital in Baghdad, and worked for eight months in England, so I was not elated at playing intern again at CCH. My consolation was that many other outstanding foreign medical graduates (FMGs) from several countries were in a similar situation. I overcame the bitterness quickly as I delved into the work and got completely absorbed by the large spectrum of the diseases I encountered.

It was around this time that I received an anxious letter containing many "whys" from my mother in Baghdad. She wanted to know why I chose Chicago for my residency, a town of gangland warfare and the Saint Valentine's Day Massacre? Why a public hospital, hadn't I had enough of public hospitals in Baghdad and suffered at the sight of poor and deathly ill patients? And was I not going to marry an Iraqi woman after all?

I sat down to write my mother a conciliatory letter. I explained that the gang wars had been in the 1920s; that I had not seen anyone killed since my arrival on May 27; that the hospital offered exposure to a wide spectrum of illnesses that would give me excellent clinical experience in a relatively short time; and that treating the poor had always been my understanding of the special merit of medical practice, as it had been for my father. Perhaps to put a smile on my mother's face, I added humorously that the rich can get any doctor they choose, perhaps even a few from another more advanced planet. Finally, I told her that marriage was nowhere on my mind at the time or in the near future. It was funny that my mother's letter had an addendum by my father praising me for my choice of hospital. I guessed he must have added it surreptitiously when he took out the letter to drop in the mail.

I was initially quite distressed by the magnitude of poverty, severity of illness, near illiteracy, deprivation, uprootedness, rampant alcoholism, and drug addiction among the patients I treated. I kept asking myself how this was possible in the richest country in the world, on a continent with untold resources, many of the best minds in the various professions, science and technology, a liberal democracy subscribing to the idea that "all men are created equal," that they are "endowed by their Creator with certain inalienable rights." Yet again the hard work of attending to these patients distracted me from the gloom of such reflections.

CCH was a mighty busy place in those days. The Emergency Room (ER) looked like a bazaar in Baghdad. It attended to thousands of usually very sick patients each month. The internal medicine program had four services or teams of house staff. Each service was on call every fourth day, admitting between six and fourteen patients, with an average of eight each time, while also covering another ward of at least twenty patients beside its home ward. Each service had an attending physician, a second- or third-year resident, and two interns, sometimes with one or two medical students (externs). The patients admitted from the ER were routed to the admitting ward, 35-South, on the third floor of the A-Building. It was where we almost lived every fourth day, and it reminded me of Dante's Purgatory.

In 35-South were patients in beds—or on stretchers when the beds were all full. Interns scuttled around to examine the patients. The ward clerk's voice boomed as she paged physicians, forgetting that she did not need to shout into the microphone. And a busy, often intoxicating din blanketed the place. Interestingly, I found the place quite exciting, like a field hospital or even a MASH unit, and I pumped out much adrenaline as I attended to my patients.

Interns examined the patients; drew blood for various tests; did electrocardiograms (EKGs); inserted intravenous lines, catheters into the urinary bladder, and tubes through the nose into the stomach; and often wheeled patients to the x-ray department because of lack or tardiness of auxiliary staff. They also performed various blood, body fluid, urine, and sputum tests in a small, busy, and congested side laboratory located in the corridor leading to 35-South. We also inserted CVP (central venous pressure) lines to judge the state of hydration in very ill patients. Like most other interns, I was not acquainted with that procedure, and I had certainly not seen it done by house staff in England. A fine and highly dedicated nurse, Virginia (Jennie) LaRoche showed me how to insert my first CV line.

I was surprised that the residents almost automatically ordered a large battery of blood tests, x-rays, and electrocardiogram for every patient who was admitted to the hospital, whereas I had been accustomed in Baghdad and England to order only tests that would confirm or refute my clinical impression. In the latter case I would consider other possible diagnoses and order the relevant tests. I suspected that the practice in US hospitals was intended to save time and avoid diagnostic errors. The country was certainly wealthy and could obviously afford the cost, but I thought that the tradition of ordering too many tests, sometimes repeated frequently, made it less imperative for young physicians to exert their mental faculties in making a clinical diagnosis first.

Every postcall morning we had to attend morning report, where we presented the most difficult or interesting cases to an assigned attending physician. Soon afterward that role was assumed by the chairman of medicine himself, representing to us the "moment of truth." We learned much at these sessions, especially when they were attended by subspecialty physicians whom the chief resident invited to discuss particular cases.

The work was hard. On many call days our service would admit fourteen patients. At one time my cointern was a pleasant and hardworking Korean whose English was hard to understand, but he was adept and fast in performing spinal taps (lumbar punctures), so I asked him on those very busy days to concentrate on those punctures and let me do the history and physical for the new admissions.

The work on 35-South brought the house staff together and engendered among them a strong bond, a sense of camaraderie as among soldiers on the battlefield. We came to know and often befriended many residents and fellows-in-training, not just in internal medicine subspecialties, but also neurology, surgery and even gynecology, when we called them for consultation on special cases.

On call days a chief resident was on hand to scout the scene, look at the patients, give advice, decide which patients could be transferred to the general wards, select cases for presentation at morning report, call up various consultants to that meeting, and search for articles pertaining to the selected cases.

Assigned attending physicians also came around to scan the patients and help us with the more difficult cases. One evening I had a patient with atypical neurologic manifestations that I attributed to an unusual stroke. When I spotted an attending physician prowling around the ward like a caged tiger, I went up to him to discuss the case and introduced myself. He introduced himself as George Dunea. He thought the patient had a subdural hematoma, a collection of blood under the outermost thick cover of the brain. He turned out to be right. Little did I know then that only five years afterward I would work with Dr. Dunea for twenty-six years in the division of nephrology (kidney diseases) at CCH.

Fellows in subspecialty training abounded on 35-South. One was Dr. Ramesh Patel, a cardiology fellow who almost lived there, an intelligent and especially friendly man, always sitting at a crammed desk on the ward, looking intently at our EKG strips while rubbing the pinna of his left ear before pronouncing the final verdict as to what particular abnormality the EKG exhibited.

There was also Dr. Demetrius Dordorikus, a gastroenterology fellow from Greece, an earnest and straight-talking intellectual. When Turkey invaded Cyprus in 1974, he was beside himself with rage and suspected the CIA had orchestrated the event for the benefit of Turkey. "Can you imagine?" he said me, his face flushed and neck veins engorged. "Kissinger is sitting with Ecevit [the Turkish Prime Minister]. They are discussing the situation in Cyprus. Ecevit then excuses himself for a minute and goes to a side room to phone his generals with the go-ahead signal for the invasion of Cyprus. Can you believe that?" So I found myself uttering many soothing phrases to calm down Dimitri. Many months later, he performed on me, under light anesthesia, an upper endoscopy because I had vomited a little blood. When I woke up, Dimitri was quite amused that I had been rolling and singing while under the effect of the anesthetic.

"We didn't give you much anesthetic, but you are obviously quite sensitive to these agents. I'll tell you, though—you really sing quite well!" he said, laughing.

"Thank you, Dimitri, I'm glad you find this amusing. So what did you find?" I asked.

"Tiger-skin gastritis," he blurted.

"A tiger in my stomach; how odd!" I murmured before I dozed off again.

One of the strange things in life, perhaps only to be found in America, is that I've never seen or heard from Dimitri or Ramesh since 1975. We've been all very busy and gone our separate ways.

Several of the medical conditions I first encountered at County I had only read about but never seen in Iraq. Prominent among these ailments was delirium tremens, better known as

DTs, a condition occurring in alcoholics upon withdrawal from or reduced consumption of alcohol. I saw it mostly among men. They would become highly tremulous, sweat profusely, and have hallucinations: "Wipe those insects off my skin" or "Get that elephant out of the room" or "Call the police; these guys are chasing me." They would become agitated and often aggressive or abusive. Their blood pressure might rise markedly and their pulse would accelerate, or they may have seizures.

The condition is quite serious. Sudden death has been known to occur. It should be promptly treated with sedation and hydration. On Ward 28 in Building B, where I was assigned early in my internship, patients with DTs often had to be placed in leather restraints tied to the bed rails, but before sedation took effect, they might be agitated that they almost raised the beds from the floor while attempting to get up. You could hear the rhythmic banging of the beds' legs on the floor on approaching the ward. The sound resembled the distant march of battle drums.

The interns at CCH had their own physical sign to check for recovery from DTs. We called it the "string sign." We would pretend to have a stretched string held on each side between the forefinger and thumb and would ask the patient, "What color is this string?" He would say it was red or yellow or any other color, which we called a "positive" string sign. We would repeat the maneuver every day. Eventually, when we asked, "What color is this string?" the patient would protest, "What string, Doc? You think I'm crazy?" This "negative" string sign told us the patient had come out of the frightening world of the DTs.

We also saw the late neurological effects of alcoholism in the form of the Wernicke-Korsakoff syndrome caused by deficiency of vitamin B1, and usually associated with chronic alcoholism. Patients may exhibit abnormal eye movements, dementia, and unsteady gait (the Wernicke component), also poor memory and impaired ability to perform manual tasks (the Korsakoff component).

Another aspect of alcoholism that was new to me was a severe lung infection, known in those days as type III pneumococcal pneumonia. Early during my internship at County, I attended to a very sick man with that condition who was also in DTs. I worked hard to get him out of the woods. Many years later I was walking along Harrison Street when I was startled by a car honking at me. I turned my head and saw a taxi driver smiling broadly, almost laughing, and waving to me. He saw I didn't recognize him, so he shouted, "I am the guy who almost died from that damned pneumonia. You saved my life." I looked harder. He was handsome and healthy, not the human wreck I had once treated, so I knew he had left alcoholism behind.

Alcoholic liver disease was another common condition I encountered at CCH. It took the form of acute hepatitis (inflammation), cirrhosis (scarring), or fatty infiltration. Of course I had seen cirrhosis in Iraq, but it was not usually from alcohol, as a majority of Muslims, especially among the peasantry, shunned alcohol. We called that condition cryptogenic (of obscure origin) cirrhosis. The alcoholic liver disease of CCH patients was usually severe, often associated with much fluid in the abdomen, bleeding from dilated veins at the lower end of the esophagus (the food pipe), liver and kidney failure, confusion, and coma. Hardly a week passed by without us admitting at least two patients exhibiting one form or another of alcoholic liver disease.

Yet another result of alcohol toxicity was cardiomyopathy, seen as marked enlargement of the heart, which fails and produces abnormal beats, some of them pernicious and potentially fatal. The experience of Cook County Hospital with this malady went back long before my time, when patients were put to bed rest for months. The patients improved significantly. This was attributed by many to the prolonged bed rest, when the more plausible explanation would have been the abstinence from alcohol.

Intravenous drug use, mostly of heroin (mainlining), was also rampant in the 1970s. This practice often resulted in blood infection from contaminated needles, whereupon the infecting agent, often the virulent Staphylococcus aureus bacteria, would at times settle on the heart valves (endocarditis), damaging them and causing poor closure of the affected valve (incompetence). Fragments of the bacterial colonies on the heart valve may also be thrown out by the blood jet into various organs such as the brain, the lungs, or even the heart muscle itself, with serious consequences of tissue death or the formation of abscesses. If not treated quickly, the condition causes death from heart failure and sepsis. The treatment with antibiotics needs to be continued for many weeks to allow the drugs to penetrate the bacterial colonies sheltered in protuberances (vegetations) adherent to the surface of the valves. Sometimes treatment fails and the valve has to be excised (open heart surgery) and replaced by a prosthetic valve.

I had not seen this condition in Iraq for there was hardly any intravenous drug abuse then or even now. The valvular heart disease I encountered there in adults was usually the result of rheumatic fever acquired after strep throat. The damaged valves in that condition might also be infected, usually by benign bacteria that normally live in the mouth (Streptococcus viridans). However, once these bacteria gain access to the blood stream through traumatic tooth brushing, extraction, or other surgical procedures, they become infective and may cause endocarditis of the rheumatic heart valves. The condition is easier to treat than the County variety because of the nature of the bacteria and their response to many antibiotics.

Another frequent disease that resulted from mainlining was the highly infectious hepatitis B, a viral affliction of the liver caused by contaminated needles and spread by the sharing of such needles. The virus may cause an inflammation of the arteries before the liver disease is manifest. The liver inflammation is acute, may linger for a long time (chronic active hepatitis), and can end up in cirrhosis and liver failure. There was at the time no treatment for the condition.

Many intravenous heroin addicts, particularly African American males, also developed scarring of the kidneys (focal segmental glomerulosclerosis) with much spillage of the blood protein into the urine, swelling of the feet and legs because of water retention, and a fairly rapid course to end-stage kidney failure which requires treatment with dialysis. When addicts have exhausted all their veins, they often inject the street drug under the skin (skin popping). This causes chronic infection and abscesses, which may in turn lead to failure of the kidneys due to the accumulation in them of an abnormal protein called amyloid, hence the term amyloidosis. These kidney complications of drug abuse came into full light a few years later, after I finished my residency and specialty training in kidney diseases.

Another common cause of admission to County was sickle cell anemia. Interestingly, it was CCH that provided the opportunity for the first description in the Western medical literature of this disease in a dental student from the island of Granada. He was seen by Dr. James Herrick, a cardiologist, who asked his medical resident, Dr. Ernest Irons, to see the patient. The resident examined a blood smear from the patient under the microscope and described the red blood cells as having the shape of sickles. When Dr. Herrick saw his resident's notes, he became interested in the case and postulated that the red cells assumed that sickle shape because they probably contained an abnormal hemoglobin. He published an excellent paper in 1910 about that case in the Archives of Internal Medicine.

Dr. Herrick was proven right much later, in 1949, by Linus Pauling, the Nobel Laureate, and Harvey Itano in their famous paper "Sickle Cell Anemia, a Molecular Disease," also coauthored by S. J. Singer and Ibert Wells, in which they described the abnormal sickle hemoglobin. In sickle cell anemia, more than 90 percent of the hemoglobin will be of this abnormal form, while subjects with only the sickle cell trait would have a combination of the normal and abnormal hemoglobins in their red blood cells, with the latter being the lesser fraction.

The gene responsible for the sickle hemoglobin evolved in Africa. It protected the red blood cells from being destroyed (hemolyzed) by malarial parasites. This turned out to be a mixed blessing because the sickle hemoglobin would precipitate during various physiological stresses, forming unwieldy "tactoids" that stretch the red cell membrane and disrupt it (hemolytic crisis), thus causing chronic anemia necessitating frequent blood transfusions. Even when the red cells were not destroyed, they would clump together, occluding the microcirculation to various organs like the spleen, brain, lungs, and bones, causing excruciating pain (pain crisis) and infarction, the death of tissues deprived of adequate blood supply. Several African languages have names denoting severe pain during such crises.

About three in a thousand African Americans in the US have sickle cell anemia, and seven in a hundred carry the trait. Many patients were admitted to CCH either in hemolytic or pain crisis or both. The pain is severe and almost always needs to be relieved with narcotic analgesics, to which many patients (sadly) become addicted. The patients also have to be given blood transfusions and intravenous fluids.

Patients with sickle anemia or the trait often have red blood cells in the urine and, unless they are tested for sickle hemoglobin, undergo several unnecessary, discomfiting, and expensive tests to determine the cause of the blood in the urine. I remember seeing a patient because he had grossly bloody urine for which he was brought to CCH from the Cermak jail. There had been no physical abuse, and he'd had many tests that were negative. He had a mild anemia that was attributed to the recurrent bleeding in the urine. I ordered a specific test that showed he had a sickle trait; about 30 percent of his hemoglobin was of the sickle variety. The blood in the urine lingered for four months before it finally cleared. I had no doubt it would recur and hoped he would not be subjected to more invasive diagnostic tests.

Another disease I encountered was tuberculosis. The Metropolitan Tuberculosis Sanatorium (MTS) of Chicago, the largest in the country, was established in 1911 and had 950 beds. By the early 1970s, the prevalence of tuberculosis (TB) declined with improved public health conditions and better treatment of the disease. MTS was therefore being underutilized and was closed soon thereafter.

Patients with TB started to stream into CCH. Some were unaware they had the disease; some had received treatment at MTS but had not finished the required course; and others had not adhered to the prescribed treatment. These patients posed a high risk to themselves, their kin, other patients at CCH, and to the house staff and required the physicians to maintain a high index of suspicion that some patients might be harboring TB. When Dr. Whitney Edington came to CCH as chairman of the Division of Pulmonary Disease, he saw to the placement throughout the hospital of posters announcing: Think TB, as a constant reminder to the house staff.

A common thread ran through the stories of most patients I saw in those years: that there was very little if any medical care before the illness that brought them to the hospital. Many, perhaps the majority, had either no health insurance or only public aid coverage and would not be serviced at most other clinical facilities. At best they would be attended to grudgingly then directed to go to CCH.

Very early after my arrival at County, I saw on 35-South a young man who had severe diabetic ketoacidosis and dehydration. He was breathing fast and deeply and was almost comatose. This happens when diabetes, especially the type 1 variety that occurs in the young, is not well treated, so various organic acids accumulate in the blood, thereby threatening the normal metabolic processes of the body. I passed in his arm vein a central line, my first one, and started the treatment.

When he woke up and started recovering, I found him to be a very intelligent and engaging youth, but he said almost nothing about his personal life. He told me, however, that he never knew he had diabetes. About two weeks after he was discharged from the hospital, I received in the mail a very nice blues record of his. I had not been interested in the blues before, but I knew he was a well-known singer of the genre. Listening to that record was a new experience for me. The tunes seemed to distill centuries of agony.

I also saw the homeless and the skid row patients, a sad picture of human wreckage. I saw a patient once in the emergency room who had infected leg ulcers. Maggots were crawling not only over the ulcers but also on his entire body. I saw another patient who had pellagra, a disease of vitamin B2 deficiency known as the 4Ds: dermatitis, diarrhea, dementia, and death. I had read about pellagra in medical school but had never seen it before. The tormenting question knocked loudly at my ears again: How does this happen in the richest country in the world?

Cook County Hospital's Main Building in the 1970's, Chicago. Courtesy of Caryn Stancik.

DR. QUENTIN YOUNG.
COURTESY OF CARYN STANCIK.

THE AUTHOR WHILE AN
INTERN AT COOK COUNTY
HOSPITAL, 1972.

# 19

# Cook County Hospital: Part III

I had company as soon as I first arrived at County. My cousin Ali and my medical school friend Mazin arrived there at the same time. Ali and I enrolled in straight internal medicine residency, which was three years, and Mazin went into the five-year general-surgery program. Moreover, Dr. Lilly Hussein, who recruited the three of us to CCH, was an attending physician in the Division of Hematology, and we saw her during the lunch hour nearly every working day. She and her warm and kindly husband, my cousin Dr. Ja'far Hussein, hosted us often at their home. Ja'far had also trained at CCH but was at the time a cardiologist at Augustana Hospital on Chicago's Near-North Side.

During the first year, we lived at Karl Meyer Hall and had lunch there, so we made friends quickly. In the early 1970s, there were four other Iraqi physicians at CCH. We lunched together often and became good friends. Our circle was very well thought of and was affectionately called the Iraqi Mafia.

Dr. Quentin Young arrived at County as chairman of medicine early during my internship. He had a personality that people took to immediately. He spoke in a low voice without much modulation. His language was enlightened and punctuated by a powerful vocabulary. His education was encyclopedic and his politics humane, socialist, and pacifist. I learned quickly from others that he'd flown to Hanoi in the middle of the Vietnam War. This had obviously not endeared him to the more conservative elements in the medical profession or the mainstream media.

He loved being at CCH, worked hard to improve patient care and services at the hospital, and attracted to the place many like-minded interns and residents who admired him and were among the best-performing house staff. His office was for a while on the main floor of Karl Meyer Hall. He often kept the door open, and I remember seeing him frequently working into the evening hours, writing or poring over piles of paper. Most of the house staff, myself included, were quite happy that he was the chief of medicine.

For a period during my internship, the second-year resident was Dr. Ronald Shansky. Ron was of average height, broad built and had a handsome face, with black eyes, long black hair, and a beard and mustache. He bore a resemblance to a jovial Karl Marx. He had a powerful voice and clear enunciation enhanced by passion and energy. We took to each other instantly and became good friends. He gifted me *The Scalpel, the Sword*, the story of Dr. Norman Bethune by Allen and Gordon, with the dedication "To Asad, in the spirit of internationalism." I found the book engrossing and compelling. Ron might have been reminded of Dr. Bethune upon seeing me, a young Iraqi physician working hard to care for the Chicago poor thousands of miles away from Baghdad, but I clearly could not do then or now what Dr. Bethune had done in caring for less fortunate humans.

My cointern at the time was Bindu Desai, an intelligent, broadly educated, and vocal woman who cared greatly about the

patients. She, Ron, and I made a dynamic trio. Another interesting and hardworking physician joined us soon thereafter as
third-year resident, Lambert (Bert) King, a quiet, soft-spoken,
perceptive, and caring man. I remember once after I'd finished
attending to a patient on another ward, I went back to our home
ward to find Bert and Ron bending over a skid row patient's feet,
swabbing and cleaning awful ulcers between his toes. They were
at it for at least two hours. As I watched them work on the patient,
they seemed to be atoning for the sins of a society that allowed
some of its members to descend into such miserable existence.

We worked hard in those days and had little auxiliary support.
One late evening I went down to the intensive care unit on the
main floor of Building A to check on a patient of ours who had
been admitted there. There was a makeshift X-ray room in the
middle of which sat a large rectangular table where the ICU patients lay down to get X-rays with a portable machine. Instead of
a patient, however, I saw Ron himself, lying on his back with his
arms and legs spread apart, his long hair fanning under the weight
of his head, sound asleep from sheer exhaustion. I was concerned
he might fall off the high table, so I woke him up, saying, "You
look like Samson in the temple. Your hair has grown long again,
and I was worried you might repeat the act of wanting to die with
the Philistines." He got up laughing, rubbing his sleepy eyes.

Bert and Ron introduced me to my first taste of Chinese
and Mexican cuisine. The Mexican restaurant was El-Hardin
on Clark Street in Chicago. The Chinese restaurant was also in
Chicago, but I don't think it exists anymore. I picked them up in
my yellow VW Super Beetle to drive to the restaurant. They were
both mortified to see me make several U-turns, as I'd been used
to doing in Baghdad, and pleaded with me to desist. They called
the maneuver the "Asad special." During the few months it took

me to shed the habit, however, I never got a single ticket. I saw Bert only once after finishing my residency at County, when he came visiting from New York.

I met Dr. Lee Meyers when I did a rotation in neurology on Ward 24 in the main building. He was a large, kindly man with a ruddy face, a generous beard and mustache, somewhat curly hair, a bald patch on the back of his head, piercing blue eyes, and a hearty laugh. He had the appearance and demeanor of a German professor but could easily pass for a nineteenth-century European psychiatrist or musician. Above all, he was an outstanding clinical neurologist with impeccable bedside manners and a caring attitude.

Once I presented to Dr. Meyers the case of a woman in her thirties and concluded by saying I thought she had MS (multiple sclerosis). He smiled but didn't say anything. He talked to the patient, examined her, told her he'd talk to her later, and motioned to us to leave the room. He took me to a side room and said, "That was a nice presentation, and you were right about MS, but you should not mention a diagnosis in the patient's presence before we've done more testing and prepared her to receive our opinion. I apologized, saying, "But, Dr. Meyers, I only said MS. I don't think she knows what that means." Not a very smart remark. He retorted with a smile, "Everyone around here knows what MS is." I never forgot that incident and forever afterward insisted that my junior staff should not discuss a patient with me until after we've left the room.

Dr. Meyers invited another brilliant neurologist, Dr. Martin Bruetman from Mount Sinai Hospital, for a once-weekly clinical session, when we presented some of our difficult or interesting cases. It was a pleasure to watch Dr. Bruetman dissect and discuss the cases. He was clinically astute, had an interesting quizzical face like Inspector Clouseau's on public television, and used facial expressions more than words to express his opinion of our analysis. He would suddenly digress to talk about Cezanne or Renoir before returning to the clinical discussion. These sessions were quite engaging, humorous, and unforgettable.

Many years later, my mother-in-law lost sensation over her right heel. I examined her but could not determine the cause of the problem. I decided to take her to Dr. Meyers. After examining her, he told me the condition was a viral neuritis (inflammation of a nerve) and that it would blow over in six months. And indeed it did.

# 20

# The Hines Interlude

My first year of internship at CCH was not easy. I worked and studied hard, learned much from my patients, read up on their particular cases in specialty textbooks and journal articles, and scurried around to discuss them with the radiologist or the pathologist. Meanwhile I had to adapt to a new society and culture and overcome my homesickness. The latter effort was rendered much easier by the hard hospital work, as there was hardly any time to brood. At the end of that first year in June 1973, I was presented with a plaque for Best Intern in Medicine. I was happy and honored to receive it from an institution that had seen many oustanding physicians.

I needed change, however, so I thought about looking at other programs for my second year of residency. I am by nature a creature of habit, so I wasn't interested in leaving Chicago. I loved the city, its lakeshore, the theaters, museums, and the public library. The people were among the nicest in the world, and I had made many friends. Two cousins and my friend Mazin were there, and although I was not yet married, I was somehow certain that Chicago was the best large US city to raise a family.

It was at this time that I got a phone call from Dr. Harold Levine, who had been chairman of pulmonary medicine at CCH but left in late 1972 or the first half of 1973 for Hines Veterans Administration Hospital, affiliated with the University of Loyola Hospital in Maywood. He said, "County is sinking in a political quagmire. You should come over to Hines. Dr. Gunner is here with his team, and there are many other good physicians. You would like the experience very much." I was at the time interested in cardiology, and Dr. Ralph Gunner was a famed clinical cardiologist, so I decided to go to Hines for my second year of residency. During my application for the position, my first contact was with Dr. John Demakis, also an outstanding clinical cardiologist and onetime CCH man. He was very kind to me and helped facilitate my application. Thus it was that I started my second year on Ward 10-East at Hines VA Hospital.

My experience on the ward was disappointing. Ward 10-East was supposed to be a cardiology ward, but there were in fact only three cardiac patients when I started. The remaining twenty or so were cases of chronic obstructive pulmonary disease (COPD) from smoking and lung and prostate cancer. I had no interns working with me, so I found myself playing the intern again. Sometimes I had two Loyola medical students who worked hard but were obviously not sufficiently experienced to lighten my load while I, on the other hand, had to spend extra time instructing them.

Every time a patient was admitted, a chart as thick as Tolstoy's *War and Peace* came up to the floor, exhibiting the glorious merits of the then much-talked-about Weed system that enumerated all the patient's problems large and small: root canal, congestive heart failure, pruritus (itching), constipation, COPD, bipolar disorder, and so on. It was as though the physician need not bother with a diagnosis of the present illness as long as he was aware of the history of root canal and itching. Very often the symptoms of a condition like heart failure, such as shortness of breath or fatigue, would be listed as separate problems, although congestive heart failure had already been listed. Acronyms abounded, challenging even the internists themselves to decipher them, and would've been impossible to fathom for a physician outside the field of internal medicine. It is astounding that these vexing issues, born out of a lack of diagnostic priorities and common sense, have actually found their way into the electronic medical records of today.

Many patients checked in at Hines shortly after Thanksgiving but did not check out until after New Year's, having received Christmas gifts from the hospital. If I wanted to discharge a patient, he would immediately produce for my benefit a letter from his congressman or senator extolling his outstanding military service. The patients with COPD or even lung cancer continued to smoke as they went up and down the elevator to the cafeteria. Moreover, I had no exposure to the illnesses peculiar to women or young people because Hines did not treat the veterans' families, a thing I did not suspect before I joined.

Dr. Mushtaq Khan made rounds in the ICU, a friendly and knowledgeable young man who contributed much to my experience. Dr. Gunnar made rounds there once a week, when we presented to him interesting or difficult cases. The sessions were quite absorbing because Dr. Gunner was a brilliant clinician, and it was a pleasure to listen to him expound on the details of cardiac disease and the relevance of clinical signs.

He had his favorite maxims like "Cardiac pain that shoots to the left arm stops at the elbow" or "If you suspect a pain to be of cardiac origin but do not hear a fourth heart sound, think again" or "If you think a patient has severe mitral valve incompetence, you better hear a third heart sound," all sayings of his that I quoted over the following years to my trainees and colleagues. On 10-East, however, the only interesting rounds were those of Dr. Jean Moffat, when she discussed the occasional interesting cardiac case. She too was a highly accomplished British cardiologist. I also liked her elegant British accent, which reminded me of my time in England.

My knowledge of coronary artery disease was enhanced by a project Dr. Gunner and his colleagues were undertaking to study the disease with angiography. This involved the delivery of intravenous contrast, popularly called *dye*, into the arteries that supply the heart. Many patients were referred from MacNeal Hospital, which I jokingly called "the chest pain center of the Midwest." The angiographic pictures and the patients' case histories were presented at special sessions attended by the attending cardiologists, headed by Dr. Gunner, the fellows, and the residents. I was nearly mortified during a session when a physician said the patient he was presenting was referred "from the chest pain center of the Midwest, as Dr. Bakir calls it." To my relief, Dr. Gunner turned around and simply gave me a wink.

I nevertheless lost interest in cardiology because I saw the fellows in training spending much more time doing tests and procedures than seeing patients and performing the meticulous physical examinations Dr. Moffat habitually undertook. They did not exert their intellect to make a clinical diagnosis but waited for the various tests to provide the answer. They were therefore more technicians than clinicians. Furthermore, there were not in those days the sophisticated echocardiograms, nuclear scans, or MRIs that have nowadays rendered physical examination perhaps less crucial to making a diagnosis.

My rotation in hematology (blood diseases) was quite interesting and useful. Among the attending physicians in that section was Dr. Manatosh Banerji, an excellent teacher, who also had a wide knowledge of topics not medical: history, politics, and philosophy—a feature uncommon among US physicians. He had prepared for the house staff an excellent "Hematology Survival Kit," a folder containing the key laboratory findings in the common blood maladies.

I still have that folder as a memento, stored in one of my many office cabinets, the papers quite yellow now. I ran into Dr. Banerji about fifteen years later and was quite surprised when he greeted me by my first name, a testimony to his sharp memory. I told him I still had his "survival kit" in storage. He laughed and was happy to hear that. My wife and I became good friends with him and his wife, Dr. Basanti Banerji, a family physician, a charming and widely educated lady.

Boredom and disenchantment, however, kept harassing me while at Hines. I saw I was still doing an intern's work after four years of postgraduate experience plus a busy year at County, where I treated hundreds of varied medical illnesses. Patient turnover was slow. I was not getting at Hines the experience of supervising younger colleagues that a physician must acquire in his formative years.

More importantly, I was not seeing the illnesses of younger people, like type 1 diabetes, or diseases of women, like lupus or the medical conditions peculiar to pregnancy, such as preeclampsia (toxemia). I had been interested in all of them. Moreover, the absence of trauma and burn units would not support a wide-ranging experience in the medical and pathophysiological complications of these potentially fatal conditions.

Therefore, I wrote a letter to Dr. Armand Litmann, the chairman of medicine at the time, detailing the reasons for my request to resign from the program at Hines. Dr. Demakis called me shortly thereafter; he agreed with some of the issues I raised and said, "You are lucky your letter stopped at my desk first. Had it made it to Dr. Litmann, he would've seen to it that you'd never get your boards of internal medicine. Just keep quiet for two weeks or so. Dr. Pine is coming back here from Vietnam, and we'll give him your place." I thanked Dr. Demakis and left his office. As I got into the elevator, I encountered Dr. Harold Levine. He looked at me guiltily and said, "I saw your letter, and I agree with what you said. I am sorry about that, but I assure you they are working on restructuring the residency program."

Two weeks later, I went back to CCH to be received like a long-lost cousin with a strong hug by Dr. Young, who exclaimed, "Stranger, welcome back."

# 21

# Cook County Hospital: Part IV

Upon returning to County, I spent a total of one year in internal medicine subspecialty rotations. An interesting period was the three months I spent in endocrinology (diseases of hormone-making glands). We went on rounds with Dr. C. Canon, who was himself an encyclopedia of endocrinology (he later wrote a textbook on the subject) and was adept at expounding at length on all the cases we saw. He was also a friendly, polite, and charming gentleman and was liked by all the house staff, who waited enthusiastically for his rounds, later known as *Canon rounds*. I formed a lasting friendship with him, and many years later he became a neighbor as well.

I saw many intriguing cases. One that I remember in particular was a young boy with what was called at the time Hurler-Hunter syndrome, or mucopolysaccharidosis, a genetic condition where complex substances accumulate in various organs of the body because of a genetic lack of enzymes that break them down. The buildup of such substances would cause growth and mental retardation, a unique facial appearance (gargoylism), dwarfism, enlargement of abdominal organs, and early death. Gene therapy has nowadays been used to treat Hurler syndrome successfully in animals, thereby holding a promise for humans as well.

The other memorable figure in the division of endocrinology was Dr. Bhatia, whose specialty was diabetes. He had studied and worked in England before coming to America, had probably seen thousands of diabetics of all stripes, and knew all there was to know about the disease and its management. His diabetes team at County consisted of two nurse practitioners, Pat Girzik and Judy Conway, and the assigned house staff. We rounded with him on all the difficult and brittle diabetic patients spread over all the hospital buildings, and the nurse practitioners kept a log of the patients we saw.

Dr. Bhatia was an engaging man and was fond of certain phrases he uttered almost habitually, his favorite being "it's neither fish nor fowl," which we found quite amusing and mimicked the way he said it when the rounds were over. I became quite knowledgeable and experienced in diabetes and how to individualize treatment. I owe that to Dr. Bhatia. I have retained all that I learned from him, and what he taught us then remains valid to this day. He and I became friends, and when I finished my training in kidney diseases, he asked me to join his busy internal medicine practice in Aurora, but I was much more inclined to pursue an academic career.

I also liked the infectious disease rotation. Dr. Harvey Kantor, the division chairman at the time, was a knowledgeable physician and a gentleman. We saw a large number of cases, many of them quite interesting. Dr. Kantor also invited Dr. Stuart Levine from Presbyterian St. Luke's Hospital across the street to make rounds with us once a week and discuss some of the more difficult cases. It was a pleasure to listen to Dr. Levine expound on such cases. At times I wondered if there was anything about infectious diseases he did not know; and teaching was his very element.

It was during that rotation that I got to know Dr. Roger Benson, a very tall, handsome, amicable, gold-hearted, hardworking, and caring physician—one of the best doctors I'd ever known. He was doing infectious diseases at the time, running from one ward to another, carrying in his lab coat pockets all sorts of paraphernalia: test tubes, plastic cups, and glass slides—and talking with passion and energy about the work he'd been doing. We became friends. It was almost impossible not be friends with Roger.

One day I gave him a ride in my VW. He sighed with relief and said, "It is amazing that there is in this little car enough space above my head, which usually butts against the roof of most large American cars." I replied, "That's German space engineering, Roger. Germans can be pretty tall as well, and I'm sure they had you in mind while designing this car." We both laughed.

Many years later, when he was medical director at the Cermak jail hospital in Chicago, he invited me to give a talk on certain aspects of kidney disease. Other doctors there (likely including some residents) had trained at CCH. I was impressed by the excellent work Roger had done at the hospital. He had the same energetic dedication he'd displayed at CCH many years earlier. I opened my talk by reminding the physicians that they, as well as the patients, were lucky to have Roger run the show at Cermak, and I recounted his tireless career at CCH. He sent me a touching thank-you letter that reflected his kind and sensitive soul. When I more recently heard of his death, I took out his letter, read it again, and shed some tears.

Another unforgettable personality at County was Dr. Paul Szanto, the chief of pathology. His forte was pathology of the liver as he had trained under the famous liver pathologist Solomon

Papper, but his knowledge and experience in the entire discipline was almost unique. He had an extensive collection of pathology slides from thousands of cases, many of them unusual and extremely interesting, and his presentations at the once-weekly clinicopathological conferences (CPCs) were a delight.

A patient's case would be presented by a resident. Then it would be discussed by an attending physician who would make a clinical diagnosis based on the resident's text, the auxiliary tests, and the relevant literature. Finally, Dr. Szanto would project the pathology slides on the screen. His Central European accent, almost akin to German, was interesting and somewhat musical. He would use similes and metaphors in his description of the pathology, and end up either congratulating the discussing physician on his clinical acumen or apologizing for him if he had missed the diagnosis because "this case is very unusual."

# 22

# The Kidney

$S$hortly before finishing my residency at County, I applied for a two-year medical subspecialty training (fellowship). I had regained my old interest in kidney diseases, so I decided to do a nephrology fellowship. I did not want to leave Chicago. After the middle of 1974, I was called for interviews at different places, including the University of Chicago, so I scheduled my first interview there. I met with Dr. Adrian Katz, the chairman of nephrology at the time. Dr. Marshall Lindheimer was also present. I knew Dr. Lindheimer by name because I had read his publications pertaining to renal disease in pregnancy, his foremost interest.

We had the usual conversation typical of such interviews. Both men were happy with me, so they asked me to start my fellowship in January 1975 instead of the more traditional first of July. I said I wouldn't finish my internal medicine residency until the end of June and was concerned I would not qualify for the internal medicine boards if I cut short my residency; I was in fact aware of several such cases. Dr. Lindheimer assured me: "Don't worry about that. This is the Harvard"—he did not pronounce the two *r*'s—"of the Midwest. We'll make sure you get your boards." I was not convinced but kept quiet.

After the interview with Drs. Katz and Lindheimer, I met with Dr. Kenneth Fisher, who talked to me about his ongoing work with isolated kidney tubules but did not discuss any clinical topics. Then I saw Dr. Victoria Lim, who specialized in the hormonal disorders of chronic kidney failure. I had known Dr. Lim during my rotation in nephrology at CCH, when she made visiting rounds on the renal ward.

After Dr. Lim, I was shown around the hospital by Dr. Emanuel, a Greek, who was a bright clinical nephrologist. I asked him how many consultation requests the renal service received daily. "Not many," he answered, "because our residents are quite capable, so they really do not need our help often." I was not comfortable with that response. It confirmed my impression that the major emphasis of the fellowship program was on basic rather than clinical research, and although I was interested in the former, my priority was to attain excellence in clinical nephrology.

Then there were the two large medical district hospitals, neighbors of CCH: the University of Illinois and Rush Presbyterian St. Luke's Hospitals. I knew Dr. Neil Kurtzman, the chief of nephrology at the former because he came to the small conference room on the renal ward at CCH once a week, when the rotating residents or fellows presented to him interesting cases of acid-base or mineral disorders, his forte. In the interview with Dr. Kurtzman, he talked passionately about work on isolated kidney tubules, a topic I was not interested in. I did not get the opportunity to see the workings of the clinical service.

My main interest lay in diseases of the glomerulus, the filtering structure. Each kidney has one million of them. At Rush Presbyterian Hospital, Dr. Robert Kark and his team had done pioneering work in that field in the 1950s. They were the first group to systematically employ kidney biopsy for the study of glomerular diseases, particularly those caused by systemic lupus erythematosus (lupus nephritis), and their published studies on the subject were a milestone and remain cogent to this day. In 1974, when Dr. Kark was about to retire as head of nephrology, Dr. Edmund Lewis came from Boston via the University of Chicago to assume the position. Dr. Lewis was mainly interested in glomerular diseases and lupus nephritis.

When I was called for an interview at Presbyterian, I met with Dr. Lewis and other members of his section and was later asked to join the team for their sign-out rounds in late afternoon. The conference room was quaint, with wood paneling and a portrait of Richard Bright, the nineteenth-century British physician and renaissance man who was among the earliest to describe what we now call glomerulonephritis. In fact this condition was called Bright's Disease well into the twentieth century.

I was impressed by the plethora of interesting cases presented at the conference and the clinical excellence of the presentations and discussion. Presbyterian Hospital was at the time one of the ten best hospitals in the nation and drew patients not only from Chicago, but also from the suburbs and neighboring states, so there was a wealth of clinical and pathological material as well as a kidney transplantation service. The day I spent at Rush decided the matter, so I accepted their offer.

What I liked most about my kidney fellowship training was the examination and interpretation of kidney biopsies. Renal pathology was then at the cutting edge, and even good general pathologists had not quite caught up with the developments in the field of renal biopsy, where kidney tissue was being examined by three different techniques. In the early months of my training, I would review my patients' kidney biopsies with Dr. Alex Miller, a fine gentleman and an excellent general pathologist who was also quite adept at kidney pathology.

I immersed myself in study and read from cover to cover the two volumes of *Pathology of the Kidney*, then the bible of renal pathology, an outstanding work written entirely by Dr. Robert Heptinstall whose impressive experience and writing style were quite rare. I have kept to this day my 1976 edition of the book to remind myself of the great pleasure I derived from that memorable text.

I found that outstanding pathologists had a natural facility for pattern recognition. Dr. Lewis himself was facile at interpreting renal biopsies. In 1976, Dr. Melvin Schwartz, who also had a special interest in the kidney, joined the department of pathology. He would attend the weekly renal biopsy conferences to present the cases, but Dr. Lewis had established the useful practice of asking the fellows or visiting nephrologists to stand up and describe out loud the renal biopsy findings. For the fellows in training, that was the moment of truth that accelerated the heartbeat and might have raised the blood pressure, but it was the best way for the trainees to understand the subject.

Fortunately for me, I seem to have had the eye for pattern recognition, so I did well from the start. In fact, a few years later, when I was a young attending nephrologist at CCH, Dr. Heptinstall himself attended the Rush biopsy conference and Dr. Lewis asked me to read one of the biopsies. Dr. Heptinstall was actually quite impressed by "the level of competence of your renal pathologists," to which Dr. Lewis replied that I was a nephrologist, not a pathologist. I never got the opportunity to tell Dr. Heptinstall that I owed much of my knowledge of renal pathology to his bible in two volumes.

All in all, I learned much form my two years at Presbyterian and saw a wide variety of renal diseases. I also encountered many cases of lupus nephritis, in which I had a keen interest. Moreover, I learned the radiological features of various renal diseases from an accomplished renal radiologist, Dr. Suresh Patel, who also did the renal fluoroscopy (X-ray imaging) for the patients we biopsied.

He coauthored my very first kidney paper, about rare cases where the diagnosis hinged on angiography (X-ray of the kidneys after injecting dye to visualize the renal arteries). We became good friends, and for many years afterward, while at CCH, I would take kidney X-rays of difficult cases to show him for an unofficial second opinion, known in physicians' jargon as a *curbside consult*, which he gladly rendered, spending time describing cases in which he also saw an opportunity to teach his trainees. He later moved to Northwestern University Hospital.

Among the senior nephrologists who regularly attended the weekly renal biopsy conferences at Presbyterian were Drs. George Dunea and Earl Smith, chairmen of nephrology at CCH, and Mt. Sinai, Chicago. In 1977, Dr. Dunea approached me at the end of one of the conferences to ask if I was interested in an attending physician position in the nephrology division at CCH, beginning July 1.

I missed CCH, the exciting time I had there during my residency, the poor patients I treated, and the interesting friends I saw at work every day. I also saw that Dr. Dunea was an intelligent and experienced physician and nephrologist who also had a wide knowledge, not just of the history of nephrology but of the world, and that he possessed an encyclopedic education. I replied that I was indeed interested in the position he offered. He invited me to his condo on Lake Shore Drive to discuss the job. I went there and the deal was done.

Many years later, Dr. Dunea related to me over supper and wine that in 1977 he had informed Dr. Quentin Young that he had offered me a position in the renal division. Dr. Young was very happy to hear the news and asked, "He is not a king slayer, is he?" Hearing the story, I laughed and said to Dr. Dunea, "George, whatever sins I've committed in my life, slaying kings has never been one of them. I have learned much from my association with you, and I'll be damned if I slew a mentor."

# 23

# My Life in Chicago

Although I have been an avid reader since my childhood, the postmedical college years of work and training robbed me of the time for much extracurricular reading and caused me a nagging subliminal discontent. The situation improved markedly after I finished my postgraduate training, when for the first time in nine years I had reasonably enough time to pursue my old interests—reading, the theater, movies, travel, museums, and the outdoor diversions of natural scenery, like walking (I've been a formidable walker since my boyhood), biking, and hiking.

I owe to my life in Chicago a clearer understanding of the history of ancient Iraq, Islam, and the Arabs. Ancient Iraq fascinated me the most, not simply because I was an Iraqi, but also because it was the cradle of modern civilization and the source of the three Abrahamic religions. After all, Abraham issued out of Ur in southern Iraq.

The Sumerians of southern Mesopotamia invented irrigation and large-scale agriculture, domesticated wheat and barely, made beer, developed organized religion, and designed the wheel. More remarkably, around 3500 BC they invented the written word, the cuneiform script, and produced the first great literature in history, the Epic of Gilgamesh and other legends that found their way down to the biblical and Koranic stories of the flood and other events. They built the first cities, looked at the heavens, studied the stars, and knew mathematics. They sailed all the way to present-day Mumbai to trade their goods for lapis lazuli and other precious stones to use in their temples. These structures were stepped (such as the Ziggurat of Ur) because they were meant to be staircases to the gods, and they inspired the pyramids of Egypt, the earliest of which were also stepped.

My high school textbook on ancient Iraq was dry, uninteresting, and poorly illustrated. The teaching I received was not much better, lacking in depth and analysis, and biased by national pride. It did not appeal to the mind of the young, so I simply memorized the contents of the textbook and got high grades for that. My interest in ancient Mesopotamia was kindled by the only book in English that I read while still in Iraq, George Roux's *Ancient Iraq*.

Timely gifts arrived when I first visited the Mesopotamian section of the British Museum and afterward, when I discovered the Oriental Institute of the University of Chicago shortly after my arrival in the city in 1972. I managed to visit it frequently, usually on Sundays. I came to know Professor McGuire Gibson at the institute, a world-renowned scholar of ancient Iraq, who also headed the Friends of Nippur Society. Nippur in southern Iraq was the Mecca or Vatican of ancient Mesopotamia. Many priceless clay tablets were dug up at the site, revealing to Western scholarship much of the period's history of religion and culture.

I subscribed to the Friends of Nippur Society and learned much from its publications and presentations. There was also a series of lectures on Sundays, some given by invited experts on ancient Iraq. Last but not least, the Oriental Institute's bookshop introduced me to landmark works by prominent scholars, works that had not been available to me during my time in Iraq. I read Samuel Noah Kramer's *History Begins at Sumer*, Gordon Childe's *What Happened in History*, Thorkild Jacobsen's *Toward the Image of Tammuz*, and Alexander Heidel's *The Gilgamesh Epic and Old Testament Parallels* and *The Babylonian Genesis* among many others. The crowning literary achievement of the Oriental Institute, however, was of course its admirable work on the multivolume Assyrian dictionary.

The Legend of Gilgamesh parades some universal themes that have always intrigued the human mind: the civilizing of the savage, the yearning for friendship and sorrow over its loss, and above all the pursuit of immortality. Gilgamesh, two-thirds god and one-third man, is the king of the prosperous Sumerian city-state of Uruk (it is claimed that the name Iraq derives from Uruk). He is handsome, strong, arrogant, and egotistic. As King he has the right to bed any newlywed woman ahead of the groom. One day he hears of the robust savage Enkidu, who roams the nearby forest, running and hunting with the wild beasts.

Gilgamesh orders the temple prostitute Shamkatum to go to the forest to seduce Enkidu and bring him back to Uruk. She takes off to the forest and, spotting Enkidu quenching his thirst at a pool, undresses and lies down on her back in a most tempting pause. They make love for a full week, and Enkidu, having thus been "civilized," agrees to accompany her to Uruk. Arriving there, he hears about Gilgamesh, who was then on his way to "initiate" another newlywed damsel. This incurs the fury of Enkidu, who decides to block the path of Gilgamesh to the bride's house. There soon follows a clash of the titans. It is not clear who wins the wrestling match, but it seems to have been a stalemate. The important outcome of the encounter, however, is that Gilgamesh and Enkidu embrace each other and become close friends.

Gilgamesh then persuades Enkidu to accompany him on a journey to kill the god Humbaba, the guardian of the Cedar Forest, probably today's Lebanon—which is interesting because the Sumerians, lacking hardwood, imported the cedar from Lebanon. After a perilous trek, the two friends encounter Humbaba and slay him, raising the ire of Innana (later Ishtar of the Babylonians), goddess of fertility but also of the netherworld. Innana in turn appeals to her father, the supreme god Anu, to dispatch down to Earth the bull of heaven to avenge Humbaba by crushing Gilgamesh and Enkidu. As the bull of heaven encounters the two warriors, a ferocious battle ensues where the bull is at last slain. The earth trembles as the mighty bull collapses to the ground. Innana is absolutely enraged, so she afflicts Enkidu with an intractable illness that eventually causes his demise.

Gilgamesh is now beside himself with grief and is inconsolable. He places Enkidu's limp head in his lap and weeps. He cannot understand how this formidable giant has been transformed into a flaccid corpse drained of courage, energy, and life itself. "Will I meet the same fate?" Gilgamesh queries. "No, I shall find the secret of everlasting life."

He has heard of Utnapishtim (the later Noah of the Bible), who had attained immortality, and decides to travel to meet him. Gilgamesh undertakes a horrendous journey to the end of Earth to meet the wise old man. Somewhere on the road, he is told of a boxthorn-like plant that bestows eternal youth on whomever consumes it. He finds it, then places it on the ground beside a lake before he dives in to wash. But alas, a snake wiggles its way to the plant and swallows it. Gilgamesh is overwhelmed by despair, but fortifies himself again to continue his hazardous voyage.

He traverses the Road of the Sun—a long, frightful, pitch-dark tunnel nobody has hitherto entered—guarded by two scorpion men until he finally sees the sun again. He has to sail across the poisonous Waters of Death where even a single drop splashing on him would snuff out his life. Finally, having survived those awesome odds, he finds Utnapishtim.

"Tell me, sage, how did you achieve immortality? I beg you to divulge your secret to me," he implores the divine man. Utnapishtim waves his hand dismissively and tells him that humans will never be immortal, that he alone was granted immortality by the gods to reward him for saving the human race from a ghastly deluge of which the gods had forewarned him. They instructed him to fashion a huge boat, to seal it with pitch and bitumen, collect his people and one male and female of all animal species around him, and board them on the boat. The flood came roaring and covered the land, but Utnapishtim heroically navigated his ship and landed it at Mount Mishnu, where he unloaded his people and their animals. For that the gods bestowed on him everlasting life.

No other human, Utnapishtim tells Gilgamesh, will live forever. "As for you, Gilgamesh, you will achieve immortality, that is, eternal renown, if you go back to Uruk, repair its old walls, and render good deeds to your subjects." And so did Gilgamesh, who thereby achieved immortality. For readers interested in delving into this great epic, I recommend the wonderful English rendition, *Gilgamesh* by Steven Mitchell.

The Legend of Gilgamesh was acquired and enlarged by the later Babylonians, who called it Enuma Elish (When Above). It influenced Homer, the Genesis stories of the ejection of Adam from Paradise, and most strikingly, the account of Noah and the Flood.

The opposite of the Epic of Gilgamesh, demigod, king, administrator, warrior, and adventurer is the Legend of Tammuz (Dumuzi), the young, handsome god who is "the quickener of the child." He is the power in the palm bringing forth its date fruit, of the sap rising in trees, of the grain and its ferment, the beer, and the nutritious power of milk. He is a passive or intransitive power, simply loved for his goodness, youth, and handsome looks. He is not the active transitive power that was Gilgamesh.

Tammuz goes through a cycle of death and resurrection. When he dies at the end of summer, the people, especially the women, weep and wail for him and pull at their hair. Men and women come out to recite heartrending incantations and poems about the departed young and noble God Dumuzi. I agree with Thorkild Jacobson when he observes in his book *Toward the Image of Tammuz* the striking similarity of that ritual to the present day annual Ashura mourning by the Shia of southern Iraq for Imam Husayn's martyrdom in Kabala. I often think that, like DNA, cultures, customs, and rituals are fairly indestructible. It's as if they are encoded in genes that serve to ensure the cohesion; hence the survival of human groups.

Tammuz is still the name given to the month of July in the Iraqi calendar. In fact, all the solar calendar months retain the names given them by the Babylonians, who acquired many from their Sumerian forerunners. The Sumerian civilization diffused eastward to Persia and perhaps even India, northward to Anatolia (Turkey), and westward to Greater Syria, thus diffusing its heritage into the civilizations of those other regions.

Migrating in successive waves to Mesopotamia, the Semitic peoples of the Arabian Peninsula inherited and further developed the Sumerian legacy. These were the Akadians, the Babylonians, the Assyrians, and the Neo-Babylonians. The Akadians established the earliest empire in history under King Sargon of Akkad, and their language became the lingua franca of the civilized world.

The Babylonians invented the sexagesimal system, based on the number sixty. They divided the year into twelve months and the month into thirty days, knew the theory of Pythagoras twelve hundred years before his birth, taught it to pupils at school, and made impressive astronomical discoveries. Their greatest ruler, King Hammurabi, inscribed the first legal code on his famous stele, now preserved in the Louvre. The code is most probably the ancestor of the almost similar but much later Ten Commandments.

The Assyrians established a mighty empire that stretched over northern Iraq, a large part of Turkey, and the Levant. They also ruled Egypt for a while by mandate. Their landmark symbol was the winged bull, with the face of a solemn bearded ruler, the body of a bull, the wings of an eagle, and the feet of a lion. They spread Mesopotamian civilization to new peoples, including the ancient Greeks who inhabited the Mediterranean coast of today's Turkey. Their most memorable king, Ashurbanipal, had the largest personal library of clay tablets in the ancient Middle East, baked clay "textbooks" that informed the modern European archeologists of his and the ancestral civilization of Sumer, and guided them to Nippur.

The Neo-Babylonians built the famed Hanging Gardens of Babylon. Their city was the Paris of the ancient world. The Ishtar Gate of the city was adorned by the famous Lions of Babylon, now in the Pergamo Museum in Berlin. That was also the time of the Jewish captivity in Babylon, where Mesopotamian civilization had a major impact on Jewish life, learning, and religious studies. Many stories of the old Bible have their origins in the Sumerian legends inherited and embellished by the

Babylonians. Even today the Hebrew solar calendar, like its Iraqi counterpart, retains the Babylonian names of the months, and several Jewish personal names derive from Babylonian origins, for example Mordecai comes from Marduch, the supreme god of the Neo-Babylonians.

In summary, the ancient Mesopotamian civilizations that flourished in today's Iraq and diffused to Persia and Anatolia, as well as the civilization of ancient Egypt, gave rise to the ancient Greek civilization, which spread far and wide under the Helenic and the subsequent Roman empires.

I also did much reading of Western scholars' books on the history of the Arabs and Islam. This was a most interesting experience because, except for the works of Ali al-Wardi and Taha Husayn, it was my first encounter with Arab and Islamic history interpreted in the light of modern Western scholarship. Books like Joseph Schacht's *The Legacy of Islam*, W. Montgomery Watts's *The Majesty that was Islam*, Marshall Hodgson's *The Venture of Islam*, John Glubb's *The Great Arab Conquests*, Juan Cole and Nikki Keddie's *Shiism and Social Protest*, and Yitzhak Nakkash's *The Shi'is of Iraq* provided scholarly and fascinating reading.

Yet it is curious that not much of this excellent scholarly literature had found its way to the lay readership or mass media. I daresay that most Americans are not aware that Islamic civilization had contributed immensely to their Western heritage and the Renaissance following the dark centuries of Europe. Muslim scholars of the House of Wisdom in ninth-century Baghdad had retrieved, translated, and enlarged upon long-forgotten Greek works in geometry, medicine, science, and philosophy. The

Baghdad public library in the ninth century AD had several hundred thousand paper books at a time when paper was unknown in Europe.

Almost a thousand years before the European Enlightenment, Ikhwan al-Safa' (the Brethren of Serenity) and the Mu'tazila movement in Baghdad attempted to marry Muslim theology to Greek philosophy and the science of the time. There was a furious backlash against them by the Hanbalis, which resulted in a small civil war in Baghdad, where horses were reported to have waded up to their knees in Mu'tazilite blood. The Hanbali sect, by the way, is the stem wherefrom sprang the branch of the violently intolerant Wahabism, which incubated and hatched al-Qa'ida and ISIS.

Arabs in India stumbled upon the then-unappreciated number *zero*, immediately recognized its revolutionary import, named it *al-sifr* (cipher) and later spread it around the world. They invented algebra (al-jabr). Al-Khawarizmi came up with the logarithms without which computers would have been impossible. And the very numbers we use today are called Arabic numerals. They also made groundbreaking contributions in optics, astronomy, and navigation. Many of the heavenly constellations still retain a modified version of their original Arabic names, and the mariner's astrolabe is derived from the Arabic *Isterlab*.

In medicine, al-Razi (Razes) in the ninth century distinguished chickenpox from smallpox, and Ibn Sina (Avicenna) in the tenth century wrote his *Al-Qanoon fil-Tib* (*The Cannon*), the most comprehensive textbook of medicine at the time and for many centuries thereafter. It was taught at the University of Paris until the seventeenth century. The first surgical removal of the thyroid gland was performed under alcohol anesthesia in Baghdad in the ninth century.

In philosophy, Ibn Rushd (Averroes) was a towering figure in eleventh-century al-Andalus (Muslim Spain). He elaborated on the tensions between religion and philosophy and influenced many European philosophers, the Averroists, who began a re-thinking of philosophy versus Christianity. Ibn Kaldun in the twelfth century was the father of sociology, and his writings on economics anticipated Karl Marx by five hundred years.

When I first arrived in the US in May 1972, I knew much about the country's literature and movies, but not as much about its political history and social movements before the presidency of Eisenhower. This sounds curious now, but I was not interested in America's early history, perhaps because it stretched back only half a millennium, compared to Iraq's age of ten millennia. What first aroused my interest in the early history of America, however, was Gore Vidal's book *Burr*. I was fascinated by Vidal's mastery of style, his wit, benign sarcasm, and his talent of rendering historic characters as though they were still living.

I could not stop reading Vidal, so I moved on to his *Lincoln*, from which the president emerges as the great man that he was, notwithstanding Vidal's habitual cynicism. In fact, that was the first time I beheld Lincoln's immense stature and his legacy. I later read Vidal's other historic novels, *1876* and *Empire*, both quite engrossing. When I occasionally chanced to see the author on television, I was not surprised that his conversation and comments readily recalled his writing style. I then took a break from Vidal's writings to read Tocqueville's *Democracy in America*. I was quite impressed by the astuteness of the Frenchman.

I found Ron Chernow's *Alexander Hamilton* to be a masterly

book, written with care and passion. It is curious that there isn't usually much public mention of Hamilton, certainly not nearly as much as Jefferson or Madison. It struck me that there were innumerable streets, bridges, parks, and libraries named after Jefferson, Madison, Jackson, and others but not many after Hamilton. Of the Founding Fathers, Hamilton receives the least acknowledgment, yet he was in fact the founding father of "modern" America.

Hamilton's genius was versatile. He rendered immense service to the country, worked long hours, and was George Washington's French interpreter and trusted emissary during the Revolutionary War, much liked by the older man. He was a major contributor to the *Federalist Papers*. Unlike the Virginian Jefferson, who envisaged America as a pastoral paradise, Hamilton foresaw its future as an industrial and financial powerhouse. As secretary of the treasury, Hamilton championed the establishment of the First Bank of the United States in 1771.

Perhaps he does not get much mention because of the tragedies that beset him later in life. There was the Maria Reynolds sex scandal. When he explained the circumstances of the affair to James Monroe, Monroe promised not to divulge it, but then told it to his friend Thomas Jefferson, who had no love lost for Hamilton and leaked the story, to be picked up by the scandal-mongering journalist James Callender.

Then there was the death of Hamilton's son Phillip in a duel to defend his father's honor. This caused his sister Angelica to have an irreversible nervous breakdown. Last but not least was Hamilton's own death in the duel with Aaron Burr. It is said that Hamilton shot at Burr's leg, not intending to kill him. Burr, however, shot to kill. Shakespeare would have rendered Hamilton's labors, ascent, his later years, and his death into another one of his great tragedies, but Mr. Chernow deserves the credit for showing me the towering genius that was Hamilton.

Another book I enjoyed immensely was Doris Goodwin's *Team of Rivals: The Political Genius of Abraham Lincoln.* I listened to the entire text on CDs. I do about an hour a day of driving between work and home, so I decided to use the time to good purpose by listening to audiobooks, which I borrow from the wonderful Oak Park Public Library, with its friendly and helpful librarians. The text is almost always delivered by outstanding narrators or actors. I feel as though I am watching a good play.

*Team of Rivals* is a scholarly labor of love by Ms. Goodwin. President Lincoln emerges out of her splendid biography as the great man that he was. He was poor as a child. He educated himself, read Shakespeare's works, studied law, and when he ran for president in 1860, he was far less known than his rivals for the presidency, William Seward, Salmon Chase, and Edward Bates, none of whom thought much of him. Yet he brought them into his cabinet as the important secretaries of state, treasury, and defense. Working with him, they all came to respect and appreciate him, especially Seward, who became quite devoted to him.

Lincoln loved good theater, and whenever he had time to spare, he went to watch a play. And he lived and ate very simply. He held up during the dark days of the Civil War, the death of his beloved son William, and the near madness of his wife. His speeches were always powerful and inspiring, and he was an engaging storyteller. He also possessed a ready wit. After Grant's victory at Vicksburg, he received complaints about Grant's drunkenness, to which he replied that he liked to know what brew Grant drank, so that he, Lincoln, could provide it for his other generals. Yet his life was not crowned with the happiness and satisfaction he so aptly deserved, but with the sudden end by assassination in a theater, one of the loves of his life. Another Shakespearean tragedy.

⁂

And speaking of the theater—this was for me among the most interesting aspects of life in Chicago. It was not just the outstanding theater establishments of the Steppenwolf, the Goodman, Second City, Victory Gardens, Court, North Light, the Shakespeare and the Looking Glass, but also Zanies and the plethora of small and extraordinarily gifted acting groups rendering in small theaters with remarkable talent the works of great playwrights, hilarious improvisations, or stand-up comedy. At the Second City Theater I saw performances by James Belushi, Bill Murray, Dan Akroyd, and Julia Louis-Dreyfus before they became stars. Second City excelled in sociopolitical satire, and the improv pieces were quite hilarious. More so was the merciless lampooning of onetime Chicago mayor Jane Burn in "Burn Baby Burn" at Zanies.

In 1976, I saw at the Ivanhoe a memorable performance by that father of modern stand-up comedy and political satire, Mort Sahl. I still remember one of his jokes that evening. He enumerated the names of three early US presidents, then three from the 1960s and '70s, paused, then asked the audience, "What does that tell you?" He waited, his face displaying its naturally sarcastic expression, and, not hearing back from the audience, blurted, "It tells you Darwin was wrong!" to much laughter.

There was more. Mike Royko's unauthorized biography of the first Mayor Richard Daley, *Boss*, made the New York Times Best Seller list for twenty-six weeks and was rendered into a play which was just as popular. Royko was a Chicago fixture.

His humorous and perceptive columns were a regular feature in the *Chicago Sun-Times*. Once he recommended the issuing of a bond to build a fence around the state of California to prevent the lunatics from fanning out to the rest of the country, for which he received much hate mail from those worthy Californians. Many also reminded him of the notoriously corrupt Chicago politicians.

When the *Sun-Times* was sold to Rupert Murdoch, Royko resigned from the newspaper staff, saying, "No self-respecting fish would want to be wrapped in a Murdoch paper." He went on to point out that Murdoch was not interested in real journalism, only in political power—a prescient remark, vindicated many years after Royko's death in the 2011 hacking scandal in London, involving the staff of Murdoch's paper *News of the World*.

I have enjoyed theater in Chicago even more than I did in London. I recall marvelous performances of Death of a Salesman, The Idiot, The Brothers Karamazov, Uncle Vanya, The Seagull, The Merchant of Venice, King Lear, Cyrano de Bergerac, and Our Town. Arabian Nights, directed by the ingenious Mary Zimmerman and performed by the Looking Glass Theater ensemble, was a masterpiece. I was borne in Baghdad, the city of One Thousand and One Nights, but I have never seen a more perceptive rendering of these tales by a Western theater ensemble, not even by an Arabic theater group. It is a wonder how Ms. Zimmerman, an American living thousands of miles away from Baghdad and a millennium removed from Arabian Nights, could so profoundly capture the spirit and ethos of those tales, their time, and place.

A particularly interesting scene in *Arabian Nights* was about the beautiful, highly talented, and widely educated young woman whose reputation had reached the Caliph Harun al-Rasheed, so she was invited to his court. In attendance were the best and brightest in science, philosophy, and theology. They all tested her with difficult questions, which she answered promptly and correctly. The caliph, quite taken by this amazing jewel of a woman, told her he would ask her one question; if she answered it to his satisfaction, she would become his wife. "What is the purpose of life?" he asked. "Enthusiasm," she immediately replied. "By God, you will be my wife!" he retorted.

One winter evening my wife and I were strolling on Halstead Street (not a safe evening stroll in those days) when we stumbled on a makeshift theater where a group of young amateur actors were playing *The Lion in Winter*. The place looked like a warehouse, and it was frigid inside, but we hardly felt the biting cold because we were so engrossed by the enchanting performance of those young actors. Indeed, there have always been many such small talented acting groups around Chicago.

Then there were the movie theaters. There was the Carnegie on Dearborn Street, the Fine Arts on Michigan Avenue (both now gone), Facets Multimedia on Fullerton, Century on Clark Street, The Music Box on Southport Avenue, and (not least) the Film Center, initially at the Art Institute complex on Columbus Drive and later in the Fine Arts district on State Street.

And there is the Chicago Film Festival. I remember some of the marvelous movies these theaters showed: *State of Siege*; Francois Truffaut *400 Blows*; *The Tin Drum*; Lina Wertmüller's *Swept Away* and *Seven Beauties*; Federico Fellini *La Dolce Vita* and *The Conformist*; Luis Bunuel's *The Discrete Charms of the Bourgeoise*; *The Year of Living Dangerously*; *Missing*; Yves Robert's rendering of

Marcel Pagnol's *My Father's Glory* and *My Mother's Castle*; *Official Story*; *El Norte*; and *Salam Bombay*.

The Chicago Film Festival has showcased many memorable movies, among them *The Blood of Husayn*, a powerful and passionate story about the death of Husayn, the youngest son of a Pakistani family. He was killed for defending the poor and powerless against a despotic regime. The plot recalls the life and death of Imam Husayn, the grandson of the Prophet Mohammad, in the seventh century. The movie was banned by Pakistan's military dictator Zia'ul Haq and has never been released in Pakistan. The director finally moved to the United Kingdom where the film was shown on British television. Other outstanding and unforgettable movies shown at the film festival were the Iranian movies *The White Balloon*, *Separation*, and *Children of Heaven*.

Radio in Chicago has likewise been a pleasure. WFMT, 98.7 FM, is a wonderful classical music station that has few parallels elsewhere. It has presented most interesting programs like *From the Recording Horn* by Andy Karzas; the Metropolitan Opera live broadcasts, sponsored by Texaco; and the simulcasts with Chicago Public Television WTTW. It also featured *The Studs Terkel Program*, where over the years Mr. Terkel interviewed a wide array of both famous and ordinary people.

I still remember some of his interviews from the 1970s and '80s, for instance with the Israeli author Yoram Binur; with the famous flutist James Galway; and with James Haughton, who in 1972 took charge of Cook County Hospital for a few years as the executive director of the Health and Hospital Governing Commission. Mr. Haughton, who sounded uncomfortable during the interview, complained that he could not hear Studs's questions. Terkel apologized, saying that others have had a similar complaint. Studs's voice was low-pitched but captivating, perhaps because you could feel his intellect flowing through it.

Mr. Terkel was a Chicago landmark, a charming humanist, and the writer of such good books as *Division Street America*, *Hard Times*, *Working*, and *Talking to Myself*. In 1998, he and WFMT donated over seven thousand tapes of his interviews to the Chicago History Museum, and in 2010 the museum and the Library of Congress announced a joint project to digitize the tapes. Dr. Quentin Young was Studs's friend and personal physician until Studs's death in 2008.

WNIB, 97.1 FM, no longer on the air now, also broadcast classical music. It featured the delightful *Adventures in Good Music* by Karl Haas. *Those Were the Days*, by Chuck Schaden, was another of its regular rebroadcasts of early radio programs and comedies, many of which I had enjoyed in my teenage years and early twenties. It was quite nostalgic to hear again those long-gone talents. I was saddened when the station folded in 2001.

Chicago Public Radio, WBEZ, 91.5 FM, is also an outstanding station with few rivals anywhere. It is always interesting to listen to its programs *All Things Considered*, *The BBC Hour*, Jerome McDonnell's *World View*, Terry Gross's *Fresh Air*, Bob Edwards's *Weekend*, *Marketplace*, Garrison Keillor's *A Prairie Home Companion* (now hosted by Chris Thile), and the comedy programs Michael Feldman's *What Do You Know* (no longer airing), and Peter Sagal's *Wait Wait Don't Tell Me*.

Then there is fabulous music. The Chicago Symphony Orchestra is beyond doubt one of the very best in the world. When I arrived to Chicago in 1972, Sir Georg Solti was conductor. I may shock many people if I confess that he was not my favorite; rather it was Bernard Haitink, Ricardo Muti, and principal guest conductor Claudio Abbado.

I think our taste for conductors forms early, when we first begin to listen to classical music, and we remain faithful to them and later to those who remind us of them. My all-time favorites have been Otto Klemperer conducting Beethoven's symphonies and Mahler's *Resurrection*, while I favor Rafael Kubelik for the *Titan* and Smetana's *Vltava*; Arturo Toscanini for Tchaikovsky's *Pathetique* and his *Piano Concerto No. 1* (Vladimir Horowitz, pianist); Sir Neville Mariner for Mozart's last five symphonies and his great piano concertos (Alfred Brendel, pianist); George Szell for Brahms's second and third symphonies and Mendelssohn's *Scottish* and *Italian*; Eugene Ormandy for Saint Saens's second and fourth piano concertos and his cello concerto; Collin Davis for Sibelius's symphonies; and Solti for Bruckner.

I like popular music, too, but I listened to it much more often in my younger days in the 1960s through the 1980s than in later years. After my arrival in Chicago, I often listened to Harry Chapin, whose lyrics and singing from the heart I quite enjoyed. He was a true talent, a humanist and philanthropist. Of his songs the most poignant to me were "W.O.L.D.," "Mr. Tanner," "Mail Order Annie," "Old College Avenue," and "Changes," all included in his wonderful album *Short Stories*, which I listen to even now. He died nine years later at the young age of thirty-eight, on the road to give a free concert.

Other popular songs I cherished and still listen to every once in a while are Jim Croce's "Time in a Bottle"; John Denver's "Rocky Mountain High"; Glen Campbell's "Rhinestone Cowboy"; Frank Sinatra's "Strangers in the Night" and "Forget Domani"; Judy Collins's "Bring in the Clowns"; Foreigner Band's "Cold as Ice"; the Carpenters; Mary Hopkin's "Those Were the Days"; Dean Martin's "Sway with Me"; and Nat King Cole's "Mona Lisa" and "Those Lazy Hazy Crazy Days of Summer."

Other Chicago landmarks are its architectural jewels that attract people from near and far, the Frank Lloyd Wright houses in the city and in Oak Park; the Magnificent Mile of Michigan Avenue between the Chicago River and Oak Street; the marvelous Lyric Opera, one of the best in the world; the beautiful lake shore; Grant Park and now Millennium Park, with its amazing *Cloud Gate* sculpture (often called *The Bean*) and wonderful outdoor summer concerts; the Art Institute, with its impressive impressionist collection; the Field Museum; Shed Aquarium; Adler Planetarium; Museum of Science and Industry; Lincoln Park and its zoo; Ravinia Music Festival; Botanic Gardens and Morton Arboretum with their interesting trees and shrubs and the incredibly beautiful autumn colors; and Brookfield Zoo. I have lost count of how many times my family and I have visited these wonderful places. Whenever we had visiting friends from overseas or other states, we would invariably take them to as many of these marvelous sites as possible.

Soon after I arrived in Chicago, I discovered the Brookfield Zoo, got addicted to it, became a member, and contributed to a fund to adopt a baby elephant, one of my favorite mammals.

Much good came out of this when several years later I went for my naturalization interview downtown. The young lady who interviewed me asked me about my favorite places in and around the city. I immediately mentioned the Brookfield Zoo and my baby elephant, who was by then approaching a healthy adolescence. She beamed upon hearing that, told me she was herself a member of the Chicago Zoological Society, and proceeded to expedite my naturalization process.

I have always been attracted to zoos because I love watching those distant ancestors and cousins of ours, noting their behavior and interactions. Moreover, I am quite interested in comparative anatomy and physiology. In Baghdad, there were many street cats and dogs. The cats would climb over the brick fences of homes and sit there for hours, then jump down on the lawn. We watched them mark their territory and fight over it and over female mates, run away from dogs, and chase mice and torture them before they killed them. No wonder we never saw a single mouse inside our home despite having at least two doors wide open in the daytime.

We watched the dogs on the street and around restaurants and cafés, their group and leadership structure, their heroic defense of their turf, and their interaction with people and benefactors. We watched birds build their nests and crows flying and alighting as though with a purpose. It is certainly not like watching restricted animals in a zoo, and it provokes a sense that these animals are not simply dumb creatures driven only by instinct. And what is instinct after all?

Even as a child, I always suspected that animals are not simply creatures of instinct, but that they possess some thinking processes, languages, modes of social interaction, hierarchies, and strategies for procuring food, hunting, and building their homes. I could certainly see that they have emotions similar to ours.

We had a pair of mallard ducks for which we placed a water basin in our lawn. One morning we found the female dead. My youngest brother started crying as if he'd lost a sibling. The green-headed male refused to eat or do anything else and simply melted away. A cat of my uncle's family would not come out from under a table in an upper-story room for at least a week whenever they left town on vacation, although my paternal grandparents and their youngest daughter lived in the same house. I am glad that many scientists are now revising the old assumptions about the mind and behavior of animals, and not just the higher apes, elephants, whales, dolphins, and crows.

I spent much time at the Brookfield Zoo and later took our two children there almost once a week, often with relations or friends of theirs. It was a wonderful education for them. Even now my thirty-four-year-old son calls me on pleasant, sunny days to say "Let's go to Brookfield, Dad."

On long weekends or short vacations we had the charming town of Geneva, Illinois, only a forty-five-minute drive from our home; Lake Geneva in Wisconsin, 120 miles away; or wonderful Door County, also in Wisconsin, a 240-mile trip to its northern tip at Gills Rock. Door County is a truly lovely peninsular appendage of Wisconsin, situated between Lake Michigan and Green Bay, where there is wonderful scenery, good walking, biking, swimming, and fresh fish to eat.

It has the wide lake, the charming little towns along the peninsula, the famous fish boil, and the ferry crossing from Gills Rock to Washington Island, where no cars were allowed. On this island we saw artists painting or engraving on slabs of tree bark. One was a beautiful scene of a seagull flying between the deep blue water and the pale blue summer sky. I bought that painting and it hung in my study for over twenty years until my wife expropriated it to my son's apartment in downtown Chicago. He loves it too. One could walk in Washington Island's woods, then climb to the top of a high tower to see the meeting of Lake Michigan and Green Bay. What a sight!

THE MARINA TWIN TOWERS ASTRIDE THE CHICAGO RIVER. WHEN
INAUGURATED, THEY WERE THE HIGHEST CONCRETE BUILDINGS IN THE WORLD.

THE WRIGLEY BUILDING, LEFT, AND THE TRIBUNE TOWER BRACKETING
CHICAGO'S MAGNIFICENT MILE, JUST NORTH OF THE CHICAGO RIVER.

Clockwise from the left: The Bloomingdale
Building, the old Water Tower, the John Hancock
Building and the Water Tower Place, Chicago.

The Chicago River.

THE OAK PARK PUBLIC LIBRARY: CAROLE HARRISON'S SCULPTURE *UNITY AND GROWTH* IN THE VESTIBULE. COURTESY OF MR. JAMES MADIGAN, DEPUTY DIRECTOR OF THE LIBRARY.

OAK PARK PUBLIC LIBRARY: *ONE BOOK, ONE OAK PARK* DISPLAY IN THE LOBBY. MY FRIEND ALBERT EXPLAINING TO ME HIS THEORY OF GENERAL RELATIVITY (A BIT OF HUMOR). COURTESY OF MR. JAMES MADIGAN.

MY FAMILY: FROM LEFT TO RIGHT: MY WIFE NADIA,
DAUGHTER MAY, MYSELF AND SON ALI.

WITH MY WIFE NADIA.

MY MOTHER AMIRA IN MOURNING AFTER MY FATHER'S PASSING IN 2001

FROM LEFT TO RIGHT: MY YOUNGER SISTER, DR.
SHATHA BAKIR, MY MOTHER AND MYSELF.

My wife and I with Ala' al-Aswani (center),
author of *The Yacobian Building*

From left to right: Dr. Lilly Hussein,
Professor Farhan Bakir and myself.

WITH MY COUSIN, DR. JAFAR HUSSEIN, RIGHT

WITH DR. NABIL OMAR ALI, MY CHILDHOOD FRIEND SINCE 1956.

WITH MY FRIENDS. FROM LEFT TO RIGHT: NABIL OMAR ALI,
MYSELF, HARITH AL-JAMALI, DR. SHAWKI AL-ATTAR.

WITH MY FRIEND DR. HAZIM ZAKKO, RIGHT.

# 24

# Cook County Hospital: Part V

I was happy to go back to CCH in July 1977 as attending physician in medicine and nephrology. I worked hard and was happy attending to kidney patients, many of whom were very ill and had other morbidities beside renal disease. I also taught the renal fellows and the residents passing through the kidney service and learned from the extensive pathology on hand.

We handled many cases of accelerated or malignant hypertension targeting the kidneys, the heart, and the brain; renal disease from diabetes, lupus, sickle cell anemia, and intravenous drug use; and neglected end-stage kidney failure. Toward the end of the 1970s, heroin-associated nephropathy almost disappeared, to be replaced by HIV nephropathy from the early 1980s. There were also several other kidney diseases, uncommon in the US but seen among immigrants from countries all around the globe.

Patients with end-stage kidney failure needed much work and attention to their physical and psychological condition. Many had seemingly been healthy people, largely symptomless until quite late in the progression of the kidney ailment. A large number had simply not known of their disease, only that they had high blood pressure or diabetes. Eventually they did develop symptoms of advanced kidney failure, the result of long-brewing uremic toxicity, went to the emergency room at CCH, and were admitted to the hospital. They then learned their kidneys were done for, that they needed long-term dialysis treatment, and if they were lucky and physically sound, that they also needed a kidney transplant. This was the hammer blow that would shatter many people, and this was the situation the renal staff had to attend to and manage.

Suddenly patients see their life turned upside down. They experience denial followed by anger (Why me?) and then depression. There is role reversal for spouses; possible loss of employment; dietary, fluid and travel restrictions; and the sense that one has become a marginal person, always in danger of dying from high potassium in the blood or water buildup in the lungs.

Furthermore, patients with end-stage kidney failure have significant dysfunction of most other bodily organs. They are almost invariably anemic. Calcium leaches out of their bones and settles in the arteries. They are more likely to have some impairment of higher intellectual function, reversal of sleep pattern, restless legs, muscle cramps, severe itching, enlargement of the heart, bleeding from the gastro-intestinal tract, intermittent nausea and vomiting, sexual dysfunction, and impotence.

When they do get a kidney transplant, they must take drugs intended to subdue the immune system to prevent it from rejecting the transplanted kidney, so they become immunocompromised, susceptible to opportunistic infections and certain types of cancer. The workload of kidney specialists is therefore quite demanding and unusually taxing, and it requires teamwork, including physicians, nurses, dietitians, and social workers.

I studied in great detail the diseases I encountered in my

patients. No two patients having the same disease will display exactly similar symptoms, for the clinical expression of a disease is the result of the interaction between the offending agent on the one hand, and on the other, factors such as age, the immune system, racial and genetic variables, environment, and diet. I researched the literature and published my own clinical studies of the patients I saw at CCH.

Every Thursday morning for over twenty years I saw at the clinic lupus patients with kidney involvement as well as others with primary renal diseases. On Wednesday afternoons I joined the other kidney doctors at the general renal clinic, and on Tuesday afternoons the hypertension clinic where at one time we treated six thousand registered patients with the help of excellent nurse practitioners.

Four of those nurses, Matlyn Blanchard, Joan Matellotto, Prima David, and especially Diana Perschke rendered much help in several of my published studies, scheduling patients, keeping track of their vital signs and laboratory test results, and recoding them in flow sheets I had drawn up. Jewel Wallace (formerly Jewel Fowler), our renal secretary, was always a loyal worker who typed the manuscripts with their tables and figures and sent the finished material to the publishers.

Our nurse practitioner for the inpatient service was Joseph Block, who also attended the clinic sessions. I called him the "backbone" of the renal division. He was energetic, dedicated, educated, and always keen on learning new material. He assumed many tasks not required by his job description. He accompanied me and my house staff team on rounds, relentlessly taking down notes. He knew all the patients with end-stage renal disease, even their whereabouts after they were transferred out to free-standing outpatient dialysis centers.

Every time a kidney biopsy was scheduled, Jo would make the advance arrangements, grab a dissecting microscope to reassure the nephrologist that the retrieved tissue specimen was adequate, and take it back to Rush Hospital where Dr. Melvin Schwartz, the renal pathologist, oversaw the processing of the specimen. Jo was also our liaison with the other specialty divisions in the hospital, and there was hardly any attending physician or trainee who did not know or like him. Moreover, Jo was an avid reader with a well-rounded knowledge. Oftentimes when I went into the renal office, I would find in my mail slot a copy of the *New York Times* that Jo had left for me. It usually contained a report or article about the Middle East. I had not been a subscriber to the journal at the time, but decided to enlist after perusing the editions Jo had kindly left for me.

Jo was always doing something. I never saw him sitting down or idling. He loved his work so much that he neglected to attend to potentially serious health problems he'd had for a while, and he eventually paid with his life for his incessant activity and engagement. It was a very sad day for me when he passed.

My observations and study of kidney disease in African Americans extended over a quarter of a century and were put in print. Some patients who developed renal shutdown from accelerated hypertension and went on dialysis treatment recovered enough kidney function within three months to be taken off dialysis. I therefore recommended that such patients not be considered for kidney transplantation up to six months after they'd gone on dialysis. Patients with sickle cell anemia sometimes developed a peculiar kidney disease with severe protein leakage in the urine and had worse prognosis for kidney function and survival than other sicklers without that renal complication.

I also found that the most common cause of the primary

nephrotic syndrome (heavy protein spillage in the urine) in adult African Americans was a scarring kidney lesion called focal segmental glomerulosclerosis; also that lupus kidney disease in its severe inflammatory forms had a worse course and outcome in these patients than in Caucasians.

Because most kidney diseases are chronic, patients would come to the clinic for many years, so they become family. They would often come with their spouses or close friends. A female patient might have brought along her child or grandchild. Patients would tell me much about their domestic problems and family dynamics. I have come to know some patients for more than thirty years—and have sadly attended the wakes of those who passed.

I saw patients of various races, ethnicities, and religions. Most were African Americans who themselves were of diverse origins, their ancestors having come from different regions of Africa. Many had intermarried with Native Americans and some with Caucasians. There were also many Hispanics from Mexico and Central America, Filipinos, South and Southeast Asians, Arabs, Poles, and other East Europeans. What becomes obvious after a short while is how similar human beings are in their reaction to illness, their anxieties, fears, love of children, and the dread of losing loved ones. I have often told my trainees and my children, perhaps half in jest, that humans are almost like cats in their intra-species similarities.

During my nephrology career, several revolutionary developments have lightened the suffering for patients with kidney failure. Anemia used to be a vexing problem requiring frequent blood transfusions until recombinant DNA technology introduced erythropoietin, the hormone that stimulates the bone marrow to make red blood cells. The natural hormone is made in the kidneys, the reason why patients with withering kidneys become very anemic, hence weak and breathless upon exertion. Recombinant erythropoietin was nearly as groundbreaking for renal patients as insulin had been for diabetics, and it solved the intractable problem of anemia in kidney failure. Furthermore, the introduction of safer intravenous iron preparations has rendered the treatment of iron-deficiency anemia much easier in these patients and the results more predictable.

Bone disease has also been a considerable problem. The normal kidney converts vitamin D into an active form crucial for calcium absorption from the intestines and for bone integrity. In kidney failure, active vitamin D is sparse or missing. The parathyroid glands in the neck gear up, producing more of their hormone, which leaches calcium from the bones. The introduction of synthetic active vitamin D, another momentous event, has improved intestinal calcium absorption and suppressed the excessive production of parathyroid hormone, further diminished by the later introduction of the drug cinacalcet.

Phosphorus (phosphate), no longer excreted by the failing kidney, is retained in the body and it, too, leads to stimulation of the parathyroid glands to make more hormone. Worse still, high blood phosphorus levels trigger a gene that converts the smooth muscle cells in the walls of arteries into bone-forming cells (osteocytes), leading to arterial calcification, which has become a merciless killer of patients. Phosphate-binding compounds are therefore given to dialysis patients to trap dietary phosphorus in the gut, thereby decreasing its intestinal absorption. For many years before and well into my nephrology career, aluminum-based phosphate binders like aluminum hydroxide were prescribed. They were effective but produced long-term adverse effects, including resistant anemia, fractures, and dementia.

To make matters worse, I discovered in 1985 that

aluminum-induced dementia may be acute and fatal when these compounds were taken simultaneously with a citrate solution commonly given to predialysis patients with kidney failure to prevent the blood from becoming acidic. I published my findings where I reasoned that citrate had facilitated more intestinal absorption of aluminum. I recommended against its use with aluminum compounds, and switching to calcium-based phosphate binders. Other nephrologists subsequently examined the issue and published similar findings. This quickly led to the abandonment of aluminum compounds for the calcium-based ones and the disappearance of the acute fatal syndrome. Moreover, another group of nephrologists later elucidated the mechanism by which citrate enhanced the absorption of aluminum from the gut.

The calcium-based phosphate binders have lately come under scrutiny for fear they may worsen the arterial calcification already common in patients with kidney failure. Although this concern has not been vindicated by airtight studies, it did prompt the development of other binders like sevelamer (Renagel and Renvela), lanthanum (Fosrenol) and iron-based compounds (Velphoro). These agents have provided reasonable alternatives for patients who develop high blood calcium levels from calcium-based binders. It remains to be seen if they will prove safe in the long run.

There have also been significant improvements in the field of hemodialysis: more biocompatible and permeable dialyzer membranes, and computerized dialysis machines. Likewise, in the arena of kidney transplantation, more targeted immunosuppressive drugs have been developed, and kidney donors are no longer restricted to immediate blood relatives, namely parents, offspring, and siblings.

During my carrier at County, my research work, teaching activities, clinical rounds, and interdepartmental conferences brought me in contact with many other physicians and PhDs outside the kidney division. I always enjoyed working with those colleagues. They were experienced and dedicated, and I learned from them. Some became dear friends. Foremost among those was the late Dr. Vincent Lopez-Majano, with whom I worked when I was doing research in lupus kidney disease. He was the head of the nuclear medicine department, a highly educated Spaniard who had come to the US many years earlier and had been a surgeon before he branched out into nuclear medicine.

Dr. Lopez was a warm, passionate, straight-talking, and intelligent man whom I immediately took to. Besides his extensive experience in nuclear medicine, he was fully versed in the history of Arab Spain, one of my favorite subjects. He gifted me some rare books and artifacts pertaining to that golden age, when Cordoba was the most advanced, enlightened, and tolerant capital in Europe. He himself was a talented artist who executed evocative sculptures and sketches. I've cherished several that he quickly drew one afternoon for my two children, and four beautiful statuettes he gifted to me.

His talent must have been embedded in his DNA, for a great ancestor of his was the famous and prolific Spanish painter from Valencia, Vicente Lopez y Portana, who became court painter to King Ferdinand VII and drawing instructor to the king's second and third wives. He painted almost every notable Spaniard of the first half of the nineteenth century, including a striking portrait of Francisco Goya, and was still court painter to Queen Isabella II when he died in 1850 at age seventy-eight. I saw a painting by him at the Prado in Madrid, and there might have been others I missed. In fact, Dr. Vincent Lopez had an uncanny physical likeness to a self-portrait of his worthy ancestor. Dr. Lopez also had a particular interest in the sculpture of the ancient peoples of Latin America and possessed a large collection of such artifacts, many of which he donated to a museum.

He was a socialist and, like many others of his generation, had been traumatized by the history of the Spanish Civil War. He was also a humanitarian who traveled several times to Central America to repair children's harelip deformities for no fee. After he retired from CCH, he spent much time reading to the blind.

His wife, Jadwiga, a Polish American, is highly interesting, educated, and perceptive. She is widely read, kind, and sociable. She was an active member of the International Women's Association, and introduced me and my wife to many interesting and engaging people. She and Vincent were very close. They traveled much together, and when I or my wife called them, they would both get on the speaker line to chat with us. We also got to know their dear late son, Paul, their daughter, Denise, her husband, and their two boys.

I was overtaken with grief when Vincent went into a coma in his last days. Neither of us was religious, but I placed my hand on his forehead and recited to myself "al-Fatiha," the first sura of the Koran, then said in a voice muffled by my tears, "Goodbye, Vincent; farewell, dear friend." I hoped he would hear me; comatose people do sometimes hear and may even comprehend. He died very shortly thereafter. It's been many years since he passed, but I still speak of him as though he were still alive, just as I do when talking about my late father and father-in-law.

The late Paul Levy was another engaging man I came to know when I was working on the subject of aluminum toxicity. At the time, Dr. Dan Hryhorczuk was running the statistical analysis of my research data. He was quite adept at that, having been a bright member of the occupational medicine and toxicology department. Dan was a real gentleman: quiet, intelligent, and possessed of an excellent analytical ability. He looked like Liam Neeson, one of my favorite actors. It was a pleasure to work with him. When he saw that I was involved in several other research projects, especially a large study of lupus kidney disease in African Americans, he directed me to Paul Levy, at the time chairman of the environmental and health sciences program at the University of Illinois School of Public Health.

When I first entered Dr. Levy's office, he was sitting at his desk next to a computer on which he had mounted a plastic statue of a dinosaur. I was quite amused by the evolutionary metaphor, but also a little discomfited because I wasn't in those days quite at ease with computers or statistical methods. I said to Paul laughingly, "I hope I'll do better than your dinosaur up there." He echoed my laughter. I was struck by his simple manner, modesty, warmth, and friendliness. He knew his statistics inside out, and when I showed him my raw lupus data, he commented that it was the work of a lifetime and recommended the most appropriate statistical methods for the study.

Paul and I developed a long working relationship. He was coauthor on several of my papers, including another one on aluminum. He perfumed the statistical analysis, and I learned from him much about that subject. We became friends and would sometimes go for a lunch break at Rodytis in nearby Greek Town on Halstead Street. I talked to him about the history, politics, and society of Iraq and the Middle East, and he told me about many epidemiological projects he'd undertaken overseas, including Africa, with its ceaseless political violence and civil wars. He was a brave humanist and a dedicated marathoner.

After Paul retired, he moved to Chapel Hill, North Carolina.

I saw him once or twice when he came back to Chicago to visit. When his health began to deteriorate, his wonderful wife, Virginia Tomasek-Levy, provided him with much care and comfort and kept me and his other friends abreast of his doings via nice holiday cards, often containing a typed script.

I had planned to visit him in Chapel Hill, but before I could do so, I received from Virginia the news of his death. I attended his memorial at the School of Public Health on May 4, 2012, and talked to his colleagues and many of his onetime students about my debt to him, his excellence in his field, his humanity, and our friendship. I also told them that one of the sorrows of my life was that I did not make my intended visit to him before he died. But then, fate mocks us all.

Another friend from my CCH days was Dr. Bruce Benin. I first met him during my internship in internal medicine at CCH, when he, too, interned in the discipline for a year before starting residency in dermatology under Dr. Len Barsky. We liked each other and became friends. He developed into an accomplished dermatologist, in my view the best in Illinois, perhaps only next to his mentor Dr. Barsky. He was outstanding at explaining the mumbo jumbo of skin diseases, but he was also possessed of a wider education in history, politics, and society. I always enjoyed talking to him about those subjects and almost always consulted him on patients with the occasional skin condition, including myself and family members.

Dr. Lilly Hussein has been one of the longest-lasting attending physicians at CCH. She has poured her soul and limitless energy into the institution. She has treated, cured, and helped countless patients with cancer, her specialty, and advised a multitude of residents, especially foreign medical graduates, who steered their way to success and recognition. She is an astute physician who always guided her treatment of patients with good knowledge, long experience, inexhaustible compassion, and much of that rare commodity, common sense. Her life-long work has been appreciated and acknowledged by all and sundry, and she was honored by the National Arab American Medical Association for her dedicated service to its members.

A dear friend from CCH days was Dr. Hazim Zakko, a psychiatrist I initially met during my internship at the hospital. We became close friends. He did not stay long at CCH before he left for private consultative practice. Hazim was an intelligent, intuitive, and well-educated man, who had worked in London for several years before coming to the US. He was an avid reader and had much interest in all fields of knowledge. His dialogue is straightforward, passionate, and characteristic, his forecasts usually pessimistic. Trademark comments of his that I always find amusing are: "Don't argue with Allah. He could always make it worse for you." Or upon seeing extravagant displays: "I wonder why God has not yet toppled the world."

I would drive to his home in the city, and we would follow our usual itinerary of walking along Michigan Avenue to the Chicago River; turn back to go to Riza's Persian Restaurant on Ontario Street; order a bottle of wine and appetizer; talk politics, literature, religion (neither of us being religious), and the latest news of our Iraqi American friends; dine at about ten o'clock at night; and then walk back to his place, where I would pick up my car to drive back home. Lately he's been stressed by the plight of his Christian community in Iraq under the mercy of ISIS, and the flight and scattering of large numbers of Iraqi Christians across the globe. In earlier days, we played backgammon at his place while having drinks and appetizers. He was better at the game and beat me most of the time.

I first met Dr. Jose Arruda, chairman of the renal section at the University of Illinois at Chicago, when we merged our renal fellowship programs in 1986 so that the renal fellows-in-training would rotate through CCH, the University of Illinois, and Westside VA Hospitals. He and I connected immediately and spoke the same language, so much so that our long conversation was a truly enjoyable event. We were natural friends.

Jose is a highly intelligent physician, trained in the best tradition, and an outstanding teacher and clinician. His forte was renal physiology, but I was impressed by his deep knowledge of all other fields of nephrology. He was meticulous and punctual about his teaching and research obligations and made sure he gave these activities due time and energy. His humor and light comments always gave our joint teaching conferences a lively aspect, often lacking in many such meetings.

Another good friend was Dr. Todd Ing, whom I met early in my career at CCH. Dr. Ing must be one of the most popular nephrologists, not only locally but also around the world, beloved by all his peers and trainees, a real gentleman and a wonderful human being. He was chairman of nephrology at Hines Veterans Administration Hospital when he invited me there to discuss a case at a clinicopathological conference. The event fostered a long-lasting friendship between us. After his retirement he remained active, and oversaw and coordinated many online and paper publications. He invited me to write two editorials about my past aluminum research and to contribute to a book chapter about the history and future of dialysis, all of which I gladly and promptly rendered. After all, who could turn down a request by Todd Ing?

I also came to know Dr. Earl Smith, chairman of nephrology at Chicago's Mount Sinai Hospital, an outstanding nephrologist, who trained a large number of well-known and successful kidney specialists. I first met him when he attended the kidney biopsy conferences at Presbyterian St. Luke's during my fellowship years. He also participated in those at CCH during my time as attending physician. We got to know each other very well and became good friends. What I most liked about him was his common sense and reluctance to jump on the bandwagon whenever a new theory or treatment became fashionable. He was a meticulous clinician who paid much attention to detail and avoided unnecessary tests.

Of my colleagues in the renal division at County, I have had a lasting collaboration and friendship with Drs. George Dunea and Suresh Hathiwala. Dr. Dunea has a superb encyclopedic education in most fields of human endeavor. I was impressed that he could recite the names of all the Roman emperors in sequence, had read Gibbon's *Decline and Fall of the Roman Empire*, knew the ancient Persian kings, the famous Muslim caliphs of the Arab golden age, the Ottoman sultans, and the Mogul emperors. He told interesting stories about the history of nephrology and the pioneer of hemodialysis and artificial organs, Dr. Willem Kolff, under whom he trained at one time.

In fact, Dr. Dunea was better informed about many aspects of past Arab civilization and religious issues like the Sunni-Shia schism than many of my Arab friends. His writing style was crisp, distinctive, and humorous, and for many years he contributed to the *British Medical Journal* a popular column, "Letter from Chicago," which later became "Sounding Board." The columns I most liked were "Socrates on Clinical Excellence," "Oplavichi," and "The Simian Medical School."

He and I often played backgammon at his home in the city. Like me, he had learned it while a child, but I beat him most of the time. I'm afraid he was a sore loser. One time he beat me pretty badly, as I was quite distracted by the car accident I'd just had on my way to his place. He would later jokingly say, "Let's do some backgammon, but please have a car accident before you arrive at my home."

Dr. Hathiwala has also been a dear friend: a highly intelligent man (he often did mental math), a gentleman, warm and compassionate, beloved of patients, house staff, colleagues and friends, and possessed of a well-rounded education. What I most admired about him and his wife Papi was their dignified stoicism in the face of personal tragedy and loss, of which they had more than their fair share. They were compensated, however, with a talented young woman and physician, their daughter Tanvi.

Another enriching experience of mine at County was of course the interaction with numerous outstanding house staff who were at one time or another medical students, interns, residents, or fellows under my supervision and who were well informed and hardworking and took their patient care duties seriously. Such house staff have always reminded me of a dedication by the author of a medical textbook: "To our younger colleagues who continue to teach and illuminate us."

I have always enjoyed teaching: curriculum subjects to many of my schoolmates, English grammar to my younger sisters, Arabic to several non-Arab friends, history to whomever was interested, and medicine since my internship in Baghdad. I've cherished the interaction with "our younger colleagues," who often ask challenging questions, forcing us to think outside the box, and whose enthusiasm further propels ours. Foremost among the pleasures that have always captivated me is the intellectual interaction between the teacher and the interested disciple.

I must mention in this context Dr. Barry Mizok, whom I knew as a medical student during his externship at CCH, and who later became an excellent intensive care physician at the hospital. He and I often lunched together at the Illini Union building of the University of Illinois, when we talked about myriad issues, large and small. His wife, Dr. Janice Benson, was also an outstanding resident who became a crucial member of the family practice department at CCH. Dr. Paul Ringle was an excellent chief resident, who later went into internal medicine practice at Illinois Masonic Hospital. Dr. Renslow Sherer established with the late Dr. Ron Sable the AIDS clinic at County. He had a sound legal mind, perhaps because of his Scottish ancestry, which is why I often jokingly called him "the man from the Hebrides."

Dr. Robert Cohen, responding to my challenge, could roll his *r*'s like a true Arab. When I expressed my admiration for his facility, he said it developed while learning Spanish. I commented that the faculty had probably been dormant in his Semitic DNA, waiting to be stirred up. He now runs the Department of Occupational Lung Disease at Northwestern University Hospital in Chicago. Dr. Avery Hart was an excellent resident, who impressed me during his kidney rotation by his ready mastery of the medical issues peculiar to renal patients who suffer from multiorgan dysfunction. He later became chairman of general medicine.

Dr. Miriam Sanati was a charming and dynamic resident, one of the few not intimated by the renal consultants. I first met her when she asked us to see a patient and was impressed by her presentation of the case, personality, and self-confidence. I asked her if she knew our renal fellow Negin, an intelligent and handsome young man. I would get into such a match-making mood every now and then, a noble pursuit, I think. She answered, "Yes I do," so I quickly turned to Negin and said jokingly, "Negin, perhaps you should invite this charming young lady to dinner sometime," upon which she burst out laughing and said, "But, Dr. Bakir, I am already married!" to collective laughter.

Many years later, when my wife Nadia and I saw her and her nice husband, Nema, in a social gathering at Dr. Dunea's home, she reminded me of that episode, relating it with relish to my wife, who glanced at me disapprovingly and simply said, "I am not surprised at all." There was again much laughter. Miriam has been for many years now one of the excellent attending physicians at CCH.

Dr. David Ansel was another outstanding resident. In my evaluation of his performance at the time, I recommended that he be offered a position as attending physician at CCH once he finished his residency—and he was. He and some of his colleagues once published an interesting article in the *New England Journal of Medicine* about the "dumping" of patients on CCH by private hospitals.

One early afternoon, David and I were involved in a tragicomical incident with a seemingly drugged patient at the Fantus Clinic. After the dust settled, I suggested to David he should write a book about County, that very interesting and bizarre behemoth teeming with suffering humanity. He did so many years later, not forgetting to render a florid description of that very incident. When I read his book I called him to remark that contrary to his claim, I had never worn an Armani suit. He pleaded poetic license and reminded me that he'd said Armani-*style* suit. He had also worked at County with Dr. Arthur Hoffman, another accomplished onetime resident of mine, and later attending physician in internal medicine.

Many excellent fellows have worked with me over the years. Some contributed to several of my publications: Drs. David Share, Francisco Chio, Chokri Alioua, Nauman Tarif, and Alfredo

Pegoraro. Other fellows were good clinicians I enjoyed working with, among them Drs. Carolyn Brecklin and Jane Vernik.

The accomplished and hardworking house staff members at CCH, not only in internal medicine but also in surgery, obstetrics and gynecology, pediatrics, the world-famous burn and trauma units, and the eternally crowded emergency room were the cornerstone and pride of the hospital. The house staff saved thousands of lives, especially of uninsured indigents, new immigrants, and even foreign middle-class individuals, including physicians, suddenly taken ill while visiting Chicago. Those trainees came to CCH instead of private institutions eager to recruit them because they wanted to serve the less fortunate and underprivileged members of our society.

They loved the practice of medicine, poured their souls into it, and were full of energy and motivation. They possessed much ATP—adenosine triphosphate, the energy battery of our cells. I would often joke with my trainees by telling them, "I wish we had a blood test to measure the ATP level. If it is high, we would immediately accept the job applicant. No need for lengthy interviews." It is to these unsung warriors that the patients owed their loyalty to CCH despite the legions of administrative shortcomings that always beset the hospital, not only during my time, but also long before and afterward.

There were frequent eleventh-hour shortages of various materials, obviously because of tardy inventory survey. The pharmacy often ran out of crucial medications like the diuretic furosemide (Lasix) and others. This evolved into a nightmare when the administration decided to get a middleman outfit to procure the drugs instead of getting them directly from the pharmaceutical companies. Many specialty clinics had long patient waiting times of six or more months. The organization and retrieval of medical records was always a horrendous headache. We kept our own renal records at the clinic, but were told the practice was not allowed, actually frowned upon, by the Joint Committee on Accreditation of Hospitals (JCAH), but we kept them there regardless, and our patients were better off for it.

A chronic problem that was particularly vexing to me and all the renal staff was our inability to get timely vascular access for hemodialysis. We received many patients from the emergency room who had not had regular medical care and were admitted with severe symptoms of kidney failure. Immediate dialysis would then be undertaken by the renal fellow or the intensive care resident, who would place a temporary dialysis catheter directly into a large vein in the neck or groin.

It is preferable if a surgeon, or nowadays an interventional radiologist, tunnels the catheter under the skin below the right collarbone before entering into the vein because such catheters are less likely to clot or get infected than the ones inserted directly into the vein. But these tunneled catheters were seldom placed early because the surgical department had neither the time nor the staff to do that, and interventional radiologists did not come on stage until many years later.

If the patient was deemed to have end-stage kidney failure, he would need long-term dialysis treatment, and a fistula connecting an artery and a vein in the arm would be necessary. It would take the fistula six weeks to three months to be ready for use, and even then may have to be revised. During this maturation period, the patient should have a tunneled catheter. At County, both the tunneled catheters and the fistulae took too long to accomplish. It is important to place a fistula as soon as possible so that the catheter would not stay in the jugular vein inordinately long, thereby raising the risks of clotting of the vein or blood infection, which may damage a heart valve. Furthermore, patients with long-term catheters do not thrive as well as those with an arm access.

Of the several vascular surgery chiefs during my time at CCH, only two were helpful and accommodating. A torrent of memos, letters, and meetings with general surgery chiefs and administration officials produced hardly any results. I must say that it was not so much the vascular surgeons' fault. They were deluged by all manner of vascular emergencies—ruptured aortas, gangrenous legs, and traumatic arterial injuries—and did not consider dialysis vascular access a priority, its being a lifeline notwithstanding.

To put it in a nutshell, successive administrations would not hire more vascular surgeons to solve our problem. Neither did the vascular chiefs themselves forcefully demand the hiring of a dedicated surgeon to concentrate on dialysis access. When they did get an additional surgeon, he too would be quickly sucked into the whirlpool of the big game, unable to allot enough time for the small fish of dialysis access.

In fact, access surgery is not easy and needs much experience and patience, and the results are often disappointing. I used to call the procedure "the humbler of vascular surgeons." The best results are obtained by those who perform it all the time, whereas many outstanding surgeons who work on the aorta and the large arteries often have poor fistula outcomes if they don't do them regularly.

When CCH eventually affiliated with Rush, I reached an understanding with Dr. Stephen Jensik, the conscientious, hard-working kidney transplant surgeon I had known since my fellowship days, to help us with vascular access. After all, he had performed kidney transplantation for most of our eligible patients. He was very helpful, and his participation went far to shorten the waiting period for access placement, but there remained a problem with patients lacking insurance coverage.

The vascular access saga distressed me immensely, placed a heavy burden on my conscience, and even disturbed my sleep many a night. It was one of the main reasons influencing my decision to take the early retirement package the Cook County Board offered in late 2002.

I retired from County in March 2003, a few months after the new hospital building opened. Its famous historic name, known the world over, was sadly changed to John H. Stroger Jr. Hospital after the chairman of the Cook County Board. It had far fewer beds than the old hospital. I had at the time been professor of medicine at the University of Illinois at Chicago since 1997 and stayed on as volunteer senior attending physician at Stroger Hospital, no longer attending to patients, but participating in the renal teaching program, especially the monthly kidney biopsy conferences. I was satisfied that I had served the patients at CCH for nearly thirty-one years, including my residency time.

After leaving County, I have spent the bulk of my time in private practice as a renal consultant, as well as making rounds on my dialysis outpatients, and being medical director of a large dialysis center in Chicago. After a few months, I began to miss CCH, the intriguing cases, the teaching and research, and the interaction with house staff. Even now, fourteen years after leaving County, I frequently dream that I am conducting rounds in the old hospital (not the new one), making a diagnosis of a challenging case, and discussing it with colleagues and house staff.

My life outside Cook County Hospital, and in private practice, and all the fine friends I made there, can only be the subject of another book, if I could summon up the time and energy to write it.

With Dr. Vincent Lopez-Majano , right.

With Mrs. Jadwiga Lopez-Majano, right.

WITH DR. GEORGE DUNEA, LEFT, AT A KIDNEY CONFERENCE.

WITH DR. JOSE ARRUDA, LEFT.

From Lt to right: Dr. Peter Hart, Dr. George Dunea, myself, Dr. Jose Arruda, and Dr. Todd Ing.

Christmas party at the Dialysis Unit of Cook County Hospital, 2002. First row, from left to right: Nurse Practitioner Jo Block, myself, Nurse Timcan, social worker Molly Older, Nurse Practitioner Joycelin.

WITH DR. EARL SMITH, RIGHT.

# 25

# Professional Excursions Overseas

## I. SOUTH AFRICA, 1996

During my time at CCH, I made several professional trips overseas, some of them quite notable. In September 1996, I traveled to South Africa with a group of thirty-four other nephrologists from the USA, Germany, Canada, the United Kingdom, Sweden, Denmark, Belgium, Poland, the Czech Republic, Croatia, Australia, Brazil, and Jamaica. The largest number of physicians was from the US, followed by Germany. The expedition was an initiative of the Citizens Ambassador Program established by President Eisenhower after World War II to facilitate interaction between US citizens and professionals with those of other countries, especially ones undergoing major changes.

The delegation was led by Professor Jacques Bourgoignie,

nephrology chair at the University of Miami School of Medicine, assisted by his kind and charming wife, Chantal, chairwoman of Voices for Children in Miami. The itinerary of the trip—the places and hospitals to visit and the choice of the guest speakers—were based on the recommendations of South African nephrologists, especially Dr. A. M. Meyers, head of nephrology at Johannesburg Hospital.

Arriving at Johannesburg, we were welcomed, oriented, fed, and warned not to venture out on our own into the city after dark. The next morning we visited the Johannesburg Hospital of the University of Witwatersand. The South African organizers had requested that five of our delegates, myself included, give lectures to the hospital's medical staff. My talk was on the course of lupus nephritis in African Americans. The lectures were followed by lively discussions, and I saw that the South African doctors were very knowledgeable, experienced, and astute. They had decided to stay in South Africa during and after the turmoil that led to the collapse of apartheid in 1994, while many of their colleagues had left the country.

A member of our team had established a philanthropic project in Soweto. He and his wife were about to visit the place, so a few colleagues and I jumped into a van with them that drove us to the famous town. I was disheartened by the scenes of poverty, undernutrition, and deprivation. The large, dilapidated city looked like a huge refugee camp, bursting at the seams with a mass of suffering inhabitants. A large section of town had only one faucet for clean water. Women, men, and children carried metal vessels, waiting to fill up, and the situation, we were told, was the same in the other town sections. Outside Soweto and along the roads leading into Johannesburg there must have been thousands of squatters—jobless and homeless people having no money and little food, an ideal breeding environment for crime, gangs, and violence. It was crystal clear that the nascent black government would certainly have a long and bumpy road ahead toward reversing the devastating ills of apartheid.

We were then driven to Louis Trichardt, 450 kilometers (281 miles) northeast of Johannesburg in the Northern Province, and checked in at the Clouds End Hotel. African porters, several of them past middle age, came out to carry our heavy suitcases, balancing them on their heads. The man carrying my bag was at least sixty years old, but tall and muscular. His face bore the vanquished but dignified expression of a Native American Sioux chief and showed the signs of determined and quiet patience during a long history of adversity.

"Please put the bag down. It's not heavy; I can carry it myself," I pleaded.

"It's nothing, sir," he answered.

"At least carry it by hand," I retorted, perhaps insensitively.

"Don't worry, sir. Please go ahead of me to your room, and I will deliver your suitcase there," he answered with a thankful smile while pointing to the location of my room. I was embarrassed and trudged ahead to the room. On the way there were large numbers of the Blauw Aap monkeys (Blue Ape), handsome, with very light blue hair, humanlike faces and peering inquisitive eyes, sitting on tree branches and studying the members of our group or chasing each other on the rooftops.

I went out for a walk outside the hotel area, along a trodden sandy path bordered on both sides by dry bushes, still thinking about the vanquished Sioux chief, when I heard a roaring car motor behind me. A Jeep swirled round and stopped in front of me. The Afrikaner hotel proprietor called out, "Sir, I will drive you back to the hotel. Please get in."

"I am taking a walk, if you don't mind. Are you afraid I might run into a lion?" I asked irritably.

"Yes. This is Africa, sir, and we are not far from the Mozambique border," he replied.

I said to myself, "By God, he is right of course; it *is* Africa, not my suburb of Chicago or my usual hiking trails." Feeling quite foolish, I boarded the Jeep. I recalled then that our tour guide had told us never to look a lion in the face if we chanced upon one, but simply to turn slowly around and walk away— hardly a comforting advice.

"We have a walkway around the hotel if you need the exercise. I'll show you where it is. There are plenty of green snakes there, but they are not poisonous," the proprietor said apologetically.

We were invited to a barbecue dinner at the Ben Lavin Nature Preserve, just outside Louis Trichardt, where we met with Dr. A. M. Meyers and physicians, students, and staff from Elim Hospital, founded by the Swiss Mission in 1899, and the oldest hospital north of Pretoria. Dr. Meyers talked about the state of health care in South Africa, the challenges of recent epidemics, and the shortage of physicians, especially in the countryside. He wanted to hear our comments and suggestions. I understood quite well what he was talking about, for I was aware of the flight of many experienced South African physicians during the few years before the end of apartheid and afterward. I personally knew quite a few doctors who'd come to Chicago and suburbs. Many more must have settled in other locales in the US and around the world.

The members of our delegation made various recommendations. Mine was based on the health care system in the Iraq of my time, where medical college was free, but graduates had to serve in the provinces for five years, a year for every year of medical school except the sixth year. I also mentioned the good experience we had with nurse practitioners at CCH. The physicians we met at Ben Lavin were engaging, enthusiastic, and intent on serving as best as they could. This was amply confirmed when over the next two days we visited Elim Hospital, the nearby Pietersberg Regional Hospital, and later the Mankweng Hospital, which is attached to the University of the North. The workload was heavy for the physicians and auxiliary staff. In one of the hospitals, one-third of all admissions tested positive for the human immune deficiency virus (HIV).

We then headed to Kruger National Park, a nature preserve 7,523 square miles large (19,485 square kilometers), more than two-thirds the size of Massachusetts. It lies in the northeastern part of South Africa and stretches 220 miles (360 kilometers) north to south and 40 miles (65 kilometers) east to west. We arrived for dinner at the Olifants (Elephants) Camp and spent the night there. We then got in a motor coach for an early morning game viewing before proceeding on a trip through the park, arrived at the Berg-en-dal Rest Camp, spent the night there, and had another early-morning game viewing before heading back to Johannesburg.

The trip through Kruger was one of my most interesting experiences. Most striking was how majestic and purposeful the animals looked in their natural habitats. A cheetah chases in the early morning a seemingly doomed impala, strategizes, gallops at a speed of eighty miles per hour, so fast that she appears quite fuzzy to the human eye, and soon enough grabs the helpless impala and goes for the jugular.

The lions, kings of the jungle, lie lazily in the shade while the females stroll around, eying the surroundings. The antelopes, the leopards, the baboons, and even the hyenas, were all so interesting and real, nothing like what we see even at the best zoos.

Of the birds, there was a plethora of species. Fortunately for us, one of the delegates, Dr. Alan Robinson, was an expert at identifying most of them. The ones he could not quickly name he would soon recognize by referring to an illustrated book he carried with him. I called him our ornithologist.

While driving through Kruger, we saw a herd of elephants about to cross the road ahead of the bus. The leader of the herd, a large female, stopped at the edge of the road with a baby elephant almost stuck to her flank, lifted up her left foot, and trumpeted. Our driver immediately stopped the bus and turned off the engine. He told us the herd wanted to cross the road but might hesitate as long as they hear the sound of the engine. The herd, headed by the leading cow, crossed the road. She and her baby protégé stopped on the opposite edge of the road until the entire herd had passed on to the field, then she lifted her foot again, trumpeted, and joined her team. Animals, especially elephants, do seem to think. Not only that, but elephants also share with us the practice of remembering their dead. We saw at the Olifant museum in the park some touching videos of elephants visiting the places where the bones of their dead kin or ancestors lie. They look at the bones mournfully and gently turn them about with their trunks.

The scenery was new to me: the vast landscape; the graceful baobab trees; the glorious night sky as I had never seen it before, with the stars glistening, twinkling brightly, seeming almost near at hand. I could clearly see the Milky Way. The Berg-en-dal campsite had nice dwellings with thatched roofs. It had no light bulbs whatsoever except in the limited area of the restaurant. When we finished dinner and headed toward our rooms, it was very dark and eerie, and we could hear the distant roaring of lions and the nearby laughter of hyenas. I carried a flashlight, so a couple of the lady delegates asked me to walk them to their rooms.

They were quite uneasy in a setting they had never experienced before.

We were driven back to Johannesburg wherefrom we flew to Cape Town, the legislative capital of South Africa and also the capital of the Western Cape Province in the south-southwest part of the country. It has a long coastline along the Indian and the Atlantic oceans. The city is nestled under Table Mountain on the shore of Table Bay at the northern end of the Cape Peninsula, a tongue that juts out of the western coastline and curves eastward toward Cape Point, where the Indian Ocean meets the Atlantic. Some of us did in fact wade in the water there and could sense that it cooled considerably as we walked from east to west. The guide told us the Atlantic Ocean was ten degrees Celsius (eighteen Fahrenheit) cooler that the Indian Ocean where they meet at Cape Point.

As is well known, Cape Town had been a beautiful city, but by 1996 its luster had faded after years of sanctions and turmoil. There were also scenes of poverty, with African women on the sidewalks beseeching us to buy their trinkets: "Please, kind sir, do take this nice bracelet. I badly need the money," they would plead. Often their little children would be around them as well. We were then taken on a tour of the Cape Peninsula, where we saw Kirstenbosch Botanical Gardens, a center for the study and preservation of South African flora; then to Boulder Beach to look at a large group of the Jackass or Black Foot penguins restricted to South Africa; and finally to the Cape of Good Hope Nature Preserve.

We visited the famous Groote Schuur (Great Barn) Hospital where Dr. Christiaan Barnard performed the first heart transplantation for Mr. Louis Washkansky in 1976. It so happened that the hospital was made a Western Province heritage site the same year we were there. We toured the hospital, and three delegates, Drs. J. Bourgoignie, E. Pedersen and I were invited to discuss clinical cases of interest. I was struck by the great similarity of much of the hospital's patient population at the time to that of CCH in the 1970s and early 1980s, with much malignant hypertension, tuberculosis, and severe lupus nephritis. The medical staff was excellent and dedicated, and was clearly working hard to attend to these severe illnesses affecting a large number of patients.

We drove to beautiful Stellenbosch, a little east of Cape Town, where we visited the Renal Unit at the University of Tygerberg Hospital. A group of us was to attend a session of clinical case presentations, and Dr. Bourgoignie and I were requested to be present at the meeting. I gave the same lecture on lupus nephritis I'd given at the Johannesburg Hospital and found that the chief nephrologists, Drs. M. R. Moosa and A. A. Walele, were quite acquainted with my work. Interestingly, lupus nephritis was fairly common and quite severe in the Malay population of South Africa, and as in Chicago—among the urban blacks, not those in the countryside. I observed the same phenomenon about severe hypertension in blacks: its prevalence in the cities, especially Johannesburg, and rarity in the provincial towns and villages.

A very pleasant aspect of the South Africa trip was my getting to know many of the outstanding delegates from the US and abroad. I was delighted to make the acquaintance of Dr. Borgoignie, whom I'd never met before, although I had read several of his publications. He and his wife were of course instrumental in making the expedition the great success it was.

I also met Dr. Jack Coburn, whose work on bone disease in kidney failure I was well acquainted with. He told me he had reviewed one of the aluminum papers I had previously submitted for publication. There was also Dr. Svend Strangaard from Denmark, who was one of the speakers at the Johannesburg Hospital. Early in my renal training I had read an interesting paper of his about the auto-regulation of brain circulation in hypertension, so I was pleased to meet him in person. He told me he and his wife had been to Baghdad many years earlier and had liked it very much.

I don't think my impressions of South Africa in 1996 will ever fade from my memory. Here was a large, beautiful, and rich country where a minority white population owned 85 percent of the best land, dominated the majority blacks, and established a heinous apartheid regime where the native Africans had no access to the country's riches and essentially no rights.

In 1996, only two years after the final collapse of apartheid, I saw the country as a bizarre combination of the First and the Third Worlds. I, like most other people, had obviously been aware of the economic and sociopolitical realities of apartheid, but I gained much more knowledge of South Africa in that visit and also from fairly intensive reading beforehand on the history and demographics of the country. The sordid details of the Boer War were interesting. Much more interesting, however, is the fact that the Zulu Kingdom in South Africa was in its time one of the best organized in the world, but, like preconquistadores Mexico, had no gunpowder and was therefore destined for defeat.

## II. SHANGHAI, 2002

A Chicago lady who had been involved in some philanthropic work in China sought a group of people, including a few physicians and surgeons, to travel with her to Shanghai. They were to give lectures, visit some hospitals to make rounds, discuss clinical cases, and perform some operations. I had not previously known her. Dr. Dunea asked me if I wanted to join her group, and I readily agreed. I had not been to China and was quite interested to see as much as I could of Shanghai and vicinity and learn firsthand about the people, economy, and the state of medical practice. We took off in October 2002.

The weather in Shanghai was moderate, but there was much air pollution, giving a dusky appearance to the city and its high-rise buildings. It reminded me of Los Angeles in the 1970s. There was robust construction going on. Cranes and forklifts were a busy part of the skyline. The city pulsated with activity. People rushed to work, and hundreds of young and not-so-young men and women on their bikes dashed forth like an army as soon as the green traffic light went on.

I gave a lecture and conducted clinical case discussions at Ruijin Hospital, formerly St. Marie, founded in 1907. A renowned hospital, it is the largest teaching facility for the Jiao Tong University School of Medicine, and had produced internationally recognized figures such as Drs. Chen Saijuan, Chen Zhu, and Wang Zhenyi.

The doctors were experienced, up to date, and hardworking. I made rounds at the hospital's dialysis unit and was impressed that the staff put on gowns, gloves, and shoe covers as though they were entering an operating room. The nursing and technical staff displayed exemplary tact and professionalism. After I finished my day at the hospital, the kind nephrology staff presented me with an exquisite green bronze ewer cased in a velvet box.

I also discussed some cases of children with kidney diseases at Fudan University's Children's Hospital, ranked as the top pediatric hospital in China, and the first in Asia to be accredited by the Joint Commission International. It was founded in 1952, has thirty-five thousand admissions and serves 2.2 million outpatients annually. This was for me another remarkable experience.

The physicians were highly advanced, and many were involved in research. A busy pediatric nephrologist took calls and slept in the hospital once a week. Meanwhile he was taking a course in molecular biology in the evenings. His wife was a busy general pediatrician. They had one daughter. A fellow-in-training in kidney disease also did research in molecular biology at a state-of-the-art center. No wonder there has been an avalanche of Chinese medical papers and presentations at kidney conferences in the US over the last decade. Interestingly, most of the Chinese physicians I met were fully versed in their ancient medicine, and many still practiced it along with Western medicine.

The pediatrician couple were kind hosts to me. They took me to the old city, where we dined at a busy restaurant, and two days later they accompanied me to the famous Shanghai Museum of ancient Chinese art. The old town was much diminished in size but quite charming. It reminded me of the pictures that thrilled me when I read "Aladin and the Magic Lamp" as a child.

On another day I took a walk in the city. I did not hear the usual chirping of birds, but I saw a street vendor selling porcelain birds to enthusiastic children who blew into a hole in the porcelain to produce an almost natural bird song. I then remembered that under Mao Zedong the birds in China were eliminated because they ate the seeds, another one of those Great Leap Forward projects that cost millions of lives from widespread famine. The worms that the birds had hitherto enjoyed eating were left free to destroy the agricultural produce. I bought one of the porcelain birds, whistled through it, and have kept it to this day.

I then walked into a large and busy park where there was

an art fair. The paintings, sculptures, and artifacts on exhibition were fine and interesting. Statues of famous Chinese philosophers and administrators stood in different parts of the park. What most attracted my attention was the sight of large families, each surrounding one child, usually a boy, pampering him and passing him on from one lap to another. They observed then and still do the one child policy. One must wonder at the coercive power of a state that can impose such a policy on a people accustomed for millennia to having many children.

I passed by two families comprising the parents, their siblings, and other relatives. The baby boy they had surrounded was adorable, so I asked them if I could hold him for a minute, and produced my camera for one of them to take a picture of me with the child. They were very excited about that, but got into an argument about who would have the privilege of taking the picture. I settled the issue by asking the seemingly older grandfather to do that, to his immense satisfaction and gratitude. I had not forgotten the veneration Eastern cultures extend to the elders. A dark thought kept nagging at me, however, as I remembered that many infant girls were secretly done away with because the parents had wanted a boy.

Visiting the Shanghai Museum in the People's Square was among my most enjoyable experiences in the city. I spent most of the day there, frequently apologizing to my two companions for the time I took to read the artifacts' legends. "No apology needed. There are too many things to see here, and we are having a good time, too. Please, please take your time," they responded with the most polite of smiles. No wonder—they were the products of five millennia of civilization and fifteen centuries of Buddhism.

The current museum building was started in August 1993 and inaugurated in October 1996. It was originally founded in 1952 and had been located in the former Shanghai Racecourse club-house and later in the Zhonghui Building, which housed insurance and bank offices. The current structure owes its existence to Ma Chengyuan, who must have been a genius at fund-raising, initially collecting $25 million, then $10 million from the Shanghai diaspora in Hong Kong, and finally persuading the Shanghai city government to allot 140 million yuan for the building. He was the museum's director from 1985, when it sat in the Zhonghui Building, until his retirement in 1999.

The building is quite interesting in that it has a circular top and a square base to symbolize the ancient Chinese concept of round sky, square earth. It is designed in the shape of a *ding*, an ancient bronze cooking vessel, an excellent example of which is the Da Ke Ding exhibited in the museum and credited with having inspired the shape of the building. It is 29.5 meters high (almost 97 feet), comprises five floors, covers a 39,200-square-meter area (almost 388,080 square feet), and contains 120,000 pieces. These encompass almost the entire range of ancient Chinese art: ceramics, bronze, jade, paintings, calligraphy, seals, sculptures, and coins. There are also many items of national significance such as a Han Dynasty transparent bronze mirror.

Even for a Mesopotamian acquainted with the artifacts of his and other ancient Middle Eastern civilizations, I was struck by the exquisite beauty of the Chinese objects, owing to the fact that such artistic mastery had been achieved four and half millennia ago, and grateful indeed to my hosts, the pediatric doctor couple.

On another day I did something on my own. I jumped into a minivan that had collected another five tourists from various hotels and headed with the group to the ancient city of Suzhou, not far from Shanghai. I was determined to see the famed classical gardens of Suzhou, also its canals and arched stone bridges, which predated those of Venice by five hundred years. That has not, however, deterred the Eurocentrics from calling Suzhou the "Venice of China."

Actually, Suzhou is quite ancient, having been founded in 514 BC. It became one of the largest cities of the world during the Han dynasty (AD 100) and has been a prominent commercial center since the Song dynasty (tenth century). During the Ming and Qing dynasties, it was a national cultural and economic center and the largest noncapital city in the world. Since the economic reforms of 1978, it has been one of the fastest-growing cities in the world.

In 1997 and 2000, UNESCO named eight of the finest classical gardens of Suzhou as World Heritage Sites. Over a millennium spanning the period from the eleventh-century Song dynasty to the nineteenth-century Qing dynasty, two hundred such gardens had been built, but only sixty-nine are preserved, and our tourist group had time to see only three. This was a marvelous experience, one that provided a close impression of paradise. Artfully constructed landscapes representing rivers, rocks, and hills, with well-placed pagodas and pavilions, evoked a sense of eternal serenity and filled me with inner peace and an awareness of the futility of many of our daily pursuits. Our group also greatly enjoyed a boat cruise on one of the city canals.

My journey to China was limited but nevertheless quite memorable. My wife and I have been planning to make a more extensive sojourn to that venerable old country, but it has not happened yet. That short trip to Shanghai and vicinity, however, was enough to show me that the dragon had begun to thump its feet on the world stage. It reminded me of a saying attributed to Napoleon Bonaparte: "Let China sleep, for when she wakes the world will tremble."

# 26

# Visits to the Homeland

In late 1977, six years after leaving Iraq, I returned there on a visit, not by myself, for I was uneasy about the fascist atmosphere under the entrenched Ba'th party, but as a member of the National Arab American Medical Association (NAAMA), for a medical convention it was to hold in Baghdad. I had at first been hesitant to sign up but eventually decided to go, prevailed upon by the longing for family and friends, a repressed deep yearning to see Iraq again, including the playgrounds of my childhood, the two houses where I grew up, the schools I went to, and the libraries and bookshops I frequented.

I still had my parents and four siblings in Baghdad, also my maternal grandfather, my larger family of uncles, aunts, and cousins, and several dear friends from the days of Baghdad College and medical school. I was also happy that my childhood friend, Nabil, was also going. He had earlier lost his parents and a sister in a car accident outside Baghdad and had not had the opportunity to go back at the time. He, too, still had a brother and his family and many friends in Baghdad.

The atmosphere upon landing at Baghdad airport was similar to many in other totalitarian states. There were not many smiling faces, and numerous "regular" people who were clearly plain-clothes security agents. As I waited to pick up my luggage, a man's voice called out "Sa'ad Abbas Bakir?" I turned around, scrutinized the man's face, and recognized him to have been a classmate in the early years of grammar school but had not seen him since. He was now working in the airport's customs section, which implied that he, too, belonged to the security apparatus. Many such people were recruited into these services and paid well because of their excellent memory for faces, a quality he obviously possessed. Not knowing his intentions, I was somewhat perturbed, but he smiled after I greeted him by name, and he expedited my passage through customs. Childhood connections do matter, I suppose.

I was of course thrilled to see family and friends again. We reconnected instantly and delved into conversation, reminiscences, and discussions as though we hadn't been separated for six years. A joyful energy suffused me, like a fish returned to the sea after hanging on the fisherman's hook, or a dry sponge immersed in water.

I saw Namik again, and we spent a wonderful evening with A'rag, reminiscences, and Mahler. I saw my friends from the days of medical school: Imad Murad, a dermatologist; Abhar Ma'rouf, an electrical engineer; and Qusay Adwa, an employee at a government-owned company. In the old days, we often went to al-Waha al-Khadhra' (the Green Oasis) next door to the Olympic Club in the center of A'dhamiya, where we had drinks and kebab and discussed all sorts of political, literary, and social matters. Except for Qusay, we were of a similar mind about most issues and arrogantly dismissive or deprecating of those who did not share our views. But then the youth know everything, don't they? Missing from the gathering this time was In'am al-Daghestani, who had been a boxer, then got a degree in English and translated into Arabic T. S. Eliot's *Murder in the Cathedral*, which did not sell a single copy, so he gave us each a copy and forgot about the whole matter.

In'am was quite eccentric but highly entertaining. In spite of his English degree, he liked to shock us by claiming the British had no real literature, certainly not much compared to the French or the Russians. He later left for Sweden, became homesick, and wrote us that, having gotten tired of the very free Swedish women, he erected in in his mind's eye a statue, "now enveloped in heavy Swedish fog," of a young Iraqi woman with shy modesty and attractive prudence.

His homesickness got so much worse that he confined himself to his room and was not seen for many days until a neighbor, an older woman, broke into his quarters and pulled him away to a hospital where he was attended to and fed. The kind woman took him back to her place and nursed him back to health. The episode impressed him greatly with the kindness of the heretofore "bland" Swedes, and he eventually got accustomed to the country. He later became a journalist and one day traveled to conduct an interview with Ayatollah Khomeini when the latter was in exile. He never got to see the old man because the plane that flew him to his whereabouts crashed.

I then visited the Medical City Hospital, where I gave a talk and discussed a clinical case that was presented to me. I was impressed by the intelligence, knowledge, and hard work of the house staff, who excelled despite the oppressive political atmosphere and the impediments the Ba'thist government had placed on physicians wanting to travel abroad for further training and specialization. While there I ran into Mizhir, my cointern in internal medicine in 1971. Upon seeing me, he let out a surprised and jubilant laugh from the heart; we hugged like long-lost brothers. Another friend, Namuk al-Khateeb, from our days in the Army Medical Reserve Corps, invited me to a popular club. It turned out to be a surprise party attended by a large number of my medical school classmates. They circled around me, asked me endless questions about America, and told me the latest jokes, both political and dirty. It was a happy riot.

I went to al-Mutannabi Street, in my days the intellectual heart of Baghdad, where I had spent endless hours at al-Muthanna Bookshop. I was disappointed this time that there were no books of current literature, politics, economics, philosophy or science. I looked for the very good *New Atlas of Iraq* by Ahmad Susa. I owned it during high school but lost it later. It was not to be found at any bookshop. Neither could I find any maps of Baghdad, Iraq, or the Middle East. Nor were there any reprints of Ali al-Wardi's books or the works of modern Iraqi poets. All I could find were books of the classical Arab poets, and too many nonsense books on the "philosophy" of the Ba'th, Arab nationalism, and the ever-elusive Arab unity—altogether an insult to one's intelligence.

The Ba'th Party had managed to imprison Iraqis by incarcerating their minds. In 1969, the Ba'th government evicted the Jesuit teachers from Baghdad College, the best school in Iraq, and its sister al-Hikma University, which the Jesuits had designed themselves in the Abbasid style of architecture. The fathers were never compensated for the properties. Victor Hugo said that to close a school is to open a prison. Under the Ba'th, Iraq had indeed become one vast prison. A few years later, almost the entire senior faculty of the University of Baghdad Medical College and the Medical City Hospital was "retired," to be replaced by their onetime students and trainees, more acceptable to the Ba'thist government. Today, the once wonderful Baghdad College of my teenage years lies in sad ruins, a microcosm of what has happened to the country, and the Baghdad Medical College, once the pride of the Middle East, is woefully lacking in experienced high-caliber physicians and teachers.

During that first visit to Iraq after a six-year absence, I was struck by the beauty of the old buildings of Baghdad and the shrines of Kadhimiya, A'dhamiya, Sammarra, Karbala, and Najaf. I was equally taken by the superb quality of the Iraq Museum of Antiquities and the Baghdad Museum, which depicts various aspects of life and crafts in the city during the late nineteenth and the first half of the twentieth centuries. It was as though I had not paid enough attention to those features before I left Iraq. But natives usually take their country's landmarks for granted.

So I was moving around like a tourist, snapping shots of buildings, mosques, and museum pieces, to the amusement of the locals who had not been accustomed to seeing many tourists in the country. Curiously, Iraq had not been a popular destination for tourists even though the first cities, urban civilization, and writing originated there. Iraqis, though generous, warm, and friendly, are not suited by temperament for the service industry of tourism. Furthermore, the abundant oil resource does not encourage the development of alternative sources of income, and Iraqi governments engaged in anti-Western rhetoric obviously were not attracting many tourists.

An oddity that immediately attracted my attention was the sight of *soldiers*—not professional museum guards—keeping watch in many of the halls both at the Iraq and the Baghdad City museums, another sign of the militarization of the country. In the Iraq Museum there was a group of grammar school girls. Their teacher was showing them the famous Sumerian harp mounted by a bull's head. I wanted to take a photo of the artifact, but the sentry would not let me because "there were women close by," referring to the schoolchildren. This came from a simple soldier from the countryside displaying his Bedouin morality in an urban center.

In fact, Baghdad had already become much less urban even back in the early seventies, with far fewer men sporting modern attire and many more wearing the countryside dishdasha, the long, flowing dress in white, gray, or black. An increasing number of people in the government were not far removed from their rural origins. They did not speak the Baghdadi dialect of the 1950s and '60s, and they favored rustic and gypsy songs. I noticed on subsequent trips that this trend had only increased over time.

Another example of this rustication was an event the Iraqi reception team had planned for our trip to Samarra, a historically important city north of Baghdad, for a brief period the Capital of the Abbasid caliphate, and famous for its spiral minaret (al-Melwiya), which I first scaled while in grammar school. Arriving there, we were taken to a performance by swirling Rifa'i dervishes, a pseudo-Sufi Sunni group. One member of this group, Izzet al-Duri, was an upper echelon Ba'thist and a close associate of Saddam Hussein.

A swirling dervish show is fairly interesting, I suppose, but this one was gory, though bloodless, in that the performers, after repetitious incantations and whirling, leaned on long spears that pierced the outer aspect of their flanks, entering from the front and exiting from the back—not a sight for the fainthearted. In fact, the American wife of one of our colleagues fainted, fell on the floor, and had to be brought back by splashing water on her face.

I visited the shrines in Kadhimiya, Samarra, Karbala, and Najaf. I am not religious, but I wanted to see the places that gave me so much wonder and excitement as a child. The crowds were much thinner than usual and almost entirely Arab. There were the usual loud pleas for the Twelve Imams to intercede with Allah to lighten the burden of the pilgrims' sorrows and deprivations, but there was not the quiet obeisance and solemn humility of the non-Arab pilgrims I had seen in my childhood.

There were hardly any foreign visitors to the shrines during my early visits in the 1970s and later, but they came back during the years of sanctions in the 1990s, when Saddam's government needed cash, but were allowed to come only in organized groups closely surveyed by Saddam's security agents. Over time during his reign, the religious personages who escorted the pilgrims around and saw to their needs were entirely replaced by government-assigned agents, most of them members of the mushrooming security service.

Iraq had become one of the most oppressive states in the world. People could not own typewriters or copying machines. I wanted to make an Arabic name stamp for myself, and was astounded to find that I had to go to General Security for the stamp contents to be cleared. I was then given a brief memo authorizing whomever was to make the stamp to do so.

Besides the intellectual imprisonment of the educated class and the jarring nonsense of the regime's propaganda, travel was highly restricted. Many of my friends and acquaintances were on the *Meni'* (forbidden) travel list for no reason at all and could not therefore leave the country.

During a subsequent visit to Iraq, I noticed that my father became perturbed upon receiving a phone call from an old friend, A. T., a seasoned pediatrician at the main children's hospital in

Baghdad and an older brother of one of my teachers in medical school who had left for the US a few years earlier. Dr. A. T. had heard I was in Baghdad and asked my father if I could see his younger brother, H. T., a Qasim-era minister who had just been admitted to the Medical City Hospital for acute kidney failure. I said I would certainly do so. Dr. A. T. picked me up at our home, and we drove to the hospital in Bab al-Mu'adham.

I went into the patient's room and saw a dignified man of polite demeanor, eyes sparkling with intelligence, a common feature in his family, and a subdued expression of pain on his face. I asked him what had happened. He was in jail, like many other distinguished professors, teachers, and ex-officials. He and the other prisoners, including a friend of his who had been a professor of physiology at Baghdad Medical College, were herded every morning on a long run under the hot sun and beaten on the back with thick bamboo sticks. One day after the run and the beating, Professor H. T. stopped urinating.

I thought he had acute kidney failure from muscle injury (rhabdomyolysis), a condition where the red pigment myoglobin is released from the traumatized muscles and clogs up the kidneys, causing them to shut down. I explained this to the patient as gently as I could and told him he would need dialysis treatment. He listened intently, not displaying any alarm, understood, and said nothing. I told him I had to return to the US the next day, and would give a full account of his condition to his physician brother in the US, which I did.

Several weeks after my return to the US, my cousin, also a physician, invited me to his house for a dinner in honor of Dr. Khalid Naji, a famous surgery teacher of ours at Baghdad Medical College. He, too, had recently been in prison and was ultimately released. Somehow he had managed to leave Iraq.

"The jailers would blindfold us and say we would be shot by a firing squad," he related, "then take us to another place in the prison and line us up against a wall. We would then hear the whizzing sound of flying bullets, followed by a deadly silence. They would then take us back to our cells. I never knew if some of us were killed or if the whole operation was just a sadistic mock execution." But the Ba'thists were masters of sadism.

"The security agents at the prison would tell me I was a communist," he continued, "then they would return the next day to say I was a Freemason. Finally I got fed up and told them they better make up their mind. I couldn't be a communist and a Freemason at the same time." He concluded with his familiar hearty laughter. I was amazed he had not lost that trademark laugh of his after the terrible prison experience.

Many years later I called Professor H. T.'s physician brother in the US to recommend to him a bright young doctor who was looking for a residency position. A man with a broken voice answered the phone. I told him who I was and asked if I could speak to the doctor. He said, "I see you have not recognized me. I am H. T. You were kind enough to visit me many years ago at the Medical City Hospital in Baghdad, when I developed kidney failure." I was overcome with emotion and asked him how he was doing. "I had peritoneal dialysis (through the abdomen); my kidneys never recovered. My brother here arranged for me to come to the US, where I got a kidney transplant, but it's now not working well," he said. He died shortly thereafter. He could not have been older than sixty.

The Ba'thist regime had instituted a reign of terror rarely matched elsewhere. It employed all sorts of techniques to intimidate the people and keep them quiet. On another visit to Iraq, I found my family, friends, and almost all my acquaintances

speaking fearfully of Abu Tabra (the Ax Man). He would reportedly enter any house he had targeted and ax his chosen victim
to death. In summer nights, when many people slept on their
fenced roofs, he would easily climb up to dispatch his victims.
Most people I knew in Baghdad abandoned that long and pleasant
nocturnal habit in summertime and slept in their bedrooms under
the air conditioner.

The regime's security agents, largely organized by Saddam,
would make a habit of knocking at people's doors at night, ostensibly looking for Abu Tabra, but instead picking up individuals on
their wanted list, labeled as CIA or Zionist agents, communists,
Arab nationalists, or simply revisionist Ba'thists. These victims
would thereafter disappear without a trace. A few came back
years later, a shadow of their old selves, broken men and women,
suffering from severe post-torture symptoms, including horrible
nightmares.

During that same visit, I looked for my friend Mizhir, but
he had disappeared. I learned he'd traveled to England to visit
his uncle, a famous physician who had contributed to a project
to build a university in Kufa, one of the Shia sacred cities 170
kilometers south of Baghdad. Mizhir's uncle had earlier been
arrested for his role in the project, tortured by suspending him
from the ceiling, placing a hungry cat in his trouser legs with the
ends tied up, and banding his penis to prevent urination. When
he was finally released, he left for England.

Upon returning from his visit to his uncle, Mizhir was received at the airport by security agents, then simply disappeared. I
have had no news of him for over three decades, and I am certain
he died in one of Saddam's terrible prisons, most probably after
unimaginable torture. In all cases, and as a matter of course,
the victim's family was warned not to speak a word about their

vanished loved ones lest they meet the same fate themselves. But all of this was only the prelude to future atrocities on a massive scale.

Before and after becoming president in mid-1979, Saddam Hussein, a poorly schooled thug with a past history of homicide, having murdered his own uncle, took with monomaniacal energy to bolstering the state instruments of terror and oppression. Upon becoming president, his absolute rule lasted almost twenty-four years and was one of the darkest chapters in the history of Iraq. The damage it caused the country, its people, and resources exceeded the devastation by Hulago's Mongolian horde in the early thirteenth century.

Saddam's blind adventurist policies—which better educated Ba'thists, the military, and the oppressed masses failed to thwart—brought upon Iraq three devastating wars and a decade of pernicious sanctions. Over two million Iraqis perished, the middle class was wiped out, and the country was left in utter ruin. In fact, very few episodes in Iraq's history had witnessed a succession of disasters as frequent as in the era of the Ba'th. I can only summarize these for readers. A thorough description would consume thousands of pages, far beyond the scope of this modest memoir.

WITH MY FATHER, RIGHT.

WITH NAMIK HAZIM NAMIK, LEFT.

With my friends from medical school years.
From left to right: Ayad Murad, Abher Ma'roof,
Imad Murad, myself and Qusay Adwa,

The author (center) with staff, trainees and medical
students at the Medical City Hospital, Baghdad, 1978.

# 27

# The Poison Grain

While working in England in 1971, soon after I left Iraq, I heard about a mushrooming disaster of mercury poisoning long before I found any published material about what rapidly became an epidemic. This was the importation from Mexico and the US of mercury-coated wheat grain and barley on the order of Saddam Hussein, the number two Iraqi official after President al-Bakr. Mercury compounds kill fungi (fungicidal) and had been used at times to coat grain seeds intended for planting. However, the toxicity to humans of even miniscule amounts of mercury was known in Europe and America. Sweden had banned its use as a fungicide in 1966, and the United Kingdom in 1971.

In late 1971, seventeen thousand metric tons of wheat grain and twenty-two thousand of barley coated with methyl mercury and colored a pink-orange hue were imported for planting by Iraq, where wheat and barley were first domesticated six millennia earlier. It came in sacks with warning labels in Spanish or English, languages unknown to the Iraqi peasantry, and many bore the black-and-white skull and crossbones emblem equally unfamiliar to that population.

Countless peasants used the poison grain to make bread, which they and their children ate. Many had washed off the pink-orange-dyed grain with water, assuming it would then be safe to consume. Their livestock was also fed the tainted barley but did not seem to sicken, as the first symptoms of toxicity take two to five weeks to appear. The farmers therefore availed themselves of milk and meat from the affected livestock, birds that had picked up the poison seeds, and fish and vegetables exposed to contaminated waters wherein the tainted grain was dumped by other more cautious farmers.

The hospitals were soon flooded with poisoned patients. More than 6,500 were admitted and over 450 deaths reported, but Iraqi doctors, among them many of my medical school classmates, were convinced the numbers of sick and dying were tenfold the official figures because patients dying at home would not have been reported. Early symptoms of intoxication were abnormal sensations such as numb extremities, progressing to loss of balance, impaired vision or blindness, and death from failure of the central nervous system. Mercury crosses the placenta. Blood levels in the newborn were the same or higher than in the mother. Infants had damage of the central nervous system. Even low levels of intoxication caused slower development in children, abnormal reflexes, and the *quiet baby syndrome*, one who never cries.

It wasn't until late January 1972 that the Ba'th government started to warn the population against consuming the tainted grain, but did not broadcast the scale of the disaster. In fact it resorted to a news blackout. When the poisoning epidemic escalated, it ordered the army to eliminate all tainted grain and threatened the death penalty for those attempting to sell it. Countless farmers were scared by these tactics and dumped the grain in the Tigris, further aggravating the scale of contamination.

Once the news of the disaster got out, the World Health Organization (WHO) rushed in to help with experts, analytical equipment, and drugs. The drugs were on the whole not very effective. In 1974, WHO and FAO (Food and Agriculture Organization) issued recommendations to prevent such disasters, emphasizing that governments should avoid or restrict as much as possible the use of mercury-treated grain, and perhaps further coat it with a bitter additive to make it inedible. They recommended clear labeling of sacks in the local language and the use of danger symbols understood by the population—all common sense measures that seem to have escaped the government.

What is particularly galling about that tragic episode is that the Iraqi authorities had either ignored or not learned from past experience. In 1956, there had been two hundred cases and seventy deaths from mercury poisoning, and in 1960, when Saddam Hussein worked at the Ministry of Agriculture, there were a thousand cases and two hundred deaths. But I am sure he was an incompetent employee, too busy conspiring with others against Qasim and awaiting the coming of the Ba'th.

The epidemic was at the time the largest reported anywhere, starting in late 1971, peaking in January and February of 1972, and subsiding by the end of March. Professor Farhan Bakir was the first author of a medical paper published in the journal *Science* describing the clinical picture and course of patients affected by the epidemic. Among the coauthors were his colleagues, the late Dr. Salem Damluji and his late pediatrician wife, Dr. Lam'an Amin-Zaki.

# 28

# Ethnic Cleansing, Murders, and Massacres

## THE ETHNIC CLEANSING OF THE FAYLEES

The Faylees (or Lures) of Iraq are Shiite Kurds who had for millennia inhabited the eastern Diyala Province of Iraq and the contiguous Kemanshah and Ilam Provinces in Iran. They speak a southern Kurdish dialect. It is estimated that before the Ba'th era, there were probably 2.5 million of them in Iraq and 3 million in Iran. In Iraq, a good number of them attained high levels of education, were endowed with talent and intelligence, achieved professional and commercial success, obtained distinguished positions, and had a significant influence on Iraqi society. It was this cream of the Faylee community that the Ba'th government first targeted in its persecution of the whole ethnic group. The authorities claimed the Faylees were Iranian subjects, but the real reason they were marked was their Shi'ism and the intellectual and social influence of their elite.

In the 1970s and 1980s, the Ba'th government and security agents stripped the Faylees of their homes, properties, citizenship, and all legal documents pertaining to their status and identity and expelled them to Iran, where they essentially became stateless refugees. Between thirteen and thirty thousand Faylees, probably twenty-two thousand, died in captivity in Iraq under horrific prison conditions and systematic murder by the Ba'th secret police. At least four thousand of their youth disappeared.

I have a Faylee friend whom I first met in Baghdad College. He had a ready wit and audacious humor and was quite popular in high school. I used to visit him at his home where we spent the time chatting and listening to records by the popular Egyptian singer Abul Haleem Hafidh. His father and siblings were all bright and successful professionals.

He is now a successful urologist in the US, with many patents to his name. His eldest sister was a prominent lawyer in Baghdad in the Qasim era, but she disappeared when the Ba'thists grabbed power. His brother, also a lawyer, lived in Algeria for a while, having probably fled the Ba'th security agents. He went to the Iraqi consulate in Algiers to renew his passport, was served a glass of milk or juice, and died shortly afterward. People naturally assumed the drink was laced with thallium—tasteless and odorless, and the favorite murder weapon in the 1980s of Saddam's killing machine.

The Iraqi Minority Council estimated that only about one million Faylees still lived in the country before the 2003 US invasion. As of 2012, it is reported that 120,000 of them remain stateless in Iraq.

# THE DISPOSSESSION AND EXILE OF THE TABA'A

In 1974, many targeted Shiites were said to be *taba'a*, meaning they had not been Ottoman citizens, but rather Iranians, during the Turkish domination of Iraq. The irony of this is that it was the Iraqi Shia (not the Sunnis) who fought alongside the Ottomans against the invading British in 1914, while the Arab Revolt against the Ottoman Empire was undertaken by the Sunnis of Hejaz under Sharif Hussein of Mecca. It was therefore amazing that Saddam and his ilk of Ba'thists, "proud" of Iraq's independence from the British and the Turks before them, were now chasing those Shia whose ancestors had not originally been Ottoman citizens.

The great majority of the *taba'a* had Iraqi citizenship and had lived in Iraq for many generations, often for centuries. A great many of them had descended from well-known Iraqi tribes but had avoided the acquisition of Ottoman citizenship for different reasons: some religious, as the Ottomans were Sunni; and others to avoid being recruited by the Ottoman rulers for the Crimean War, a meat grinder that meant almost certain disability or death.

Sixty thousand Iraqi Shia were thus deprived of their homes, property, and identity documents, bundled up in buses, not even allowed to contact their relatives or friends, and dumped across the border into Iran. The majority of them did not even speak Persian. Many—nobody knows how many—died beyond the borders from hunger, fatigue, illness, and exposure. The organizer of this atrocity was—who else? Saddam Hussein. But he must have had the approval of President Ahmed Hassan al-Bakr. Saddam, as president in 1979, deported yet another thirty-five thousand Shia under the label of *taba'a*.

# THE TWAIREEJ MASSACRE

Before and during the war with Iran, the persecution of the Shia attained a truly gigantic scale. A Shia procession from the southern town of Twaireej was on the march to commemorate Ashura. They were shouting slogans like *"Saddam jur eedek, sha'b al-Iraq mayreedek"* meaning "Saddam, pull back your hand. The people of Iraq don't want you," whereupon they were attacked by armed helicopters that strafed them with bullets, killing some three hundred souls.

After the Twaireej massacre, the ritual of the Ashura processions, especially dear to the Shia peasantry and the urban poor, was banned by the Ba'th government—this in a country where the Shia easily comprised two-thirds of the population. Hundreds of Shia were arrested and many tortured for ignoring the ban. The Shia clerical leadership in Najaf (al-Hawza) was placed under tight surveillance, and Ayatollah Ali al-Sistani was confined to house arrest, notwithstanding the fact that the Najaf Hawza professed the "quietist" school of Shia theology, which does not advocate Wilayet al-Faqeeh (a state governed by a religious council) or violent political action.

# THE SAVAGE WAR ON THE DA'WA PARTY

In the 1970s and thereafter, a savage campaign of imprisonment, unimaginable torture, and executions of actual or presumed members of the Da'wa (the Call), a Shia religious party, proceeded unabated. The favorite torture methods of the Ba'th included the avulsion of finger- and toenails, burning of limbs, applying live cigarette butts to the skin, crushing of bones and toes, beating with brass knuckles and wooden bludgeons, gouging of eyes, electric shock to the genitalia, inserting red-hot metal rods into body orifices, raping women in in the presence of their husbands and family, amputation of tongue, ears, and limbs, unleashing hungry dogs upon prisoners, immersing prisoners in nitric acid tubs, and thallium poisoning.

Thallium was an acquisition from the East German STASI, tasteless and odorless, given with yogurt or Kebab to prisoners before they were released. It worked somewhat slowly but relentlessly to cause paralysis, kidney failure, and death. Thousands of the relatives and friends of the victims of these atrocities fled to Iran or Syria and the ones having more professional qualifications to England, Australia, or New Zealand; so did other thousands of Shia who suspected that they too were targeted.

On one of my visits to London in the 1980s, I went, as a matter of habit, to al-Saqi bookshop off Queen's metro station to look at the latest Arabic literary output (it was ebbing fast) and was surprised to stumble upon a very large volume cataloguing the names and photos of over four thousand Iraqi Shia, almost entirely men, said to have been Da'wa Party members, who were executed or simply disappeared without a trace. They were young or middle-aged men. A great many had finished college or postgraduate education. I did not have a restful night sleep for a long time afterward.

## THE MURDER OF AL-SADR AND HIS SISTER

Mohammad Baqir al-Sadr was a Sayyid (descendant of the Prophet Mohammad) and an Islamic scholar, widely known all over the Muslim world for his erudition and outstanding scholarly output. His most famous publication was a two-volume book on Islamic economics, but he also produced excellent works in the fields of logic, theology, philosophy, jurisprudence, fundamentals of Islamic Law, Koranic commentaries, and Muslim history and culture. His books were to be found in both Shia and Sunni academic centers.

His sister, Amina Haydar al-Sadr, also known as Bint al-Huda in recognition of her virtue and descent from the Prophet, was very learned and dedicated to study, good works, and most of all to educating young Iraqi women. Baqir and Amina al-Sadr were arrested by Saddam's security henchmen, thrown into prison, and tortured to death in April 1980. This series of crimes naturally caused a tense relationship with the Islamic Republic of Iran on Iraq's eastern border.

These unspeakable atrocities and the much larger-scale ones that followed were not denounced by Arab political leaders or their media. Moreover, it was these crimes, not the 2003 US invasion of Iraq, that opened the sectarian rift in Iraqi society, which only worsened after the invasion, when the virulent Saddamists and later Al-Qa'ida and ISIS unleashed mass murder on the Shia population with suicide and truck bombings in mosques, bazaars, wedding ceremonies, and funeral processions, killing thousands every year. These, too, were not denounced by our Arab brethren. On the contrary, hundreds or even thousands of wealthy Saudi and Gulf individuals were financing the murderous gangs.

Neither was there much mention in the world media of Saddam's monstrosities. Quite the opposite, his government obtained lethal anthrax and botulinum toxins from the United States Center for Disease Control (CDC) for "research" purposes. Phillips Company and affiliates sold Iraq a previously unheard-of amount—five tons—of poison gas precursor. Donald Rumsfeld, who oversaw the war against Saddam's regime in 2003, had actually visited him in Baghdad in December 1983, and in 1984,

Ronald Regan hosted at the White House Tariq Aziz, Saddam's face to the outside world. The Soviet Union continued to do business with the Iraqi government and provide it with advanced weapons, and the French were to supply Saddam with their sophisticated Super Étandard strike fighter planes during the coming war with Iran.

# 29

# Eight Years at War with Iran

Toward the middle of 1979, Saddam Hussein had accumulated much power and was clearly eyeing the presidency. President Ahmed Hassan al-Bekr was given to understand that he was "not well" and should step down. So he did, and Saddam became the fifth president of Iraq on July 16, 1979. Six days later he convened a large videotaped meeting, took the speaker's stand, smoking a long cigar, and announced that a large conspiracy by traitorous Ba'th Party members had been uncovered. (Remember Stalin?)

He then proceeded to call out the names of sixty-eight alleged conspirators who were immediately grabbed one after another by armed security agents and taken away. The remaining members, shaken by mortal fear, applauded and shouted out their support for the "leader." Twenty-two of the "conspirators" were executed by a firing squad of high-ranking party members, and by August 1979, hundreds of prominent members had been likewise executed. Saddam had become the absolute dictator.

Frightened by the Shia religious revival during and after the Iranian Revolution, and alarmed at its contagious effect on the oppressed Shia of Iraq, Saddam, ever obsessed by retaining absolute power for himself and his Tikriti relations, was quite open to the inducements by the US and its client Arab regimes to attack Iran. Several US media commented "knowingly" that the "formidable" Iraqi Army will "cut into Iran like a knife through butter," thereby fortifying Saddam's megalomania and grandiose delusions.

The US was quite frustrated by the American hostage crisis and angry about losing a client state as important as the Shah's Iran. Shortly before the start of the war in September 1980, President Carter commented that Iran was about to have a hot autumn. The Saudis, being Shia-hating Wahabis, had oppressed the majority Shia population of the eastern province of Ahsa, the richest in oil, and treated them like third-class citizens. The authorities were therefore quite apprehensive lest their Shia subjects begin to stir.

To make matters worse for the Saudi rulers, the Iranian revolution induced a resurgence of religious fervor among their own Wahabi citizens, manifested by Intifadhat al-Haram, the uprising led by Juhayman al-Utaybi, who took over the Ka'ba itself, the holiest site in Islam, causing the Saudi government to use maximum violence against the rebels, even to employ foreign mercenaries to literally gas the rebels out of the Ka'ba.

Furthermore, Kuwait had a sizable Shia population, Bahrain; a disadvantaged Shia majority of easily 75 percent; and the United Arab Emirates, with significant numbers of Shia—all three small countries ruled by long-running Sunni families. These ruling sheiks knew from their tribal traditions to ally themselves with a big tribe to protect their rule and the interests of their flock, so they went with the Portuguese during the waning days of Ottoman hegemony, then the British, then the US.

The Saudis and those sheikdoms to their east promised monetary and other support for Saddam, who, true to his impetuous character, attacked Iran. There was nothing in Iraq remotely akin to a dissenting national assembly, opposition political parties, or institutions of third thought to reject that foolish endeavor. All opposition to Saddam and his dirty dozen had been physically eliminated, and the surviving remnants had gone underground or into exile.

There was no longer a mature and experienced military high brass to render advice or caution restraint. The army had been purged of its best elements and cowed into submission to the Ba'th apparatus. Saddam himself did not possess the knowledge of history or the political insight to recognize that it was foolhardy to attack a country in revolution because the aggression would immediately unite all contending political factions against the external enemy and make it actually easier for the clerical regime in Iran to dispose of its critics and further consolidate political power. He had probably not read the history of the European incursion into revolutionary France following 1789 or the Western support of the "Whites" in the Russian civil war of the early 1920s.

Furthermore, like the Iranians, the majority of Iraqis are Shia who would have viewed the war as a sectarian project. Before the war, Saddam saw to it to visit towns and villages in southern Iraq, and would sit down with the locals and chat. "How do you like the TV reception nowadays?" he would ask. "For we have worked to improve the service." One or more men would then answer, "May Allah extend your life, sir. The service is much better now. We can even see and hear the Sayyid on television." The Sayyid they referred to was Ayatollah Khomeini, speaking on the waves from Teheran. For the record, he was in fact a Sayyid (descendant of the Prophet).

Iran has three times the area and population of Iraq, hundreds of miles of common border, a martial tradition, and imperial history. It was not about to disappear; it would always be there, abutting Iraq. No sane Iraqi leader, certainly not during the monarchy, would have chosen a confused history over real geography. As things turned out, when Saddam, disregarding common sense and his country's security, launched his reckless war against Iran, he soon found himself grabbing a tiger by the tail.

The war against Iran was also accompanied by the most fatuous propaganda. It was named al-Qadisiyya, and often Qadisiyat Saddam, in reference to the victory of the Muslim Arab army over the Persian Sassanids at the battle of Qadisiyya in southern Iraq in AD 636. Saddam commissioned a very large painting of the Qadisiyya Battle to be hung in a museum adjacent to the Arch of Ctesiphon (Taq Kisra) in Salman Pak, twenty-two miles (thirty-five kilometers) southeast of Baghdad. Salman Pak, officially called al-Mada'in, is the site of the ancient Ctesiphon, the winter capital of the Parthian and Sassanid empires (247 BC–AD 651) and the largest city in the world from AD 570 until its fall to the Muslim armies in AD 637.

Saddam's Qadisiyya was trumpeted as a battle against al-Furs al-Majoos (the Zaroastrian Persians), ignoring the obvious fact that the Persians had been Sunni Muslims after the Arab conquest in the seventh century, and only converted to Shiism during the Safavid period in the sixteenth century. The Persian Abu Muslim al-Khurasani recruited his Persian countrymen to join the Abbasid movement and was therefore an integral player in the triumph of the Abbasids over the Ummayads and the establishment of the Abbasid Empire in AD 750. He was later murdered by the third Abbasid caliph, Abu Ja'far al-Mansur.

The Persian Barmakids were the actual administrators of the

Abbasid Empire in its golden age during the reign of Harun al-Rasheed, who had grown up among the Barmakids in Iran until he was nine years old. When he came to Baghdad, his Arabic speech had a Persian accent. After he became caliph, the Barmakids often presented to him on Nawruz, the first day of the Persian (originally the Babylonian) New Year, the head of an Alawi rebel (follower of Iman Ali) on a silver platter. Harun later liquidated the Barmakids and expropriated all their properties.

The majority of Muslims, the Hanafis, follow Imam Abu Hanifa al-Nu'man, whose father and grandfather were Persian merchants from Kabul. The revered Sunni, the Sufi Shaykh Abdul Qadir al-Gilani, who has a beautiful mosque in Baghdad, was from Gilan in Iran. The Persian Seebawayh was the greatest grammarian of the Arabic language. Al-Razi (Razes) was the most famous Muslim physician of his time, the first to differentiate smallpox from chickenpox. The United Nations has a Razi Day to commemorate him and his works.

The Persians contributed the most to Islamic civilization. They were in the vanguard in the disciplines of astronomy, mathematics, philosophy, calligraphy, geography, the arts, architecture, and science. The philosophers of the Savafid era carried down and enlarged the legacy of the great Andalusian philosopher Ibn Rushd (Averros). The Persians built the amazing Blue Mosque of Isfahan, and the chief architects of the Taj Mahal and Humayun's Tomb in India were Persian. They produced the legendary Omar al-Khayam, who, besides his world-famous quartets, was one of the most eminent mathematicians and astronomers of his time. Persian workers built the Blue Mosque of Bursa in Turkey, and Persian was the literary and court language of the Ottomans during the first two centuries of their dynasty. The great civilization of Mughal India was Indo-Persian and Persian was the language of the royal court, the literati, and administrative bureaucracy for a very long time before it became a major component of Urdu.

It is evident, therefore, that the epithets lobbed at the Iranians by Saddam's regime, and to this day, by the Wahabi Saudi propaganda have only to do with Iran's endorsement of Shiism during the Safavid period. They are the same epithets darted at the Shia in Iraq and elsewhere— a pure example of sectarian bigotry. No Arab with the least measure of education and respect for Islamic civilization should repeat these idiocies about Iran. Sadly, too many do.

Incidentally, Zoroastrianism, the pre-Islamic religion of the Persians, was the first monotheistic creed in the Middle East, noble and enlightened, the religion of a great Empire, and it influenced all three Abrahamic religions. A great number of Iraqis' pre-Islamic ancestors in central and southern Mesopotamia had actually been Zoroastrian, while in the north and northeast they were Christian.

That aside, the majority of the Shia in Iraq and worldwide saw the offensive anti-Iran propaganda as an insult to Shi'ism emanating from hateful chauvinism. After all, the Sunni Turks to the north were never called Byzantines or Hittites, and as Ottomans, they had ruled and often abused Iraqis and Arabs for many centuries. Later, as modern Turks, they never renounced their claim to the Mosul Province of Iraq, now called Nineveh.

The Iraq-Iran cataclysm lasted eight years, from September 1980 to August 1988, longer than the First or Second World War, and was among the ghastliest catastrophes of the twentieth century. In fact, it was reminiscent of World War I, with its trench warfare, the astronomical fatalities sustained in the gain or loss of thin slivers of land, and the unrestrained use by Saddam of chemical weapons against Iranian troops. There were, how-ever, two major differences from World War I. The first was that Saddam also used the chemical weapons against his own Kurdish citizens, notoriously in Halabja, in March 1988 after the town fell to a combined force of Iranian troops and Kurdish guerrillas; and in the genocidal Anfal campaign from 1986 to 1989. The second was Saddam's use of large-scale air and missile bombardment of Iranian population centers.

The war exacted a terrible toll on both countries. The reported number of deaths has varied from one source to another. Ra'ad al-Hamdani, one of Saddam's generals, stated that 250,000 Iraqis died, of whom 53,000 perished just in the battle for Shatt al-Arab. The "Battle Deaths Dataset," a product of a team of political scientists, put the combined fatalities of both sides over 600,000. A scholarly data set from the "Correlates of War Project" placed the figures at half a million Iraqis and three-quarters of a mil-lion Iranians. The latter two data sets do not reconcile with the numbers of fighting-age men counted in Iraq's 1997 and Iran's 1996 census.

The Iranian Basij (the Organization for Mobilization of the Oppressed), a volunteer paramilitary force, put the Iranian bat-tlefield deaths at 155,081 plus 16,154 killed during the bombard-ment of the cities, while a scholarly publication placed the total number of Iranian fatalities at 183,623, based on statistics from the Veteran and Martyrs Affair Foundation, an Iranian gov-ernment bureau. This last figure may be more reliable since this government agency would be responsible for compensating the widows and orphans of the war dead. These grim statistics, how-ever, do not give an accounting of the Iraqis and Iranians injured, maimed, disabled, or left with debilitating post-traumatic stress disorders and the adverse consequences thereof for their families.

In Iraq hardly any family was not affected by the conflagration. A young cousin of mine had married a twenty-six-year-old engineer who disappeared at the front early in the war, only six months after their marriage. Nobody knew if he was killed or taken prisoner of war. She, a previously cheerful young woman with a constant smile, waited mournfully for news of her husband and did not remarry for another twelve years, after she was certain her young spouse had been killed.

My brother was recruited to the front during a bloody stage of the war when the casualty figures were quite grim. All of us, especially my mother, were in unremitting anguish about his fate. It was a miracle that he came back home in one piece. A cousin of my friend Mazin was killed in the war, and an old friend of mine, a surgeon, died during a bombardment of Basra. The city, caught in the cross fire of the two belligerents, lost vast numbers of its famed palm dates. Over four hundred kinds of dates were grown in Iraq, the very best in the world. Since it takes an average of thirty years for a date palm to bear fruit, after the war ended, Iraq was importing dates from Jordan.

There were reports in Western news journals of Iraqi boys in their mid to late teens being rounded up for eluding conscription, arranged in a semicircle, trembling, some wetting themselves, before being shot by Saddam's military police. Iraqi women had to surrender their sparse jewelry for the "war effort." So many Iraqi men were drafted to the Iranian front that Saddam had to import several million Egyptians to till the land, attend to the date palms, and perform municipal jobs. Many even worked as gravediggers and were seen all over Karbala and Najaf where the coffins of the Shia war dead were brought daily to circle the holy shrines before burial. A great number of Egyptians had been jailed criminals who were released and sent to Iraq, whereupon the number of thefts and violent crimes increased considerably—a gift from one Arab brother, Hosni Mubarak, to another, Saddam Hussein.

The Iraqi soldiers at the front lines could not retreat because there was always a firing squadron in the rear, often including Jordanian soldiers, that would immediately shoot them. The soldier's corpse would be returned to his family and his coffin would be labeled "traitor." It contained a bill to be paid by the family for the bullet that killed him and the coffin holding his dead body. In the trenches, the soldiers were tied to each other with ropes to make it impossible for them to retreat or escape.

Many senior Iraqi Army officers were opposed to the war, but would not articulate their views for fear of liquidation and the resulting destitution of their families. Worse things still could happen to them. Hamid al-Juburi, who was at the time Saddam's information minister, related not long ago on YouTube the story of a senior officer in the Basra sector of the war zone who was suspected of not being adequately loyal to Saddam, who therefore immediately dispatched some of his henchmen to the officer's home in Baghdad. They raped his wife while videotaping the beastly crime. The officer was then summoned back to Baghdad, shown the video and ordered to spy on his colleagues. Failing that, he was warned, the video would be distributed to all and sundry. He chose to spy on his comrades-in-arms and was rewarded with a big promotion.

The large, modern, and expensive petrochemical plant in Basra was destroyed. The wide Shatt al-Arab was no longer navigable, clogged up with sunken ships and war debris. Iraq therefore lost its outlet to the Persian Gulf and had to direct its trade with the outside world and export its diminishing oil output via the port of Aqaba in Jordan. It also sold oil to Jordan at greatly discounted prices.

Moreover, Saddam gifted to Jordan extensive Iraqi territory east of the border between the two countries, as though he'd inherited the land from his ancestors. Jordan was therefore the main beneficiary of the Iraq-Iran war. It flourished, and its capital, Amman, expanded dramatically. In 1964, when my friend Mazin, my brother and I visited Amman on our way to Syria, it was not larger than one district of Baghdad. During the Iran war, however, it came to rival Baghdad, eventually surpassing it in many respects.

In the final analysis, the war ended with very little change in the antebellum Iraq-Iran border. The main events of the long war were the initial seizure by the Iraqi Army of Khuzistan; its recapture by Iran and the surrender of thirty thousand Iraqi troops; the seizure by Iran of the Fao peninsula south of Basra and later the oil-rich Majnoon Islands; and their subsequent retrieval by Iraq. These battles consumed a horrendous number of soldiers. In Iraq itself, the war was associated with atrocities by the Saddam regime against the Shia in Dujail in July 1982 and the Kurds of Halabja in March 1988.

The war might have ended much differently had it not been for the active US involvement on the side of Saddam. The US was neutral in name only. Both the US and the UN looked the other way when companies in the US and allied countries supplied Saddam with chemical agents or their precursors. When the war dragged on, US AWACS surveillance planes and spy satellites provided Saddam with crucial information about Iranian troop concentrations and movements. Then the US launched Operation Earnest Will, where American navy vessels escorted reflagged Kuwaiti oil tankers along the Persian Gulf to protect them from Iranian attack.

In September 1987, US Navy helicopters fired on Iran Ajr,

a landing and mine-laying ship, killing some of the crew and chasing the remainder into the water. Navy Seals then boarded the ship, found some mines, and detained the surviving sailors. Four days later, a US Navy detachment scuttled the ship in international waters. In October, US Navy forces destroyed two Iranian oil platforms in Operation Nimble Archer, in retaliation for an Iranian missile attack on a reflagged Kuwaiti oil tanker anchoring off Kuwait.

In April 1988, the US frigate Samuel B. Roberts was damaged by a mine. Its serial number matched those of other mines in the surrounding waters and the ones previously found on Ajr. This led to the launching that month of naval Operation Praying Mantis, the largest since World War II. For those unacquainted with the wantonness of the names of military operations, the mantis is a species of insect that preys on other insects, clasping them with forelimbs held up as if in prayer.

The operation was larger than the Battle of Chumonchin in the Korean War, the Gulf of Tonkin incident, the Battle of Dong Hoi in the Vietnam War, and the operation in the Gulf of Sidra off Libya in 1986. Praying Mantis resulted in the sinking of one Iranian frigate and the damage of another along with three speedboats and one gunboat, and the destruction of two oil platforms. Fifty-six Iranian crewmen were killed in the process. The US lost only one helicopter, which crashed, killing three Americans.

On November 6, 2003, the International Court of Justice ruled that the actions of the USA against Iranian oil platforms in October 1987 (Nimble Archer) and April 1988 (Praying Mantis) "cannot be justified as measures necessary to protect the essential security interests of the United States of America."

On July 3, 1988, an Iranian Airbus passenger plane was flying from Tehran to Dubai. The pilot had seven thousand hours of flight experience. It was still within Iranian airspace and over its territorial waters when it was struck by a guided missile launched from the USS Vincennes under the command of Captain William C. Rogers III. It splintered in the air and fell down into the Persian Gulf. All 290 people on board, 16 crew members and 274 passengers, including 66 children, died instantly. All but 38 victims were Iranians. The Vincennes's commander was described by other senior US Navy officers as super aggressive and always itching for a fight. Post-tour-of-duty medals were given to Captain Rogers (the Legion of Merit), the Vincennes's crew (Combat Action Ribbons) and the Air Warfare Coordinator (a Navy Commendation Medal).

Eight years later, in 1996, the International Court of Justice dropped the Iranian Airbus case after the US paid reparations to the tune of $61.8 million for the families of the dead and another $70 million for the price of the plane. The US regretted the loss of life but never acknowledged the wrong or apologized. In August 1988, five weeks after the Airbus disaster, Vice President George H. W. Bush, talking to a group of Republican politicians, said, "I will never apologize for the United States. I don't care what the facts are" and "I am not an apologize-for-America kind of guy."

In the final analysis, the Iraq-Iran war, most importantly and sadly, deepened the Sunni-Shia divide in Iraq and beyond. It was clear, even to politically unsavy eyes, that the Arab states, mostly Sunni, stood by Iraq during the war, with the exception of Syria, ruled by an Alawite elite and Qaddafi's Libya.

The Alawites were acutely aware of the Arabs' sectarian and chauvinistic proclivities and the centuries of neglect and persecution by Sunni rulers and the Ottoman sultans, especially the notorious Selim the Grim. Qaddafi was more balanced in the 1980s and recognized that Iraq's war against Iran was a misguided endeavor that would only harm the cause of Arabs and Muslims. The other Arab rulers and their obedient media did not decry the launching of the war against Muslim Iran, the aerial bombardment of its cities, the gassing of its troops and of the Iraqi Kurds in Halabja, the massacre of Iraqi Shia in Dujail, or the relentless liquidation of actual or presumed members of the Iraqi Da'wa Party.

# 30

# More Mass Crimes

## THE DUJAIL MASSACRE

In July 1982, during the Iran-Iraq war, there was an attempt, reportedly by some Da'wa Party operatives, to assassinate Saddam Hussein as he was returning to Baghdad from a visit to Dujail, a largely Shia town of some seventy-five thousand souls, located 53 kilometers (33 miles) north of Baghdad. His motorcade was driving along the palm tree-lined road when about a dozen men emerged from behind the palms and fired at it. The gun battle lasted a few hours, during which most of the assailants were killed and a few captured.

Rounded up were 393 men and 394 women and children, who were sent to the notorious Abu Ghraib prison where they were subjected to horrendous torture. Their homes and farms in Dujail were demolished, and the palm orchards lining the road between Dujail and the nearby town of Balad razed.

Under torture, 148 prisoners, including 8 juveniles, "confessed" to having participated in the assassination attempt and were executed. Another four men were added to the list of the condemned by mistake. Of the remaining 639 detainees, 40 died from torture, and around 400 men, women, and children, mostly family members of the executed prisoners, were sent to another fearsome prison in a remote site in southern Iraq. The Arab media, which over two decades later loudly reprobated the Americans for the Abu Ghraib prison revelations during the US occupation of Iraq, had been mute about Abu Ghraib in 1982.

After 2003, Saddam was brought to trial for the Dujail massacre. He exhibited no regret whatsoever. On the contrary, he displayed his usual swagger, insulted the judges, shouted the usual slogans (Long live Iraq; Long live the Arab Nation), and took transparent delight in the heartrending testimonies of the Dujail victims' relatives. He was convicted and later hanged.

## THE HALABJA GAS ATROCITY

Halabja (Helebche) is a town in southern Iraqi Kurdistan, only 14 kilometers (9 miles) from the Iranian border and 240 kilometers (150 miles) northeast of Baghdad. In March 1988, toward the end of the Iraq-Iran war, it fell to a combined force of Iranian troops and Kurdish Peshmerga (guerrillas). An Iraqi Army base on the outskirts of the town was besieged. Two days later, on March 16, the Iraqi Army, commanded by Saddam's cousin Ali Hassan al-Majeed (Chemical Ali), subjected the city to indiscriminate rocket and napalm attacks and in the evening employed French Mirage and Russian MIG planes to drop chemical bombs on residential parts of the city far from the besieged army base.

The chemical weapons killed between thirty-two hundred and five thousand Kurds, including women and children, and injured between seven thousand and ten thousand others. Most victims were civilians. The poisonous chemicals included mustard, nerve, and cyanide gasses. The surviving victims, who were taken for treatment in Teheran hospitals, suffered from mustard gas exposure, causing tremendous difficulty to breathe and excruciating pain in the airways. Many died in horrible agony. Thousands more died later from exposure complications, diseases, and birth defects.

Following the gas attack, the town was littered with corpses of men and women, many hugging their dead children. Nevertheless, the Iraqi Army flattened the city with explosives and bulldozers. After some time, many Kurds returned to rebuild the city although there was persistent contamination of soil, water, plant, and animal life. The Japanese donated $70 million to provide for safe drinking water for the returnees.

Halabja was thus the site of the largest ever use of poison gas against a civilian population. It is almost incredible how many countries supplied Saddam with the precursors or ingredients of the lethal chemicals. Around thirty-six thousand tons of precursor chemicals came from Singapore, the Netherlands, Egypt, India, West Germany, France, and the USA. Culprit companies included Kim al-Khleej, a Singapore-based company affiliated with the United Arab Emirates. It sold Iraq forty-five hundred tons of VX, mustard, and sarin gas precursors and production equipment. The Indian company Exomet Plastics and the West German company Karl Kolb GmbH were also among the suppliers. The US companies Phillips and Alcolac provided Iraq with thiodiglycol, the precursor of mustard gas.

The thiodiglycol transaction was exposed by a leak from Iraq's own "full, final, and complete" disclosure of the sources of its chemical arsenal. The transfer of these weapons of mass destruction was immensely facilitated by President Ronald Reagan's removal of Iraq from the list of state sponsors of terrorism. No wonder then that a mere fifteen years later, President George H. Bush had good reason to believe the reports of Iraq's possession of weapons of mass destruction (WMDs).

Iraq accused Iran of using the chemical weapons in Halabja. Tariq Aziz emphatically denied that Iraq was the responsible party, even when the Kurdish political leader Jalal Talabani, who later became President of Iraq in 2003, was at the time screaming on CNN that it was the Iraqi Army that employed the poison gasses. And why would Iran use chemical weapons against its allies? The US government and intelligence services intimated that Kurdish civilians were not the intended target and hinted that Iran was responsible for the attack.

The British Commonwealth Office stated that dialogue would provide the route to changing Iraq's actions. Punitive sanctions would not be effective and would damage British interests to no avail—as though Chemical Ali's action in Helebja was a routine military operation, not a flagrant war crime. Likewise, Dieter Backfisch of the West German company Karl Kolb said in 1989 that Germans see poison gas as something quite terrible, but it does not worry customers abroad. The ludicrous allegations that Iran was the perpetrator of the gas attack proved, as expected, to be baseless.

The International Crisis Group, in its 2002 communication number 36, "Arming Saddam: The Yugoslav Connection," concluded that many national governments had approved the provision to the Iraqi regime of weapons of mass destruction because it was engaged in war against Iran, the reason why today's Iranian officials call the Iran-Iraq war, World War III.

In December 2005, a Dutch court sentenced Frans Van

Anraat to fifteen years in prison for having bought chemicals on the world market and sold them to Saddam. The court ruled that Saddam had committed genocide in Halabja. In March 2010, the World High Court decreed officially that the Halabja episode was an act of genocide. The Canadian Parliament voted that the episode was a crime against humanity. In March 2008, Iraq announced that it would pursue litigation against the entities that supplied the chemical agents used in Halabja. And in 2013, a group of Kurds initiated legal action against two French companies that helped Saddam build his lethal gas arsenal. Alcolac of the US, too, was a defendant in US District Court Case No. 1:09-CV-00869-MJG.

Chemical Ali was the immediate instrument of Saddam, not only in the Halabja monstrosity, but also the genocidal Anfal campaign against the Kurds in 1986–89 and against the Shia after their revolt in 1991 at the end of the Kuwait war. He was also accountable for the large-scale killings of Shia in Medinat al-Thawra, later named Sadr City, in 1999.

After the toppling of the Saddam regime in 2003, Chemical Ali was brought to trial. He showed no sign of remorse and was anything but repentant. He declared that the Halabja episode was necessary to guarantee the security of Iraq. He was convicted and hanged.

## THE ANFAL GENOCIDAL CAMPAIGN

The poison gas attacks on Halabja and on the Iranian troops during the eight-year war were only the most glaring examples of chemical warfare, but Saddam's regime had actually employed chemical agents in twenty-one smaller-scale attacks against the Kurds and during the March 1991 Shia revolt in southern Iraq.

In the case of the Kurds, the gas attacks supplemented traditional weapons in the Anfal campaign, which spanned three years, from 1986 to 1989.

This too was a genocidal campaign where the brutality of the Saddam regime knew no bounds. One outrageous example among many was the shipment by the regime's security agents to Sulaymanyia of fifty-seven boxes, each containing a very pale Kurdish child with the eyes gouged. The extreme pallor of the children indicated they had been bled to death. Their families were not allowed to claim them. They were instead buried in a mass grave, and each family had to pay ID 150 for the burial expense.

The Anfal campaign resulted in the destruction of 4,500 Kurdish villages (and 31 Assyrian ones), the dislocation of 1,000,000 of the 3,5000,000 Iraqi Kurds, the demise of 180,000 Kurds, and the disappearance of more than 17,000 in 1988. This, including the 21 gas attack episodes, likewise raised no international uproar until after the Kuwait war. It would have been politically inconvenient for the big world powers to make any fuss while the war with Iran was still afoot.

# 31

# The Kuwait Debacle

In the disastrous Iran war, Iraq not only consumed all its foreign currency reserves but also became heavily indebted to Saudi Arabia and Kuwait. Saddam had somehow assumed the two countries would forgive the debt because he had spent Iraqi blood and treasure to fight their Shiite nemesis Iran. In fact, the war was a double blessing for those Arab brethren because most of the Iraqi war casualties were Shia, constituting as they did the bulk of the army's rank and file. Khairallah Tilfah, Saddam's father-in-law and a fierce sectarian, had said about Iran early in the war, "We will field against them their own dogs," meaning the Iraqi Shia soldiery. To Saddam's chagrin, both Saudi Arabia and Kuwait refused to forgive Iraq's debt.

Shortly before the Iran war, Saddam might have been further incentivized to wage the battle by the promise of a sliver of Kuwaiti land to provide an access for Iraq to the Persian Gulf. After the end of the war, he demanded the fulfillment of that arrangement, but Kuwait rebuffed him. To add insult to injury, Kuwait began to steal Iraqi oil by cross-border slant drilling from the northern Rumaila field in Iraq. This inflamed Saddam, who was never known for good anger management, so he began to make loud, threatening noises.

He also alienated Egypt when the Iraqi government, the security forces, and the men returning from the Iran war began to harass the large Egyptian workforce that had filled a great many jobs vacated by the Iraqis at the front. There was at least one large demonstration in central Baghdad by Egyptian workers whose payments had been stopped. It was brutally suppressed by the military, who sent in tanks to the area. Eventually most Egyptian workers were expelled from Iraq. Most were not allowed to take with them even their electric appliances and other modest possessions, which piled up in Baghdad's airport. Last but not least, Saddam alarmed Israel, America's staunchest Mideast ally, by declaring he would burn half the country if it dared attack Iraq.

A tense situation thus developed between Iraq and its onetime Arab allies and war financiers. On July 15, 1990, the Iraqi government complained to the Arab League that Kuwait's extraction of oil from the Rumila field had not ceased and was denying Iraq $1 billion a year in revenue, and that Kuwait's and the United Arab Emirates' loans to Iraq should not be regarded as debt. Saddam also accused both countries of being US stooges bent on implementing an American plan to damage the Arab world. He threatened to use force against them. The US responded by sending warships and aerial refueling planes to the Persian Gulf. By July 23, Saddam had amassed thirty thousand troops at the Kuwaiti border, whereupon the US placed its Gulf fleet on alert.

Saddam then met with the US ambassador to Iraq, April Glaspie, who was about to leave on vacation. He complained about the border issue and Kuwait's stealing of Iraqi oil, and he attacked American policy for being pro-Kuwait and UAE but harmful to Iraq. He said, "But we too can harm you" and "We cannot come to you in the US but individual Arabs may reach you." She said she understood Iraq's need for cash to rebuild after the war, that it was not US policy to interfere in border disputes between neighboring Arab states, but that she was concerned about the Iraqi troop buildup at Kuwait's border and the threatening language of recent Iraqi government statements.

It is still debatable how Saddam interpreted Ms. Glaspie's statements at that meeting. Some analysts argued that he saw her giving him a green light to settle the matter as he saw fit. Others contended that she did not purposely intend to do anything of the sort. Tariq Azziz, Saddam's minister of foreign affairs, who was present at the meeting, said later that Saddam did not think Ms. Glaspie was indifferent to the possible use of military action against Kuwait. What is clear, however, is that the US ambassador did not give Saddam a stern and unequivocal warning that the US would certainly intervene in the event of any Iraqi attack on Kuwait. Significantly, Ms. Glaspie was never heard from afterward.

On July 31, talks were held in Jeddah, Saudi Arabia, mediated by Egypt's Hosni Mubarak on behalf of the Arab League. Iraq demanded $10 billion for the lost income from the Rumaila oil field. Kuwait offered $9 billion. It was also reported that a Kuwaiti delegate made remarks offensive to the Iraqis. Saddam responded by ordering the immediate invasion of Kuwait, which began on August 2, 1990, with the bombardment of Kuwait City, the capital. He was probably driven by his usual maniacal rage and the tribal impulse for the raid (*ghezwa*), meanwhile forgetting what Iraqis had always known, that the quest for Kuwait spelled the demise of Iraqi rulers. Neither did Saddam know or remember an old Arab proverb, "Foolishness is the cause of manifest anger, and regret is its sequel."

At the time of the invasion, the Kuwaiti rulers (except the Emir's youngest brother, Ahmad), many professionals, and other citizens had already fled the country. Ahmad was killed during the Iraqi attack on the royal palace. Six days later, Saddam appointed Chemical Ali military governor of Kuwait and declared the country to be Iraq's nineteenth province. Iraqi military forces were now at the Kuwaiti-Saudi border and not far from the major Saudi oil-rich eastern province.

Initially it seemed that President George H. W. Bush was undecided as to how exactly to respond to the situation, but the UK prime minister Margaret Thatcher was all for robust military response by the US and its allies, so she gave Bush a "a transplant of the spine," according to one newspaper comment. But then it was Britain that created Kuwait after World War I by drawing a line in the sand, wasn't it?

The invasion of Kuwait was yet another stupid gamble by Saddam, even worse than the Iran War, for it obviously never occurred to him that the US and the UK would never sit idly by when he had seized the oil assets of Kuwait and was threatening those of Saudi Arabia, both countries US and UK protégés and providers of the majority of Persian Gulf oil. The unfortunate Iraqi people were to pay a heavier price for this adventure than they did even for the Iran War.

Thus started Operation Desert Shield, from August 21, 1990, to January 17, 1991, when US forces landed in Saudi Arabia. President Bush recruited thirty-four countries to contribute military forces or funds or both—the largest alliance since World War II. US Army General Norman Schwarzkopf was appointed commander. The overwhelming majority of forces were from the

US, followed by Saudi Arabia, the United Kingdom, and Egypt, which was enticed by a US promise to forgive a $7 billion debt.

Besides Saudi Arabia and Egypt, the other Arab countries contributing forces to the coalition were Syria, Kuwait, Bahrain, Qattar, UAE, Oman, and Morroco. All except Syria and Oman were staunch supporters of Saddam during the Iran War. Of the English-speaking countries there were Canada, Australia, and New Zeeland. Of the European countries besides the UK were France, Belgium, Holland, Norway, Denmark, Spain, Portugal, Italy, and Greece. Asian countries participating were Pakistan, Bangladesh, Singapore, and South Korea. South America was represented only by Argentina. Germany and Japan did not contribute troops, an act prohibited by their constitutions, but donated funds. Germany contributed $2 billion and Japan $12 billion. This and the $36 billion from Saudi Arabia amounted to $48 billion of the $61.6 billion cost of the First Gulf War.

United Nations Security Council Resolution 678 gave Saddam a deadline of January 15, 1991, to withdraw from Kuwait. The Russians, long friendly with Saddam's regime, warned his circle that the US was now serious about military action to drive Iraqi forces out of Kuwait. The Russians were told that all Iraq asked from them was not to help the US in this conflict. Saddam did not see the writing on the wall or heed the warnings and became ever more obdurate after President H.W. Bush announced, "We will kick his ass off," undoubtedly knowing full well that this would only strengthen Saddam's obstinacy.

After all, Saddam's personality profile was well known to Bush and the CIA, who had recruited Saddam in the 1960s, and it was well described in several publications. Saddam saw himself as an Arab sheik. He had even donned the *Aba* (cloak) of a sheik many times. One does not get an Arab sheik to do something by insulting him. Bush also pronounced Saddam's name like the biblical city of Sodom.

Saddam declared that no foreign nationals in Iraq would be allowed to leave the country because they were "guests"—another "Shaikly" gesture. The implication that they had become hostages was not lost on anyone. Moreover, he had a nice "chat" on TV with a young British boy, while placing his big hand on the boy's shoulder. Saddam, speaking amicably to a British boy? That too sent another shiver through the media.

Operation Desert Storm was launched on January 17, 1991, with a massive five-week aerial and naval bombardment of Iraqi troop concentrations, military command and communication facilities, and stationary and mobile rocket launchers. Supply lines were cut off for many Iraqi units that had been poorly provided with food. A large number of soldiers resorted to eating grass to fend off starvation. One Iraqi commander said that in eight years of war with Iran, his unit had not been subjected to a small fraction of the pounding it got from Desert Storm. Iraq is only twice the size of Illinois, yet more bombs were dropped on it in six weeks than all the bombs used in World War II: 142,000 tons, including 350 tons of depleted uranium shells. This was indeed Colin Powell's "shock and awe."

The bombing was not restricted to military targets. It wrought massive destruction on civilian infrastructure; 80 percent of oil refining capacity; 92 percent of electric power generation; 135 phone networks; more than 100 bridges and radio and TV stations; and railroads, highways and food processing facilities. Hard hit were factories producing medicines, textiles, cement, electric cables, and aluminum. Even sewage processing stations were struck, the equivalent of germ warfare. Sewage flooded the streets in Baghdad, Basra, and other cities, thereby triggering an epidemic of diarrheal diseases that claimed thousands of lives, especially of children, the most vulnerable.

I remember watching on CNN the burning of Baghdad, the fabled city of *One Thousand and One Nights*, hardly restraining my tears and struggling against a dry, gripping, choking sensation in my throat and the weight of a mountain crushing my chest. I had usually been hard of tears until that moment. Untold thousands of Iraqis went hungry, suffering terribly under sanctions and bombardment. Many more thousands died from common illnesses for lack of medicines and damaged health care facilities.

A brother of mine in Baghdad had to drag his diabetic wife, in near coma from very low blood sugar, eighty-four steps up to the doctor's office because the elevator, as most others in the city, was disabled by the loss of electric power. Other diabetics simply died from a shortage of insulin. The French diplomat Eric Rouleau commented in *Foreign Affairs* that the Iraqi people were never consulted about the invasion of Kuwait for which they were being so severely punished, that they understood the use of military power to evict Iraqi troops from Kuwait, but they could not comprehend why the bombing aimed to destroy the country's infrastructure. Neither could I.

This ferocious bombardment lasted five weeks. A US general, quoted before the war, had threatened that Baghdad would be leveled into a parking lot. The US ground offensive followed on February 24, and two days later Iraqi troops began retreating from Kuwait after they'd set fire to 737 oil fields on Saddam's orders.

US bulldozers and tanks carrying antimine plows overran Iraqi trench works at the Saudi-Iraqi border, burying hundreds of Iraqi soldiers alive. Thousands surrendered to avoid this terrible fate. News reporters were banned from the scene, but Patrick Sloyan of *Newsday* somehow managed to see Bradley vehicles and Vulcan armored carriers cross over the trenches and fire at the Iraqi soldiers as the tanks buried them in the sand, their arms sticking out. Defense Secretary Dick Cheney stated that 457 Iraqi soldiers were thus buried during the ground assault.

As the Iraqi troops retreated into Iraq itself, they were hounded and fired at by military aircraft. A large number were thus killed or wounded. This "highway of death" stretched for 60 kilometers (37.5 miles). American, British, and French forces pursued the retreating Iraqis up to 240 kilometers (150 miles) south of Baghdad. Saddam's "elite" Republican Guard suffered the least as they withdrew more swiftly than the unlucky rank and file.

Just a hundred hours after the start of the ground war, President Bush announced the liberation of Kuwait and a cease-fire. A peace conference was held in occupied Iraqi land, and a cease-fire agreement was signed whereby Saddam was not allowed to use fixed-wing aircraft but could use armed helicopters and tanks. Saddam declared Iraq had triumphed in this "mother of all battles." Fringed by his henchmen, he stood erect on a balcony looking down on a crowd and fired from his gun several shots in the air, the usual tribal celebratory gesture. I remembered then that when the Japanese captured Singapore during WWII, Churchill called the event a disgrace, not "the mother of all battles."

Iraqi combat casualties were heavy. Estimates range between twenty to thirty-five thousand deaths. Based on Iraqi POW testimonies, a US Air Force report put the death toll at twenty to twenty-two thousand. A study by the Project on Defense Alternatives placed the combat figures at twenty to twenty-six thousand killed and seventy-five thousand wounded, and the civilian deaths at thirty-five hundred. The latter figure is the same as that given by Beth Daponte's report on the civilian bombing fatalities, but she added a hundred thousand who died from other effects of the war, and there were certainly plenty of those other effects, as I will explain later.

The Kuwait war revealed yet again Saddam's impulsive behavior, poor judgment, lack of knowledge of the actual strength of his military and the loyalty of the ground troops. It showed also his appalling ignorance of the might of the US war machine, with its high technology and modern tactics and strategy. The Iraqi Army rout in Kuwait reminded me yet again of the trouncing by the Israeli forces of the Egyptian army in Sinai in 1956 and again, along with the Syrian and Jordanian armies, in 1967. Saddam, however, was either oblivious of those major events or had not learned their lessons.

The Iraqi Army had no good generals after the 1958 coup and certainly not after the Ba'th takeover in 1968. Almost all the experienced officers were let go and replaced by junior ideologues or opportunists who had little or no combat experience. Furthermore, the army's modus operandi, if any existed, was based on the Soviet defensive entrenchment model and lacked the offensive or surprise initiative. Perhaps even more importantly, the Iraqi rank and file were predominantly Shia who had no love for Saddam, having seen his killing and persecution of their kind and the suppression of their religious leadership and rituals. They were drained by eight years of the Iran war, which had ended only two years before the Kuwait war. No wonder they simply did not want to fight yet another one of Saddam's wars. They died regardless.

# 32

# The Shia Spring Holocaust

On February 15, 1991, nine days before the start of the US ground assault on the Iraqi troops in Kuwait, President H.W. Bush broadcast a speech on Voice of America urging the Iraqi military and people to force Saddam to step aside and for Iraq to comply with UN resolutions and join the family of nations. On the same day, the Voice of Free Iraq, a CIA-sponsored radio station in Saudi Arabia, broadcast a call to the Iraqi people by Salah Omar al-Ali, an exiled member of the Ba'th Revolutionary Command Council, to rise against the dictator Saddam Hussein and dispose of him in order to save themselves from destruction by foreign forces. On March 1, two days after the liberation of Kuwait, President Bush declared again that the Iraqi people should remove Saddam, thereby facilitating the resolution of all problems as well as the acceptance of Iraq back into the family of peace-loving nations.

On March 3, which happened to coincide with the Arabic lunar month of Sha'ban, a tank gunner, back from the Kuwait war, fired at an oversized picture of Saddam staring down over the main square in Basra, to the acclamation of returning soldiers crowding the square. This fairly simple but brave act sparked a popular explosion in southern Iraq, which came to be known as the *Sha'ban Intifadha.* The leader of this Basra revolt was Army officer Mohammad Wali, who assembled a number of military vehicles and attacked government buildings and the main prison, with the overwhelming majority of Basrawis supporting the action.

The revolution spread to the other southern Iraqi cities like fire in dry hay: Amara, Diwaniya, Nasiriya, Samawa, Kut, Hilla, and the holy shrine cities of Karbala and Najaf. All government control in these cities melted away in a few days. A large number of Ba'thist security and government officials were killed. The gates of Saddam's awful prisons, sites of torture and oblivion, were opened, and the ghosts of men, feeble and confused, were released. Many thought that al-Bakr was still president of Iraq, so long had they rotted in those dungeons of no return.

The US troops in the area did nothing to help the revolutionaries. They had their orders to do the opposite. There was an attempt by the rebels to march en masse on Baghdad, but they were blocked by the US military, which allowed an Iraqi division advancing on Basra to slip through US lines. US troops blew up massive stores of Iraqi arms and ammunition to prevent their falling into the hands of the insurgents. They disarmed as many rebels as they could. This was a clear signal to Saddam to mount his counterattack, which he promptly undertook with all the satanic force within him and his "dirty dozen," whose souls no God had ever touched.

Thus began the genocide against the Shia of southern Iraq, the Mesopotamia of old. Without delay, Saddam, now certain the US forces in Iraq would not intervene, dispatched his Republican Guard southward. They had tanks, heavy artillery, and helicopter gunships. The tanks carried signs declaring *"La Shi'eta be'del ya'om,"* meaning "No Shia after today." I saw the photo of such a tank on the front page of the *New York Times* and was horrified by its message of genocide.

The cities of southern Iraq were attacked indiscriminately. Entire sections were leveled by artillery. The Republican Guard, using women and children as human shields, swept through neighborhoods and rounded up all males older than fifteen for mass executions, detention, and torture. The bodies of the dead were mined and left on the streets to rot, be eaten by hungry dogs and rats, or be buried en masse by bulldozers. Thousands others were sent away to prisons outside Baghdad where they were subjected to unimaginable torture. A great many died, and many others were never seen again. The entire population of southern Iraq was terrorized. Fleeing civilians were strafed by helicopter gunships, which also dumped on them phosgene, mustard, and CX poison gases.

The *Christian Science Monitor* published a painful account by a US pilot who was flying his military aircraft over the southern Iraqi town of Soug al-Shiukh. He watched in anguish as Saddam's helicopters were flying below his squadron, firing indiscriminately at a crowded marketplace in the town. He felt great guilt for not intervening to stop the massacre because his orders were crystal clear—not to intervene.

These genocidal acts were ordered by Saddam and executed by his Republican Guard under the command of Chemical Ali and Saddam's son-in-law Kamel Hussein. I saw Chemical Ali on US television delivering a destructive kick with his heavy military boot to the face of a captured man brought to him for interrogation and had been forced to kneel on the ground with his hands tied behind his back.

The holocaust reached its darkest peak in the sacred city of Karbala, home to the shrines of Imam Husayn and his half-brother al-Abbas. The rebels had taken over the city. After furious bombardment by Saddam's heavy artillery and firing by helicopter gunships, his Republican Guard entered the town in their big tanks displaying the signs that said "No Shia after today," where-upon a great number of the rebels and their leaders took refuge in the two shrines. All the atrocities I described earlier were repeated in a more savage manner. Untold numbers of people were summarily executed. Men were picked up from the streets and hung by the neck from the tanks' gun barrels; clerics caught walking or fleeing were showered by automatic gunfire.

Loud speakers instructed the population to leave the city. When they did, they were fired upon from helicopters, which also dumped poison gas on them. The sister of an Iraqi American friend of mine joined thousands of others who sought shelter in the fabled date palms and orange groves of Karbala. She, all her children, and hundreds of others were killed by helicopter gunfire. The tops of the palm trees were destroyed by artillery to render them useless for sheltering fleeing civilians. A cousin of my father-in-law had barely stepped out of the front door of his home when a cannon shot lacerated his abdomen. His intestines tumbled on the ground in view of his panic-stricken family. He died instantly. The main hospital, al-Husayni, was overwhelmed by the deluge of dead and wounded. It, too, was targeted by the Republican Guard. They stormed it, killed the patients, threw others out of the windows, and executed the doctors and nurses.

The entire section of town surrounding the shrines was leveled by artillery, and the shrines were encircled. They had heavy doors. Kamil Hussein scanned Imam Husayn's shrine and shouted, "You are Husayn and I am Hussein; let's see who will prevail," then ordered the cannoneers to smash the gates. They entered the sacred places in both al-Husayn and al-Abbas shrines and killed the thousands of people sheltering there with automatic weapons. A Western visitor to Karbala after the disaster described the devastation as being worse than post–World War II Dresden.

It is ironic that a few years later Kamil Hussein himself was brought by the Republican Guard to circle the Iman Husayn shrine before being taken to Jordan for an operation for a head injury. Saddam had hit him on the head with the butt of his handgun for failing to detect a military plot against the regime. Sometime later he and his brother, a namesake and another son-in-law of Saddam, fled with their families to Jordan after a rupture with Saddam's notorious son Uday and perhaps with Saddam himself.

They were interviewed by the CIA in Amman and divulged some state secrets. They were later sweet-talked by Uday into returning to Baghdad, assuming Saddam would not widow his daughters and orphan his grandchildren. It is a sign of their stupidity that they had not taken the measure of Saddam during all the years they'd served him. They were both killed shortly after they returned to Baghdad. Most Iraqis had no doubt the brothers' fate was divine punishment for the desecration of the Karbala shrines.

The other sacred city, Najaf, is eighty kilometers (fifty miles) southeast of Karbala and is the home of the shrine of Imam Ali himself. It houses the religious hawza (the top five Shia religious figures) and seminaries attended by students from all over the Muslim world. It is also the birthplace of some of the greatest Arab poets, including al-Jawahiri, whom I mentioned earlier. The city, moreover, has Meqbarat al-Salam (the Cemetery of Peace), which had for many centuries received the Shia dead for burial. Among their other atrocities, the Republican Guard overran the cemetery with bulldozers, overturning the innumerable graves contained there, a mass desecration of the dead perhaps not seen since the beginning of human history.

After the toppling of Saddam in 2003, mass graves containing thousands of skeletons were discovered all over southern Iraq. One in particular was believed to hold ten thousand victims. Heartrending videos and pictures showed men and women crying, grieving, and digging, some with their bare hands, in and around the graves for a piece of clothing, an earring, a bracelet, a hair clip, or any artifact that might identify a skeleton as belonging to a loved one.

The lucky Shia who somehow survived the holocaust fled on foot toward the southern marshes, Kuwait, Syria, and Iran—men, women, children, and the elderly. Thousands perished from hunger, fatigue, sickness, and the elements. A Chicago surgeon, a friend of mine and a relative of my wife, was watching television when he spotted his brother, also a physician, among the masses of Shia refugees in the Iraq-Kuwait border town of Safwan. The brother later went to Iran, then moved to England with the help of the humanitarian Lady Emma Nicholson, who was then a member of the British Parliament.

A great number of the Safwan refugees were transferred by the Americans to camps in Saudi Arabia where they were terribly mistreated. Many were beaten and raped by the Saudi overseers even though they were the victims of Saddam whom the Saudis had helped evict from Kuwait with their $50 billion contribution. The Americans could not have fathomed the pernicious hatred the Wahabi Saudis harbor for the Shia.

I met one of those rape victims at Cook County Hospital, an Iraqi pathologist and a fine man who was eventually allowed to come to the US as a refugee. The Iraqi refugees at the notorious

Saudi camps mounted a protest against their awful mistreatment. The result was a shocking scene I watched on CNN where some of the protesters were buried in the desert sand up to their chins and had their lips sewn by harsh jute threads.

The Shia fleeing on foot to Iran died daily by the hundreds along the hazardous trek to the east. Many were killed by land mines laid by the Iraqi Army during the Iran war. Luckier were those who fled to Syria and settled in Damascus around the shrine of Sayyida Zaynab, the sister of Iman Husayn. Other desperate tens of thousands took refuge in the Haweeza marshes close to the border with Iran. This triggered a protracted vicious campaign by Saddam's military against the marshes, their refugees, and their indigent inhabitants. They wreaked destruction using heavy artillery and helicopter gunships. They burned the reed huts that had housed the marsh people for millennia, killing and forcing relocation of the people. They poisoned the waters to exterminate man, buffalo, fish, and fowl, and dried up the marshes by diverting the river waters. But more about this human and ecological disaster later. Thus ended the Shia rebellion after a month of massive war crimes by Saddam's Republican Guard and loyalist troops.

I can hardly suppress a sad smile when nowadays much of the mass media and several of my friends reiterate that the 2003 US invasion of Iraq triggered the sectarian divide and the civil war that followed. Such statements are characteristic of "blame the foreigner, not ourselves" syndrome, endemic in the Arab world. Have they not read the modern history of Iraq? Have they had their heads in a hole during the dark era of the Ba'th, culminating in the barbarous rule of Saddam? In fact and quite sadly, a majority of non Iraqi Arabs still consider Saddam a hero. A golden statue of his is to be erected in Amman, Jordan, with money provided by his daughter, money stolen from the people of Iraq.

# 33

# Another Anfal for the Kurds

The Kurdish uprising in the north of Iraq occurred almost simultaneously with that of the Shia in the south after the official end of the Kuwait war. It started in Rania on March 3, 1991, when the Kurdistan Democratic Party (KDP) and the Patriotic Union of Kurdistan (PUK) joined forces with more than fifty thousand deserters from the army and the home guard militia (Jahsh). They fanned out to take most cities in the north, including Kirkuk, but not Mosul, within ten days. The crowds shouted the slogans Democracy for Iraq, and Autonomy for Kurdistan. Jalal Talabani, who twelve years later would become president of Iraq, proposed a southward march on Baghdad.

In the city of Sulaymaniya, the rebels took over the notorious Directorate of General Security, obtaining fourteen tons of documents pertaining to the genocidal Anfal campaign of the 1980s and other barbarities and delivered them to Human Rights Watch for the world to learn of Saddam's crimes. There was general jubilation in Kurdistan, but it did not last long. As in the South, the

US allowed Saddam to march his Republican Guard and other loyalist troops for the counterattack.

Tanks, heavy artillery, and helicopter gunships headed north and there began a repetition of the atrocities committed in the south. The Peoples Mujahedeen of Iran (MEK), a great number of whom had been living as refugees in Iraq after the Khomeini revolution, assisted Saddam's forces, not only in the north, but also in the south. A prominent member of the group, Maryam Rajavi, declared, "Take the Kurds under your tanks and spare your bullets for the Iranian Revolutionary Guard." About 750,000 Kurds fled toward Iran and 300,000 toward Turkey:—women, children, and the aged.

The Kurdish region of Iraq is mountainous and remains cold in early March. Five hundred to a thousand civilians died daily from exposure, hunger, and disease at the Turkish border. The refugees in Turkey, a NATO member and US ally, were treated very badly by the Turkish military. Blankets, food, and water sent to them by the UN and other organizations were stolen by Turkish soldiers and police, and victims of diarrheal diseases, including cholera, were denied treatment by the Turkish authorities. This led to a confrontation between the British Royal Marines in the area and the Turkish military in the town of Yaroshiva.

The UN Security Council took its time until April 5, 1991, to condemn the Iraqi government for oppressing the Kurds (but not the Shia) and to call on it to respect the human rights of its citizens. The timing of the declaration was quite interesting in that it coincided with the Iraqi government's announcement the same day of the crushing of the uprising in all of Iraq.

The number of Shia and Kurds killed and injured during the March 1991 rebellion is surely over one hundred thousand, but accurate statistics are not available for obvious reasons. Tens of thousands of Shia victims were buried in mass graves or died during their flight. Thousands of others died in jail or from injuries they sustained during the rebellion. The Kurdish victims faced similar circumstances.

Altogether, figures from 20,000 to 130,000 are cited for the Shia dead, not including the tens of thousands who perished in the southern marshes' operations, and claims are for 20,000 to 100,000 Kurdish fatalities in the north. The higher figures in the two ranges are much more likely. The real numbers of Shia and Kurdish deaths are probably higher still if one considers the victims who perished subsequently from diarrheal and other diseases, hunger, and exposure. These numbers do not include those who were injured and maimed, often for life. Relief for the Kurds, however, came fairly quickly when, in mid-April 1991, the US forces drove sixty miles into Iraqi Kurdish territory to build camps for the displaced Kurds, and (much more importantly) when the US declared a safe hamlet and a no-fly zone over Kurdistan. No such protection was given to the Shia.

The US silence about the genocidal atrocities Saddam committed while crushing the March uprising is a black chapter in the history of US foreign policy and a resonant indictment of the concept of realpolitik that, like Henry Kissinger before them, Messers Bush, Brent Scowcroft, and Colin Powell subscribed to. Furthermore, I have no doubt whatsoever that Saudi Arabia had also prevailed on its longtime friend President Bush to allow Saddam to quell the rebellion lest Iran gain more power in the region. After all, the Saudis did contribute the lion's share of the Gulf War cost. And did the lives of millions of Iraqis really matter to them?

Pronouncements by US officials to explain their inaction during Saddam's counterattack on his people lacked honesty, defied credulity, and left little room for trust in the steadfastness of US foreign policy. As Saddam's forces were about to finish off the Shia and Kurdish rebels at the end of March, President Bush stated that he had made it clear from the beginning that it was not an objective of the coalition or the United States to overthrow Saddam Hussein, that he did not think the Shiites in the south, those in Baghdad, or the Kurds in the north felt that the United States would come to their assistance to overthrow Saddam, and that he had not misled anybody about the intentions of the United States.

In fact, the prewar statements by President Bush and others left no doubt among Iraqis that the US would come to their aid if they rose up against the regime. However, it became very clear from the beginning of the rebellion that, far from aiding the rebels, the Bush administration actually worked against them and allowed Saddam to crush them. The deputy director of operations for the Joint Chiefs of Staff, Major General Martin Brandtner, stated that there was no intention on the part of US forces to let any weapons slip through to the rebels or to play any role in assisting either side. A grammar schooler would understand that by not helping the rebels achieve victory, the US was actually helping Saddam's regime to survive, and so it did.

When the Shia uprising erupted, the US secretary of defense, Dick Cheney, said that he was not sure whose side he'd want to be on. I was reminded of that statement many years later when Mr. Cheney received a heart transplant. Some local newspaper I happened to glimpse at declared in bold print, "Innocent Heart Confined to Cheney for Life." Coalition commander Norman Schwarzkopf later regretted that the ceasefire agreement allowed Saddam to use helicopters, but intimated that helping the rebels would have strengthened Iran.

US State Department spokesman Richard Boucher said on March 6, 1991, that he did not think outside powers should be interfering in the internal affairs of Iraq, as though those "internal affairs" did not constitute genocide. Moreover, the Bush administration accused Iran of arming the rebels, as though it was a bad thing to do so. Furthermore, the chairman of the Joint Chiefs of Staff, Colin Powell, explained in his book *My American Journey* that while Bush might have given encouragement to the rebels, the practical intention was to leave Baghdad enough power to survive as a threat to Iran.

In 2006, the president of the Washington Kurdish Institute called the US stance during the March 1991 rebellion a betrayal of Iraq, and attributed it to a dangerous illusion of maintaining stability in the Mideast, purchased with the blood of its people and resulting in such horrors as the massive 1991 bloodletting of Iraqis seeking to overthrow Saddam. Likewise, the late Ahmed al-Chalabi said in 2011, "Prompted by realists in his administration such as Colin Powell, Brent Scowcroft, and Richard Haas, Mr. Bush allowed Saddam to fly military aircraft to put down the uprising. While thousands of US troops were on Iraqi soil and in some cases were close enough to watch, the tyrant unleashed the power of modern weaponry against men, women, and children."

In 2011, the US ambassador to Iraq, James Jeffrey, apologized officially to Iraqi politicians and southern tribal sheiks for the US attitude in 1991, whereupon Adel Abdul Mehdi, a Shiite political figure, responded that had the US aided the 1991 uprising, it would have achieved a much better outcome than that of the 2003 war, because the role of the Iraqi people (not a foreign invasion) would have been paramount in toppling the regime. Ayatollah Basheer al-Najafi, a prominent member of the Shia Hawza, said the US apology had come too late. It did not change what happened and did not bring the victims back to their wives, sons, and siblings.

Those of my readers who prefer audiovisuals over text would be well advised to see Michael Wood's 1993 documentary *Saddam's Killing Fields* and Abbas Fadhil's film *Dawn of the World*.

# 34

# The Marsh Arabs

The marshes of southern Mesopotamia (*al-ahwar* in Arabic) had originally covered 7,700 square miles (20,000 square kilometers) of freshwater lakes and wetlands in southern and southeastern Iraq. Before the era of dams and water diversions, al-*ahwar* constituted until fairly recently the largest wetland ecosystem in West Asia.

The marshlands comprise three main water bodies. The largest is the Hammar Marsh, just south of the Tigris River but largely supplied by the Euphrates River, which often flowed into it near the city of Nasiriya. It stretched eastward, often overflowing onto Shatt al-Arab, the confluence of the Tigris and Euphrates rivers at Qurna north of Basra. The Haweezeh Marsh, just east of the Tigris wherefrom it gets its waters, extends eastward across the border into Western Iran. The Central Marshes, between the two rivers, are also supplied by the Tigris, which, augmented by tributaries from Iran, continues on a southeasterly course to empty into Shatt al-Arab.

The marshes have been home to an extensive variety of animal and plant life, several species of fish, millions of birds of many species, as well as millions of other migratory birds, including herons, flamingos, and pelicans stopping over during their winter journey from north to south.

The Marsh Arabs are the descendants of the ancient Sumerians. They live in sophisticated reed homes erected on the many islands in the marshes and commute by canoe-like boats (*mesh'hoof*) between the numerous islands. They entertain visitors—tribal sheiks, hunters, and foreigners—in elaborate reed reception halls (*diwans*). They live on rice, fish, fowl, and the milk from their water buffaloes, from which they make delicious (and nowadays deemed unhealthy) white butter (*gaimer*), very popular among Iraqis, who eat it mixed with date syrup. Even the Iraqis in the diaspora have somehow managed to procure this taste bud pleaser.

The draining of the marshes had started in the early 1950s, during the monarchy, when the British engineer Frank Haig recommended in 1951 a network of canals and dykes on the lower reaches of the Tigris and Euphrates to drain some of the marsh waters to bare more land for agriculture. The theme was consistent with the passion for dams in the four decades from the 1940s through the 1970s and the desire to increase cultivable land and generate hydroelectric power. This was not tempered with due awareness of unintended negative consequences. For instance, there was the salting of the Nile delta of Egypt after the construction of the Aswan High Dam. The silt carried by the Nile was much reduced, allowing the salty Mediterranean to creep up onto the delta. The Iraqi marsh waters, however, had been reduced by only 10 percent before the time of Saddam.

After 1988, the process of water diversion from the marshes picked up pace, but the work accelerated greatly after the Shia uprising of March 1991, when tens of thousands sought refuge in the marshes to escape the Republican Guard's genocidal campaign. I have already described the atrocities Saddam's forces committed in the marshes immediately after defeating the uprising, but these crimes continued unabated well into 1994 and afterward. The United Nations announced plans to set up a post in the Hammar march to render humanitarian aid to the thousands of marsh indigents and estimated two hundred thousand rebel refugees. The relief workers sent there were blocked from entering the area by Saddam's forces. The US military, still heavily present in the Gulf region, did not intervene.

Lady Emma Nicholson, British member of parliament in 1991, was alarmed at the plight of the Shia of southern Iraq, especially the Marsh Arabs. Unable to enter Iraq from Kuwait after the end of the first Gulf War, she traveled to Iran and, with considerable help from the Iranian authorities, crossed the border into Iraq, finding herself among the Marsh Arabs. She witnessed the massive suffering and the destruction of a five-thousand-year-old way of life. She said she was surprised the international community, while working hard on behalf of the Kurdish victims in northern Iraq, was almost unaware of the Shia suffering in the south, so she founded the nongovernmental organization AMAR, acronym for Assisting Marsh Arabs and Refugees, to publicize the human and ecological disaster and enlist the help of the UN and other organizations.

In only two months, from December 1991 through January 1992, seventy marsh villages were destroyed, the homes burned down, and fifty thousand dwellers removed. In April 1992, Saddam's government, in violation of the ceasefire agreement with the US, began to use fixed-wing aircraft in the attacks on the marshlands, an escalation no doubt observed by US AWACs and satellites monitoring the region. The US State Department declared that Iraq had dumped toxic chemicals in the marshes, but stopped short of threatening Saddam with any punitive action.

In July 1992, the draining of the marshes continued, with work proceeding at a fast pace to complete a drainage system consisting of a large river and three long canals. Earthen barriers were being built to block the Tigris tributaries feeding the Amara marshes, and the Euphrates was dammed below Nasiriya. A curfew was enforced throughout the south. Marsh Arabs were again ordered to evacuate and their homes were burned. Helicopter gunships strafed escapees, and large numbers were rounded up and taken to grim detention facilities in central Iraq.

In August 1992, the US, Britain, and France accused Iraq of undertaking a systematic military campaign against the Marsh Arabs and warned the Iraqi government that it could face consequences. President Bush had waited until this same month, fully a year and a half after Saddam's onslaught on southern Iraq, to announce that the US and its allies would enforce a no-fly zone south of the thirty-second parallel to protect dissidents in the south from attacks by the regime. In fact, Bush was not about to intervene because he did not want Iran to get stronger, and Cheney "did not know" which side he should be on.

Saddam must have understood Bush'es announcement to be merely window dressing, for in March 1993, the UN reported that in the preceding months, hundreds of executions had been carried out in the marsh areas. Saddam's forces did not use aircraft after the establishment of the no-fly zone in the south, but resorted to long-range artillery and ground assaults, causing heavy casualties and destruction of living quarters. Mass executions continued. President Bush was not angry this time, presumably because Saddam had not challenged the ban on aircraft. In October 1993,

Michael Wood produced an excellent film on the Marsh debacle in *Viewpoint* on Britain's Independent TV.

In November 1993, Iran reported the Marsh Arabs could no longer fish or cultivate rice and that 60,000 of them had fled to Iran since 1991 and appealed to the world community to provide help. Not much help was forthcoming, certainly not from the US. Many Iraqi Americans donated money for the cause, but it must have been a drop in the bucket. By the mid-1990s there were between 80,000 and 120,000 marsh refugees in Iran.

In the same month (November 1993), the UN reported that 40 percent of the marsh waters had been drained. Satellite pictures showed the entire central marshes to be dry. A month later, the US State Department issued another toothless warning that Iraq was using indiscriminate military operations in the south, which included the burning of villages and forced relocation of noncombatants. The US could have stopped the genocide if it put its mind to it, but it did not.

In February 1994, Saddam's military and forced laborers managed to divert the Tigris water south and east of the main marshlands, causing ten-foot-high floods in the surrounding farmland to render it useless and force the people hiding there back to the already dried-up marshes, where they would be easily eliminated. In the following month, a team of British scientists stated that 57 percent of the marshes were drained and that the entire wetland ecosystem in southern Iraq will completely disappear within twenty years. In the following month, US officials put out yet another report that Iraq was still conducting military operations in remote areas of the marshes.

Seven animal species went extinct during the drainage of the marshes, including the gray wolf, the Indian crested porcupine, and the Bunn short-tail bandicoot. Other species are at risk of extinction: 90 percent of the Basra reed warblers are gone and half of the world's marbled teal species. Also dying out are the African darter, the sacred ibis, the Maxwelli subspecies of the smooth-coated otter, and the Eurasian otter.

By the time of the 2003 US invasion of Iraq, 90 percent of the marshes had been drained, the Hammar and the central marshes almost completely, and the Haweezeh 65 percent. After the invasion, the local population destroyed Saddam's dikes. The new Iraqi government together with UN and US agencies, and record rains in Turkey, combined to reinundate the dry marshes. By late 2006 they regained 58 percent of their original water volume and large numbers of the displaced Marsh Arabs flocked back.

But this was not the happy ending because of the later onset of drought; the building of dams at a furious pace on the Tigris and Euphrates in Turkey, and on the Euphrates in Syria; and also because of ISIS (Da'esh) control of dams on both rivers in Syria and Iraq. These have combined to reduce again the marsh waters to 30 percent. Perhaps worse still, the much-reduced Tigris and Euphrates waters, hence of Shatt al-Arab, have caused a marked reduction of silt deposition at the outlet of the Shatt, causing the Persian Gulf waters to creep up past the confluence of the Tigris and Euphrates and into the marshes themselves. This salting has caused the death of many fish species, obliging many Marsh Arabs to leave the area again.

One can only hope this will not be the sad ending, the loss of millennia-old wetland ecosystem.

THE MARSHES: TWO MARSH ARABS ROWING IN A BOAT
(MASH'HOOF). US ARMY CORPS OF ENGINEERS.

# 35

# Twelve Years of Lethal Sanctions

As I have explained, the Kuwait war brought extensive damage upon Iraq's civilian infrastructure. During the war, 142,000 tons of bombs were dropped on Iraq, more than in all of World War II, including 350 tons of bombs coated with depleted uranium. This was followed by Saddam's genocidal campaigns against the Shia and the Kurds, both encouraged to rise but later betrayed by President George H. W. Bush. Sadly, what succeeded those appalling events was to prove even more lethal over the next twelve years: the sanctions regime from 1991 to 2003.

Five months after the end of the war, the UN Security Council, prompted by the US, issued Resolution 661, imposing harsh economic sanctions and a strangling trade embargo on Iraq, such that the country could no longer sell oil, almost its only source of income, and could not import items essential to repair the damaged infrastructure of agriculture, industry, health care, and education. Only food, medicine, and a few humanitarian necessities were allowed.

The problem was that the list of proscribed items included almost everything considered to have the potential for dual civilian and military use. This included graphite pencils for students; nitroglycerine to treat impending heart attacks; fertilizers and spare parts for machinery and medical equipment, ostensibly because graphite could be used in nuclear furnaces; nitroglycerine to make dynamite; fertilizers to produce poison gas; and industrial spare parts to fix military hardware.

Even more perplexing was the prohibition of such items as X-ray films and machines, radiation therapy equipment, transportation vehicles, and even women's sanitary necessities. Individual Americans could not use US mail to send a meaningful quantity of essential drugs, medical supplies, journals, or textbooks because there was a twelve-ounce limit on packages to Iraq.

In the absence of oil revenue and with almost no foreign reserves, Iraq could no longer import essential items even if they were not prohibited. What money was available Saddam would obviously spend to guarantee the loyalty of his military, security services, and the inner core of the regime. After all, he'd not only gone to war against Kuwait but also against his own population. Consequently, Resolution 661 and even the later "Oil-for-Food" Resolution 986 of April 1995 resulted in massive suffering and death that considerably exceeded that of the Gulf War itself and its immediate aftermath.

In the early period of the sanctions, not much of their devastating consequences was reported in the US or Western media, but gradually the facts began to surface. In 1991, toward the end of the Gulf War, I gave a talk at Cook County Hospital about the catastrophic effects on Iraq of the massive bombing campaign to a large assembly of attending physicians, medical residents, and other concerned individuals in the Chicago area. The audience was shocked by the gruesome facts, and many people pledged to spread the word in their communities.

In 1997, I met with Drs. Quentin Young, then no longer at CCH; Peter Orris, a friend and a member of the Department of Occupational Medicine at County; Ronald Shansky, the friend from my residency time at the hospital; Linda Murray, a physician who had been a medical resident of mine many years earlier; and Kathy Kelly of Voices in the Wilderness, a humanitarian organization dedicated to publicizing the condition of and rendering help to various victimized communities and individuals around the world.

I was asked by this group to contribute an article about Iraq under the sanctions regime to *Physicians Forum*, a Chicago Bulletin. It was published in the 1997 fall issue under the title "The Children of Iraq Are Dying." I followed this with "Iraq: The Tragedy of Disease, Deformity, and Death," published in the 2000 spring issue of the *AAUG Monitor* (Arab-American University Graduates). In June 1997, I participated in a symposium on Iraq at the National Convention of the Arab-American Anti-discrimination Committee (ADC) in Washington, DC, to present a talk and video, "Iraq: A Human Tragedy."

What happened to the Iraqi people, especially the children, during the sanctions regime is a horror story that occupies a front seat in the hall of twentieth-century calamities. What is even more disturbing is that the sanctions were sustained despite the common knowledge that they destroyed only the ordinary people and had no impact on the heavily armed Saddam regime that had killed over a million of its citizens, and despite the obvious impossibility for the people to topple that regime, having been betrayed by our government and its allies after the March 1991 rebellion.

In 1995, the sanctions had caused the death of a million Iraqis, 570,000 of whom were children under five years old; toddlers had "old man faces," and four million people, one-fourth the total population at the time, were starving (UN Food and Agriculture Organization, FAO). The children were being felled by diarrheal diseases, malnutrition, and terribly underfunded hospitals lacking intravenous fluids, drugs, and vaccines. A United Nations report described the children's condition in Iraq as worse than sub-Saharan Africa, that an Iraqi child was dying every ten minutes, and of the survivors a third were stunted, another third underweight, and one in six wasted.

A 1995 FAO mission to Baghdad sampled twenty-five clusters totaling 2,120 children from different neighborhoods of the city. The findings, published in the British medical journal *Lancet*, were as follows: Compared to prewar levels, infant mortality had increased twofold; the death rate of children under five years fivefold; and diarrheal conditions threefold. Stunted growth had increased from 12 percent to 28 percent, the same as in the Congo; low body weight from 7 percent to 29 percent; and wasting from 1 percent to 12 percent, similar to Madagascar's.

The United Nations International Child Emergency Fund (UNICEF) conducted interviews in Iraq and concluded that among children younger than five years, forty-seven thousand excess deaths had occurred during the initial seven months of sanctions. In 1997 it declared that the age-adjusted relative child mortality rate in Iraq was 3.2 times the prewar level and that 960,000 children, a third of all Iraqi children, were chronically malnourished. The Swiss Society of Preventive Medicine reported in 1995 a doubling or greater of the rates of polio, neonatal tetanus, cholera, leishmaniasis, and malaria, all diseases conquered many years before I finished medical school in 1968.

There was also a large outbreak of brucellosis, also known as Malta fever, which causes a painful enlargement of lymph nodes and fever and may involve the joints, spine, and heart valves. There were so many cases that in only one city, 369 patients were reported by Dr. Jawad al-Khafaji to have been admitted to Ibn Sayf Hospital in al-Musayab city in Babylon Province in the year 2000, a full quarter of them children ranging from less than one to five years old. There was also a large outbreak of the disease in Baghdad itself, described by Drs. A. al-Abbasi and S. Alwan. My friend and medical school classmate Dr. Namuk al-Khateeb told me he'd seen hundreds of cases of brucellosis while practicing in Baghdad. Like too many other physicians, he left Iraq during the sanctions regime for New Zeeland, then moved on to Australia.

Also in 1995, the World Health Organization (WHO) stated that there was a sixfold rise in the death rate for children under five years old and that the majority of Iraqis were on a semistarvation diet. Furthermore, Dr. Leon Eisenberg of the Harvard team visiting Baghdad described epidemics of gastroenteritis, typhoid, cholera, and marasmus, a wasting malnutritional disease I had only read about but never seen in Baghdad before I left it. He declared the sanctions represented a war against public health and that they had no basis in law, morality, or humanity. He appealed to the American Medical Association to oppose them.

The condition of the hospitals was abominable. They were empty and dirty and lacked important medicines, intravenous fluids, and vaccines. Abdominal surgery was being performed without prior X-rays or sterile gloves. There was no heating, and patients were asked to bring their own blankets and heaters if they had any. Mothers were often told to take their children home to die.

In 1997, a delegation of British physicians visited major

hospitals in Iraq, then published its findings in the prestigious *British Medical Journal*. One-third of hospital beds had been closed. One-third of medical equipment was nonfunctional for lack of spare parts. Heating, lighting, clean water, and sewage disposal were seriously lacking. And the average patient stay had been reduced by 50 percent.

In Ibn al-Atheer Hospital, quite modern and advanced before the sanctions, the cleaning staff was reduced from twenty to only two. The monthly cleaning budget was cut down to 1,500 Iraqi dinars, the equivalent of $1 US at the time. And bedsheets and blankets were used to clean the floors. Many wards lacked working toilets and sewage drains, and were infested with vermin, flies, and other insects. In the main general hospital in Mosul, Iraq's second largest city, surgical operations were cut down from the already reduced figure of fifteen per week to only two. Surgeons opted for operations taking less than one hour and requiring fewer sutures. And only three sutures were used to close an appendix operation.

The introduction of Resolution 989, the Oil-for-Food program, in April 1995, four years after the implementation of the sanctions regime, was largely a window dressing maneuver, for it did not stop the people's misery. Iraq was allowed to sell some of its oil for food. Much of the money thus raised, however, was paid out for war reparations to other governments and private companies. What ultimately trickled down to the Iraqi citizen was a mere twenty-five cents, providing only 25 percent of the calories needed to maintain reasonable health and functionality.

Arthur Holdbrook, the head of the food program in Iraq, declared that Resolution 989 had not solved the problems of unsafe drinking water, lack of hospital equipment, or infrastructure disrepair. Furthermore, two top UN aid officials in Iraq placated their conscience by resigning because they could not operate meaningfully under the sanction regime.

Saddam's government imported low-quality foodstuff. Rice sacks often contained tiny stone pebbles. Poor quality or sham medications were procured from Third World companies, often of nascent lineage, poor quality controls, or fraudulent practices. Better medicines and foods were hoarded by Saddam's sons, relatives, Republican Guard members, and other loyalists and introduced into the black market to earn windfall profits.

Another tragic event of the Gulf War was the use by the US of depleted uranium to coat projectiles intended for high penetration, the metal having replaced titanium for the purpose. Although depleted uranium has low-level radioactivity, it is nevertheless "eternally" radioactive. The half-life of a radioactive metal is the time it takes for half of the radioactivity to dissipate. For uranium-238 the rate is 4.468 billion years, roughly the age of Earth, a decay rate of one part per million every 6,446 years, longer than the age of urban civilization. The corresponding figures for uranium-235 are 700 million years, one part per million every 1,010 years. Put another way, the time it takes for the radioactivity of uranium-238 to disappear completely is twice the age of our earth.

Upon the coated projectile's impact, the uranium burns and atomizes into tiny particles that are inhaled by people and animals, contaminates the soil and water, and enters into the food cycle. This most probably accounted for an astounding rise in the incidence of cancers, especially of the blood, brain, and soft tissues, particularly among children. Many such cancers were fast-growing.

I saw a twenty-four-year-old refugee from southern Iraq at the Fantus Clinic of CCH. He had fled after the March rebellion of 1991, was herded with other refugees to the inhospitable camps in

Saudi Arabia, and was then allowed to come to the US. He had a tumor of the thyroid gland the size of a lemon. When I asked him how long he'd had the growth, he exclaimed, "By Allah, Doctor, it was the size of a chickpea only three weeks ago!" I referred him to the oncology service at the hospital to treat what was a rapidly growing thyroid cancer.

There was a tenfold rise in the incidence of lymphoma and forty-fold increase in the rate of brain cancer in soldiers returning from the area around Basra, which was subjected to the heaviest bombardment. Studies by four Mosul universities documented a tenfold rise in cancers after 1991. Most of the victims could not be given radiation therapy because the necessary equipment was barred by the sanctions. A classmate of mine from grammar school and another from Baghdad College both died of brain cancer. Dr. Carol Sikora of the WHO Cancer Program and Professor of Cancer Medicine at the London Imperial College School of Medicine protested loudly against this prohibition and declared that physicians should not keep quiet about such grave matters.

Another sequel to depleted uranium was a tremendous rise in the frequency of amenorrhea (cessation of the menstrual cycle) in young women, miscarriages, intrauterine fetal demise, and (most awfully) congenital birth defects, many quite grotesque. Such birth defects were also noted in families of Gulf War veterans from the US and allied nations. Dr. Jenan Ali of the Basra General Hospital had a whole album of pictures of babies born without limbs, genitalia, eyes, or brains, or having frightful deformities of the head or spine. In Mosul, there was a report of 120 families having twenty malformed newborns whose fathers had served in the Gulf War.

Then there was also the Gulf War syndrome, affecting many Gulf War veterans from the US, Canada, Britain, Australia, and New Zealand. This was an insidious illness that sapped the strength of victims, leaving them weak and disabled, and culminating in some cases in death or suicide. Medical and radiation experts suspected the syndrome resulted from low-level radiation illness, but Western governments muddled up the discussion, leading many to suspect they wanted to sweep the matter under the rug. Doctors and scientists were subjected to pressure or actually fired, and many veterans' medical records and computer disks were "lost."

It wasn't until August 1996 that the UN Sub-Commission on Human Rights declared that depleted uranium was a weapon of mass destruction. Its use, however, continued and it was sold to seventeen countries.

Add to that the scourge of the screw worm fly. The insect was indigenous to the US, Mexico, and Central America but unknown in Iraq until it suddenly appeared north of Baghdad in 1996, then it rapidly spread to twelve of Iraq's eighteen provinces. Livestock was devastated, as the insects' larvae can actually consume a whole cow in one week. The flies can be packed in boxes and dropped from the air. Only US, British, and UN military aircraft could fly in and out of Iraq. A biological war expert in the German Bundestag stated that Iraq is the latest victim of what appears to be a deliberate introduction of the screw worm fly.

A major factor in the destruction of Iraq by the sanctions was the collapse of the Iraqi currency, the dinar, and the resultant inflation, resembling the nosedive of the German mark after World War I. The Iraqi dinar fell like a rock. It was worth $3.30 US before the Gulf war, whereas after the war $1 US became worth ID 4,500 in 1994 and ID 2,000 five years later. This made it extremely difficult for the government and Iraqi charitable foundations to purchase food, medicine, and other necessities, and far more so for individuals and families, even among the once affluent professional class. People had to carry sacks of nearly worthless high-denomination bills to purchase ordinary items or conduct simple commercial transactions. Most Iraqi Americans were constantly sending cash contributions to family and friends who had been well off before the sanctions.

On a visit to Iraq, I was quite appalled by the misery and deprivation all around. Households were selling much of their furniture, home appliances, and even room doors and windows to procure food, also (especially) medicine for their children and loved ones. Many widows of the Iran and Kuwait wars were selling themselves to scrape a living for their children. Some were executed by the regime, which had made a cynical tilt toward religiosity.

In the Kadhimiya shrine I saw many women, their heads and faces covered, begging surreptitiously. One approached me and said under her breath, "Kind sir, Wlaidi [my son] was in the Iran war, and we hadn't heard from him for a long time until he sent word that he was coming home. My husband is ill and out of work, and I don't have any money to cook a meal for my son. Could you help me, please? May Allah give you health and long life." I was touched by the word *wlaidi*, a loving miniaturization of *waladi*, which reminded me how Iraqis, especially from the south, modified words to describe their loved ones.

The educated and professional middle-class people, suddenly finding themselves impoverished and seeing no future promise for their children, started to emigrate whenever and wherever the opportunity arose. They went to Jordan, the United Arab Emirates, even Sudan and Yemen. The ones with higher qualifications headed to England, Canada, and Australia. New Zeeland was the most welcoming. So many Iraqi professionals ended up there that a street was named Khan Della after a district in Baghdad. The US was the least welcoming.

A medical school friend and classmate of mine had gone into private practice in Baghdad and done extremely well until the sanctions hit. Since his father-in-law was a Canadian citizen, he decided to sell off and take his family to Canada. He sold everything he had, fetching only $5,000 US, but this equaled 22.5 million Iraqi dinars, for the dollar was worth 4,500 dinars at the time. Canada accepted him on the condition that he would not practice medicine in the country. He agreed and for a while worked as a peritoneal dialysis technician before leaving for the United Arab Emirates.

A young nephew of mine got a job as a ship hand on a vessel headed to Singapore and from there boarded another ship that took him to Taiwan. He got a job in a battery factory, and being sharp and hardworking (like most middle-class Iraqis), was quickly promoted to a section head. He fell in love with a young Taiwanese woman and married her. He told me the women there were smart, loving, and made exemplary wives and mothers. Many years later he took his wife and their little child to live in Vancouver, British Columbia. I have uncles, cousins, nephews, and nieces living now in Canada, the US, England, Holland, UAE, and Jordan.

During Saddam's reign, but especially in the time of sanctions, four million Iraqis emigrated out of the country, almost the entire middle class. This was a sinister sign for the future of Iraq, for it takes at least a generation to replenish the lost human resource. Moreover, and more importantly, any hope of some future democracy and political stability after the Ba'th era was greatly diminished by the flight of the middle class. This was to be amply demonstrated after 2003.

The prevalent want and destitution under the sanctions also led to massive corruption among government workers and in the small private sector. Bribery became a fixture of everyday life. Teachers would give private lessons in the evenings to augment their meager incomes. Some desperate ones would even fail students who would not sign up for their private tutoring sessions. Regular citizens took to burglary, and bands of thieves sprang up all over the country. This and the widespread official corruption in the government, army, secret service, and the police would become an established pattern that would haunt Iraq after the demise of Saddam in 2003.

A close physician friend of mine, a classmate in Baghdad College and medical school, came to see me when I was visiting Baghdad. He told me the story of a neighbor of his, an old widow who had a helper during the day but was alone at night. She was awakened by the sound of some falling object and was terrified to see a masked man, gun in hand, walking toward her. He ordered her to give him whatever valuable artifacts she possessed. She pleaded with him, invoking her old age and human mercy to no avail. She offered to give him food and all her departed husband's clothes, to which he responded with a hysterical laugh.

She then led him around her little home, and he picked up what he thought were money-fetching objects and the little jewelry she had. When he was done, he saw she was beside herself with grief, sobbing uncontrollably but suppressing her voice with her hand on her mouth. He sat down, took off his mask, and said, "Don't cry, old woman. I am not a thief. I was in fact an army officer before I was let go. I have a wife and four children, one of them ill, and we are all hungry." He suddenly started sobbing himself, dropped his loot on the floor, and left the house.

The endemic deprivation and loss of hope in the future drove most people back to religion—the opium of the dispossessed and the balsam for the sick and disabled. But this time it was an obsessive pursuit taken up by Iraqis who had previously been the least religious of Muslims. Modern women who had been to college and graduate school discarded makeup, covered their heads, stopped shaking hands with men, even male relatives, and sometimes sold their chairs and sofas and sat on pillows on the floor. Men, previously Marxists, Arab nationalists, or even Ba'thists, grew beards and lined up in mosques to pray behind imams who spoke a tenth-century language.

More ominously, Saddam's government began to condone Wahabi activism in Iraq to confront the restive Shia population. Wahabi literature could be found lying on desks in government offices. Wahabis financed by Saudi Arabia were at work to convert as many people as they could, especially in the Anbar Province, enticing them by paying each convert $50 US per month, the equivalent at the time of ID 200,000, a handsome sum in the impoverished Iraq of that period. Men wearing a beard but no mustache, clad in only knee-high dishdashas, the emblems of the Wahabi sect, were seen even in the Shia province of Karbala, which in Ottoman times had been pillaged and burned by the Wahabi hordes from Najd in today's Saudi Arabia.

During my visit to Baghdad, I saw Saddam on TV speaking the language of religion. Someone asked him what he'd do about a certain problem, I cannot remember what it was, and he answered, "We would do what al-Khulafa al-Rashidun did," the four successors to the Prophet Muhammad in the seventh century. It was quite obvious that Saddam and his Ba'thists, the cynical opportunists they've always been, had read the mood of the Iraqi and Arab populace in general and decided to make a 180-degree turn to religion. Up to the 1960s, Baghdad was so liberal it even had a red light district in the center of the city, but in the 1990s Saddam was executing destitute widows who went into prostitution to hold on to dear life for their children.

In April 1999, I was invited by Professor Shams Innati of the faculty of Villanova University in Philadelphia to give a talk "The Crisis of Deformity and Death" at a two-day symposium at the university. The symposium was titled "Iraq: History, People, and Politics." I readily agreed. The event was cosponsored by the American Friends Service Committee and the Quakers' Peace and Concerns Standing Committee of Philadelphia.

When I arrived, I was picked up by an elderly Quaker lady, white-haired, thin, wiry, energetic, and friendly. She jumped into her car and drove me to where I would be staying for the night. It was a quaint blue wooden house, probably from the early twentieth century, and very clean. I had a small upstairs room to myself. A second room was to house another speaker. I lay down in bed and tried to imagine how Philadelphia looked when the house was built, then dozed off into oblivion. I woke up the next morning to find my lady friend waiting cheerfully to drive me to the university.

The two-day symposium was well organized and attended by several hundred students and faculty members, not only from Villanova, but also from several other universities. The speakers were faculty members of the universities of Chicago; Illinois at Chicago; Ohio State; Dartmouth; North Carolina State; South Carolina; Vermont; New York; American University of Washington, DC; Massachusetts; McMaster of Ontario, Canada; and Nanterre of Paris, France. The topics were varied and quite interesting. Notably, the common theme that ran through many of the presentations was that the sanctions on Iraq amounted to genocide. The speakers were outstanding and had a thorough grasp of their subject. In my talk, "Crisis of Deformity and Death," I concentrated on the medical, public health, and radiation aspects of the Gulf War and the sanctions, particularly the devastating effects on children.

Professor McGuire Gibson of the Oriental Institute at the University of Chicago had done outstanding archeological work in Iraq and was quite enthralled by the ancient Mesopotamian civilization. In his talk "Ancient Mesopotamia: World Heritage under Threat," he highlighted the problem of destruction of ancient Iraqi sites in search of artifacts for sale. This in fact was the reality on the ground, and it is nearly impossible to know how many artifacts were stolen and sold, not just by criminal bands, but also by desperately hungry and forlorn people. To the anthropologists, the sad aspect of such theft is that they don't learn very much from artifacts removed from the place where they had been found.

I was impressed by the Villanova University symposium on Iraq and saw that it had enlightened a large group of graduate students and other attendees, who would undoubtedly communicate what they heard to others. In fact, the Iraq sanctions were eventually criticized or condemned by many organizations and individuals of diverse political and moral persuasions: WHO; UNICEF; FAO; the *Wall Street Journal*; the *Chicago Tribune*; US, British, and other physician groups; the American College of Physicians; the Pope; the World Council of Churches; the International Action Center (established by former US Attorney General Ramsey Clark); the Arab American Anti-Discrimination Committee; and Voices in the Wilderness.

On the other hand, Leslie Stahl, in a 1996 interview on *60 Minutes*, asked our UN representative Madeleine Albright if the death of 570,000 Iraqi children—more than those who died in Hiroshima—was a worthwhile price to pay to remove Saddam. Mrs. Albright said yes, it was. If these were Western European or

North American children, a massive uproar would have obliged our UN representative to resign her office. There was no uproar, and she did not resign. In fact, she was later promoted to the highest position a woman had occupied at the time, US Secretary of State.

In her new post, Mrs. Albright later admitted that in many cases sanctions have been imposed for years, even decades, without achieving their objectives but that good intentions do not automatically translate into good results. I find this mind-boggling and often wonder if our high officials had ever studied logic in school. If the sanctions were meant to remove Saddam, why did we not help the millions of Iraqis who rose up against him in March 1991? US officials, including those at the CIA, must have known full well that the sanctions would not remove Saddam. They would only destroy Iraq and its people. Was that the real motive for the sanctions? I am afraid the answer must be yes, since the sanctions continued happily on despite Mrs. Albright's latter-day confession.

The sad irony of this story is that the Iraqi people had never elected Saddam, and were in fact his major victims. His Ba'th party was launched to power in 1963 and again in 1968 with CIA funds (US taxpayer money). Yet the people of Iraq were subjected to mass punishment for crimes he committed in Kuwait. Saddam and his regime were spared by our policy makers at the end of the Kuwait war and allowed to massacre hundreds of thousands of Iraqi Shia and Kurds, and devastate the marshlands and its inhabitants. Then the US instituted lethal sanctions on Iraq to remove him when it hadn't done so during the immediate post-Kuwait war uprising the US itself had prompted, and when there were some 150,000 US and allied boots on Iraqi soil. If this tale is not for a theater of the absurd, I don't know what is. A tragic absurdity.

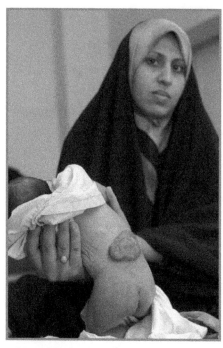

DEPLETED URANIUM: IRAQI CHILD WITH TUMOR OVER THE LOWER
SPINE. COURTESY OF PHOTOGRAPHER JENNY MATTHEWS.

DEPLETED URANIUM: IRAQI CHILD WITH HUGE COLLECTION OF FLUID
IN THE ABDOMEN (ASCITES). COURTESY OF JENNY MATTHEWS.

# 36

# Another Twelve Years of Despair

The condition of the Iraqi population under the sanctions regime was getting worse by the day. The suffering was much the worse among the Shia who were now ready to listen to a distinguished religious leader, Ayatollah Mohammad Sadiq al-Sadr, the father of today's Muqtada, and cousin of the other Sadr and his sister Bint al-Huda, both killed by Saddam in 1979. Mohammad al-Sadr had established a network of workers and volunteers to provide food, medicine, and vaccines for the poor, orphaned children and widows, and to render medical care at various clinics. He was a man of great learning, high morals, and much charisma.

Saddam at first tolerated al-Sadr's activities because he had intended to use him to blunt the influence of the religious hawza in Najaf. Al-Sadr quickly gained a huge following among the Shia poor. His sermons were attended by thousands of people. The crowds flowed outside the mosque and onto the street, and his speeches became more challenging to the regime. He was warned by the secret service to desist but continued to give his Friday noon sermons, henceforth attired in a shroud.

He knew he would be liquidated—and indeed he was—in broad daylight, by agents who attacked his car with automatic gunfire. Two of his sons, older than Muqtada, were likewise assassinated. This led in early 1999 to another eruption of unrest in the Shia provinces but especially in al-Sadr City in Baghdad, then called Saddam's City. These uprisings were again suppressed brutally, and many people were killed or rounded up for the regime's dark dungeons.

In May 1991, less than three months after President George H. W. Bush denied that the US intention in the Gulf War was to remove Saddam, he signed a directive to the CIA to create conditions facilitating the dictator's removal. This led to the formation of the Iraqi National Congress, INC, which received US financial, media, and political support. Spearheaded by the exertions of Ahmed al-Chalabi, a brilliant alumnus of the Massachusetts Institute of Technology and the University of Chicago, the INC rallied for the first time diverse political and ethnic groups and individuals opposed to Saddam's regime: secular Sunni and Shia Arabs, including ex-Ba'thists and military officers, communists and monarchists; and the two Kurdish parties, the Kurdistan Democratic Party (KDP) headed by Mas'ud al-Barazani, son of the late Mulla Mustapha al-Barazani, and the Patriotic Union of Kurdistan (PUK) led by Jalal Talabani.

In June 1992, two hundred INC delegates met in Vienna. In October of the same year, two major Shia religious parties, the Supreme Council of the Islamic Revolution in Iraq (SCIRI), headed by Mohammed Baqir al-Hakeem, and al-Da'wa Party also joined the INC, which then convened an important and highly publicized meeting in Iraqi Kurdistan, where leadership and executive councils were formed and Mr. Chalabi chosen as the head of the organization. The INC's platform professed the protection of human rights in Iraq, pluralistic democracy, the rule of law, guarding the country's territorial integrity, and complying with international law and the UN resolutions pertaining to Iraq.

Not surprisingly, the INC almost collapsed because of significant ideological and political differences between the various constituent parties, their inability to compromise, and, most importantly, the breakout of civil war in Iraqi Kurdistan between the KDP and the PUK, which lasted over three years, from May 1994 to November 1997.

When the safe haven and no-fly zone were established in northern Iraq in the aftermath of the Kuwait war, the protected area included Dhok and Erbil, strongholds of Barazani's KDP, but not Sulaymania, the traditional territory of the PUK, or Kirkuk. Violent clashes, therefore, continued in the unprotected areas between the Iraqi Army and Kurdish fighters until a balance of power was reached that allowed the Iraqi Army and government officials to withdraw from Kurdistan in October 1991. The region therefore gained de facto independence from Saddam's rule, was governed by the KDP and PUK, and adopted its own flag and national anthem.

In 1992, parliamentary elections in Kurdistan returned a majority of the votes for the PUK in Sulaymaniya and the Kurdish parts of Diyala, and for the KDP in Dhok and Erbil. The Kurdish parliament was thus divided evenly between the two parties. The PUK generally represented a more middle-class, urban, and educated following. The KDP had in its ranks tribal, largely uneducated and insular country folk. Kurdistan suffered economically because Saddam enforced a blockade to cut off oil and food supplies to the region and R-688 did not exempt the Kurdish government from the sanctions regime. The Kurds, therefore, could only trade with the outside world on the black market.

As is often the case, the poor economy was a major factor in the eruption of hostilities between the KDP and the PUK in May 1994. In the ensuing civil war, three to five thousand combatants and civilians were killed, but other estimates put the number of the civilian dead at more than eight thousand. There were clashes over territory when the PUK occupied Erbil, and also over tax income.

Barazani's KDP had allowed Saddam to smuggle oil for export through the Khabur River basin into Turkey, thereby collecting from the Iraqi government several million dollars weekly in taxes. It took the PUK more fighting with the KDP before the KDP agreed that both parties would share the tax income equally. However, the KDP persisted in its efforts to have the upper hand in controlling the flow of oil and goods through Kurdistan. During the civil war, the INC played a large role in negotiating a temporary truce between the two combatants, with Chalabi bravely commuting between the two warring camps at great peril to himself.

In January 1995, the CIA, represented by officer Robert Baer, linked up with an Iraqi general plotting to liquidate Saddam. This amply suited the CIA's temperament, always in favor of replacing ungrateful and no-longer-obedient dictators with a new, preferably military person. Saddam, like Diem of South Vietnam and Noriega of Panama before him, had to go because he bit the hand that had fed him. The CIA, like President George H.W. Bush and many of his realpolitik companions, was not interested in the lofty ideals of democracy and nation building overseas, and welcomed the notion of fast military coups, which they had expertly engineered around the globe, from Argentina and Chile to Greece, Iraq, Iran, and Indonesia. I suspect this long-standing tradition of the CIA was the reason for the mutual hatred between it and Ahmad Chalabi.

The initial plan was for a unit of Iraqi troops to kill Saddam as he crossed a bridge in Tikrit, but this was later changed to a scheme where Kurdish forces would go on the offensive while rebel troops would use tank guns to destroy a house where Saddam was expected to be residing at the appointed time. However, Saddam, ever on the lookout for conspiracies, got wind of the plot from his well paid able infiltrators. As the Iraqi Army went on high alert, Tony Lake, the US national security adviser, informed Baer that the planned operation had been uncovered, and Baer quickly conveyed the message to the Iraqi collaborators and the KDP's Barazani, but not to the PUK's Talabani; I suspect because his party was perceived as friendly toward Iran.

The plotting army officers were expeditiously rounded up by Saddam's security forces and executed. Barazani suspended the planned offensive, leaving the PUK forces to launch it alone. In a few days, they destroyed three Army divisions and took five thousand war prisoners. Baer appealed for US military support for the PUK offensive to no avail, and the Kurdish forces were compelled to withdraw. Predictably, Baer was recalled to the US and investigated for the attempted assassination of Saddam, but was let go later.

Military hostilities between the KDP and the PUK continued. In 1996, Talabani forged an alliance with Iran, permitting it to enter northern Iraqi territory to pursue operations against the Iranian KDP. Alarmed by the prospect of confronting both Iran and the PUK, and forgetting Saddam's genocidal campaigns against the Kurds, Barazani appealed for help from Baghdad.

Hoping to retake northern Iraq, Saddam readily obliged by dispatching to the north thirty thousand troops led by the Republican Guard.

The Iraqi Army attacked PUK-held Erbil and prevailed against the three thousand Kurdish Peshmerga defenders. True to itself, the Republican Guard undertook the mass execution in a field outside Erbil of seven hundred captured PUK fighters and two hundred Iraqi National Congress members. Another two thousand were taken prisoners to Baghdad. Six hundred fifty mostly INC members survived and were later evacuated to the US.

This episode awakened the hitherto hands-off Clinton administration to the possibility of yet another murderous campaign by Saddam's troops in the north, so it initiated Operation Desert Strike on September 3, 1996, launching cruise missiles from B-52 bombers and ships at air defenses in southern Iraq, extending the southern no-fly zone up to the thirty-third parallel, and dispatching an aircraft carrier to the Persian Gulf.

After securing Erbil for the KDP, the Iraqi Army withdrew to its original positions, and the KDP evicted the PUK from its other territories, even taking Sulaymaniya with Baghdad's help on September 9. Talabani and his PUK withdrew to near the Iranian border to rally and retook Sulaymaniya on October 13, possibly with Iran's help.

The lack of cohesion within the INC—its increasing weakness made worse by the Kurdish civil war—and the abiding loathing the CIA had for Chalabi resulted in the US promoting the National Iraqi Accord, headed by Ayad Allawi, a Shiite Ba'thist who had worked with the CIA for some time and was more acceptable to the US Sunni Arab allies, especially Saudi Arabia, the Gulf statelets, and Jordan. Funds for the INC from the US and other donors dried up and were not resumed until the signing by President Bill Clinton in 1998 of the Iraq Liberation Act, where-upon Congress authorized $98 million to go mainly to the INC.

In the same year, the KDP's Barazani and the PUK's Talabani signed the Washington Agreement, a peace treaty facilitated by the US, whereby the two parties agreed to share power and reve-nue and keep the PKK, active in south and southeastern Turkey, out of Iraqi Kurdistan. The US, on the other hand, promised to protect the Iraqi Kurds from Saddam.

In February 2003, shortly before the US invasion of Iraq, there was a big commotion over Chalabi's desire for the INC to form a provisional government at the start of the invasion, which would then assume its full official functions at the end of the war. This was opposed by Chalabi's backers in Congress and the Pentagon. Instead, a governing council, including Chalabi, was established after the end of the war, but he was not made prime minister. The position was given instead to Ayad Allawi, the head of the rival CIA-favored Iraqi National Accord. Jalal Talabani of the PUK was made president of Iraq, and his onetime enemy, the KDP's Mas'ud Barazani, president of Iraqi Kurdistan. Both par-ties had closely cooperated with the invading US forces, defeating the Iraqi Army out of a large area in the north, including the city of Mosul and the oil-rich city of Kirkuk.

# 37

# Notes on the 2003 Invasion

I do not intend to review the events of the US invasion of Iraq in March 2003 because they are fairly recent and have not faded from memory. It was, of course, the third major war Iraq witnessed in less than twenty-five years. I merely like to present my humble opinion regarding some of the controversies, serious or superfluous, that have raged since the invasion.

There is no doubt that most Iraqis were absolutely jubilant over the overthrow of Saddam in 2003. The Iraqi Americans I know were ecstatic. Many drank toasts and smashed their glasses. Saddam's army and Republican Guard did not even make a stand to defend Baghdad. They melted away like salt in water, while Saddam himself took off like any other common criminal and was nowhere to be found. His role models were Stalin and Hitler, but at least Hitler killed himself rather than run away or surrender.

We keep hearing that Paul Bremmer, the head of the Coalition Provisional Authority in Iraq, was wrong to dissolve the Iraqi Army. Actually, the memorandum he issued to that effect was redundant. The Iraqi Army was no longer there to dissolve. The army officers and Republican Guard were tools of Saddam. They discarded their uniforms and disappeared among the masses to emerge later as terrorists, calling themselves the "Resistance," a label repeated by al-Jazeerah and other Arab media. The rank and file of the army were predominantly Shia soldiers who hated Saddam and had suffered immense casualties fighting his foolish wars, so the last thing they were willing to do in 2003 was to fight to save Saddam and his gang.

Iraqis did not give a hoot about the reason George W. Bush and his team gave for going to war, namely the presence of weapons of mass destruction (WMDs). They were simply brimming over with joy over the demolition of the mountain of terror that had settled on their chest for thirty-five years. Not long afterward, they headed by the millions for the poll box to cast their votes in free elections for the first time in their history. They came out of the election booths smiling, laughing, their eyes sparkling with joy, their dyed fingers raised in the air with pride. Millions were for the first time in decades, marching with exhilaration toward their sacred shrines for spiritual succor in Karbala, Najaf, and Kadhimiya.

The Iraqis, as well as Bush and Tony Blair, knew of Saddam's WMDs. He had used them against Iraqis in Halabja and southern Iraq and against Iran. The US and its European allies had allowed him to acquire the ingredients for chemical weapons and looked the other way when he deployed them frequently for many years. It was natural, therefore, for Bush and Blair to believe the reports about Saddam still possessing WMDs. How much of this banned weaponry the regime had actually destroyed remained a mystery, and certainly Saddam himself had kept the issue quite murky.

It is likely that many of the WMDs were stealthily smuggled

to Syria. Saddam's henchman Izzat al-Duri traveled shortly before March 2003 to Syria, hitherto the nemesis of the of the Iraqi Ba'th, probably to facilitate the transfer of WMDs and solicit Syria's help to host and train the jihadis Saddam had already recruited under the name of Feda'iyeen Saddam (Saddam's Martyrs). After all, Saddam and the Ba'th had always been accomplished opportunists. When Saddam invaded Kuwait in 1991, he sent military aircraft to Iran, the country he had loathed and fought for eight years, to spare them destruction by the US forces of Desert Storm.

As their tragic history would have it, however, the Iraqis' great joy was not to last very long. The war was not "mission accomplished" because Saddam's virulent followers had simply gone underground. This was most certainly a plan drawn up by Saddam and his acolytes before the invasion. The US operation was militarily successful in the sense that it caused the collapse of the regime, and most Iraqis were grateful for that. However, as the medical lingo goes, the "preoperative" and "postoperative" care left much to be desired.

During the Clinton administration, many members of the INC and Iraqi American professionals met frequently with American officials in Washington, DC, and committees were set up to draw contingency plans for Iraq in the case of a US invasion. The Bush administration, including Donald Rumsfeld, seems to have paid scant or no attention to those plans before launching the invasion of Iraq. Furthermore, Rumsfeld and Paul Wolfowitz, both civilians with no past military background, pooh-poohed the respected US army's chief of staff, General Eric Shinseki, when he correctly stated that it takes about half a million US troops to hold and secure a country as large as Iraq. Consequently, with the postinvasion disappearance of the Iraqi Army, the security forces, and much of the police, the US Army could not maintain security, safeguard Iraq's long borders, and control the Sunni insurgency.

Immediately after the fall of Baghdad, there was massive looting by marauding mobs and local and foreign criminal gangs of vital government ministries, institutions, and, perhaps most sadly, the National Iraq Museum, which contained artifacts dating back to the beginnings of agriculture and urban civilization. True to his criminal nature, Saddam had moreover released thousands of hardened criminals from Iraqi jails shortly before the US invasion.

When newsmen kept asking Mr. Rumsfeld why the US forces did not even attempt to control the pillage, he exclaimed, "They are free. They are free." He also displayed angry frustration over the persistent questioning, saying that TV kept showing the same person carrying away a vase over and over again. Sadly, much more than a vase was carried away. Computers, electric equipment, furniture, lighting fixtures, and invaluable ancient artifacts all disappeared. On the other hand, Mr. Rumsfeld had seen to it that the Oil Ministry was well guarded by US forces.

The Iraq National Museum would not have been pillaged if the US force stationed in the area had been ordered to fend off the looters. Likewise, the ministries and important historic landmarks did not require a large commitment of US troops. The mere presence of a few GIs and a tank or two would have deterred criminals bent on looting. This regrettable oversight by Mr. Rumsfeld and the US military leadership conveyed to the Iraqis an unfavorable message—that the US invasion was not about "liberating Iraq" from the shackles of Saddam, but about oil, and that the US did not care about safeguarding Iraq's vital institutions and had no respect for its ancient history.

The looting of the Iraq National Museum in the middle of Baghdad was especially painful, not just to Iraqis, but to people everywhere, most of all the archeologists. In an interview on CNN, Professor McGuire Gibson of the Chicago Oriental Institute was beside himself about the episode and the negligence it represented. He told me that he and his staff had met with US government representatives several times before the invasion and had given them a priority list of thirty Iraqi sites and landmarks to protect. The National Iraq Museum was at the very top of the list. He said the same thing when he spoke at an annual meeting of the Iraqi Medical Sciences Association (IMSA-USA).

The invasion and toppling of the Saddam regime was an earthquake for Iraq's Sunni Arabs, who had ruled the land for most of thirteen centuries. Especially in Ottoman times, from the mid-fifteenth century until the collapse of the Ottoman Empire in 1918, they were the Arab constituent of the Ottoman armed forces, police, and the administrative bureaucracy of Iraq. Suddenly after the 2003 invasion, they were stunned by the 180-degree turn of their political fortunes when the majority Shia came to positions of real power in the state.

The rulers of modern Iraq before the 1963 Arif-Ba'th takeover were not oblivious to the country's ethnic and sectarian mix. Under the monarchy, positions of hard power were held by the Sunni Arabs: the monarch, most prime ministers and the military high brass. But it was recognized that the majority Shia Arabs and the Kurds must have representation. The speaker of the senate, albeit a largely ceremonial post, was often a Shiite; a large number of Shiite landlords were members of parliament; three prime ministers and a number of cabinet ministers were also Shia. There were also a few prime ministers, several ministers, and high-ranking military officers among the Kurds.

After the July 1958 coup that ended the monarchy, the Presidency Council triumvirate had a Shiite, a Sunni, and a Kurd, and General Qasim behaved like a national leader, not a Sunni General. It was only after the 1963 coup, and especially after that of 1968 and the subsequent ascendency of Saddam, that the Shia were ever increasingly marginalized so that their condition just before the 2003 US invasion was worse than any other time in the modern Iraqi state. The Sunni Arabs, especially the Tikritis, had therefore become accustomed to almost unbridled political power for thirty-five years.

The Sunni insurgency in the wake of the US invasion was, therefore, not a struggle against the "invader," as portrayed by the Arab media, but an armed insurrection by Saddamists to recover absolute power. Prominent Sunni Arabs participated in the postinvasion government, but they were largely ignored by ordinary Sunnis and dismissed as American stooges. At least two of their prominent figures, Tariq al-Hashimi and Mithal al-Alusi suffered the loss of loved ones murdered by Saddamists, the former a brother, and the latter two young sons. The Sunni Arabs boycotted the first-ever authentic parliamentary elections in Iraq's history, and when some of them did run for the elections, several were assassinated in broad daylight.

In fact, Sunni Arabs who worked with the Americans as translators or in other professional roles were targeted and often murdered by their own kin. An appalling example was that of one Anbar Sheik, who killed his own son because the young man was making a good livelihood interpreting for the Americans. A prominent lawyer from Anbar, the father of a physician friend of mine, was also assassinated because he, like other educated Iraqis, saw working with the Americans as a promise of a much better future for a country that had, under Saddam's dictatorship, spun from one disaster to another and suffered three devastating wars.

There was no postapartheid South Africa–type "Truth and

Reconciliation Commission" to heal the recent and old wounds of the Shia and the Kurds. On the contrary, the usual bigoted slogans of Majus (Zoroastrians) and Safawis (the Shiite rulers of medieval Persia), widespread during Saddam's rule, were hurled again at the Shia. These inflammatory epithets were also displayed boldly on large posters carried by Sunni demonstrators in Baghdad in a procession headed by Sunni Arab notables and clerics, including Adnan al-Dulaymi, ironically the leader of the Iraqi Accord Front. The demonstration was of course captured by the cameras and shown in newspapers, but the pictures did not provoke any disapproval by the Arab rulers or press.

Neither Saddam, when he finally appeared in court, nor any of his henchmen expressed any regret or apologized for their past crimes. On the contrary, Saddam maintained his usual swagger and bravado in court, displaying contempt for the judge and the witnesses, seeming totally unmoved, perhaps even delighted, by their recounting of the horror and loss they had experienced during his rule. He kept wagging his right index finger at the judges and calling upon the "revolutionaries" to continue their "struggle" against the invaders, essentially urging his underground thugs to continue their terrorist operations. His cousin, Chemical Ali, explained away the Halabja gassing of the Kurds as having been necessary to protect Iraq.

During Saddam's ravings in court, too many Sunnis in Baghdad were glued admiringly to their TV sets, applauding, clenching their fists, and shouting support. This prompted an article in the *New York Times* (or was it the *Wall Street Journal*?) titled "Will the real Sunnis please stand up?" The real Sunnis did not stand up. Perhaps some if not most of them feared for themselves and their loved ones from their own ruthless extremists.

The absolute worst of it all was the resumption of mass murder of Shia and destruction of infrastructure by the Saddamists and ex-security and Republican Guard members, who had, after the fall of Baghdad, melted away amongst the civilian population and implemented a virulent preinvasion plan of urban terror and sabotage. The highlight of this conspiracy was displayed shortly after the toppling of Saddam, in the truck bombing outside the Imam Ali shrine in Najaf that instantly killed the head of the Supreme Council of the Islamic Revolution in Iraq (SCIRI), Mohammad Baqir al-Hakeem, who had lost five brothers and a dozen relatives murdered by Saddam's regime. At least seventy-five, but probably more than a hundred men, women, and children were blown to smithereens.

These mass murders continued unabated almost daily. Thousands of Shia were blown up by truck or suicide bombs in mosques, marketplaces, busy city squares, colleges, wedding ceremonies, and funeral processions, often held for people killed the day before by terrorist bombs. Entire market squares were engulfed by fireballs from high-power explosives, creating huge craters, collapsing nearby buildings, and burning cars into a hulk, often with their occupants incinerated into charred bones. The worst example of these genocidal crimes was the inferno of the shopping mall in the Karrada district of Baghdad in 2016.

There was a much broader scope to this relentless terror campaign. Water pumping stations, electricity grids, and bridges were blown up. Some Baghdad landmarks were burned down, a tragic example being the famous al-Mutanabbi Street, the main book market, almost a second home to me in my youth and an emblem of the bygone Arab renaissance in Iraq. Thousands of Iraqi professionals, scientists, physicians, and engineers were killed, kidnapped, or simply disappeared.

It was as though there was a premeditated plan to take Iraq

back to the Dark Ages. The aim was to terrorize, demoralize, and cow the population; to demonstrate that neither the Americans nor the Iraqi authorities could guarantee their safety; and ultimately to topple the government. Failing those objectives, the country was to be destroyed. Saddam had once said that if the Ba'th Party were ever to be dislodged from power, "we will hand them a land without people." The statement always reminded me of a similar one attributed to Hitler: "If Germany were destined for defeat, we would surrender the keys of Earth to the angels of heaven."

The Saddamists evolved into various violently fanatical groups like the Army of Mohammad and others. They recruited members of al-Qa'ida, which found the security vacuum ideal for its operations. A large number of Saddamists actually joined al-Qa'ida or worked very closely with it, and Saddam's officers later constituted the majority of the military leadership of ISIS (Da'esh).

A particularly murderous leader of the Iraqi Qa'ida was the Jordanian Abu Mus'ab al-Zerqawi, who had been sentenced by a Jordanian court in absentia for his involvement in the bombing of three hotels in Amman. Known as the "Sheik of the slaughterers," he declared war on the Shia, launching an unremitting campaign of suicide and truck bombings in congested Shia towns, beheadings, and cold-blooded murders.

He succeeded well in turning the so-called jihad against the US troops in Iraq into a Sunni-Shia civil war, which became so grim that even al-Qa'ida Central was alarmed. The Qa'ida's second man, Ayman al-Zawahiri sent him a letter strongly admonishing him for his bloody campaign against the Iraqi Shia and diverting the jihad away from the American "enemy." Yet no Arab government or mass media ever protested his crimes. He met his demise at the hands of a joint US force in June 2006.

The Saddamists later formed the nucleus of the Islamic State in Iraq and Sham (ISIS), *al-Dawla al-Islamiyia fi al-Iraq wel-Sham*, with the Arabic acronym of DA'ISH. Sham is the name the Arabs had used for Greater Syria. Until very recently and perhaps even today, Saddam's army officers have comprised the bulk of the military leadership of ISIS.

The aim of all these criminal organizations was to trigger a full-fledged civil war between the Shia and the Sunnis by killing as many Shia as possible because they knew it was only a matter of time before the Shia would begin to retaliate. After all, al-Qa'ida and later Da'ish were operating from Sunni lands. The overwhelming majority of suicide bombers were foreign to Iraq, did not even speak Iraqi, and were sheltered, fed, and given directions to their targets by Iraqi Sunni hosts.

There was certainly plenty of money at hand to recruit terrorists and buy weapons and expensive cars to explode. The Ba'thists had stolen trillions of Iraqi petrodollars during their long rule of Iraq, and there were always the ever-willing donors among the rich Wahabis and their "charitable foundations," especially in Saudi Arabia, but also in Qatar, the UAE, and Kuwait. In 2016, UN officials stated that ISIS had some 140,000 Toyota cars and wanted to know who had paid for them. Toyota cooperated by examining serial engine numbers that revealed the cars were purchased either by private citizens of those countries or front companies doing business with them or their governments. Still more funds came from ransom money for kidnapped victims, smuggling, and narcotics trafficking.

Meanwhile, the Wahabi clerics in Saudi Arabia and the hundreds of Saudi-financed mosques and madrassas throughout the world intensified their sermonizing to demonize the "apostate" Shia and declare it was *halal* (permissible) to shed their blood and destroy their property. Neither then nor now did the US, the European community, the United Nations, or the Arab rulers and media label the activity as incitement to genocide, which it quite obviously is. On the contrary, the Qatari government-owned al-Jazeera and the plethora of Saudi-owned satellites and print media continued to fan the flames of sectarianism in Iraq and around the Islamic world.

Contrary to widespread assumptions, the Iraqi Shia are not a monolith but comprise various factions, some of which are antagonistic. Shortly after the US invasion, Abdul Majeed al-Khoo'i visited Iraq. He was a highly educated and modern Shia cleric, the son of the Grand Ayatollah Abul Qasim al-Khoo'i, the head of the Shia hawza during Saddam's rule. Abdul Majeed oversaw the reputable al-Khoo'i foundation in London and was much respected by British media and officials. Just one day after Saddam's overthrow, while al-Khoo'i was visiting the Imam Ali shrine, accompanied by the shrine guardian Sayyid Hayder al-Rufay'i, they were both hacked by Shiite assailants and left to die from their bleeding wounds.

The Shiite Sayyid Muqtada al-Sadr is somewhat of an enigma. His father, two older brothers, and parents-in-law were murdered by Saddam's henchmen. Yet, Muqtada saw the Americans as a lethal enemy and decided to go against them. Most middle-class Iraqis, the Shiites among them, consider him a simpleton, but Patrick Cockburn, in his book *Muqtada*, views him as a shrewd politician and a consummate organizer. He maintains that Muqtada managed to stay alive during Saddam's rule by pretending to be obtuse, the reason why Saddam spared him. Mr. Cockburn also states that the young Muqtada had been a competent organizer of his father's grassroots movement, its charitable activities and clinics for the poor.

Sayyid Muqtada, whom the US mainstream media are addicted to calling "the firebrand cleric," has a huge following of five million souls among the Shiite poor, dispossessed and uneducated. Many among them, especially the youth, are militant and comprise Jaysh al-Mehdi (the Mehdi Army), in reference to the Shia's Twelfth Imam Mohammad al-Mehdi (the guided one) and a descendant of the Prophet.

In December 2004, Muqtada sent his fighters to join the Sunni rebels in Fallujah in the battle against US forces. He maintained his relationship with anti-American Sunni elements after the Fallujah rebellion was crushed, but asked the Sunni clerics and religious parties to denounce the persistent violence of Sunni extremists against the Shia civilians. No such denunciation was forthcoming.

On February 22, 2006, al-Qa'ida operatives blew up the Asqeri'yeen mosque in Samarrah, north of Baghdad. The religious site is sacred to the Shia because it contains the grave of their eleventh imam, and more importantly the site of the disappearance of the twelfth imam, Mohammad al-Mehdi. The sacrilegious act was particularly galling to Muqtada's Mehdi Army, whose central theological theme is the return of Imam al-Mehdi, the Shia's equivalent of the Messiah. The destruction of the site was calculated by Iraq's al-Qua'ida's Emir, abu Mus'ab al-Zarqawi, to trigger a civil war between Iraq's Shia and Sunnis, a plan he had espoused in his earlier memoranda. And civil war there was. Terrorists flourish and usually succeed in the environment of civil strife and chaos.

Most of Sammara's population is Sunni, and a large number of them went out in a demonstration against the crime, with their leader shedding tears. Nevertheless, civil war took off like fire in a haystack. In the two years of 2006 and 2007, thousands of

Iraq's Shia and Sunnis perished in the slaughter. Three thousand souls in a month was not an unusual statistic. Corpses were found floating in rivers and sewers, murdered and mutilated people on sidewalks and in abandoned buildings. The Baghdad central morgue received hundreds of corpses a day along with a long line of anguished families looking for missing members.

Parents did not know if their children would come back from school. My nephew, a medical student at the time, was leaving for school when he saw in front of his home a convulsing man, blood spurting out of his neck. He rushed to him, hastily placed a bandage around his neck, laid him down in his car, and drove like a madman to the medical school teaching hospital. Before he arrived, the man exhaled his last breath. His head fell in my nephew's lap. What does an experience such as this do to a young man's psyche?

My sister, her husband, and her son (a dentist) fled from Baghdad along with thousands of others heading to Kurdistan in the north, usually to Erbil but also Sulaymania. The civil war strengthened Muqtada al-Sadr, his Mehdi Army, and followers, as they—not the Iraqi government and army, nor the US forces—were seen as the protectors of the Shia community against an existential threat.

The Sadr forces, thus dizzied by power, began to lord it over the Shia urban populace. They set up their own Islamic courts to try those accused of irreligious behavior, harassed middle-class professionals as well as unveiled women, and murdered alleged prostitutes. Reacting to attempts to curb them by the US and the Iraqi government, they waged in March and April of 2008 a serious and far-reaching rebellion in Sadr City, their main stronghold in Baghdad, and in Kufa, Najaf, Kut, and Basra.

The US forces battled and bombarded the rebels in Sadr City

and Najaf, and Prime Minister Nuri al-Maliki was compelled to send government troops to quell the rebellion in Basra. Al-Sadr later made peace with the other Shiite politicoreligious parties but has nevertheless remained quite unpredictable. Incidentally, his party is not the only Shiite force opposed to the US. Other smaller but militant parties are also fiercely anti-American, examples being Asa'ib al-Haq and Hezbollah of Iraq.

On the other hand, Saddam's loyalists reassembled by Izzet al-Duri, al-Qua'ida, and other militant groups remained intensely active in the provinces of Anbar (main cities Ramadi and Fallujah), Nineveh (main city Mosul) and Diyala (main city Ba'quba) and in the collar counties southwest of Baghdad. They exploded cars, sent in suicide bombers, killed Shia civilians and travelers, and intercepted and murdered pilgrims on their way to Karbala and Najaf.

Eventually President Bush decided on the "surge" operation where more US troops were dispatched, mainly to Anbar. Local Sunnis, calling themselves the al-Sahwa movement (the Awakening) were recruited and paid to fight al-Qa'ida, which had alienated the Sunni population under its hegemony by its Wahabi interpretation of Islamic law. Its followers had murdered barbers, bombed music shops, forced female students out of school, and killed members of Anbari tribes that did not succumb to their dictates.

The troop surge operation succeeded to a large extent in greatly curbing the Qa'ida presence, and the Sahwa fighters were supposed to be subsequently integrated into the Iraqi Army, police, and security forces. The latter process, however, was slow, impeded by bureaucratic incompetence and a lingering fear by the Shia elements in government that the armed and seasoned Sahwa members might turn against the central authority. After all, a great many of them had previously participated in terrorist acts against the government and the Shia population.

The continuation of violent acts against the Shia, the fact that many Sunni politicians had one foot in the government and another with terrorist groups, that they used the threat of more violence to press their demands, and the inability of the Shia politicians to overcome their centuries-old victimization complex all contributed to the failed incorporation of the Sahwa members. Even those among them who did actually get government jobs went without pay for months, but then large numbers of Shia employees likewise missed their salaries because of endemic incompetence, massive corruption, and the decline in oil revenues.

The Sunni Iraqis at large and their politicians have never been happy with a majority Shia government. They were the rulers of Iraq for centuries and have always had a majoritarian psychology, especially during the centuries of Ottoman rule. It is telling that after the 2003 US invasion, a prominent tribal sheik in Anbar told a US general that the Sunnis would rather be ruled by the Americans than by the Shia.

Hence since 2003 the Iraqi Sunnis have kept up the talk of marginalization because they cannot see themselves as lesser participants in Iraq's government. Added to their frustration was the *de-Ba'thification* program, which attempted to eradicate all Ba'thists from the state machinery. Since a great many prominent executive positions during the Ba'th regime were held by Sunnis, de-Ba'thification hit the Sunnis the hardest, although many Shiite Ba'thists lost their jobs as well.

The de-Ba'thification program was undoubtedly excessive. During the Ba'th regime, too many people, especially in the military and the police, as well as in the middle-class professions, signed up as Ba'thists simply to sustain their careers and livelihood. Since the government ran almost the entire national economy, one could not get a scholarship abroad, be promoted in the job, or obtain permission to trade unless one "signed up" with the Ba'th, a situation not much different than other totalitarian one-party states like Hitler's Germany or Soviet Russia.

It was expected and understood that Ba'thists who had committed crimes against the people would lose their positions and be brought to justice, but de-Ba'thification overreached and included all those other Ba'thists who had simply signed up to keep their livelihood. Hence qualified professionals left the country in droves, depriving Iraq of their knowledge and experience, and large numbers in the military and police joined the rebellion, where they were well paid by various parties and countries. The realization finally dawned that this extreme de-Ba'thification had caused damage to Iraq, and attempts were undertaken to water it down, but it was too late; the horse had already left the stable.

Many among the Shia politicians recognized the importance for a unified Iraq of the Sunnis and their political depth in the mostly Sunni Arab and Muslim world. These politicians tried to accommodate and co-opt the Sunni forces. The onetime prime minister after 2003, Ibrahim al-Ja'fari, emphasized in a news conference the value of Sunni participation in the Iraqi state, and Ahmed al-Chalabi said Iraq could not remain one nation without the involvement of its Sunni population. Even Nuri al-Maliki, early in his tenure as prime minister, reached out to Sunni politicians and had allies among the Anbar tribal sheiks.

But those Shia politicians and other like-minded officials were stymied by the continued violence against the Shia by extremist Sunni elements and were therefore unable to justify their stance to their constituents and disadvantaged vis-à-vis the more strident and uncompromising Shia factions. Moreover and importantly,

when Maliki saw that President Obama had no interest in Iraq
and was unable or unwilling to get the US Arab allies to cooperate
with the Iraqi government, he began to nurse a sectarian agenda
and got closer to Iran to consolidate his position.

Another huge problem was the endemic corruption among
the entire political class, ministers, parliamentarians, the judi-
ciary, the military, police, and security forces. As I mentioned
much earlier in the book, the Iraqi state institutions under the
monarchy and the succeeding Qasim regime were the cleanest in
the entire Middle East, but corruption began to creep in as the
Tikritis assumed more power after the Ba'th second coming in
1968. Under Saddam, and especially during the sanctions regime
from 1991 to 2003, corruption, nepotism, and bribery became
the norm. And the pattern persisted after the 2003 US invasion.

While high corruption in Saddam's time was largely restricted
to the ruling mafia, and outsiders embezzled at their own risk,
it became commonplace after 2003. It spread by example from
one department to another, even involving high US civil and
military officials. Iraqi government ministers and officials took
large bribes—so-called "commissions"—from foreign and local
companies contracting for various civilian and military projects
of which the stated costs were highly inflated to allow the official
to pocket the difference. Some projects, approved and paid for,
were entirely fictional, submitted by companies that existed only
on paper. Billions of dollars have "disappeared," unaccounted for
and nowhere to be found.

The consequences of this cancerous corruption were obviously immense. Hardly anything was repaired or built—not
roads, bridges, power grids, water purification plants, sani-
tation stations, or schools. Southern Iraq, destroyed by wars
and Saddam's depredations, has remained in ruins. Long

interruptions of electricity and water became routine daily events—this in a country where summer temperatures may easily climb to 131 degrees Fahrenheit (55 degrees Celsius). When I called on my brother or sister in Baghdad, these shortages were their immediate and recurring complaints. Eventually private companies began to put up large electricity generators in many neighborhoods where the inhabitants would pay for the service but the poor could not afford it.

The security and intelligence services, crucial in combating terrorism, have been lacking in modern equipment and organization. Wands for the detection of missing golf balls have been used to search for explosives in cars. They were purchased for millions of dollars from a British company whose owner was indicted for high fraud and jailed in England, but nothing happened to the Iraqi official (or officials) who purchased the wands. They are still in use even though everyone knows they are useless.

Not until the immense July 2016 terrorist atrocity in the Karrada district of Baghdad, where 300 people were incinerated and another 250 badly injured, did Prime Minister Haydar al-Abadi prohibit the use of these wands. Iraqis reasonably suspect that some of the guards manning security checkpoints have been bribed to let suspicious cars or trucks pass through, yet no security personnel to my knowledge have been brought to account until the Karrada tragedy.

I watched on the internet an interview with Mr. Dhia al-Shekerchi. He had been a high Da'wa Party official but left the organization not long after the US invasion, and now lives in Germany. He stated that during the terrorist scourge shortly after the US invasion, a brilliant engineer recommended a reputable high-tech company to set up electronic security fences to guard Baghdad and critical stretches of Iraq's borders. His proposal was turned down because the company's rules forbade the payment of bribes to facilitate the selling of its services.

Meanwhile Iraq's high officials and parliamentarians live royally in the Green Zone, surrounded by their security details. Their salaries are unimaginably high, supplemented by extra funds for their bodyguards and travel expenses, including pilgrimages to Mecca. Parliamentarians have a poor attendance record while vital issues await discussion and a vote. Absences often last for weeks or months, especially before and after the Mecca pilgrimage.

For a long time now, the Iraqi populace, especially the poor, has been convinced the government does not care about its security and welfare. In one of Mr. Maliki's travels to Karbala and Najaf, he met with Grand Ayatollah Ali Sistani before he returned to Baghdad, but he never stopped to visit a refugee camp of widows and children living in steel cargo train carriages under the burning sun. They were among the tens of thousands internally displaced by terrorist violence and sectarian bloodshed.

The several militia leaders have in fact taken better care of their followers, providing them with money, food, medicine, and shelter. Ayatollah Sistani for his part has issued several memoranda prodding government officials and parliamentarians to honor their responsibilities, but he was not heeded. However, the religious hawza, of which he is the grand cleric, regularly disperses funds to the needy widows, orphans, and men disabled in Iraq's three wars and the terrorist carnage after 2003.

Massive corruption continues unabated. It is evident that Iraq will not make any progress or even survive as a nation if nothing happens to stem this endemic disease. Ahmed al-Chalabi declared he had files upon files detailing the extensive aspects of corruption and its perpetrators and promised to make the documents public. But he died suddenly in November 2015 at his home in Kadhimiya, presumably of a heart attack, though his family stated he was poisoned. At the time of his death, he was a member of the Iraqi Parliament and in charge of the finance committee.

The Sunni poor were not worse off than the Shia's, but (perhaps naturally) they felt they were singled out for neglect. And as I explained earlier, they thought they were underrepresented in the government and the military. Their disaffection was fanned by scheming and ambitious politicians; the governments of Saudi Arabia and Qatar, with their numerous paper media and satellites—Qatar's al-Jazeera prominent among them; and last but not least, the Saddamists, al-Qa'ida, and later the growing Da'ish (ISIS) movement. Protests and demonstrations erupted in Anbar, but Prime Minister Maliki did not handle the situation with the wisdom or style of a national leader, thereby further aggravating an already explosive situation.

For a year and a half before the fall of Fallujah to ISIS, the terrorist organization's leaders and fighters had been commuting back and forth between Syria and Iraq, preparing for an invasion of Iraq. Prime Minister Maliki kept warning President Obama about the imminent danger to Iraq, but Mr. Obama treated the correspondence with the same apathy he displayed toward the expanding ISIS control of Syrian towns and oil fields. This naturally gave rise to a widespread (perhaps justified) belief in Iraq that the US had condoned the presence and expansion of ISIS in order to topple the Syrian regime and also to exert pressure on the Iraqi government.

Meanwhile ISIS ranks were swelling by volunteers from different Muslim countries and the Muslim communities of Russia, Western Europe, and North America. The Saudis recruited fighters from different central Asian countries, flew them at the Saudis' expense into Turkey, a NATO member, whereupon they were escorted by Turkish police and security officers to border crossings into Syria and Iraq. The Obama administration (including Hillary Clinton) and the CIA were well aware of all this recruiting and financing of Wahabi terrorists but looked the other way.

When ISIS finally attacked, they were received with open arms by the Arab inhabitants of the Sunni provinces so that the cities of Fallujah, Mosul, Tikrit, and Ramadi fell to them in a blitz-like speed. The people of Mosul and Fallujah were jubilant. There were in those cities large Iraqi Army contingents composed mostly of the local population. They simply dropped their arms and surrendered to ISIS. According to testimony by Iraqi Army soldiers, other troops in Mosul not wishing to capitulate were ordered by their commanding officers to drop their guns and "go home."

The atrocities ISIS committed in the areas it conquered in Iraq are well known around the world. There was the mass rape and sex slavery perpetrated against the Yazidi women and girls from Mount Sinjar and its surroundings; the cold-blooded execution of seventeen hundred unarmed Shia air force cadets at Camp Spiker in Saladdin Province near Tikrit; the rape of Shia Turkwomen, many of them dying from the violation, the mass killing of members of a Sunni tribe that would not pledge allegiance to ISIS; the use of chemical weapons at least two dozen times, notably against the Shia of the village of Taza in March 2016; countless beheadings; the use of civilians as human shields; and the destruction of famous landmarks of the ancient civilizations of Nineveh and Nimrud. ISIS fighters were well rewarded with salaries and sex salves.

ISIS also spread to areas near Baghdad and undoubtedly had many sleeper cells in the city. In fact, the capital itself was in danger, prompting Grand Ayatollah Ali al-Sistani to issue a fatwa for all able-bodied men to join the Popular Mobilization Forces (*al-hashd al-Sha'bi*) to defend the Shia sacred places, but also to emphasize they must not attack innocent civilians and noncombatants. It was the Popular Mobilization Forces, not the so-called "Iraqi Army," that with the help of the Americans and the Iranians finally pushed ISIS out of Tikrit, Ramadi and Fallujah, and is now playing a crucial role in the ongoing liberation of Mosul, giving in the process thousands of dead and injured. Hardly a day passes by without the sight of the coffins' procession in Najaf.

Besides the sectarian agenda of Saudi Arabia and its rich Gulf allies, another major contributor to the disintegration of Iraq, Syria, and Yemen was the Obama hands-off and rudderless foreign policy and its "leading from behind" Saudi Arabia and Qatar whose Wahabi citizens and front companies were aiding and arming ISIS and other terrorist groups, many of them off-shoots of al-Qa'ida. I will concentrate here on Iraq, my ancestral land and the subject of these memoirs.

"If you break it, you own it," Colin Powell once said. Yet the US in effect broke Iraq in 2003 but did not "own" it as it did West Germany and Japan after World War II and South Korea at the end of that peninsular war. All three countries were dictatorships, Japan a military one at that, but they have evolved into successful and prosperous democracies under US stewardship and commitment. It is true the US no longer had the notable statesmen and generals in 2003 that it did in the 1940s and 1950s, but that does not change the fact that the current abominable situation of Iraq is to a large extent the result of US foreign policy failure.

President Obama lacked any interest in being involved in the Iraqi scene. He saw it as Bush's war, not a major US concern, forgetting that Iraq had become an issue of extreme importance to the stability of the Middle East and the credibility of US foreign policy, standing, and prestige after the 2003 invasion. It was as though he was still the senator from Illinois, not the US president and commander-in-chief of the armed forces.

He was disinterested in pursuing the Status of Force Agreement (SOFA) that President George W. Bush had initiated and Prime Minister Maliki had favored. But Maliki perceived President Obama's lack of enthusiasm about the matter and decided naturally that the US interest in post-2003 Iraq had waned, so he set out to cultivate other allies. President Obama, on the other hand, used the issue of immunity for US troops in Iraq, a matter that could have been successfully negotiated, as the cause for the failure to implement SOFA. Furthermore, to drive home the message to the Iraqis, Mr. Obama declared his intention to speedily pull all US troops out of the country.

With Erdoghan's Turkey and many Arab states (chief among them Saudi Arabia) highly chagrined about a Shia majority government in Iraq, the only potential allies of Iraq were Iran, Syria, and perhaps farther afield Russia. Those Arab countries, especially the Wahabi Saudi state, keep harping on the issue of Iran's influence in Iraq, seemingly not recognizing that if they continue to block the Shia and their right to political representation, the Shia will have no option but to cooperate with Iran, regardless of the significant differences between the Arab Shiites of Iraq and Persian Iran. It just seems that, as usual, the Saudis and other Arabs do not understand that they cannot have it both ways, to "have their cake and eat it."

The obvious proof of the failure of Obama's Iraq policy is that he had to go back to Iraq to drive out ISIS, not just with the help of advisers and technicians but also with military personnel near battle front lines and pilots in the air. It is interesting in this context that while al-Qa'ida and later ISIS were wreaking havoc and terror, not just in Iraq, but almost everywhere else, most of our politicians were focused on imaginary threats from Iran instead of at least considering the logical option of collaborating with Iran to crush ISIS. After all, we had worked with Stalin to defeat Hitler. ISIS is no less evil than Hitler, while the Mullahs are far milder than Stalin.

President Obama did not seem to fully understand that the resolution of the crisis in Iraq is contingent on the defeat of ISIS in both Iraq and Syria. He and the European leaders continue to look at ISIS as a local phenomenon, not as an evil ideology that has metastasized worldwide and is a threat to world peace. The military struggle against it, even when successful, would only be local and likely transient. The frontal and decisive attack has to aim at the cradle of its ideology, namely the Wahabi Saudi state, its clerical establishment, and its school curriculum.

President Obama, as the US president and commander-in-chief, should have "owned" Iraq after the US "broke" it in 2003, regardless of what the commitment might have augured for his reelection prospects. But a real statesman was needed for that undertaking. The US should have seen to it that Iraq would develop into a functioning nation with a government responsible for all its citizens: Arab Shia and Sunnis, Kurds, Turkmen, Christians, Jews, Mandians, and Yezidis; that it would become a nation of laws not personalities, tribalism, sectarianism, and corruption. The effort might have required fifty years, but that's only a short spell in Iraq's multimillennial history. In comparison, South Korea in the early 1950s was a terrible backwater compared to Iraq at the time. Now it is a democracy that has produced Samsung and Hyundai, hosted the Olympics, and prosecuted its leader for corruption.

I am not Voltaire's Dr. Pangloss, but perhaps it's not too late to pick up the broken pieces of Iraq and glue them back together. Or is it? There is now no "state" in Iraq, according to the definition of the word in the political dictionary. The Kurds have established a de facto state of their own in the north. The Sunni Arabs are being used by ISIS in Mosul as human shields and are scattered in refugee camps, but are unlikely to reconcile themselves to a majority Shia government. And the Shia are divided into violently contending politicoreligious parties, each with its own militia.

There are no reliable national army, police, and security institutions that answer only to Prime Minister Abadi, who is an honest nationalist technocrat and an excellent engineer with many prizes to his credit. Unlike the various large militias, he has no teeth. As prime minister and the head of the Da'wa Party, he should be able to steer it toward his vision of national unity and progress, but it seems that he has not succeeded on that score so far. Maliki, on the other hand, remains a potent political figure despite his past failures, and he has continued to thwart Mr. Abadi's plans.

Corruption, as I mentioned earlier, is appalling and widespread among the Shia, Sunni, and Kurdish authorities, but at least the Kurds have developed their cities and spent money on infrastructure, whereas the Shia and Sunnis have had nothing to show for the billions of "disappeared" dollars. This phenomenon has severely compromised the country's security, borders, education, health care, and the development of water and mineral resources.

Corruption has also caused further loss of human resources because many expatriate professionals who returned to the country after 2003 eventually became demoralized and left Iraq, and the brain drain continues among those who could not leave the country during the sanctions years before the US invasion. Meanwhile, members of the political establishment sit in the Green Zone or undertake frequent expensive trips, not seeming to care about the daily suffering and violent demise of the people.

What then can the US, the UN, and its Security Council do to make it up to the anguished people of Iraq? The US has the main responsibility to repair the damage since it was the invading and occupying power. It needs to make a solid commitment to work with Prime Minister Abadi, who seems to have his heart in the right place. He said when he assumed the premiership that he wanted to set things right, even at the price of his own life.

First and foremost, the US needs to press on with its belated but most welcome plans to help the Iraqis expel ISIS from the country. That should be part of a larger plan to drive it out of Syria as well. The gigantic effort in Iraq and its expected casualties would be a terrible waste if ISIS retains its caliphate in Syria. It will also be helpful if the US and Iraq could revive negotiations about a SOFA agreement and a commitment by the superpower to defend Iraq in case of military aggression by any of its neighbors.

The US can meanwhile and in the longer term work closely with the Iraqi government to improve and modernize internal and border security, providing the necessary expertise, training, and equipment. It should help Iraq negotiate with neighboring states water treaties crucial to the survival of the country and its southern marshlands, recently declared a UNESCO World Heritage site. These and other necessary measures will require a larger nonmilitary US presence than has hitherto been the case.

Then there is the massive corruption problem, where the US can help Mr. Abadi and honest officials in monitoring money flows and suspicious bank accounts, providing legal expertise to facilitate the prosecution of embezzlers, freezing their assets and retrieving money that was stolen or laundered, both during

Saddam's rule and after his fall. No such retrieval has occurred yet. If this effort is even partially successful, it will restore the people's faith in the government and the good will of the USA. Iraqis have been demonstrating almost daily against the rampant corruption.

The US also has the responsibility to press its client states, particularly Saudi Arabia, Qatar, and Kuwait, to cease their machinations and interference in Iraqi affairs through various extremist or opportunistic groups. This will make Iraq much less willing to seek the protection of Iran and more resistant to its interference in Iraqi politics through its various acolytes. As long as the Shia are blown up in Iraq and oppressed and killed in Saudi Arabia, Bahrain, and Yemen, Iran will always make political capital of the situation. Eventually and almost certainly, there will arise among the Shia population militant organizations that will perpetuate the current cycle of violence, thereby creating dangerous instability in a region floating on oil and in the heart of the Middle East.

The US can also persuade Iran not to interfere in internal Iraqi politics and to end its training and arming of certain militias, the case being presented as an indispensible component of the continued normalization of relations between the US and Iran. The latter needs the US for better integration into the world economy and as a damper to the increasing ambition and assertiveness of the big Russian bear to its north. The US and Iran had collaborated during the US invasion of Afghanistan after 9/11 and also against ISIS in Iraq, and Iran could render much assistance to the US in its fight against Wahabi terrorism in the region and in central Asia. For the US, Iran is too strategic to ignore and too stubborn to bully. All US administrations, Democrat and

Republican, before that of George W. Bush war had done their best to keep Iran in the US camp.

Naturally, I cannot close this chapter before discussing the future of the "map" of Iraq. Lately a significant number of Shia and Sunni politicians have come to recognize the pressing need to transcend sectarian agendas and to preserve the territorial integrity of Iraq. On the Kurdish side, moreover, the alliance of the PUK (Talabni's party) and Goran (the reform party), unlike Barazani's KDP, have been open to the idea of Kurdistan remaining within a federated Iraq rather than being totally independent. They recognize the latter option as being unrealistic at this time.

The PUK-Goran alliance, having a more educated urban membership, senses that Kurdistan is likely to do much better economically as a member of a federal system than on its own, and is quite cognizant of the real difficulties it will encounter with a chagrined Turkey to the north and an uneasy Iran to the east. The US is best situated to facilitate such a federation, oversee the lengthy negotiations it is certain to involve, and guarantee, along with the UN, the durability, peace, and prosperity of the constituent federal regions.

The current state of affairs makes it unlikely that Iraq will survive as one nation if it is to be governed by a central authority in Baghdad. As it is, the notorious Sykes-Picot Agreement (cooked up by the British and the French after World War I) had drawn the map of so-called modern Iraq and Syria without regard to ethnic, religious, commercial, agricultural, or socioeconomic realities. The Hashemite monarchy and, after July 1958, the Qassim regime labored to forge a nation out of the disparate and contending population groups within the Syke-Picot Iraq. They achieved significant success. However, the project stumbled with the beginning of the war in Kurdistan and collapsed with the coming of Saddam, who maintained Iraq's unity only by ruthless oppression of the Shia and the Kurds.

The question for Iraq, then, becomes division or federation. The better choice, I think, is federation. However, a referendum of the entire Iraqi population must be conducted as to whether they want a single state, federation, or division. The question is certainly crucial for the future of Iraq and the Mideast, and the leaders of the various communities of Iraq should study the matter with the seriousness and wisdom it deserves, uninfluenced by personal egos and ambitions, but strictly by the interest of their constituents; I can only hope that is not too much to ask of them; their track record so far has not been inspiring.

But such a referendum cannot be undertaken before these things happen: ISIS must be evicted from Iraq. Other terrorist groups must be flushed out. The various militias have to be disbanded or incorporated meaningfully into the national army, and adventurist politicoreligious demagogues must be sent home. This will take time. The referendum will have to be conducted under the eyes of vigilant UN observers and Iraqi representatives of all parties and denominations.

Be it federation or division, it will involve lengthy negotiations between the various Iraqi groups about the federated states' boundries; water rights; revenue allocation from oil, sulfur, and natural gas; taxation; foreign policy and defense; and cooperation to ensure the nation's security, and the relentless pursuit of remaining or newborn terrorists—a nightmare of an undertaking but a must. Furthermore, there are even today mixed populations of Shia and Sunni Arabs in Baghdad, Diyala and Babel provinces, and of Sunni and Shia Turkomen in Kirkuk province. These people must have the freedom to relocate if they wish or, if they decide to stay put, they must have all the rights and privileges of the rest.

Federation or division is difficult to safeguard in a region beset by the Mideast problems of widespread illiteracy, tribalism, ethnicity, sectarianism, and zero-sum politics. Any final arrangement, as in the Balkans, must therefore be monitored by UN presence and guaranteed by US and UN Security Council commitments that are solid, durable, and not subject to the whims of US election politics.

May Allah help Iraq.

# 38

# Reflections on Global Terrorism

The 1963 Ba'th Party takeover in Iraq, especially its return in 1968 and the subsequent ascendancy of Saddam, terminated the era of the Renaissance and dashed the high hopes that the Iraqis and the international community had for a country that had been developing, emerging into modernity, and promising to move on to Second World status. It had two great rivers with many tributaries, good agricultural land, plenty of oil and sulfur, and, importantly, an intelligent, well-educated, and hardworking middle class, the largest of any other in the Mideast as a percentage of the total population.

Instead, Saddam's Ba'th established ironclad dictatorship, strangled free thought, dragged Iraq into three wars, and destroyed its human and natural resources. Ba'thism took the country back to what most other Arab and Muslim states exhibit today: poverty of the masses versus unimaginable wealth of the few, government corruption, widespread illiteracy, tribalism, atavism, cultural and economic backwardness, and resurgent fundamentalism and extremism.

To make matters much worse, Saudi Arabia (in particular) and Qatar have managed with their petro and gas dollars and media to divert these overriding Arab issues into a sectarian agenda of Sunni versus Shia. They have thereby accelerated the fragmentation of important Arab states like Syria, Iraq, and Yemen, impeding real religious and political reforms and opening the door for historical rivals Iran and Turkey to intrude yet again on the Arab scene.

There has also been the scourge of terrorism. Beginning in the 1970s, but especially after the Islamic revolution in Iran, the Saudi rulers and their Wahabi clerical establishment became increasingly nervous about their position as a tiny but very wealthy sect among the enormous Arab and non-Arab Muslim populations.

They therefore embarked in earnest on a worldwide program of proselytizing to convert Muslims into Wahabism. They spent billions of petrodollars on building Wahabi-run religious schools (madrassas) and mosques in Pakistan, Afghanistan, the central Asian states, the Arab world, Western Europe, Bosnia, Albania, and North America.

The Wahabi madrassa graduates and mosque attendants became Wahabis or were much influenced by the intolerant theology. It is among these converts and the original Wahabis of Saudi Arabia that the terrorist ideology grew and bore its poisonous fruit. Our political leaders have been well aware of this ongoing activity. In fact, the CIA trained bin Laden and his group of *mujahideen*, who were fighting the Soviets in Afghanistan in the 1970s. It is ironic that the future leader of al-Qa'ida and the engineer of 9/11 was once on the CIA payroll. But we did not learn our lesson and continued to work with such groups on and off to achieve fast results while ignoring the long-term consequences to us and to humanity.

Members of the US and European political class and media keep mouthing the phrase "Islamic terrorism" instead of "Wahabi terrorism," which is what it really is. Regular Muslims, be they Hanafis, Shafi'is, Malikis, Shia, or Sufis do not commit acts of terror and mass murder of innocents, women and children. Such crimes are only perpetrated by Wahabis or Wahabi-influenced groups like al-Taliban (the name means "students," the products of Saudi *madrassas*), al-Qa'ida, ISIS, Boko Haram, al-Shabab, and Abu Sayaf. Th e best evidence for that is that Muslims, not Christians, Jews, or others, have been the biggest victims of these Wahabi-raised and inspired global terrorist organizations. Tens of thousands of Muslims of all denominations, but especially the Shia, have been killed and maimed by these groups.

Thousands of other victims included the Christians of Iraq and Egypt, the Yazidis of Iraq, Europeans in England, France and Spain, and our fellow Americans here. As I said earlier, our political leaders are well aware of the Saudis' role in graduating and supporting these Wahabi elements. They have been briefed by our diplomatic and intelligence services and reputable sources, including the Rand Corporation, but they remain mum.

By not exposing to the public the actual theology of Wahabism and its offspring, Arab, Muslim, US, and Western leaders clearly bear responsibility for the untold thousands of terror victims among their citizenry. The Muslims themselves have been by far the most numerous victims of Wahabi ideology.

The *New York Times* published a long article about the Los Angeles Saudi consul-cleric, who received two of the 9/11 conspirators, put them up at an apartment, provided them with money, and helped them register for flying lessons. Sixteen of the nineteen 9/11 operatives as well as bin Laden himself were Saudi citizens. When all US passenger planes were grounded immediately after

9/11, a plane carrying bin Laden's family and relatives was allowed to take off to fly them back home. The American victims of 9/11, among them some four hundred Muslims, have not yet received any compensation from the Saudi government and have not been aided in that pursuit by the George W. Bush, Obama, or Trump administrations. All of that and the missing twenty-nine pages of the 9/11 committee report provide further evidence of the obfuscation by our leaders about the nature of the real enemy, this metastasizing violent ideology, the most serious threat in this century to world peace and political stability.

But then there is the oil of Saudi Arabia and the gas of Qatar, the two countries' huge investments in the US and Western Europe, the massive arms purchases, the generous donations to various Western entities like the Clinton and the Blair foundations, and the "strictly personal" fabulously expensive gifts to our current CEO, Donald Trump. They bribe governments in Muslim and non-Muslim countries in the guise of donations, loans, aid, or investment. Moreover, Saudi Arabia and Qatar now possess a huge propaganda machine comprising numerous newspapers (Saudis now own a third of Reuters News), regular and satellite TV stations, internet websites, and a mercenary army of news reporters and commentators.

The Saudi practices in their own kingdom are no different than those of ISIS. The Saudi authorities had in the past destroyed hundreds of landmarks of early Islam in the Hejaz. They forbid the erection of shrines at sites where Muslim saints and prominent past figures are buried. The great majority of Muslims, like Christians, Jews, Hindus, Buddhists, and other humans love to visit religious and historic landmarks for spiritual succor and to connect with their history. Saudi Arabia, however, is the only country in the world that prohibits that most human of rituals, except the visitation of the Ka'ba itself and the Prophet's mosque. The Wahabi state has its own "moral" guard, al-Mutaoa, to enforce the prohibition, by force if necessary, on the millions of pilgrims who flock there every year. Hence the Wahabis, through their control of the Hejaz, facilitated by the British in the early twentieth century, have imposed their antihuman prohibitions on 1.5 billion Muslims.

Al-Baqee', the burial place in the Hejaz of the Prophet's first three successor caliphs and many of the prominent early Muslims, is surrounded by a wire fence that blocks the innumerable pilgrims pouring into Mecca from visiting it. It has been neglected, is unclean, and has stray animals roaming around outside the fence. The situation was so unfathomable that the area was later cleaned up and the wire fence replaced by a glass barrier.

The Wahabis destroy historic landmarks, Islamic and otherwise, because they do not want people to be aware of their history; this would make it easier to brainwash people into Wahabism. This is why they forbid the visitation of shrines and destroy the landmarks and artifacts of ancient civilizations, as the Taliban did in Afghanistan and ISIS in Iraq and Syria. This concept has close resonance with the behavior of suicidal Wahabi terrorists who blow themselves up, killing scores of innocents in the process, and demolishing entire structures into nothing.

In a nutshell, Wahabism has given a bad name to Islam, the second largest world religion, with 1.5 billion people, the origin of past civilizations surpassing all others for eight hundred years, and ultimately the source of the European Renaissance.

Moreover, in Saudi Arabia they treat women like chattel, oppress the Shia and kill their leaders in the oil-rich eastern part of the country, prohibit free speech, and abuse female home help workers from the Philippines and southeast Asia. They flagellate and behead dissidents in "Chop Chop Square" and hang their corpses there for many days as a lesson for all. Two BBC correspondents managed a stealthy trip to the country, where they documented these ISIS-like practices. Unsurprisingly, the online video of the correspondents' risky adventure soon vanished from the web.

Anyone who's been to Saudi Arabia, watched Arabic TV, or gone online would be shocked by the Wahabi clerics' incessant hate-laden incitement to genocide against the Shia, a majority population in the eastern oil-rich province of Saudi Arabia itself and nearby Bahrain, in Iraq and Iran, and with large numbers in Kuwait, Pakistan, Afghanistan (the Hazaras), and India, totaling in all two hundred million souls. The Wahabi theology is responsible for the killing of untold thousands of Shia all over the Muslim World.

The Turkish massacre of Armenians and Kurds, the holocaust against the European Jews, the Hutus' slaughter of Tutsis in Rwanda, and the Serbian massacre of Muslims in the Balkans were genocidal crimes. Why not then the massacres and mass graves of Shiites in Iraq, Pakistan, and Afghanistan? And why is their brutal suppression in Saudi Arabia and Bahrain not a violation of human rights? Why then are the Saudi establishment and its hydra of Wahabi clerics not brought to justice at the Hague? These questions must be answered by the US, the strongest ally of the Saudi monarchy and the main guarantor of its nearly century-old reign, and by the United Nations and its Security Council.

Egypt's ambassador to the UN, Yasser Rida, published an article in the *Wall Street Journal*, "Countering the Pontiff of Terror," about Yusuf al-Qardawi, a vocal Sunni cleric widely featured in Saudi, Qatari, and Emirati-sponsored media and satellite TV networks. Al-Qardawi condones bin Laden, al-Zarqawi (the sheikh

of slaughterers), and Abu Bekr al-Baghdadi of ISIS, and also suicide bombings if they are "approved by the Jama'a (the community
of Muslims)."

Mr. Rida cogently mentions that Articles 19 and 20 of the
"International Covenant on Civil and Political Rights" state that
freedom of expression carries special responsibilities for state
governments to prohibit hatred-inciting speech, extremism,
and violence, and that the UN Human Rights Committee has
been charged with monitoring states' compliance with the ordi-
nance. Examples of such hate speech are the broadcasts by Joseph
Goebbels that brought on the Holocaust and the radio broadcasts
in Africa that facilitated the Rwandan genocide. These were no
different from the pronouncements against the Shia of Qardawi
and the Wahabi clerics.

Furthermore, the UN Security Council unanimously adopted
Resolution 1373, obligating all member states to undertake legislative and administrative measures to prevent the financing of
terrorism. Other resolutions of the council call for states to establish watch lists of individuals and entities suspected of having
links to terrorist organizations. All of this should apply to Saudi
Arabia and Qatar.

The Wahabi ideology of hate is also directed at other Muslim
sects, especially the Sufi schools, Muslim reformists and intellectuals, advocates of women's rights, Christians, Jews, and against
most norms of human civilization. The religious curriculum of
Saudi schools is an appalling catalog of rigid intolerance, bigotry,
and animus. A great many Muslim workers and professionals from
other countries had found employment in Saudi Arabia, where
their children were schooled in Wahabism and grew up with its
tenets, which they then took back to their mother countries.

The plethora of Wahabi imams in mosques across the Muslim

world, Europe, and North America has tenaciously propagated the creed, eventually breeding terror and mayhem in Europe and graduating fanatical Muslim groups among the previously tolerant Muslim populations of Bosnia and Albania. Readers who are curious to learn more about the workings of the Saudi state can go to Google Search, enter "kernel of evil," and read on. There are umpteen results.

In Nigeria, Saudi Arabia has managed with money and imams to ignite a sectarian war between the Sunni Izala and the Shiite IMNA groups. Wahabi ideology had spawned Boko Haram, al-Shabab of Somalia, and terrorist groups in Egypt's Sinai, Libya, Tunisia, and Algeria. Most of these gangs have more recently declared allegiance to ISIS. Saudi petrodollars have been used to turn Muslims against each other, tearing the fabric of Muslim and Arab societies. Certainly the Arab states are now weaker than they've ever been in modern times.

The Arab Spring had finally come to Syria, too—young and not-so-young educated people calling for more open and representative government. Not surprisingly, they met with brutal suppression by a minority government steeped in the Ba'th tradition of violence and zero tolerance for dissent. Mr. Obama looked on, declared that unarmed students and professionals were not going to unseat a heavily armed dictatorial regime, and did nothing. A vacuum was thus created that the jihadists, true to their customary strategy, took advantage of and sprang to action. There was the Qa'ida affiliate Nusra Front in Syria, terrorists streaming in from Iraq, others coming from central Asia via Turkey, and recruits from Western Europe and North America.

The Saudi rulers had been most unhappy about the secular Arab Spring anywhere because the people's quest for democracy threatened the foundation of their own regime. But when it came to Wahabi terrorists filling the gap, private Saudi money and especially the statelet of Qatar itself rushed in to help with money and arms. They hoped the fighting jihadists would unseat Bashar al-Asad (his surname means "the lion;" my first name means "happier"), and the US looked the other way. The game worked against the Syrian secular opposition because it lent credence to Asad's declarations that the resistance was comprised of terrorist groups, thus pouring cold water on any Western initiatives to support the original protest movement.

President Obama and Mrs. Clinton had seemingly not calculated that those terrorist organizations would mushroom into a bigger nightmare than the Asad regime. Incidentally, Qatar has also supported terrorist militias in Libya, thereby prolonging a chaotic and violent situation where militias were fighting each other over land and oil resources, and accelerating the fragmentation of the country. This caused a tidal wave of refugees who braved the sea. A great many of them drowned, and the survivors flooded the southern European shores.

The tragedy of Syria, with its five-thousand-year history of civilization and the world's oldest continuously inhabited capital, stands out as one of the worst catastrophes of the past and present centuries. What befell Iraq over thirty-five years happened in Syria in just five years: the destruction of ancient cities like Aleppo, Homs, and Palmyra; the nearly half a million killed and the countless maimed; the brain drain and the millions of refugees, thousands of them swallowed by the Mediterranean sea. And yet, while Germany took in a million refugees, the oil-rich Saudi state, its king, the "custodian of the two sacred mosques," the rich statelets of Qatar and the UAE—all Arab and Muslim brethren—took none.

Last but not least, there is now the sectarian war Saudi Arabia is waging against the Houthis of Yemen, killing in the process thousands of innocent civilians and children, bombing Doctors without Borders clinics and destroying the infrastructure of this already-impoverished country. In an ISIS-like operation, the Royal Saudi Air Force bombed a building housing a large funeral ceremony, killing 140 and injuring 400 people, including children. Ten thousand civilians have been killed and many more injured; eleven million are displaced; 80 percent of the population is now nearing starvation; and a child dies every ten minutes. When a prominent Arab journalist, Abdul Bari Atwan, lambasted the Saudis for the atrocious war on Yemen, he was no longer allowed to air his views on any of their media. Our US political leaders maintained an eloquent silence.

Meanwhile, amid the painful poverty and daily suffering in Yemen, Syria, Iraq, and much of the Arab world, the Saudi King travels to Southeast Asia with a retinue of over fifteen hundred people, five planes to carry five hundred tons of royal paraphernalia, and a fleet of top-class Mercedes salon cars as though this is money he'd inherited from his ancestors. The obscenity of this act comes into a blinding glare when contrasted with the allotment of over $50 billion to the world's sick and hungry by Warren Buffett and the Gates foundation.

When the UN announced that the Saudi actions in Yemen were a breach of the Geneva Convention and listed the kingdom among the countries that target children in war, the Saudi government threatened to withhold their financial contribution to the UN, unfortunately causing the latter to water down its indictment.

The Houthis of Yemen constitute 45 percent of the population. They are an offshoot of Shia Islam. Unlike the Twelver Shiites of Iraq and Iran, they follow only five Shia imams. They are called the Zaydis in reference to Zayd, son of Ali, son of Imam Husayn, and are concentrated in the northern mountainous region of Yemen, called Sa'da, bordering on southwest Saudi Arabia. They produced many consecrated rulers of Yemen, the last of whom was Muhammad al-Badr, who ruled before the military coup by Abdullah al-Sallal in 1962.

There had been constant clashes and intermittent warfare between Saudi Arabia and the Houthis, and Saudi air force and artillery had time and again bombed their towns and villages in Sa'da. Shortly before the current Yemen war, the Houthis took the lead among many other Yemeni factions and political parties protesting against the rampant corruption of the regime. Eventually the government agreed to have the protesting parties get together to hammer out an agreement about power sharing and reform. The Saudis, however, pressured the Yemeni government to renege on the agreement because they worried the "apostate" Houthis may become a significant political power in Yemen. Consequently the Houthis stormed the capital, San'a, and President Abd Rabbu Hadi fled to his benefactors in Riadh.

The war in Yemen has violated every rule of the Geneva Convention, killing thousands of people and a staggering number of children. The Saudi-led coalition has used starvation as a weapon, by blockading the ports of Yemen. The resulting famine, infrastructure destruction by non-stop bombing and the scarcity of clean water have resulted in a cholera epidemic that has killed thousands of people, especially the children. The UN has declared the situation in Yemen as being one of the worst catastrophes of our time.

Yet the Obama and the Trump administrations have not only been silent about this massive war crime, but have in fact worked with Saudi Arabia and its Gulf allies to coordinate so-called "legitimate" bombing targets, and have participated in enforcing a sea blockade on Yemen that has only worsened the human tragedy of hunger, disease, and death. Furthermore, the United Kingdom has continued to sell arms and cluster bombs to the Saudi military.

It is distressing to see that just as Obama's passive policies regarding Iraq and Syria had facilitated the destruction of their citizens, his active policy in Yemen was achieving the same result. How do the Houthis represent any threat to the US, and is there any sane or humane reason to curb them at the price of the thousands of killed and injured civilians and the many more thousands of internally displaced and starving people? Is not the Qua'ida in the Arabian Peninsula, entrenched in southeastern Yemen, the mother of al-Awlaqi and the bomber of the USS Cole, the real threat to the US and the region? And are not the Houthis the only credible force against the Qua'ida in Yemen?

Do the answers to those questions pertain to the realpolitiks of oil? But we no longer need Saudi oil as much as we did in the past. In fact, the continued overproduction of oil by Saudi Arabia, aimed at bankrupting Iraq, Iran, and perhaps Russia, has also driven many US producers out of business and caused untold economic suffering in Third World states that are largely dependent on oil revenues. In their blind hatred of Iraq and Iran, the Saudis have forgotten that their practice will eventually damage their own economy as well.

Talking of realpolitiks, I was quite surprised to learn that President Obama subscribes to that concept and that he is an admirer of its proponent Brent Scowcroft, considering that the ideology contradicts his professed humanitarian morality. President George H. W. Bush and Henry Kissinger were the prototypes of realpolitiks, and Niccolò Machiavelli its philosopher. The pursuit of realpolitiks notwithstanding, a superpower has the obligation of curbing its client states when it comes to crimes against humanity or acts that destabilize a large strategic region of the world.

The problem, I daresay, is that President Obama did not really see himself as the leader of a superpower or that he fully recognized the importance of opposing mutually deterrent superpowers in the conduct of global politics and the maintenance of world peace. He outsourced important tasks in Libya and Syria to tiny Qatar and not-so-tiny Saudi Arabia, both Wahabi states with their own bigoted and backward agendas. And the results are there for all to see. Furthermore, the other superpowers—Russia and China, both semidictatorships—had taken Mr. Obama's measure and become much less restrained.

Let's consider this scenario. The Saudi state and Bahrain continue to suppress their Shia citizens, a majority in Bahrain, killing, banishing, and withdrawing citizenship status from their leaders and imams, blocking their participation in governance, fencing off their villages, and treating them like third-class citizens. Meanwhile the Saudi clerics continue the call for the extermination of the Shia. Sooner or later there will be a major convulsion of this population and a bloody struggle to separate and form their own state in eastern Saudi Arabia and Bahrain. If the Saudi state contemplates this scenario and sees that the US may actually sympathize with the cause of such separation, it may very well change its behavior and curb its genocide-inciting clerics.

Think about it. Such an independent state would be the end of petrodollars flowing into the coffers of global Wahabi terrorism. Unfortunately, President Obama and now Trump and the Congress have remained mostly silent about the internal and foreign policies of our allies. Mrs. Clinton called them "our Sunni Arab allies." Of course they are, for they contributed hundreds of millions of dollars to the Clinton Foundation, even in the years when Mrs. Clinton was our secretary of state. The foundation graciously accepted the donations from the Saudis and the Gulf Arabs despite their financing of terrorist groups in the Arab world and their miserable record on human and women's rights. There were also outlandish gifts bestowed on our current president, Mr. Trump, who was not above accepting them. The bribery of our high officials, if we call a spade a spade, differs only in its packaging from that seen in the Third World, Russia, India, and China. US federal and state employees would go to jail for accepting bribery, but our top officials seem to be above the law.

Our leaders have shamelessly practiced the double standard we denounce in the behavior of other nations. Their policy, furthermore, contributes much to what I call the "Great Obfuscation", the misleading of the public about the identity of our and civilization's real enemy. Worse still, when Mrs. Clinton was confronted during her presidential election campaign by the fact that she knew about the arming by "our Arab allies" of extremist groups in Syria, she retorted that she thought it better than our own men having to do the fighting. What cynicism. Interestingly, the supposedly maverick President Trump has continued the obfuscation by excluding Saudi citizens from his ban on Muslims' entry to the US, notwithstanding the fact that Saudi citizens have been responsible for the overwhelming majority of terror casualties in the US, including those of 9/11.

In fact, the Obama administration, the CIA, Russia, and the whole world knew about the financing and arming of terrorist groups by Saudi Arabia, Qatar, and Turkey. This is why a great many Arab intellectuals and laity believe the Saudi and Qatari actions are actually prompted by the US for its own purposes. Saudi Arabia and Qatar are US client regimes and would not take up such serious adventures without US consent. Whether these skeptic Arabs are conspiracy theorists or not, it is impossible to deny the logic of their argument.

Next I would like to discuss the more-than-three-decades' obsession of successive US administrations with Iran because the issue has great relevance to the US national interest, and stability, and peace in the Mideast. Iran is a vast country of 636,400 square miles (1,648,000 square kilometers), larger than the US eastern seaboard. It has eighty million people, 615 miles (989 kilometers) of Persian Gulf shoreline, six thousand years of civilization, and an imperial history going back four thousand years. It has the fifth-largest oil reserve—the third if you exclude Canada's unconventional reserves. It sits in a uniquely strategic position. Going clockwise from the west, it is bordered by Iraq, Turkey Russia, Asian Muslim countries, the Arab Sea and the Persian Gulf. It has an intelligent and forward-looking population, over 60 percent of which is young and US-friendly. The country is too large and strategic to ignore and too stubborn to bully.

In much of Iran's long history before the early twentieth century, the Ottoman Empire and later Russia, not the USA, had been the traditional threats. No US administration with its gaze fixed on the national interest can afford to keep Iran for long on the list of antagonists or push it by misguided political strategy toward alignment with opposing superpowers. Iran has already been pushed much closer to Russia than it has ever been.

The problem is that we no longer have statesmen, only politicians careless of our national interest, but very careful to cultivate various special-interest lobbies to guarantee their election and reelection. They throw out empty slogans to the crowds and carry on uncivil debates in glaring TV studios. Debates should be about governance, not electioneering, and ought to be conducted by members of elected assemblies as was done by Daniel

Webster and Robert Hayne in the US, Edmund Burke and Winston Churchill in Britain, Cicero in Rome, and Demosthenes in Athens. Otherwise ours will soon become a democracy of the mob, when dangerous demagogues take the helm. Let's not forget that Adolph Hitler was elected. So was Donald Trump.

Nor is it in the interest of the Arab states, presently seduced by Saudi petrodollars, to antagonize Iran, a large and (like them) a Muslim county, offering them political depth into central Asia and vast trade and cultural exchange opportunities. But the Arabs seem to have forgotten their own relatively recent history. Did they not fight with the British against the Ottomans but only got in return Sykes-Picot and the Wahabi Sa'ud dynasty as "custodians of the two sacred mosques?"

But history has a way of coming back to haunt us. Sharif Husayn of Hejaz, once a World War I British ally against the Ottomans, saw that the British had reneged on their promises to him after the end of the war. He therefore refused to endorse the Treaty of Versailles, the Balfour Declaration, the British mandate over Iraq and Palestine, and the French one over Syria; and he did not sign the Anglo-Hashemite Treaty.

In punishment for the Sharif, the British did not support him against the advancing horde of Ibn Saud who overran Mecca, Medina, and Jeddah, thereby becoming the "custodian of the two sacred mosques." This was obviously a better option for the British than ousting Sharif Husayn themselves and occupying the Hejaz. Imagine a Muslim power occupying the Vatican! The Saudis would do the bidding of the British, and later of the Americans. Remember that an Arab tribe would always seek alliance with a much stronger tribe to safeguard its interests. To the Saudis, the British and, later, the Americans were the stronger "tribes." Now, a century later, we and the British are witnessing the mayhem the offspring of Wahabism have unleashed in both countries and around the world. "He who sows the wind shall reap the whirlwind."

I have strayed from the Iran issue, but never mind. The retrogressive and autocratic clerical rule in Iran notwithstanding (and regimes ultimately undergo positive internal change), it must be clear to all and sundry that normalized relations between the US and Iran will greatly facilitate US policies in the Mideast and Central Asia. It will check Wahabi terrorism, stabilize the Arab Middle East, and curb the resurgent aggressive encroachment of Russia, whose kleptocratic regime will only strengthen the existing ones in the Mideast and thwart the popular forces seeking freedom and clean and transparent governance. These forces are now subdued but will certainly rise again. Iran had actually cooperated with the US during the invasion of Afghanistan and looked the other way during the expulsion of Saddam's troops from Kuwait in 1991. But then President George W. Bush came out to declare Iran a member of the Axis of Evil, along with North Korea and Syria.

In my view, the opening to Iran, if not derailed, was the only outstanding achievement of the Obama administration, and will be acknowledged as such in the annals of US history.

# 39

# Back to Medicine

The Hippocratic oath was first written in Ionic Greek in the late fifth century BC. A modern version used in many medical schools was composed in 1964 by Dr. Louis Lasagna, academic dean at Tufts University Medical School. I will not repeat it verbatim, but will modify the wording a little to accommodate it to today's lingo, while preserving the sequence of the themes comprising the oath.

A graduating physician takes an oath to respect the scientific achievements of his mentors; to follow their example; to impart willingly his knowledge and experience to others; to apply to the sick all necessary treatment, avoiding overtreatment or nihilism; to understand that medicine is part art and part science; that the benefits of empathy may exceed those of medicines or surgery; and to admit that some illnesses are beyond his grasp and to be ready to consult a more experienced or specialized colleague.

The physician further undertakes not to divulge a patient's problems to others; to approach matters of life and death carefully, not to play God; to understand that he is not simply treating symptoms and signs but a human being whose illness may well affect his family's future and livelihood; that his responsibilities include attending to these "nonmedical" problems; that it is always better to prevent a disease than to treat it; and that he should remain involved in his community's affairs and honor his obligations to his fellow human beings.

Finally the physician acknowledges that only by adhering to his oath and preserving the best traditions of his discipline will he enjoy the pleasures of life, be respected in his lifetime, and be remembered after his death.

Throughout the ages, the physician had been what we call today a *family physician* in the US and *general practitioner* in the UK. He knew his patients since their infancy, and may have actually delivered them himself. He treated their spouses and children. He knew their family history firsthand and a great number of their secrets.

Patients told their longtime physician almost everything because they saw him as a priest. In Arabic he is called *Hakeem*, the "wise one," or *Tabeeb*, the "curing one." Patients went to see him at his office, but often in cases of emergency, the family brought their sick one to his home in the wee hours of the morning. My father, for example, was such a physician. He was also a consummate internist.

I have always emphasized to my trainees that the best way to understand a patient's illness is to let her tell her story, to be patient and listen, and when she is finished, we will have a reasonably good idea what's ailing her. We could then ask some questions for clarification or further pursue a symptom she mentioned more than once. We should not shoot questions at patients like darts to satisfy some inane list of items on a paper or electronic page. Sadly, I have seen this done far too often by trainees as well as some attending physicians.

If the patient's complaint is a stomach pain, we should begin by examining the abdomen lest the patient think we are obtuse or inattentive. The pain may well be radiating from another organ, but that is beside the point. We need to perform a careful and as painless an examination as possible. We have to look out for nonverbal clues of pain, embarrassment, or fear. Afterward we will be in a much better position to make a clinical diagnosis and confirm it by relevant tests, not umpteen tests that usually turn out to be negative.

Physicians are too rushed nowadays. They have to finish paperwork mandated by a mushrooming government bureaucracy and attend usually redundant hospital meetings that dry up the soul and fossilize the mind. There is no longer time enough to pursue many of the tenets of the Hippocratic oath. Moreover, our endless health care "reforms" and "innovations" have resulted in untold numbers of patients no longer able to see their physicians of many years, who would obviously not take too long a time to follow up on their various problems.

Many patients complain that they are not being examined but are only sent to have tests done. They give me a look of grateful surprise when I take their blood pressure and pulse myself or ask them to say "ninety-nine" while listening to the chest. My brother had anemia and weight loss, so he went to see his physician at a reputable hospital in a Chicago suburb. Many tests were ordered, but he was surprised the doctor did not lay hands on him. Endoscopy was scheduled, but a preceding simple stool test for blood was omitted.

A patient of mine began to complain that her shortness of breath was no longer responding as well to the medicines she'd been taking. Many years earlier, she would become short of breath while walking up a slight incline of only ten degrees. She never had any wheezing, but on percussing her chest it reverberated like a drum because of trapped air. Lung function tests I ordered at the time showed that her breathing difficulty was reversed by an inhaler that dilates the air passages. Her shortness of breath would get worse when her face was under the shower or exposed to cold wind. She had infantile eczema as a child and a strong family history of asthma.

I concluded that she had nonwheezing asthma, and a lung specialist agreed with the diagnosis since the account I've related is classic for asthma except for the absence of wheezing, which is very unusual but not unheard of. She was given medication for asthma and her symptoms disappeared. After her first pregnancy, she no longer needed the asthma drugs, another frequent feature of the disease. Later in life, however, her symptoms reappeared, and she resumed taking the asthma medication.

Because she was now much older and was not responding to medications as well as she had in the past, I referred her to a lung specialist, a university professor whose main interest was asthma. A fellow-in-training saw and examined her first, then presented her case to the professor. Tests were done. The professor told her she did not have asthma and that she could in fact donate a lung. "He never examined me or listened to my lungs," she told me. I naturally never again referred any patient to him.

My sister is a family practitioner in California. An elderly man came in to her office with his wife, and the first thing he said was, "We heard Jesus has come to town—that you actually examine your patients. So I brought you this old lady of mine to look at." In fact patients derive a psychological benefit from the mere act of physical examination, especially when no abnormal findings are detected. It is a tradition that goes back for centuries and is immortalized in too many paintings.

Another physician friend of mine works for a private company that hires physicians to treat US army veterans. The patients are supposed to come in once a year for physicals and follow-up. It turns out, however, that many have had chronic problems like unexplained anemia or an abnormal test result that has not been pursued. So he had to spend much extra time at the office to follow up on such cases. The company discourages but does not block more frequent patient visits.

The medical director of the outfit saw my friend and said his performance got top scores by the patients, but that his notes were too long; that he did not have to do full physical exams, but only concentrate on the area relating to the patient's symptoms; that there are studies showing physical exam doesn't make any difference for patient outcomes; that he did not have to waste time explaining things to patients and would do better to leave that to the nurse. His colleague at the office asked him, "Do you really want to be a doctor or leave at 4:00 p.m. to enjoy life and the good weather?" He is now looking for another job where he can continue to be a real doctor.

The ancient physician-patient relationship has changed considerably in the US since the 1950s for other reasons. Increasingly, more young people have left their birthplace in the countryside or small towns and gone to larger cities in pursuit of career opportunities. If they fall ill, they visit a physician they've never seen before, one who had not known them or their families. Eventually they may form a long-term relationship with that physician, assuming they do not relocate again.

When the Clinton administration gifted us the Health

Maintenance Organizations (HMOs), a great many patients lost their longtime physicians because the latter were not on the roster of the particular HMO company. The same happened, perhaps to a lesser extent, in the case of the PPOs (point-of-service care) because patients had to come up with much higher out-of-pocket payments (copays) if their established physicians and hospitals were "out-of-network" for the PPO outfit.

At other times, insurance companies would terminate a contract with a hospital and its affiliates or with individual doctors, thereby causing a huge number of patients to lose their longtime physicians. A friend of mine, a family practitioner, told me he once had fifty new patients assigned to him because their insurance company had terminated its contract with another practitioner. Several years later the reverse happened, and he lost two hundred patients whom he'd been seeing for many years. This is what I call playing musical chairs with patients, whereby their choice of doctors, the physician-patient relationship, their comfort, and their long-term health status become subsidiary issues. Incidentally, doctors are no longer called doctors or physicians. They are "providers," like service providers at McDonald's or auto parts shops.

Another factor in the weakening of the primary physician-patient compact has been the breakneck expansion of medical knowledge and therefore the need for more specialists and super-specialists in the various fields of medicine and surgery.

Diseases and cancers of the various body organs now require the attention of specialists with certified training and experience in those fields. Patients need to follow up frequently with these physicians, so they cut down on visits to their primary doctors, sometimes ceasing to see them altogether for reasons relating to finances, convenience, or transportation hurdles. Good family physicians and internists, however, still act as the "conductor of the orchestra," referring their patients to competent specialists. And they continue to see those patients, meanwhile staying in touch with the specialists.

The interaction between the primary physician who needs to admit a patient to an academic center quickly and the receiving doctor is often rocky. Having been in both worlds myself, academic and private, I have often noticed that many academic physicians and their trainees regard primary physicians in community hospitals with arrogant dismissal. They mouth phrases like "The patient was referred by Dr. X from St. Elsewhere Hospital," and they pooh-pooh the primary physician's diagnosis and his reason for sending them the patient. This has always reminded me of an old adage: "The greater the ignorance, the greater the arrogance."

The phenomenon also reminds me of a story my friend Mazin al-Khateeb told me a long time ago. He was at the time a surgeon at an El Paso, Texas hospital. One evening he was crossing the emergency room when a patient collapsed. Mazin jumped on the patient to resuscitate him, giving him mouth-to-mouth breathing, but the patient succumbed quickly and could not be saved.

Two days later, two somber state health officials came to the hospital and asked urgently to see Dr. Khateeb. They informed him he had to take an antibiotic they fetched for him because the patient he had tried to resuscitate had bubonic plague. Mazin was shocked to hear that, as he never knew plague still existed, and we had certainly never seen any case in Iraq.

It turned out that the primary physician who sent the patient to the ER had actually written in his referral note the diagnosis of bubonic plague, which the ER physicians laughed off. Everyone subsequently learned that bubonic plague was endemic in that area of El Paso. The primary physician was aware of that and had made the correct diagnosis.

In fact, primary physicians and internists in the community work harder than most academic physicians, and many are more astute clinicians. They see their hospitalized patients every day and witness the course of illness and its response to treatment, often variable from one patient to another. In academia, on the other hand, the first encounter of the patient is usually with a medical resident-in-training who then presents the case to the attending physician the same or the following day. The attending physician sees the patient, but the daily follow-up is often undertaken by the resident or the fellow and reported to the attending physician. Furthermore, primary physicians work long hours every day and are paged about their patients day and night, while in academia the residents usually handle such calls. Finally, rather than typing a long, time-consuming note after seeing the patient, the academic physician usually types a few lines at the end of the trainee's long note, agreeing with or modifying the latter's diagnosis and treatment plan.

Ever since I came to Chicago in 1972, controversies have raged about the optimal system of health care the US should adopt. The recommendations of the "experts" have included single payer, Medicare and Medicaid reform, HMOs and PPOs, and the implementation of the Affordable Care Act (ACA), also called Obamacare, which did not intrude on the choice of private health insurance but expanded the scope of private companies, accountable to their shareholders for returns, in participating in the Medicare and Medicaid programs.

As far as I can see (not as an expert in health insurance matters—I am not—but as a practicing physician), none of these plans has been satisfactory. The Affordable Care Act has thankfully removed the "preexisting condition" clause as an obstacle to patients signing up with insurance companies. The clause was certainly outrageous, hardly ever known in other countries, and incompatible with the definition of health insurance. However, the dispersal of many Medicaid and even Medicare patients among various private insurers has created an administrative and paperwork nightmare for patients and health care professionals.

Medicaid patients with dialysis-dependent kidney failure previously had coverage for drugs crucial for ensuring their health, rehabilitation, and survival. Most disabled ones also had coverage for transportation by a "medicar." After signing up with ACA-participating companies, a great many of these patients have lost coverage for the essential but expensive drugs and struggle with the help of social workers, nurses, and physicians to obtain them, usually unsuccessfully, through various other channels. Many have also lost their transportation coverage.

President Obama had promised that patients signing up for the ACA would be able to keep their existing physicians if they wished. This did not materialize. The companies participating in ACA have so far offered patients limited networks of physicians and hospitals to serve them, often depriving them of their customary doctors and greatly narrowing their choice of physicians and hospitals. My physician colleagues tell me that public aid patients used to come regularly for their scheduled visits, but not anymore, because they have large deductibles in their so-called affordable care contracts that they have to satisfy before they get full coverage for services. They therefore disappear with their hypertension, diabetes, or other ailments and suffer the consequences. Some who have a little money keep coming but pay cash. The physician would usually give them a significant discount.

In the larger perspective, ACA has provided inadequate insurance to millions who had none while making such insurance much more expensive, often unaffordable, for other millions of small business owners and low and middle income people. To make matters worse, several large insurance companies are now bolting out of Obamacare.

As for Medicare patients (those sixty-five years and older) who have signed up with the ACA-participating companies, a great many can no longer stay with their customary health care providers if the latter are "out-of-network" for that company because to do so would entail significant copay for services. Moreover, patients often discover that some drugs they'd been taking for years are not "approved" by the company, which in turn would direct letters to busy physicians requesting "prior approval" and justification for the drugs, including laboratory test results, and so on—a process that interrupts the continuity of treatment and consumes much of the time and energy of health care professionals, time far better spent in direct patient care, not redundant time-wasting paperwork. A more manageable (though ridiculous) situation is when the company turns out to cover essentially the same drug in question but one with a different brand name—depending of course on the contracts insurance companies make with the various pharmaceutical providers.

I told a long-term dialysis patient of mine that her blood pressure was well controlled after I had raised the dose of the drug nifedipine. She retorted, "But now I have to come up with forty dollars out of pocket." I was astounded since the drug has been on the market for many years and gone generic. I called her pharmacy, had to listen in the middle of a busy day to commercials first, then nice music, interrupted many times by "Your call is very important to us," and finally the voice of a real human being.

I explained my patient's situation to the pharmacist and asked her what the problem was. "The patient was getting three months' worth of thirty milligram nifedipine tablets, then sixty and now ninety milligrams," she said. "She has Medicare Part D (drug coverage), but her insurance company would not pay fully for the ninety-milligram strength tablets. Well, it's open enrollment season now, and the patient can sign up with another company."

Really? The patient is ninety-two years old and has been a retiree since before the internet era. There are millions of others like her, including older physicians and other professionals, blind diabetics, and illiterate people. We seem to have "experts" who think most patients can navigate their way through the electronic convolutions of often unwieldy and user-unfriendly websites to make reasonable choices about which company would best satisfy their medication needs.

Going back to the ACA, I think all President Obama had to do was to illegalize the "preexisting condition" clause barring access to private health insurers and, more importantly, work on reforming Medicare and the state-sponsored Medicaid programs. After all, the big health insurance companies like United Health Care, Aetna, and Humana are about to flock out of the ACA program, and the local Blue Cross Blue Shield providers have largely constricted the networks of providers to ACA patients.

I, like a great many other physicians, believe health care to be a right of all citizens regardless of their income or condition of employment. The federal Medicare and the states' Medicaid programs, with some fine-tuning, elimination of waste, containment of runaway health care and drug cost and emphasis on preventive care would provide good coverage for a large segment of the US population. People not eligible for these government-funded programs would be free to choose among the private health insurance companies.

My own opinion (one shared by millions of others) is that health care is a human right. Remember Thomas Jefferson's words: "We hold these truths to be self-evident: that all men are created equal; that they are endowed by their Creator with certain unalienable rights; that among these are life, liberty, and the pursuit of happiness." Life and the pursuit of happiness are impossible with poor health. A single-payer system is possible and more equitable and is a better guarantee against a multitiered health care system. After all, US citizens certainly pay enough federal and state income taxes, and a portion of that huge tax revenue could be allotted to a single-payer national health insurance rather than to various pork barrel and special lobbies-driven expenditures or futile wars. Absent such a system, I do not see how future US administrations can end multitiered health care coverage, which in fact has now existed for many decades.

⁓◦⑧◦⁓

The cost of health care in the US is close to the highest in the world. This is true for the cost of laboratory tests, emergency room visits, hospitalization, surgery, drugs, and long-term care. Pharmaceutical companies protest that it takes hundreds of millions of dollars to develop a new drug, which is why it would be very expensive for several years after launching. Yet, the cost of the drug made by the same company is much cheaper in other countries. Some years ago, during a trip to Barcelona, an expensive city, I walked into a pharmacy and purchased a seven months' supply of Zocor, a patented brand-name cholesterol drug, for the price of a single-month supply in the US.

Even out-of-patent drugs that have been on the market for many years are more expensive in the US than in other advanced countries. Prices have more recently come down because many drugs are now covered by health insurers, governmental or private, who can negotiate lower prices, or they are available at significant discounts by the likes of Costco and Walmart. Insured patients may, however, have to come up with a copay that may be large. My own health insurance policy, for example, has drug coverage, but the only time I had to use a steroidal nasal spray I paid $50 for a mere 15 cc (half an ounce) bottle. I was quite surprised, however, when the pharmacist told me insurance paid the balance of $100, as the spray cost $150. Tinfoil-wrapped Claritin tablets for allergy still cost $1 a tablet.

I now have Medicare Part D drug coverage with an outfit called Silverscript. My supplemental health insurance for medical care and drugs is with United Health Care, which has a contract with the Cook County Pension Board. The latter pays me my pension salary after deducting the supplemental insurance premium. Every month Silverscript sends me a three-column list of the drugs I had purchased. An eye-arresting example from the month of January 2017 was as follows: Among other drugs I had purchased was a two-week supply of erythromycin, an antibiotic on the market for over four decades. I paid $10.00 for it, which is fine, but Medicare Part D paid $394.85 and supplemental insurance paid $121.61.

This is simply outrageous. How do the government and the supplemental insurance company agree to pay $516.45 for a drug that should not cost more than $10.00 to $15.00 at most? This must be one of the main reasons why I and millions of others pay hefty Medicare and supplemental insurance premiums. If, for example, I had lost that erythromycin bottle during a trip, would

I have to buy another for the price of $526? And what about poor and limited-income Americans? It is clear that shenanigans must abound along the path that eventually delivers the drug to the consumer, and "middleman" outfits must be making a windfall in the process. Why can't our government and Congress get down to business to rein in these astronomical drug prices? Is it again the lobbies and their election campaign contributions?

EpiPen, a preloaded syringe of epinephrine, which highly allergic individuals need to carry with them to reverse severe and potentially fatal reactions, costs between $150 and $300. Epinephrine should be cheap. It's been available for many decades. Likewise, deflazocort, a drug helpful to twelve thousand US boys with Duchenne muscular dystrophy, was recently manufactured by a US company. The price? It is $89,000 a year. The drug has been available in Europe since the 1990s, and our countrymen have been buying it for $1,600 a year from an online pharmacy in London. The pharmacy has recently stopped providing it to US citizens because of our FDA's regulation banning the importation of drugs already available in the US.

To bring the issue into a sharper focus: Many dialysis patients would not obtain a drug I've prescribed if the copay is as little as three to five dollars. Furthermore, over-the-counter drugs are usually not covered by insurance, and most patients with limited budgets would not purchase them if the price is unreasonably high, which it often is—for example, fifteen dollars for cough syrup.

Then there are the "me too" drugs. A company produces a successful drug that sells well, but soon thereafter one or more other companies make their own brand of essentially a similar drug, perhaps tweaked at some side-chain of the molecule, market the drug aggressively at great cost, and sponsor "comparison" studies by academic investigators purporting to show the superiority of the new drug over the original one. The medical study is then discussed in journal clubs for trainees at university hospitals, and hospital-based pharmacists get busy at the Pharmacy and Therapeutics Committee, citing that same article and comparing cost in order to decide which drug they should adopt for their formulary. They must do so because it does not make sense to adopt two essentially similar drugs, especially if one is less expensive than the other.

When a drug approaches patent expiration, the company that holds the patent may produce a new, slightly modified version of the parent drug to get a new patent protection. Needless to say, all these activities pose a considerable expense to consumers. Furthermore, studies of new drugs rarely compare them to effective older drugs that have gone generic and are therefore much cheaper. I often tell my colleagues, busy and bewildered by the avalanche of new drugs, to refer to the *Medical Letter*, a useful and succinct publication that started long before my medical internship days. It gives a useful comparison of the new drugs to the existing ones in terms of their mode of action, efficacy, toxicity, and cost, with a summary at the end. The publication also offers a test, if one desires to take one, that counts as a CME (continuing medical education) credit, and is also available online. (This is not an advertisement.)

Private physicians in their offices are accosted by pharmaceutical sales representatives who expound on the merits of a new largely "me too" drug or another that produces the same effect as the older one but works through a different physiologic pathway. Many physicians are "seduced" by such presentations, especially when augmented by lavish multicourse dinners in expensive restaurants, and begin to prescribe the drug, often not cognizant of its cost. The new drug, however, may ultimately turn out to be not as effective as proclaimed, or less effective or more toxic in certain racial groups. In the past, pharmaceutical companies had much more attractive incentives for physicians and investigators, such as free trips in the US and overseas, including famous and expensive skiing resorts like Innsbruck in Austria. Fortunately, over the last several years, US authorities have introduced regulations that greatly limit such outlandish marketing.

Some useful drugs have been so aggressively and successfully marketed that their side effects, often serious, have been glossed over. A prime example is the family of renin-angiotensin-aldosterone system (RAAS) blocking drugs. The chemistry of these drugs is irrelevant to you as a reader. Suffice it to say that they do block RAAS, mainly by two different mechanisms. One family of the drugs is called angiotensin-converting enzyme inhibitors; the other is that of angiotensin II receptor blockers. They are useful for the treatment of various kidney diseases, congestive heart failure, and hypertension. However, the RAAS system is about 450,000,000 years old, having evolved to protect the blood volume and pressure, so it comes into quick action when we lose blood or become dehydrated or hypotensive. The system also increases potassium disposal by the kidneys.

Elderly patients often have impaired thirst sensation and may not drink enough liquids even when dehydrated. Many take diuretic drugs, which cause loss of water and salt. Many are in nursing homes and subject to diarrhea. Some have stroke, dementia, or serious disability and cannot themselves have access to water. Other patients, young or old, have chronic kidney disease. In all such patients, RAAS blockers have the potential of causing acute kidney failure or dangerous accumulation of potassium. While at Cook County Hospital, I saw at least four such cases a week, and now at a far smaller private hospital I see four to six a month.

Yet in medical conference after medical conference and in board review courses, speakers always sing the praise of RAAS blockers to high heaven, and little if any mention is made of their potentially serious side effects, especially in the elderly. Many years ago, at one of the annual meetings of the American Society of Nephrology, I was listening to a talk about one of the ACE inhibitors. At the end of the talk, a physician in the audience walked up to the microphone and said to the speaker, "We have a large physicians' group, and we see at least one case a week of acute kidney failure from ACE inhibitors. Would you please comment on that?" The audience immediately gave the questioner a round of applause.

The story of the RAAS blockers has been a stellar model of marketing success. Studies sponsored by pharmaceutical companies and published by notable scholars in respected journals, CME lectures, and sumptuous dinners at plush restaurants, as well as aggressive marketing by salesmen to general practitioners have accomplished the mission. As a kidney disease consultant, I sometimes recommend against the use of a RAAS blocker for certain patients. I often spend at least ten minutes arguing with another physician before I win my case. Often the patient is discharged but is readmitted later with kidney failure or high blood potassium because the RAAS blocker was resumed or prescribed by a different physician.

A somewhat similar case applies to antibiotics. When a new antibiotic with a broader activity spectrum is developed, it is marketed aggressively as well, and physicians begin to use it increasingly, even for infections susceptible to older antibiotics. What happens then is that the smart bacteria eventually mutate into resistant forms. They are cooperative, too, because they often donate their resistance factor to other species of bacteria. The food industry also plays a large part in this process by feeding antibiotics to livestock and poultry. We consume the antibiotics in meat, milk, and eggs, and some of our own natural bacteria on the skin and in the gut develop resistance to these antibiotics.

Antibiotic resistance has become a serious, sometimes life-threatening problem. Some bacteria in the nursing home or hospital environment have become resistant to all antibiotics or susceptible only to a few that have serious toxic side effects, including kidney failure. Thousands of people in the US die each year because of infections with resistant bacteria. Much more emphasis needs to be placed on this matter in medical schools and public forums.

Physicians also need to be more cognizant of the price of the drugs they prescribe. The notion that middle-class Americans are sufficiently well off to afford new patented drugs is simply that—a notion, not reality. I see many Medicare dialysis patients who worked a lifetime and are now retired. Their home mortgages are usually paid off. However, they get (net after taxes) less than fifteen hundred dollars per month in social security payments and may also get less than two thousand dollars a month from an ex-employer-sponsored pension plan. On the other hand, they have considerable drug expenses.

The average number of drugs a dialysis patient uses happens to be eight a day. The spouse, also old and likely not in good health, would be on numerous medications as well. Many patients tell me their monthly drug costs are easily four hundred dollars or more. Then there is the cost of food, clothing, utilities, gasoline, necessary travel, and intermittent expenses for home or car repair, so they end up with negligible or no savings. In other words, they live hand-to-mouth, are vulnerable, and are often taken ill because of vascular disease of the heart, brain, or the legs, or complications related to kidney failure.

Then there is TV drug advertising. Often the drugs being advertised may be effective for certain diseases refractory to traditional medicines, but have potential serious or even lethal side effects and are usually prescribed by specialty physicians after much deliberation. The ads are flashy, picturing men and women suffering from terrible or debilitating symptoms and not benefiting from established treatments, turning suddenly happy and healthy, smiling from ear to ear after taking the advertised drug. They are now playing tennis, swimming, cuddling their babies, grandchildren, or dogs, or absorbing with their spouses the beauty of natural scenery. Simultaneously, however, the announcer—obeying FDA rules—is enumerating *rapidly* the toxic effects of the drug. The companies understand, of course, that seeing the happy pictures is more effective than hearing the fast recital of toxicity.

I am not aware that this kind of TV drug advertising is practiced in any other advanced country. Even if it were, it cannot be condoned because it gives false hope to patients for whom such drugs are contraindicated. Only the physician can determine if they are suitable for a particular patient. Such patients are often desperate for relief and insist that their physician give them the drug, with the result that the doctor spends a long time explaining why it is not advisable in their case. Even then, patients may seek a second physician's opinion. It is tragicomic, on the other hand, that while the happy TV ads deluge the patients, other ads by legal firms prompt patients to contact them if they suffer any of the untoward effects of the drug in question.

Hospitalization costs are also out of sight. A hospital room can easily cost over \$1,000 a day, more expensive than first-class hotels. Materials used for patient care are billed at inflated prices, and the charges for tests such as computed axial tomography (CT scans), magnetic resonance imaging (MRIs) and angiography procedures are astounding. A patient of mine recently visited a cardiologist at a famous university hospital. The charge for a routine electrocardiogram (EKG) that has been available for over sixty years plus an echocardiogram (ultrasound test for the heart) was \$4,500, of which the insurance company paid \$3,000.

The cardiologist ordering the tests had a spell of disbelief when the patient told him about the charge. The hospital refused to reduce the bill but agreed that the patient could pay the balance of \$1,500 in monthly installments of \$100, hence for another fifteen months. Even laboratory tests that have been done for over half a century are still expensive. A complete blood count (CBC), for instance, is often billed by hospital laboratories at \$50 or more. It is a simple test for the numbers of the different cells in the blood, and has been performed decades before I went to grammar school.

Here is just one example among many I've regularly encountered over the years. A dialysis patient of mine came in for her regularly scheduled dialysis treatment, but I found the vascular dialysis access in her left arm to be occluded. The access is a connection made between an artery and a vein in the arm, creating a vascular loop to be stuck with two needles when performing dialysis. I sent her to a hospital that had a team of interventional radiologists for restoring the patency of the access, usually done with a balloon-tipped catheter. The procedure failed, so a catheter for interim dialysis was placed in a large vein through a needle stick below the right collarbone. The patient felt well and wanted to go home, but was told she had to stay in the facility for a twenty-three-hour observation. She was discharged sixteen hours after the placement of the catheter.

When I saw her back at the dialysis center and asked how she was doing, she said with a subtle smile, "I'm okay, but I want to show you something." She pulled out the bill she received from the hospital. It was for $25,000. Medicare would pay 80 percent of what it considers a standard charge, but the patient was perturbed that she had to come up with the remaining 20 percent of the bill. I could not believe my eyes. The charges for all items were simply beyond reality.

I sent a letter to the CEO of the hospital in question with a copy of the bill. I never received an answer. I called a surgeon friend at a university hospital to ask him what he thought of that bill. I was quite surprised when he said, "That's what they charge here, too—actually more—but remember that Medicare would only pay half or even a third of the charge."

This mutual game between the hospitals and the government-run Medicare and Medicaid programs is stressful for patients, especially those who are conscientious about paying their bills. It causes patients to distrust the health care system and the government and is demoralizing for the physician. Patients end up negotiating with the hospital to lower the balance, often without success, and eventually pay what's owed in monthly installments.

Hospital administrators claim they inflate the bill because they know the government will pay them only a portion of it, barely enough to cover the cost of service, and that they treat many patients who have no insurance or money. Most hospitals I know, however, are making money and pay their administrators and other officials high salaries. They are "not for profit" entities and therefore tax-exempt, something I cannot quite understand, since their net income could be very large, and they have extensive investments in the stock and real estate markets.

Another huge contributor to the cost of health care is the treatment, often futile, given in intensive care units to critically ill elderly patients approaching the end of life. It has been reported that 60 percent of Medicare funds are disbursed during the last six weeks of a patient's life. Many or most of such patients have no advance directives as to how aggressive physicians should be when there is stoppage of the heartbeat or breathing or shock (extremely low blood pressure) in the setting of a heart attack or overwhelming infection.

Modern medicine and public health have undoubtedly prolonged greatly people's lives. The average longevity of the American male at the turn of the twentieth century was forty-nine years and that of the female fifty-two. Nowadays the corresponding figures are seventy-five and eighty-two. This stretching of life span has in many cases gone beyond its bio-physiological limits—its DNA code if you like—and the body organ systems run out of reserve so that they would fail even against modest challenges.

People have been living long enough to become afflicted by serious vascular disease, resulting in heart and kidney failure, dementia, and loss of limbs. Degenerative changes of the spine result in falls and incontinence of stool and urine. They are then placed in nursing homes where they are often exposed to dehydration, diarrhea, and infectious diseases. Many develop bedsores that get infected and bore down into the bone. Therefore they get admitted to the hospital, where modern medical technology is unleashed upon them.

In the hospital they may undergo cardio-pulmonary resuscitation, the insertion of a tube into the airway and mechanical ventilation, the administration of drugs to prop up vanishing blood pressure, the use of powerful antibiotics that often cause the kidneys to fail if they had not already from infection or shock, and the performance of dialysis. Patients, often having no advance directives, may not be in a state where they can express their own wishes. The next of kin may or may not have power of attorney to make definitive decisions on behalf of the patient, so the aggressive but often futile treatment goes determinedly on.

The Illinois Surrogate Act, however, allows the next of kin to ask the physicians to terminate aggressive treatment. So can a state-appointed power-of-attorney if there is one. In that case, the patient will be given end-of-life or hospice care and will be kept free of pain and anxiety until he or she passes in peace and dignity.

The problem, however, is more complex than what I've hitherto described. Death seems to have become a taboo, and many patients and their families think modern medical technology can bestow a new life. "Doctor, do everything," they plead. Religious precepts play a large part in this situation. The next of kin, insisting that the physician must "do everything," explains, "The Lord sent her down here, and the Lord will call her back when He wishes it." So we enter what I call the "zone of agony," primarily for the suffering patient, but also for the family and the physicians. Often the family member who had been the closest to the patient, given her daily care and seen her deteriorate beyond hope would agree to rendering end-of-life comfort care, but would then be fiercely opposed by others in the family who had lived far away and had not seen the patient in many years.

Theoretically, the treating physician and another involved in the care of the patient can make a decision to suspend treatment when it is clearly futile, and is prolonging pain and suffering more than anything else. Both physicians may sign a statement to that effect. But to implement this decision against the family's wishes is a nightmare that most physicians shrink from. And not to be ignored is the concern—sometimes the dread—of litigation prompted by ambulance-chasing attorneys.

Sometimes the physician in charge asks for an "ethics consultation" where another physician and his ethics team look at the patient and medical record and may recommend comfort care only. Even that is difficult to undertake in the face of solid resistance by the family, but it provides added support for the treating physician's decision to suspend aggressive treatment. All of these measures may take a long time while the patient remains in the ICU. The treatment often fails, and the patient suffers greatly before dying. The medical bill in such a case will be simply unfathomable.

When I see a patient hopelessly beyond salvage, either in consultation or someone who happens to be a dialysis patient of mine, I have long sessions with the family. I explain to them that the most difficult thing is to draw a line between their love for the patient on the one hand and the patient's best interest on the other. It is a difficult endeavor indeed, but one that needs to be undertaken if the patient is not to suffer unnecessarily. Death is inevitable, and we have a right to death no less than the right to life—death without pain, in peace and dignity, commensurate with the good life we've had. When life has been extended beyond its biological limits, it becomes painful, with one calamitous illness following on the heels of another—the zone of agony.

I would go on to say that treatment would either fail or would only succeed partially, leaving the patient in a vegetative state or a condition lacking any meaningful consciousness of the surroundings or the joy of family and friends. I would add that loved ones pass away but they never leave us, and we often talk about them as though they were still alive. Parents have worked hard, spending the productive years of their life to raise and ready us for our own future, and we owe it to them to enable them to die a death worthy of their life of labor and love.

Quite often families respond to such argument and make a decision in their loved one's best interest. Furthermore, families have lately been more accepting of the idea of end-of-life and hospice care when they are persuaded that active treatment has become useless. Informed patients and their next of kin are much more likely to do so than the less informed, but there remains much education to be undertaken in this field, not only for the public, but also for medical students, the future doctors.

If, on the other hand, a patient is lucid enough to express his or her wishes, or has already drawn up advance directives, none of the aforementioned difficulties arise concerning medical management of refractory critical illness, advanced cancer, end-stage heart or airway disease. Typical advance directives include items like "Do not resuscitate;" "Do not intubate," or "Terminate life-supporting measures if they would not restore a wakeful and functional state."

Adding to the cost of medical care is the currently prevalent metabolic syndrome. This is a condition that results from overeating, especially of junk food high in carbohydrates and fat, resulting in severe obesity, with the subsequent development of type 2 diabetes (maturity-onset), hypertension, high cholesterol, and high uric acid with or without gout. Nowadays we increasingly see type 2 diabetes even in teenagers, whereas type 1 diabetes with insulin deficiency and weight loss had been the usual type of the disease in children and teenagers.

Atherosclosclerosis (cholesterol deposition in the walls of arteries) is a common sequel to the metabolic syndrome, culminating in devastating vascular disease affecting the brain, eyes, heart, kidneys, and the lower extremities. Recently US health authorities listed obesity as a disease qualifying for health insurance coverage. What is needed, however, is a strenuous public education campaign equal to that launched in the cause of hypertension treatment and smoking cessation, because the metabolic syndrome is now a dreadful epidemic with grim health consequences and spiraling health care cost.

The endemic use of illicit (street) drugs, especially in large urban centers, is another strain on the health care budget. Injecting drugs in the veins (mainlining) may cause infection of the blood and heart valves, with serious damage to the heart, often requiring surgery to remove the damaged valve. Other consequences include infection with the viruses of hepatitis B, which peaked in the 1970s; HIV, which followed suit in the 1980s; and later hepatitis C. These three viruses may also be transmitted by injecting drugs under the skin (skin popping).

The human immunodeficiency virus (HIV), besides destroying the immune system, is a frequent cause of kidney failure (HIV nephropathy) in young African Americans, and brain disorder (encephalopathy) regardless of race. Hepatitis C virus has become a common cause of cirrhosis, failure and cancer of the liver, as well as kidney disease. A new and expensive drug has been very effective in eliminating the virus. Skin popping may result in chronic deep-seated abscesses under the skin, often resulting in kidney disease and failure.

The use of illicit drugs through smoking or snorting may cause acute and chronic airway disease, muscle injury, and acute kidney failure in the case of heroin and cocaine. Cocaine also causes constriction of the arteries, sometimes resulting in severe hypertension, stroke, heart attack, and acute kidney failure. The use of oral drugs such as Ecstasy, especially in "rave parties," may cause high fever, dehydration, muscle injury, and acute kidney failure.

The illicit drug industry, while generating billions of dollars for its barons, has also led to mushrooming gun violence and homicide, especially in the large cities—four thousand incidents in Chicago in 2016. The violence, whether drug-related or not, is another cost burden on the health care system. Cook County Hospital has had one of the largest and best trauma units in the US and has kept quite busy. In the twenty-six years I spent at the hospital, a great number of the patients in the trauma unit were victims of gunshot or stab wounds. They needed intensive surgical and medical treatments to save their lives, often requiring airway intubation, dialysis for kidney failure, and long-term care for their wounds. Many died. Others were left with long-term disabilities, including paralysis of the legs (paraplegia) from spinal cord injury.

Not surprisingly, the US war on drugs under successive "drug czars" has so far failed to produce tangible results because there is still a large market hungry for the drugs, one that is shaped by social conditions: poverty; young people without education or jobs, trapped in ghettos and having nothing to look forward to; successful people whose lives are devoid of spirituality, morality and meaning; and finally, alienation, loneliness, and fragmentation of the family unit.

Whatever the argument is for combating the drug scourge, it is clear that the illegality of drugs is the main generator of the barons' unimaginable wealth and the unending violent deaths and destruction of civil life in many cities. The barons possess fleets of airplanes and ships, even submarines, and large processing factories deep in the jungle. They have armies of guards and assassins and extensive arsenals of heavy weapons. They buy judges, policemen, and politicians to protect their interests and assassinate in broad daylight officials who are intent on catching and prosecuting them. Moreover, terrorist groups like al-Qa'ida, the Taliban, and ISIS generate huge sums from the illegal drug trade that they use to finance their murderous projects.

Gun control in the US has not even begun in earnest. Ours is the only country of "law and order" where people are allowed to own not only several handguns, but also automatic assault rifles, weapons of war that have been used to kill school children and high school and college students. There was a time in the early history of this land when people had to carry guns to protect themselves from native Americans, highwaymen, and wild animals, and when militias fought in the American War of Independence. It is quite interesting how this early history was somehow reborn in the shape of the second amendment to the US Constitution so that in the twenty-first century millions of our countrymen are armed to the teeth in this advanced and civilized nation of laws.

President Ronald Reagan once said that guns do not kill; only people do. It had not occurred to him that a man with a knife, a dagger, or a sword cannot easily commit mass murder in a few seconds. Attempts at reforming gun laws, let alone prohibiting guns, have failed, largely thanks to Republicans who remain indebted to the National Rifle Association for donating large sums to their election campaigns. Mr. Trump, in his acceptance speech as the Republican Party nominee, did in fact thank the NRA for its endorsement of his nomination. Incidentally, people can nowadays order weapons online.

Lest the reader think I have digressed from the subject of health care (I have not), I will now point out a major contributor to its high cost, namely the rampant litigation against doctors and hospitals, very often for bogus claims. Lawyers, often referred to as "ambulance chasers," promise patients in need of cash lucrative monetary compensation, often enticing them to sue dedicated physicians who had attended to them for a long time. The legal process can take many years while the lawyers charge hourly fees far exceeding those of most physicians and handsomely pay "expert" witnesses. The process is lengthy, costly to the taxpayer, stressful, and often damaging to physicians, most of whom are hardworking and conscientious.

Judges nowadays do not disqualify for trial even grossly frivolous claims because they presumably want to give the claimant the benefit of the doubt. When a case finally gets to trial, a jury of lay people is assembled to pass the final verdict. The outcome of the case depends to a considerable extent on the skill of the lawyers and their theatrical talents.

The jury system came about in England in the twelfth century. Many cases had to do with land and water disputes. A twelve-member jury from the locale would be assembled to pass a verdict. They were not informed by lawyers in court, but had to investigate the cases themselves. The system was eventually adopted by most of Britain's dominions, including the thirteen American colonies, which evolved into the United States. It is surprising that the same system of lay jurors is still being applied in the twenty-first century to highly complex medical, biological, engineering, and high-tech cases.

In October 1989, Dr. Howard C. Snider, a urologist, published a book titled *Jury of My Peers: A Surgeon's Encounter with the Malpractice Crisis*, which was so well reasoned, logical, and touching that the Chicago Medical Society distributed it free to many of its members. The urologist had seen a patient with a refractory problem of the ureter, the tube that drains urine from the kidney into the bladder, and offered to do a new procedure of plastic repair, explaining to the patient the pros and cons of the operation. The plastic repair did not succeed—not an unusual outcome—and not the result of negligence. Nevertheless, the urologist was sued.

Dr. Snider explains that the jurors were laymen. One was a baker, another fixed flat tires, and so on. He argues convincingly and logically that justice demanded that he be tried by a jury of his peers, especially since the procedure he undertook was new and complex. The book portrays the trauma such lay jury trials inflict on physicians and indeed on society itself, and the disconnectedness of the trial lawyers from the medical world.

I myself have made several depositions in cases of so-called medical malpractice involving physicians and surgeons and was astounded to see that some cases were completely frivolous and that many lawyers lack basic knowledge of medical issues that require some understanding of biology and physiology. Such cases sometimes take years to get to trial. I once made a deposition in a case involving matters of internal medicine where the medical adviser to the claimant's attorney was a retired obstetrician who could not possibly have had a clear understanding of the case. The sued physician has to spend long hours poring over the details of the case and the deposition of expert consultants for his and the claimant's attorneys, enduring recurrent cycles of stress and financial worries during the years it takes for the case to get to trial.

Damages awarded by juries can be astronomical, pushing up liability insurance premiums for physicians, surgeons, and obstetricians and driving many to flee to states such as Indiana, where damage awards are capped. I know many highly qualified and experienced doctors who left Chicagoland for Indiana and other states that have placed a ceiling on damage awards.

Physicians, especially those manning emergency rooms,

surgeons, and anesthesiologists, often order unnecessary tests and request "clearance" by various consultants before undertaking even minor procedures, all to protect themselves against litigation, a practice referred to as "self-protective medicine." Hospitals take similar precautions by devising treatment pathways for conditions like pneumonia, heart failure, and others.

These *pathways* are cookbooks that ignore the physician's experience and assume that patients having the same condition are all alike and should be treated in exactly the same cookbook manner. This intellectual totalitarianism has now been endorsed by the government (Medicare and Medicaid) and private insurance companies. It has found its way in one form or another into the electronic medical record systems. Physicians, therefore, order tests and treatments that may not be necessary for a particular patient but are mandated by the pathway. Consequently the system, rather than containing health care cost, may actually compound it.

It is interesting in this context to touch on the findings of a recent large study published in the *Journal of the American Medical Association* (JAMA). The authors looked at the practice of twenty-two thousand hospitalists (physicians who see only hospitalized patients) and 485,000 hospital visits by Medicare patients over a three-year period from 2011 to 2014. The outcomes of patients seen by "high-spending physicians," those who ordered many tests and interventions, were no better than those seen by "low-spending physicians." This finding suggests the high spenders were perhaps less experienced, therefore needing the reassurance of more test results, or that they practiced more "self-protective medicine," always minding the ambulance chasers. The findings of the study are consistent with common sense and the impression of most experienced physicians, but perhaps it was necessary to conduct this research since our culture has been enthralled with citing study results and shunning common sense.

If an experienced physician who had known a patient for many years deviates from the pathway, he has to spend precious time explaining why he did so. Even then, the physician may find his "score" wanting in some system or another devised by the hospital or some government agency and displayed online for all to see. Furthermore, this scoring system may show that his treatment of hypertension, for example, is not up to par because he has patients who run systolic blood pressure values over 140 when the actual numbers may be 141 or 142. And so the ludicrousness goes on.

The fact remains that no two patients with the same ailment are exactly the same because the disease process and manifestations are not products only of the disease-causing agent, but also of the interaction between the agent and the patient's immune system, influenced by heredity, age, race, gender, pregnancy, physical or mental stress, nutrition, environment, and preexisting diseases like diabetes, hypertension, or kidney failure, and the drugs prescribed for them. It behooves us all to remember that no two humans having the same disease are identical, certainly not like Coca-Cola cans on a conveyor belt.

In my experience, observation, and reading during forty-five years of medical practice in Chicago, self-protective medicine easily adds at least 15 percent to health care cost, quite possibly much more. Tort reform has been advocated by many groups, but has come to naught largely because the Democrats are as resistant to the idea as the Republicans are to gun control.

Over the last twenty-five years, government intrusion into the practice of medicine has been on a steady rise. A mushrooming bureaucracy of regulatory and inspection agencies has grown to gigantic proportions. They've come up with diagnosis-related groups (DRGs) like pneumonia, congestive heart failure, and others to determine the length of hospital stay (LOS) for patients in specific DRG categories. They examine physicians' compliance with the various pathways and cookbook treatment recipes. When an experienced physician decides to forgo certain items in the recipe because they are irrelevant or unnecessary for a particular patient or to delay an unstable patient's discharge beyond the DRG time limit, he has to document the reasons for doing so, both to pacify the all-knowing grim inspectors and fend off the ambulance chasers.

Therefore, physicians spend inordinate time documenting this and that action or inaction. Nurses do the same because they, too, have their cookbooks, so they click away their documentations at computer keyboards on wheels instead of spending more time on direct patient care. Patients are no longer Mr. Jones or Mrs. Smith. They are the patient in room 1 and the patient in room 6, partly because the Health Insurance Portability and Accountability Act (HIPAA), the body of rules that jealously guards patients' privacy, is looking down upon all with eagle eyes, even when the physician inquiring about a patient happens to be a consultant called in on the case.

HIPAA and myriad other government regulations have predictably spawned a parasitic multimillion-dollar industry of books, training courses, workshops, and conferences, all ostensibly to protect physicians against the wrath of government bureaucrats or the greed of unscrupulous lawyers. Various physician associations have come up with their own practice guidelines in a maneuver known as "the regulated capturing the regulator."

Hospitals now have case management teams and utilization review committees, lovingly called UR by physicians. Their personnel as well as employees of the patient's health insurance company may call the physician almost daily and bombard him or her with all sorts of often unintelligent questions when the physician exceeds the "length of stay" limit for a patient, usually for a good reason. The physician may delay making a final diagnosis because of waiting longer than necessary for a test result, especially when the test is sent out to another lab (called a *send-out test*), or when the patient's past medical record is not available because of HIPAA constraints or staff laziness.

When the record does finally arrive, it may contain umpteen test results, informed consent forms, directions for the patient upon discharge, and a dozen other things—except for one lucid paragraph describing what the patient was admitted for, what diagnosis was made, what treatment was given, what was the outcome, and what is expected in the future, namely the prognosis. This happens because clerks fax the record without much physician input. I have long suffered from this phenomenon when I needed to peruse patients' records before accepting them for outpatient dialysis or when I examine records of my dialysis patients discharged from hospitals I don't practice at.

Because of the various pressures put on busy practitioners, some may discharge a patient prematurely in the hope that rehabilitation units or home visiting nurses will keep a good follow-up of the patient's condition. This may work reasonably well if the physician is kept abreast of the patient's progress. If not, the patient will be readmitted to the same or another hospital.

Hospitals have become obsessed with patient satisfaction scores, which are advertised in various publications and online and looked at by other patients, the public at large, and the inspecting agencies. Patients must have no pain whatsoever, even when some pain is a useful clue to the treating physician and surgeon or a deterrent to the patient against attempting certain harmful body or limb movements. Almost every other patient I see in consultation is prescribed Norco PRN (which stands for pro re nata, meaning as needed). The drug is a combination of hydrocodone (an opiate cousin of morphine) and a large dose of Tylenol. Hydrocodone is addictive, constipating, and depresses respiration in patients with lung disease or severe obesity. Many patients do become quickly addicted and, when discharged, seek the drug from their primary physicians. Opiate addiction has now become a national epidemic, and has resulted in thousands of deaths from overdose.

Also in the pursuit of high patient satisfaction scores, emergency room (ER) physicians are urged to reduce waiting time as much as possible, something patients obviously like. The patients, and often the staff, may fail to recognize that rapid processing entails perfunctory history taking and physical examination, more reliance on expensive tests, and more faulty diagnoses, frequently resulting in hospital admissions for relatively minor problems or sending home patients with more serious conditions.

A patient complaining of chest pain is almost routinely admitted to the hospital to "rule out" a heart attack unless an experienced ER physician takes the time needed for a good history and physical, perhaps augmented by an EKG and a simple blood test. Even then physicians must be sufficiently self-assured and immune to lawyer-phobia to tell patients that their problem is not a heart attack but only heartburn from eating hot peppers or nerve root pain from a rotted spine or chest wall pain or pleurisy. In the last case, the patient may have to be admitted for pneumonia, but not to rule out a heart attack, with its requisites for a cardiology consultation and further testing, some of which may be invasive and very expensive.

⚬⦿⚬

Disease entities are now coded according to the International Classification of Disease, ICD-10, launched by the World Health Organization (WHO) in 1989 to replace the older ICD-9 system. The US adopted ICD-10 in October 2015, adding a clinical modification, ICD-10 CM, and procedure code modification, ICD-10 PSC. The ICD-10 code includes the name of the disease or the procedure and a specific number representing it, for example, end-stage renal disease (ESRD) is code N18.6. Health care providers, health insurance carriers (whether governmental or private), governmental agencies, medical billing services, and electronic medical records all use this system, which may be useful in terms of standardization, especially when it comes to billing for health care services.

All US citizens with ESRD (ICD-10, code N18.6) are eligible for coverage for dialysis or kidney transplantation by Medicare, Medicaid, or private insurance. The problem arises when a patient with normal kidney function or chronic kidney disease not requiring dialysis develops acute kidney failure that does not reverse in good time. Such a patient cannot nowadays be kept in the hospital for a long time and will be discharged home to have dialysis at an outpatient unit. The companies owning these units have managed (after lengthy negotiations) to treat such patients under a special code. If the kidney failure does not resolve after ninety days, the patient is considered to have ESRD for billing purposes.

If such patients are too weak or disabled to be sent home from the hospital, they cannot be dialyzed in an outpatient setting and will need to go to a nursing facility that offers both rehabilitation and dialysis services. Such facilities will not be reimbursed for dialyzing these patients unless they are labeled as ESRD. The nephrologist is therefore impelled to use the ESRD diagnostic code. A situation where physicians must lie in order to help disabled patients cannot be ethical or good. In fact, in a perverted bureaucracy, as is often the case, the well-meaning physician could be accused of fraud by the insurance company or, worse still, by the government. Furthermore, the use of the ESRD code will almost certainly raise the patient's private insurance premium. The government must come up with a special code to cover dialysis services in this situation, and not expose the physician to the humiliation of having to lie or the fear of being accused of fraud.

The ICD-10 system may be misleading in the realm of medical education in that it may not reflect the pathophysiology of disease. For example, the kidneys would normally respond to dehydration or blood loss by holding on to salt and water and excreting a much smaller volume of highly concentrated urine. The blood concentration of certain substances like urea, normally excreted by the kidneys, will rise, a condition termed prerenal azotemia (high blood urea), with the *prerenal* adjective meaning that the event is triggered by factors outside the kidneys, which are not themselves damaged but are responding normally to the state of low blood volume.

If, on the other hand, the state of dehydration is prolonged or a substance toxic to the kidneys has been administered, there would occur actual renal damage (acute tubular necrosis), which may or may not resolve. Yet both this and the previous condition of prerenal azotemia would go under the ICD-10 of AKI (acute kidney injury) despite the fact that the kidneys are only injured in the latter example. This code is therefore not useful for the medical student struggling to understand renal pathophysiology or for purposes of medical research and accurate clinical statistics. It mislabels the patient's medical diagnosis and may well push up his future health insurance premiums.

Personally, I have not bothered with ICD-9 or ICD-10 codes and have never discussed them with my medical trainees. I have them in my iPhone, only to refer to them occasionally for billing purposes. My billing service, on the other hand, knows them by heart.

More recently we have been blessed with the electronic medical record systems. My experience had been with the earlier Meditech system and later with EPIC, which was widely advertised before it actually arrived in hospitals. Posters popped up in doctors' lounges and other hospital areas declaring "EPIC—It's here." Unlike any car or gadget one buys, it did not come with a user's manual, but many classes and courses were given to doctors, nurses, pharmacists, medical records and billing personnel. Some physicians had to pay as much as forty thousand dollars to install the system in their offices.

To be fair, there are many advantages to these systems, but saving the rain forest has so far not been one of them, seeing how much of these electronic records and other materials are printed out, with the churning sound of the printers going on ceaselessly. These records are much more legible than the handwriting of most doctors and are almost indestructible. They are accessible to physicians from different affiliated hospitals that can therefore share the same data, and from the doctors' offices and homes. They gladden the hearts of HIPAA fanatics because they safeguard patients' privacy in the best ways possible—unless they attract the interest of Wikileaks or teenage hackers. The system also has other useful features like information on drug-drug interactions and allergies and useful tools like calculators and links to good publications like *UpToDate*. (This is not an advertisement.)

Although these systems were designed by humans, they don't operate like the human mind. Clinical entities are placed in sacred boxes that do not allow easy but often necessary crossovers. I often have the impression that they have been almost specifically programmed for billing purposes, to fend off the ever-prowling litigation lawyers, to please constipated inspectors, and sometimes to perform the clever function of "the regulated capturing the regulator."

Let's look at a consulting physician opening a patient's chart in EPIC. This expert often sees a long problem list enumerating conditions entered over months or years by attending physicians, consultants, residents, fellows-in-training, physician assistants, and nurse practitioners. For example, the physician may see congestive heart failure, often in addition to other problems like dyspnea (shortness of breath), edema (swelling of the feet), and fatigue, which are all symptoms of the original disease of heart failure. This may be repeated with other diseases or clinical syndromes with entries of the syndrome as well as its components.

Then there are results of lab tests, imaging studies with the quite useful ability to retrieve the pictures via the PAX system connection, EKG reports, as well as the actual tracings and echocardiograms (dynamic ultrasound of the heart), all current and from past encounters with the patient. Nowadays it seems that every other patient admitted to the hospital has the benefit of an echocardiogram, even when no heart disease is clinically evident.

Our consultant then sees and examines the patient and goes back to *enter* his note, diagnosis, and recommendations. We don't say "write" anymore since the note is typed, and writing is a thing of the distant past. While entering his note, he uses the right click (mouse button) to include all the test results in EPIC, regardless of whether they are pertinent to his focus, and that they are already in the computer for all to see. He may also have to call the primary physician and other consultants on the case to discuss with them his findings and opinion. Finally, he marks the time it took him to do all that as "60 minutes" or "90 minutes" because it relates to the billing for his service, a practice encouraged by government and private insurers, and perhaps inspired by attorneys' clocking of their conversations with clients.

The same routine of the right click and test result translocation into the note is repeated in physicians' daily progress notes. Often a note is exactly the same as the one from the day before, as though nothing had actually changed in the patient's condition. Sometimes "the right big toe is getting better," when it had actually been amputated the day before. Acronyms are used profusely, such as N&V, meaning nausea and vomiting. Standard acronyms are used almost universally, although they may read like Sanskrit to physicians not in the field of internal medicine, and the word "multiple" is much preferred to "many," "several," or "numerous," although it actually means a multiple of a base number. For example, eight is a multiple of two.

It does not seem that Medicare and private insurance personnel know how long it takes a physician to undertake all that work, so the physician has to yet again document the time spent. Likewise, it does not seem to occur to anyone, least of all the insurers, that when a physician makes a diagnosis and gives his treatment recommendations, he must have examined the patient and reviewed the other consultants' notes and the ancillary test results.

When the physician is typing a note or orders, a sign may suddenly pop up proclaiming the patient has septic shock. The computer assumes that the physician is too feeble to recognize the signs of septic shock so he must scroll down a number of items to click on the item "The patient does not have septic shock." Otherwise the computer will not let the physician finish typing. More vexing still is that when the physician sees a need to order a test like a simple urine culture, another pop-up appears of several questions usually asked only of medical students. This maneuver has been invented by hospitals to show that a urinary tract infection was not hospital acquired in order to avoid the wrath of the all-knowing government agencies—a fine example of the "regulated capturing the regulator," at the expense of common sense and good practice.

So the game goes on. Consultants often have to answer yes to a pop-up question even when the real answer is no, because they know better and think the test they are ordering is necessary to make or fine-tune the diagnosis. It seems that the all-encompassing computer is now telling the physician how to practice medicine, enforcing in the process the prevalent intellectual totalitarianism. Should we perhaps shut down the medical schools and training programs and employ technicians or, better still, robots to treat human illnesses? Is it George Orwell's *1984*?

Talking about the computer brings me to handheld devices, the ubiquitous iPhone being the prime example. I had resisted the Palm Pilot and then succumbed to acquiring one. Then I resisted the iPhone but was defeated by my son, who insisted I should certainly purchase the famous gadget lest I be left behind and out of touch with the times. So I did. These are obviously wonderful devices and so much fun, especially the camera component. Now I stop during my walks or hikes to take pictures of flowers, butterflies, and even squirrels busy gnawing on nuts, and to snap photos of festive occasions or friends I haven't seen in years. I'll admit to having become dependent on them to the extent that I often wonder how it is that Homo sapiens has survived three hundred thousand years without them. And the companies keep upgrading them to stimulate a continuous stream of sales.

I have also downloaded various medical applications (apps) to my iPhone: Medimath, Epocrates, and others. Medimath has all the formulae I use in my kidney and internal medicine practice. All I have to do is plug in the necessary lab results, and eureka— the answer is instantly there. Most of these calculations—and there are many in the field of renal disease—I used to do in my head or scribble numbers quickly on a piece of paper. I can no longer do so with the same alacrity now that I'm dependent on my dubious friend the iPhone. It's a shame. I have also been abbreviating and adulterating my good English and Arabic to accommodate the requirements of fast texting.

I have learned that many schools have abandoned teaching kids good handwriting and that the *Oxford English Dictionary* has dropped a number of words from its lexicon. This saddens me. Handwriting is a skill that took humans millennia to invent and develop. It is an art probably akin to drawing, and it emanates from an area in the brain adjacent to the area of speech. Words, on the other hand, have distinct cultural or aesthetic associations in the brain and in many languages possess subtle meanings beside their regular usage. I wonder what in future millennia will happen to brain centers that process these wondrous skills. Perhaps this high-tech revolution will far outstrip the writing, printing press, and the industrial-scientific revolutions in their impact on the human brain and destiny.

I am not sure what shape medical practice will take in the future. But I and most of my peers are much less happy and more stressed and frustrated than ever before in my memory. The endless government regulations and the intellectual totalitarianism suffocate independent thinking and discourage, even punish, the application of experience, common sense and wisdom to the care of patients (Knowledge comes, but wisdom lingers). The results so far have been the increasing harassment of doctors, and the reign of computer and pathway-directed medical practice.

All of this has robbed many outstanding physicians of the fun of medicine, the often challenging diagnostic process, and the good old-fashioned interaction with patients. I for one have had to wage quite a few small and not-so-small battles against the enslaving tide. Naturally, as with all such totalitarian systems of thought, there are the Big Brother agents within the medical profession itself to enforce the rules.

The phenomenon of mushrooming blind bureaucracies in medicine and elsewhere is the hallmark sign of declining civilizations. I must remain optimistic, however, because I know civilization is a swinging pendulum, that there will come a time when enlightenment and common sense will prevail again. They must if the human spirit is to survive and flourish and humans not turn into the Weenas of H. G. Wells's *Time Machine.*

I must now take leave of you, dear reader. I hope I have not bored you and apologize for taking up so much of your time. I bid you farewell.

# INDEX

# ACKNOWLEDGMENTS

I am grateful to Mrs. Sally Dunea for suggesting this book's main title. I had initially chosen *An Interesting Life after All*, but Sally's recommendation was more pertinent and attractive. I am indebted to Michael Benigno of the Northeast US Jesuits and Dr. David Miros and Ann Rosentreter at the Central US Jesuit Archives for so kindly granting me permission to publish the images from my five Baghdad College Al-Iraqi yearbooks, 1957–61; to Matthew Murphy, Jennifer McFadden, and Lori Boyd at *National Geographic Magazine* for the pictures of the Samarra Spiral Minaret, Baghdad's al-Rasheed Street, and the women yogurt sellers; to Michael Shulman at Magnum Photos and photographer Steve McCurry for the photo of the Kadhimiya Shrine; to Caryn Stancik for the pictures of Cook County Hospital main building, and of Drs. Fantus, Meyer, and Young; to James Madigan for the images from the Oak Park Public Library; to Joanne Baker and photographer Jenny Matthews for the pictures of the Iraqi child victims of depleted uranium.

I am indebted to my wife, Nadia Killidar for contributing her active advice and superb taste to the book's spine design and coloring. I am also grateful to my son Ali Bakir for managing to quickly transmit all images with their captions to the publisher through Google drive, a task beyond my limited computer skills.

I am also grateful for Mr. L. Newton at Archway Publishing for his kind and thoughtful editing of my manuscript. I also wish to thank Kayla Staubough, Lauren Holmes, Rick VanDeventer, Adalee Coonie, Joy Travis, Eric Sackson and the production and art teams at Archway for their kind and patient support during the long publication process.

# ABOUT THE AUTHOR

Dr. Asad Bakir was born in 1944 in Baghdad, Iraq, where he finished medical school, served in the Iraqi Medical Reserve Corps, and did an internship in medicine. Then he left for England, where he worked for eight months before coming to Chicago. There he did his residency in internal medicine and fellowship in kidney disease. He then spent twenty-six years at Chicago's Cook County Hospital (CCH) as attending and senior attending internist and nephrologist, and director of the hospital's dialysis unit. He was made a fellow of the American College of Physicians and the American Society of Nephrology, and professor of medicine at the University of Illinois at Chicago.

This book is an interesting memoir of Dr. Bakir's rich experience of life, schooling, and work in the three countries. In it he surveys the modern history of Iraq, the 150 years of the Arab renaissance before it gave out its last breath in the 1960s, the violent toppling of the Iraqi Hashemite monarchy, the dark chapters of Saddam's tyranny, his genocidal policies, and the three devastating wars he invited upon Iraq. He discusses the lethal twelve-year sanctions regime imposed on Iraq, the 2003 US invasion and its bloody aftermath, and expounds on global terrorism, it origins, and the duplicity of political leaders in dealing with terrorists and their supporters and financiers. He devotes five chapters to his years at CCH and a long chapter to life in his beloved Chicago. He ends with an extensive and provocative discussion of medical practice and the state of health care in the US.

Dr. Bakir's book makes for an engrossing reading, for it passionately presents a panoramic range of interesting topics covering history, politics, literature, sociology, the arts, and the science and practice of medicine.